犬夜叉

INUYASHA

ANI-MANGA™ Vol.22

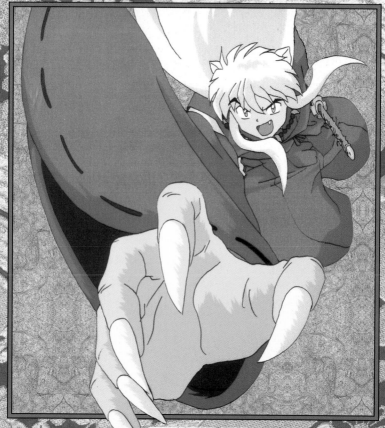

CREATED BY
RUMIKO TAKAHASHI

Inuyasha Ani-Manga™
Vol. #22

Created by
Rumiko Takahashi

Translation based on the VIZ anime TV series
Translation Assistance/Katy Bridges
Lettering & Editorial Assistance/John Clark
Cover Design & Graphics/Hidemi Sahara
Editor/Ian Robertson

Editor in Chief, Books/Alvin Lu
Editor in Chief, Magazines/Marc Weidenbaum
VP of Publishing Licensing/Rika Inouye
VP of Sales/Gonzalo Ferreyra
Sr. VP of Marketing/Liza Coppola
Publisher/Hyoe Narita

Printed in the U.S.A.

Published by VIZ Media, LLC
P.O. Box 77010
San Francisco, CA 94107

10 9 8 7 6 5 4 3 2 1
First printing, August 2007

www.viz.com
store.viz.com

Story thus far

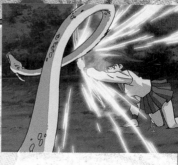

Kagome's mundane teenage existence was turned upside down when she was transported into a mythical version of Japan's medieval past! Kagome is the reincarnation of Lady Kikyo, a great warrior and the defender of the Shikon Jewel, or the Jewel of Four Souls. Kikyo was in love with Inuyasha, a dog-like half-demon who wishes to possess the jewel in order to transform himself into a full-fledged demon. But 50 years earlier, the evil shape-shifting Naraku tricked Kikyo and Inuyasha into betraying one another. The betrayal led to Kikyo's death and Inuyasha's imprisonment under a binding spell…and Inuyasha remained trapped by the spell until Kagome appeared in feudal Japan and unwittingly released him!

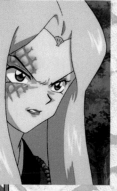

In a skirmish for possession of the Shikon Jewel, it accidentally shatters and is strewn across the land. Only Kagome has the power to find the jewel shards, and only Inuyasha has the strength to defeat the demons that now hold them, so the two unlikely partners are bound together in the quest to reclaim all the pieces of the sacred jewel. To prevent Inuyasha from stealing the jewel, Kikyo's sister, Lady Kaede, puts a magical necklace around Inuyasha's neck that allows Kagome to make him "sit" on command. Inuyasha's greatest tool in the fight to recover the sacred jewel shards is his father's sword, the Tetsusaiga, but Inuyasha's half-brother Sesshomaru covets the mighty blade and has tried to steal it more than once.

Naraku's ally Tsubaki flees to the ancient temple where she trained as a youth. Momiji and Boton, two naïve priestesses trained by the same priest who once trained Tsubaki, believe her when she claims she's being pursued by an "evil demon" and set out to confront Inuyasha and the others. The two guardians of the temple now gone, Tsubaki reveals the true reason she's returned—to gain an evil power that's been sealed away for generations…

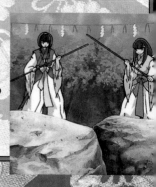

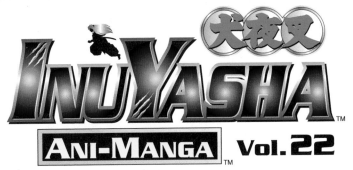

INUYASHA™

ANI-MANGA™ Vol. 22

Contents

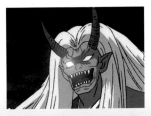

64
**Giant Ogre of
the Forbidden Tower**

.... 5

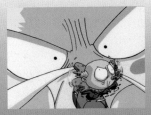

65
Farewell, Days of My Youth

.... 73

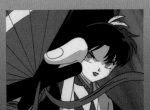

66
**Naraku's Barrier–Kagura's
Decision**

.... 137

64 Giant Ogre of the Forbidden Tower

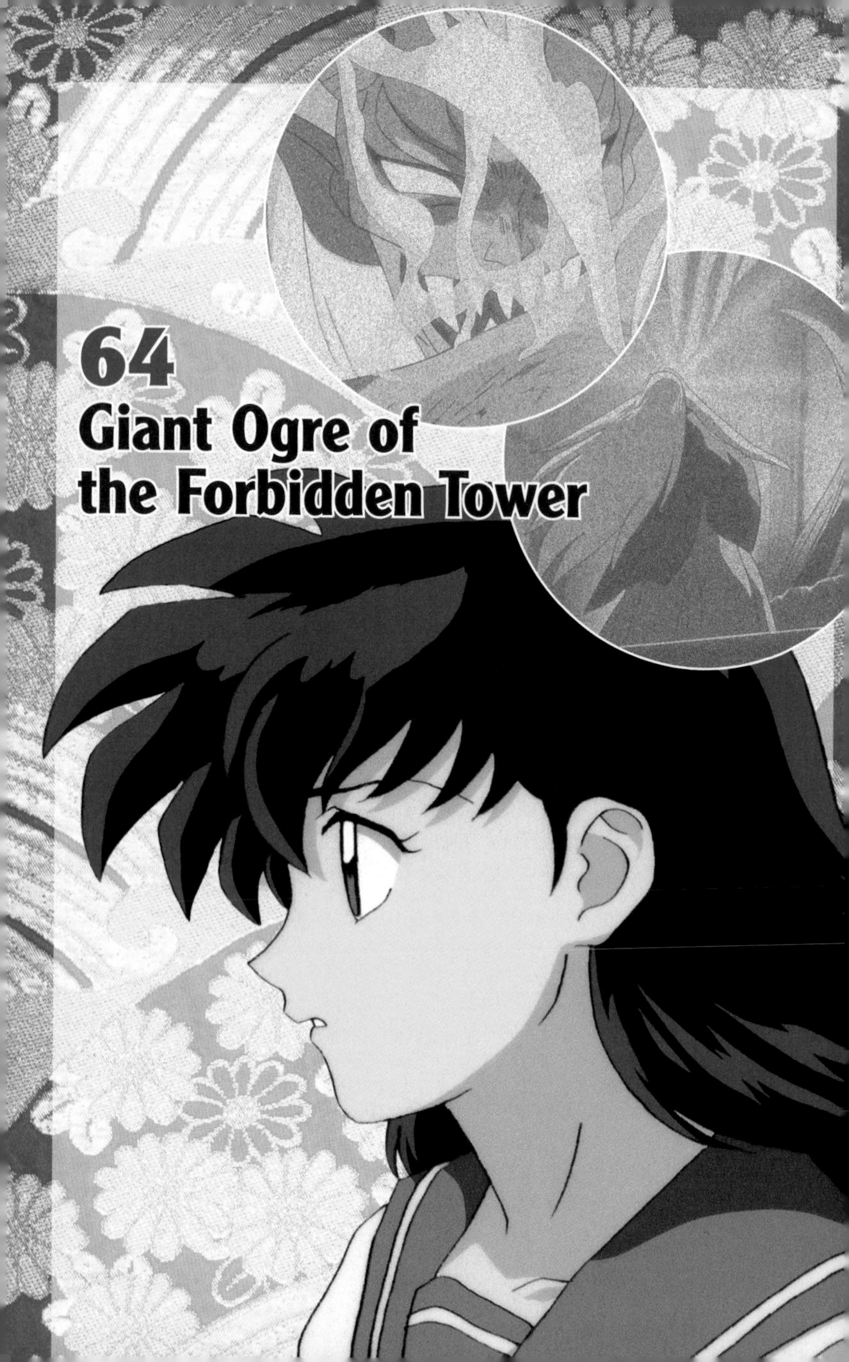

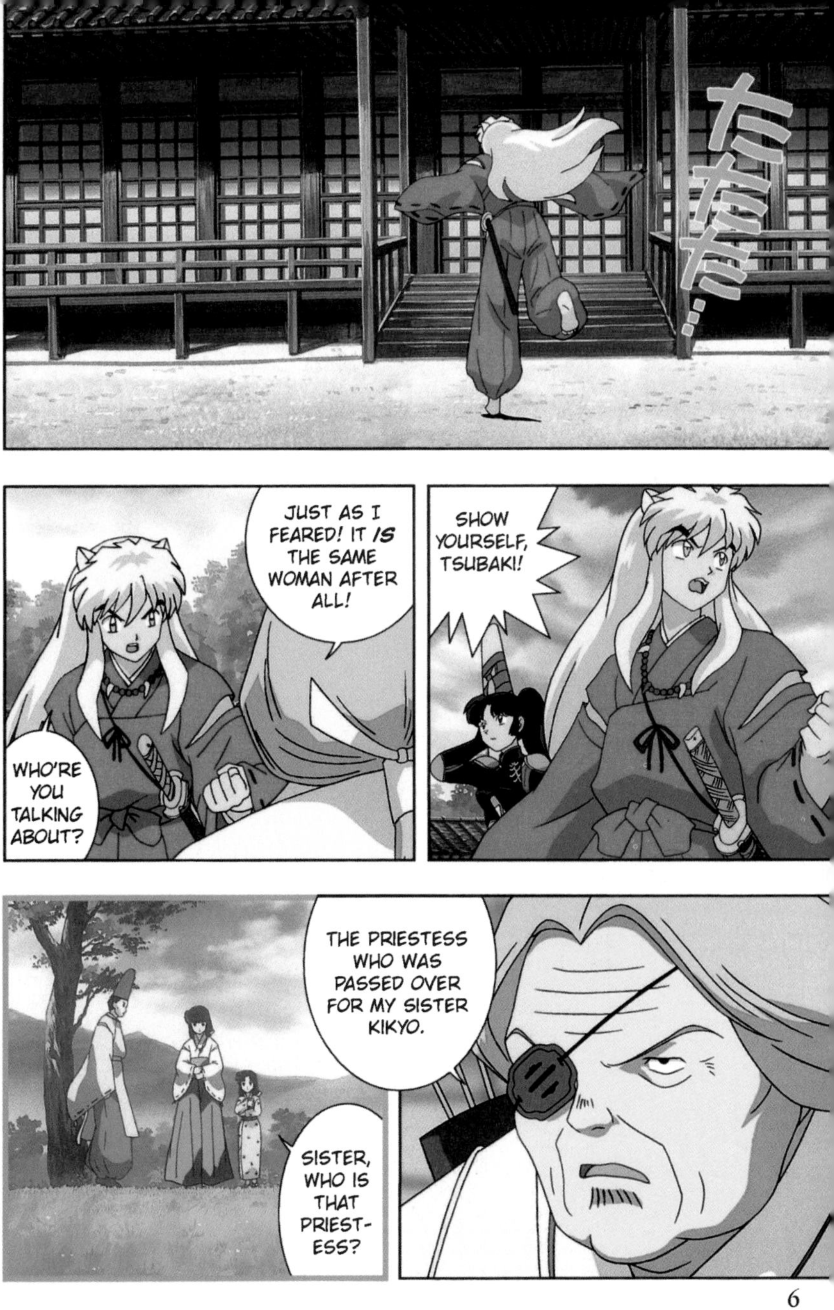
たたた…
SHOW YOURSELF, TSUBAKI!
JUST AS I FEARED! IT *IS* THE SAME WOMAN AFTER ALL!
WHO'RE YOU TALKING ABOUT?
THE PRIESTESS WHO WAS PASSED OVER FOR MY SISTER KIKYO.
SISTER, WHO IS THAT PRIEST-ESS?

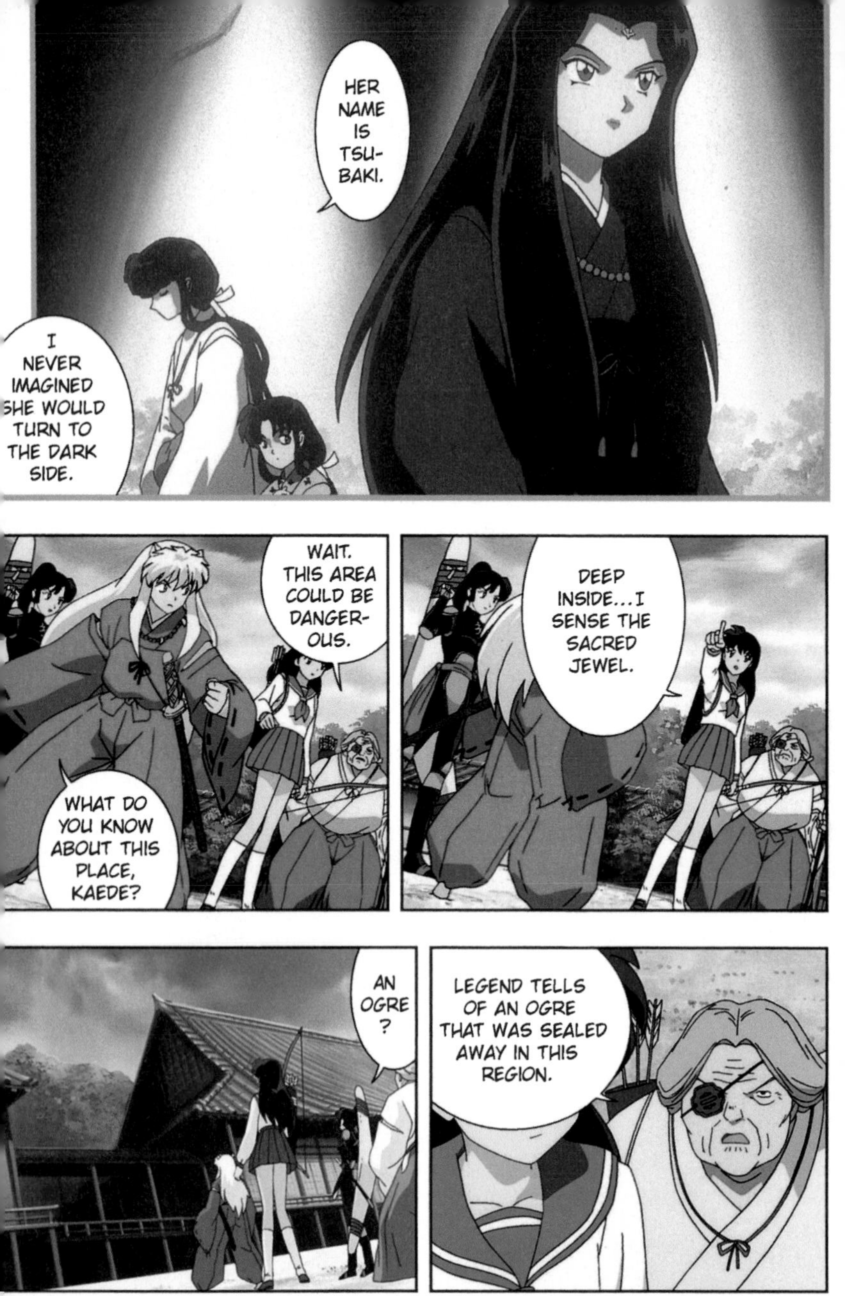
HER NAME IS TSU-BAKI.
I NEVER IMAGINED SHE WOULD TURN TO THE DARK SIDE.
DEEP INSIDE...I SENSE THE SACRED JEWEL.
WAIT. THIS AREA COULD BE DANGER-OUS.
WHAT DO YOU KNOW ABOUT THIS PLACE, KAEDE?
LEGEND TELLS OF AN OGRE THAT WAS SEALED AWAY IN THIS REGION.
AN OGRE?

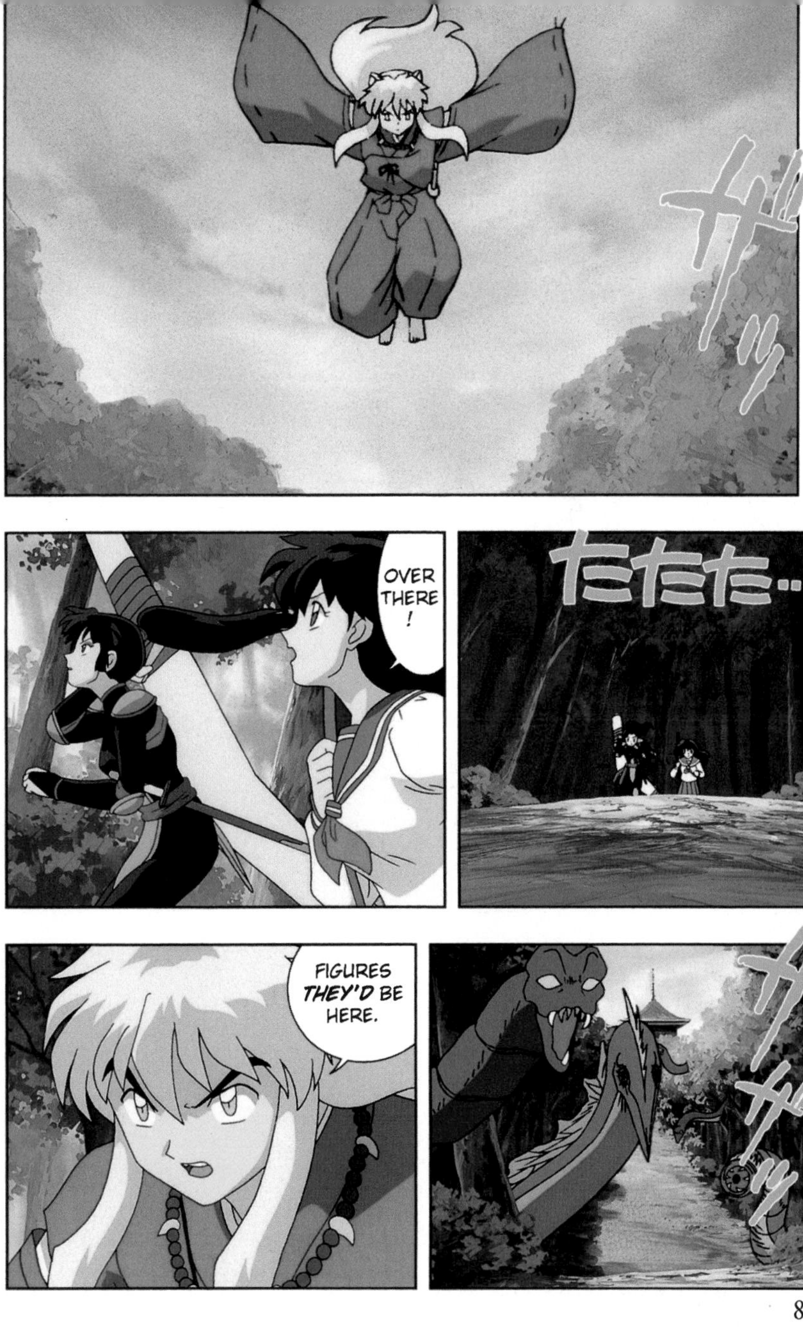
ザザッ
たたた…
OVER THERE!
ザザッ
FIGURES *THEY'D* BE HERE.

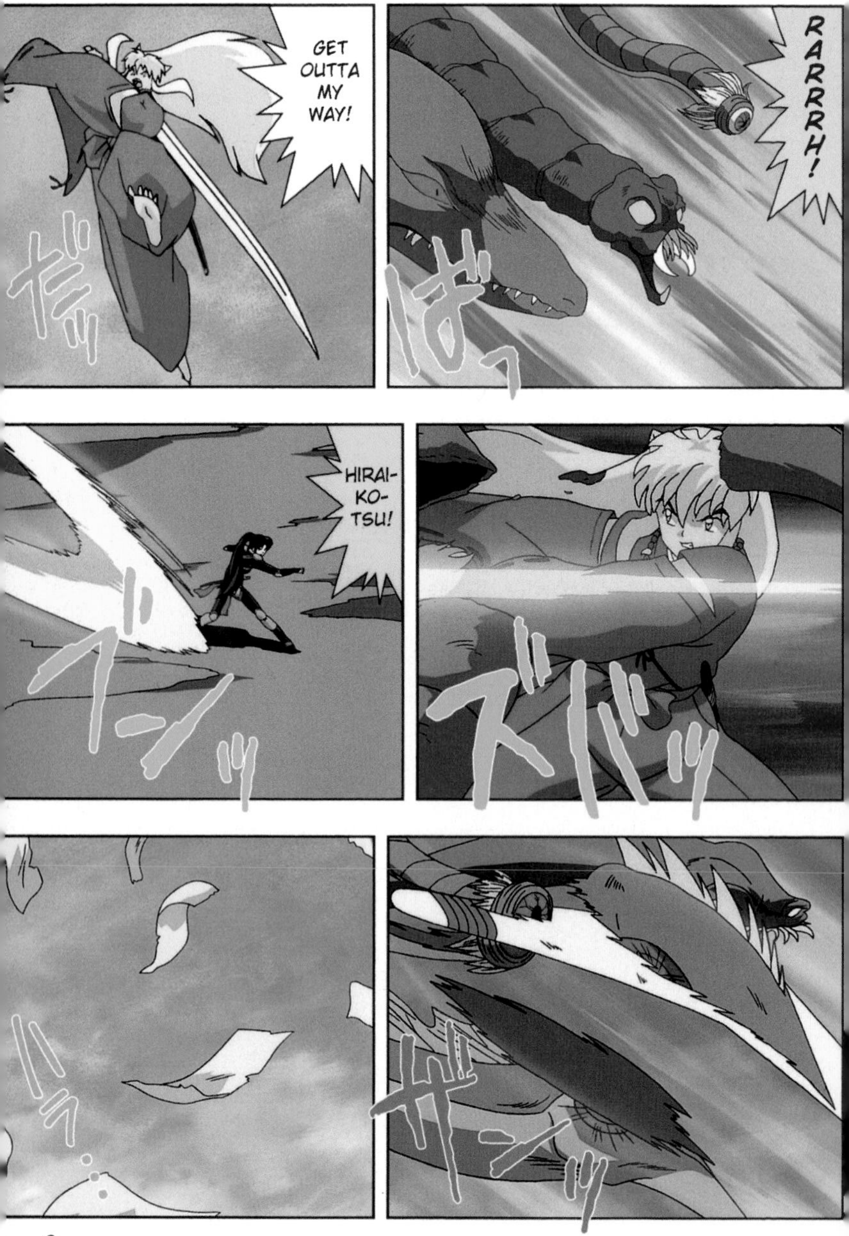
RARRRH!
GET OUTTA MY WAY!
HIRAI-KOTSU!

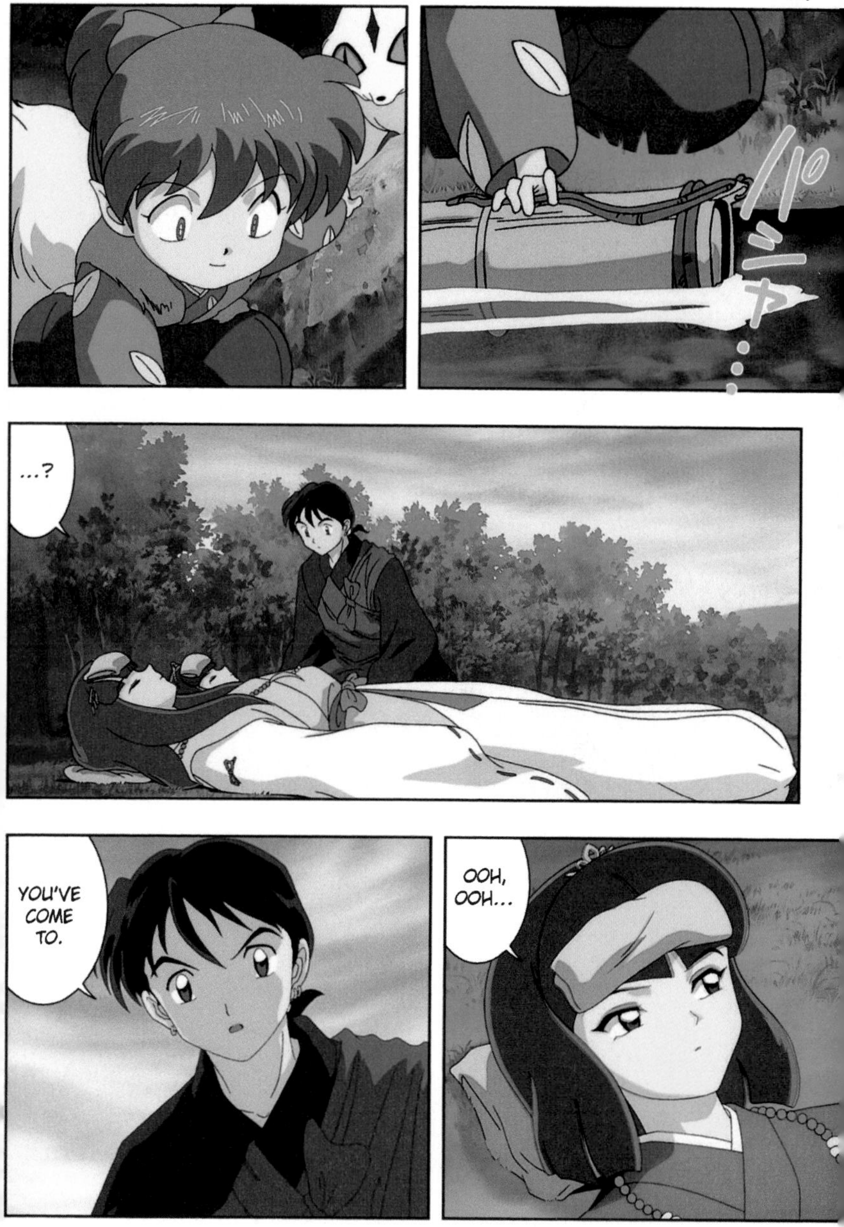

パシャ…
...?
OOH, OOH...
YOU'VE COME TO.

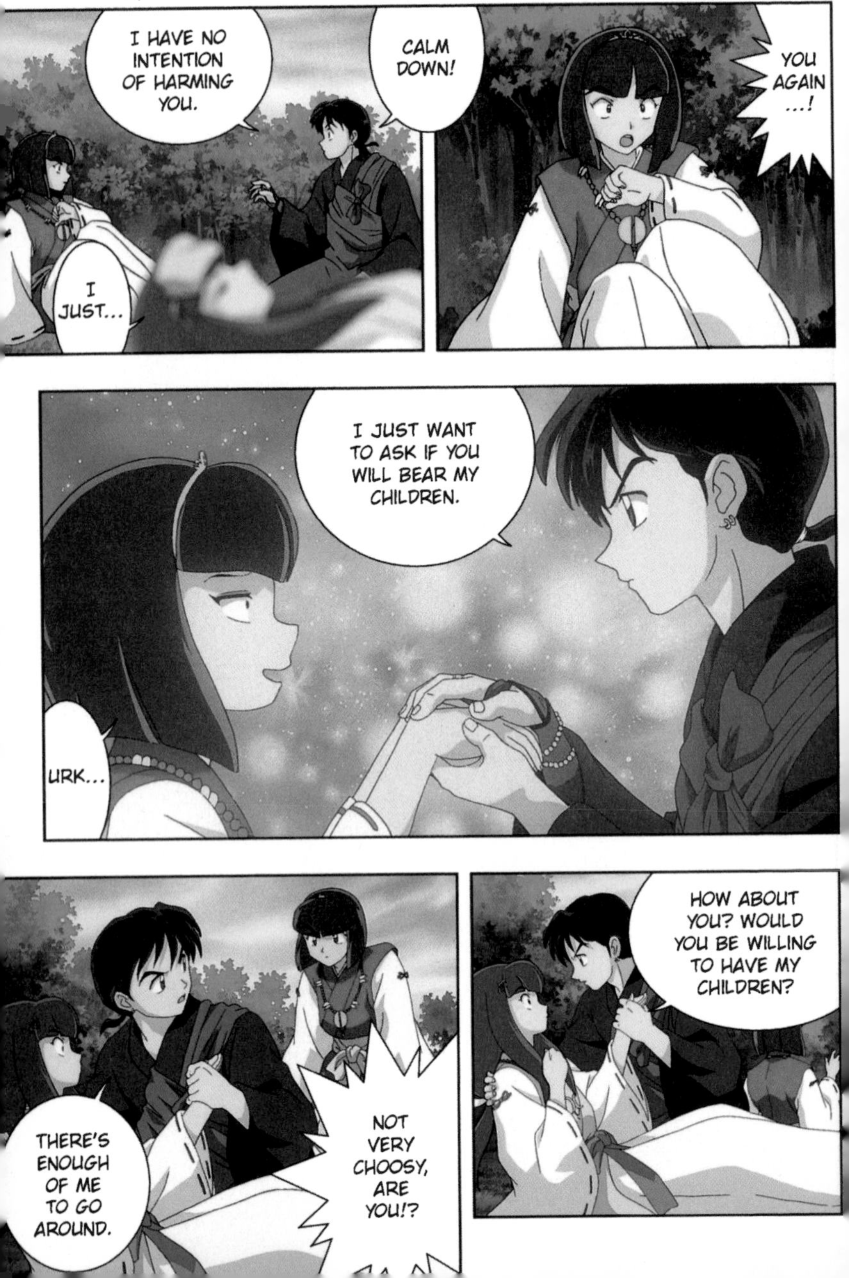

YOU AGAIN ...!
CALM DOWN!
I HAVE NO INTENTION OF HARMING YOU.
I JUST...
I JUST WANT TO ASK IF YOU WILL BEAR MY CHILDREN.
URK...
HOW ABOUT YOU? WOULD YOU BE WILLING TO HAVE MY CHILDREN?
NOT VERY CHOOSY, ARE YOU!?
THERE'S ENOUGH OF ME TO GO AROUND.

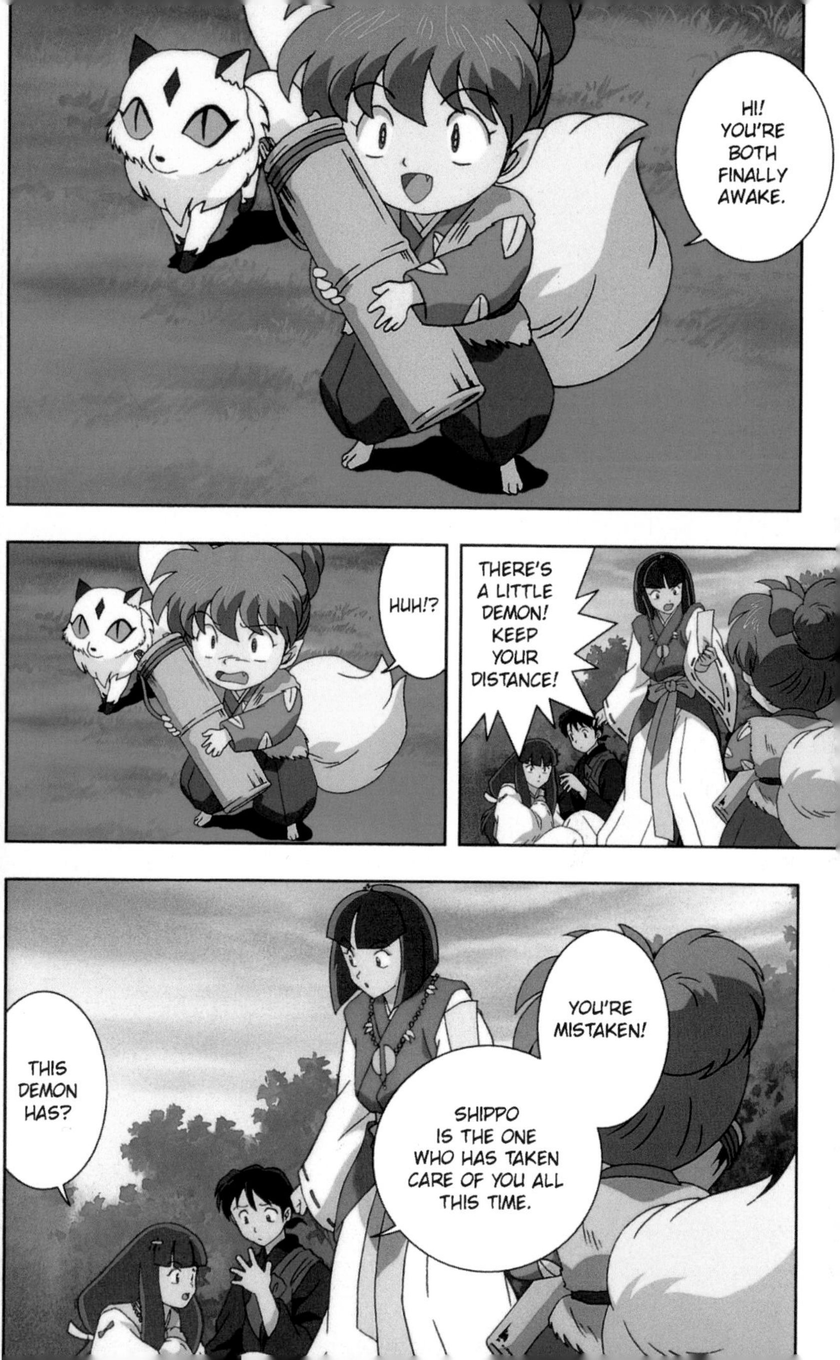
HI! YOU'RE BOTH FINALLY AWAKE.
THERE'S A LITTLE DEMON! KEEP YOUR DISTANCE!
HUH!?
YOU'RE MISTAKEN!
SHIPPO IS THE ONE WHO HAS TAKEN CARE OF YOU ALL THIS TIME.
THIS DEMON HAS?

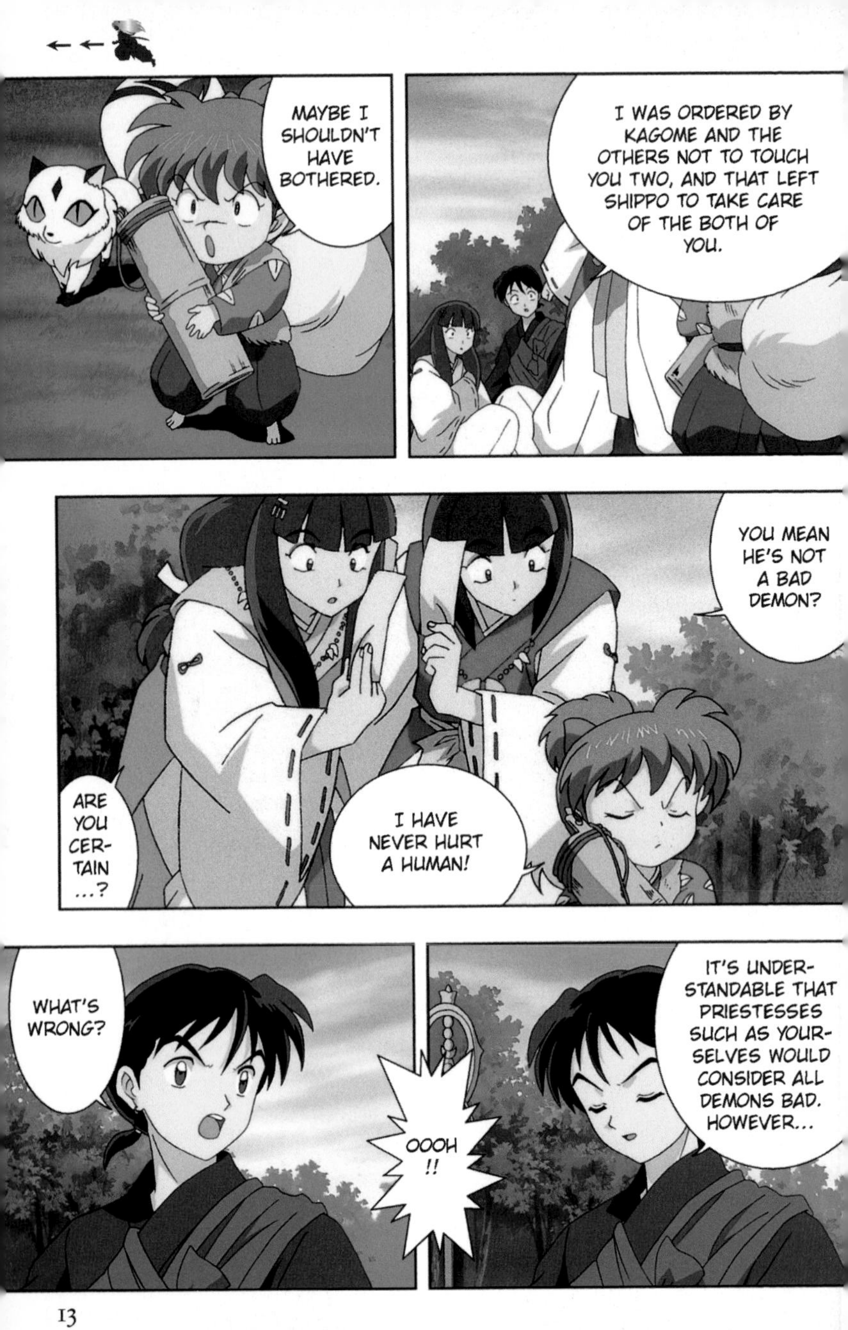
I WAS ORDERED BY KAGOME AND THE OTHERS NOT TO TOUCH YOU TWO, AND THAT LEFT SHIPPO TO TAKE CARE OF THE BOTH OF YOU.
MAYBE I SHOULDN'T HAVE BOTHERED.
YOU MEAN HE'S NOT A BAD DEMON?
I HAVE NEVER HURT A HUMAN!
ARE YOU CER-TAIN ...?
IT'S UNDER-STANDABLE THAT PRIESTESSES SUCH AS YOUR-SELVES WOULD CONSIDER ALL DEMONS BAD. HOWEVER...
OOOH !!
WHAT'S WRONG?

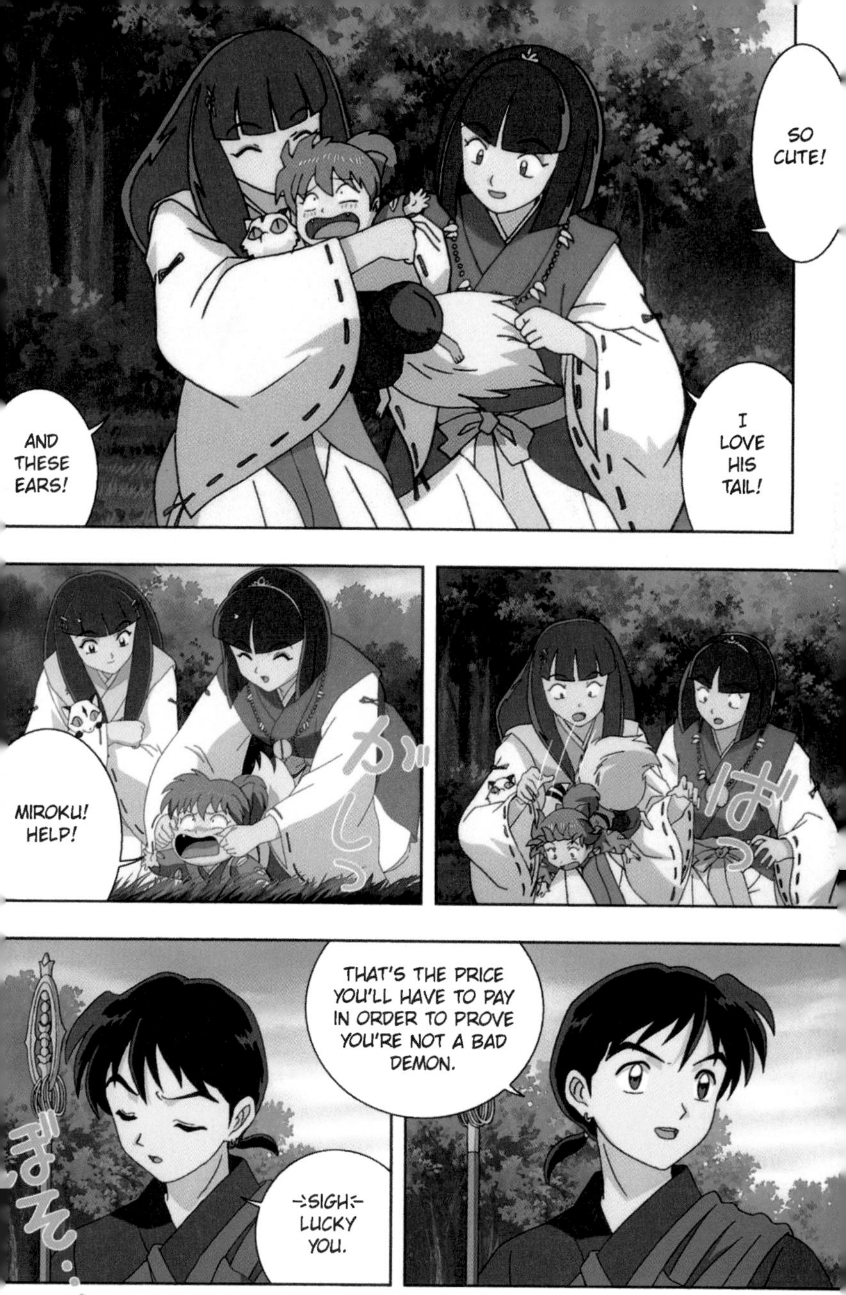
SO CUTE!
I LOVE HIS TAIL!
AND THESE EARS!
はっ
がしっ
MIROKU! HELP!
THAT'S THE PRICE YOU'LL HAVE TO PAY IN ORDER TO PROVE YOU'RE NOT A BAD DEMON.
ぼそ…
-SIGH- LUCKY YOU.

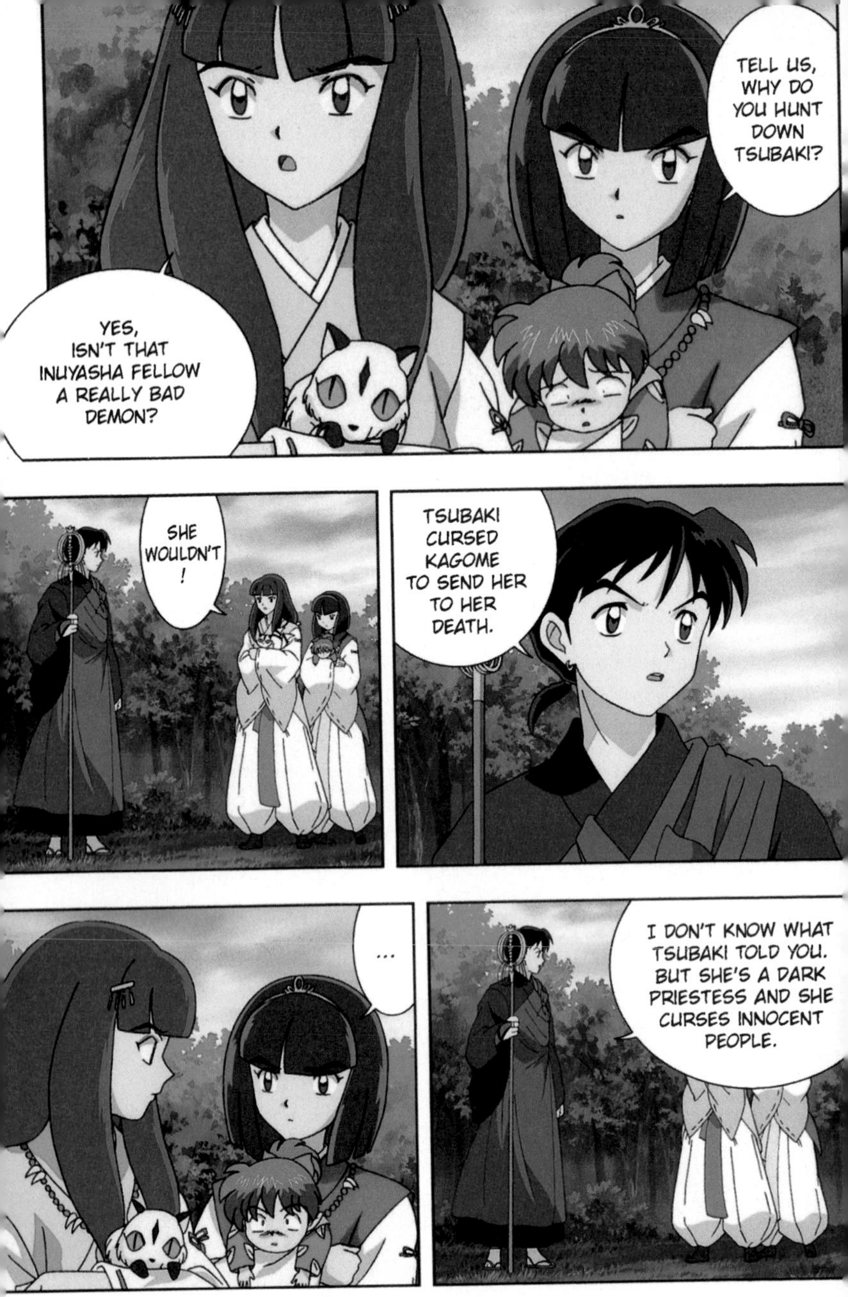
TELL US, WHY DO YOU HUNT DOWN TSUBAKI?
YES, ISN'T THAT INUYASHA FELLOW A REALLY BAD DEMON?
TSUBAKI CURSED KAGOME TO SEND HER TO HER DEATH.
SHE WOULDN'T !
I DON'T KNOW WHAT TSUBAKI TOLD YOU. BUT SHE'S A DARK PRIESTESS AND SHE CURSES INNOCENT PEOPLE.
...

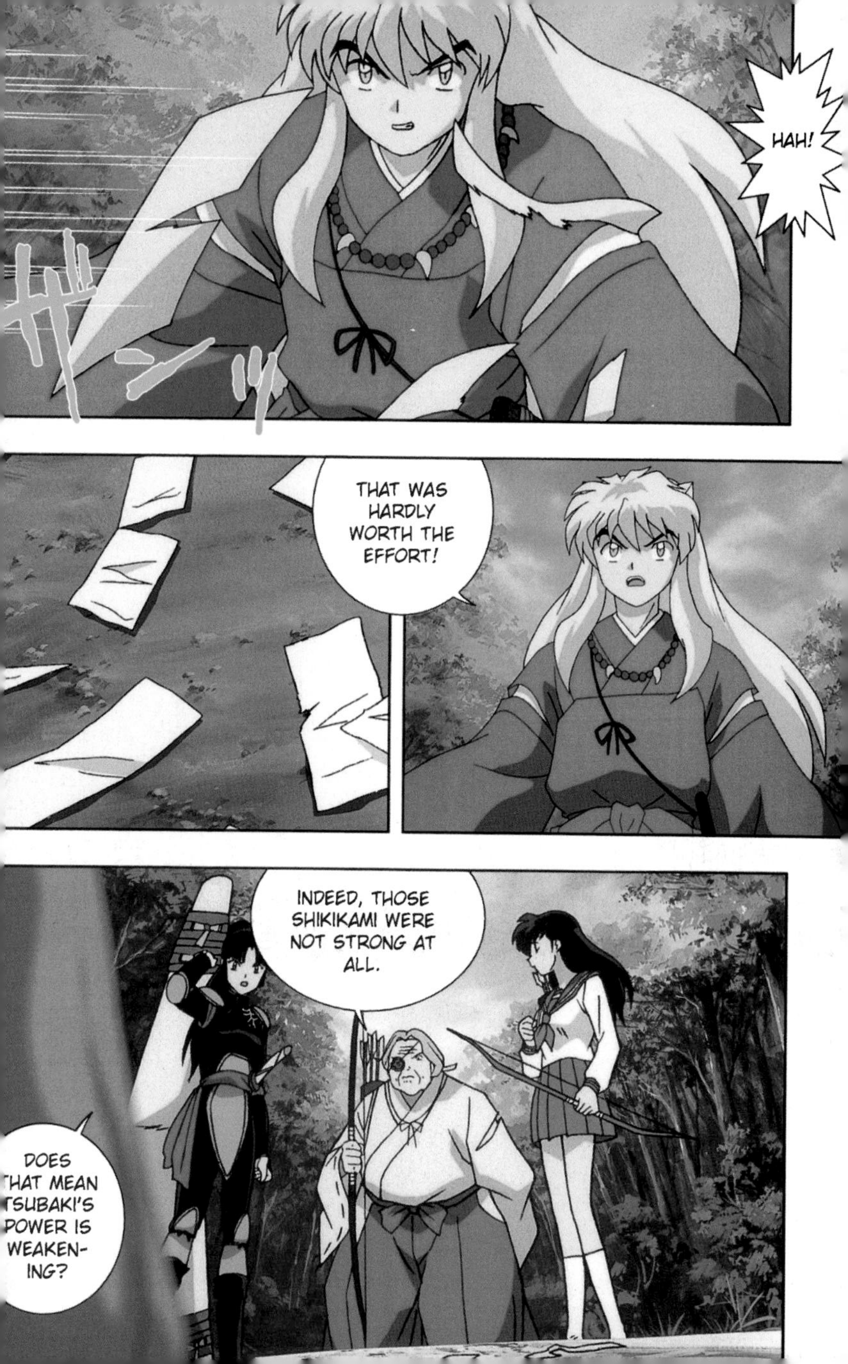
HAH!
THAT WAS HARDLY WORTH THE EFFORT!
INDEED, THOSE SHIKIKAMI WERE NOT STRONG AT ALL.
DOES THAT MEAN TSUBAKI'S POWER IS WEAKEN-ING?

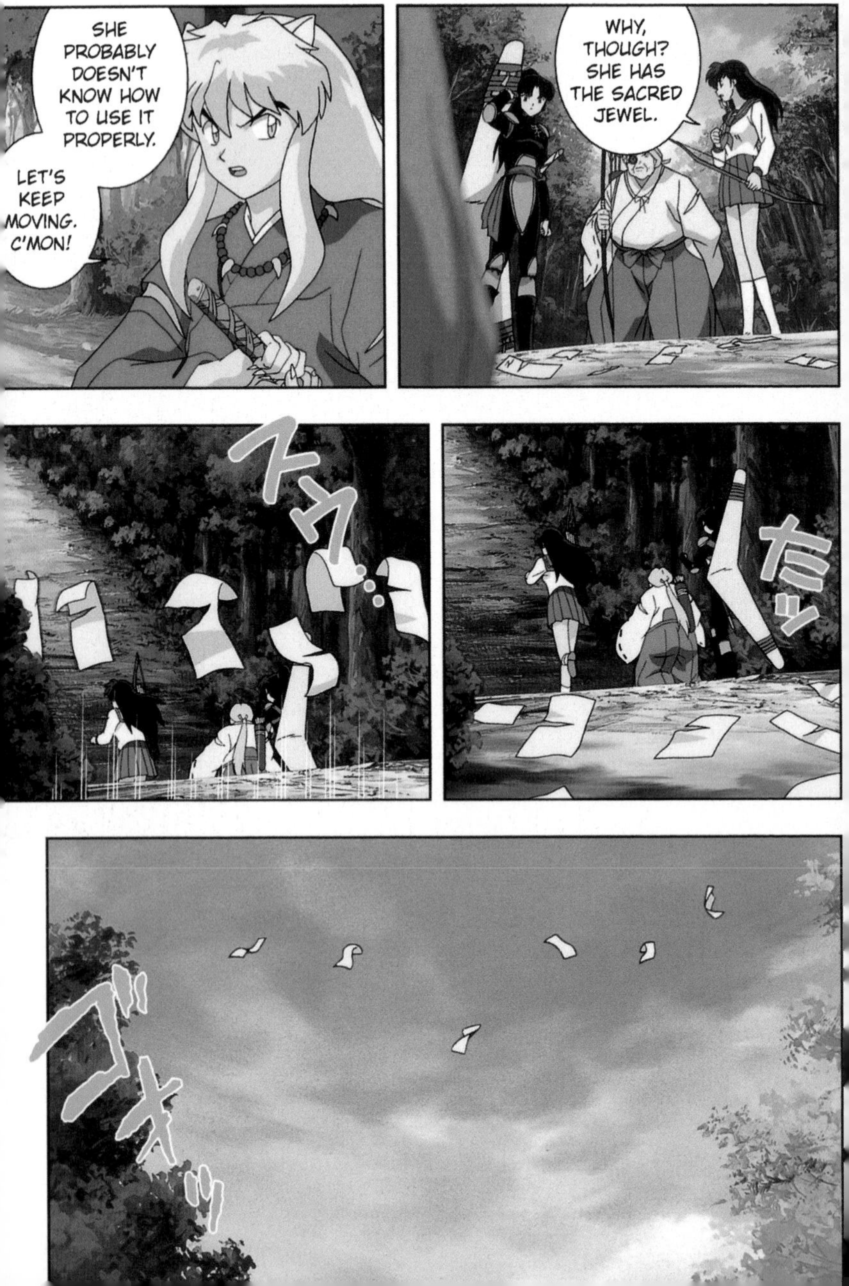
WHY, THOUGH? SHE HAS THE SACRED JEWEL.
SHE PROBABLY DOESN'T KNOW HOW TO USE IT PROPERLY.
LET'S KEEP MOVING. C'MON!
タッ
スゥ…
ゴォッ

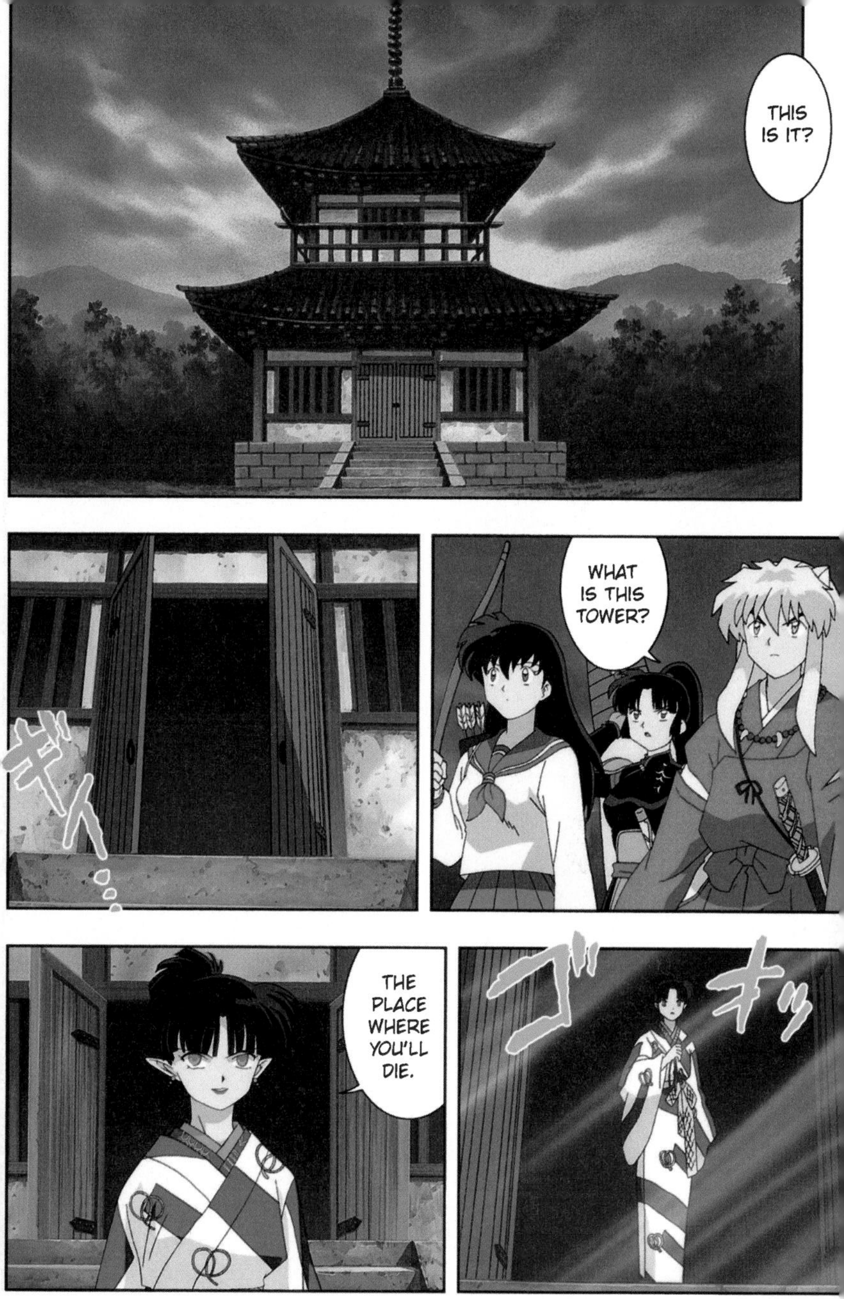
THIS IS IT?
WHAT IS THIS TOWER?
ギィ
ゴォッ
THE PLACE WHERE YOU'LL DIE.

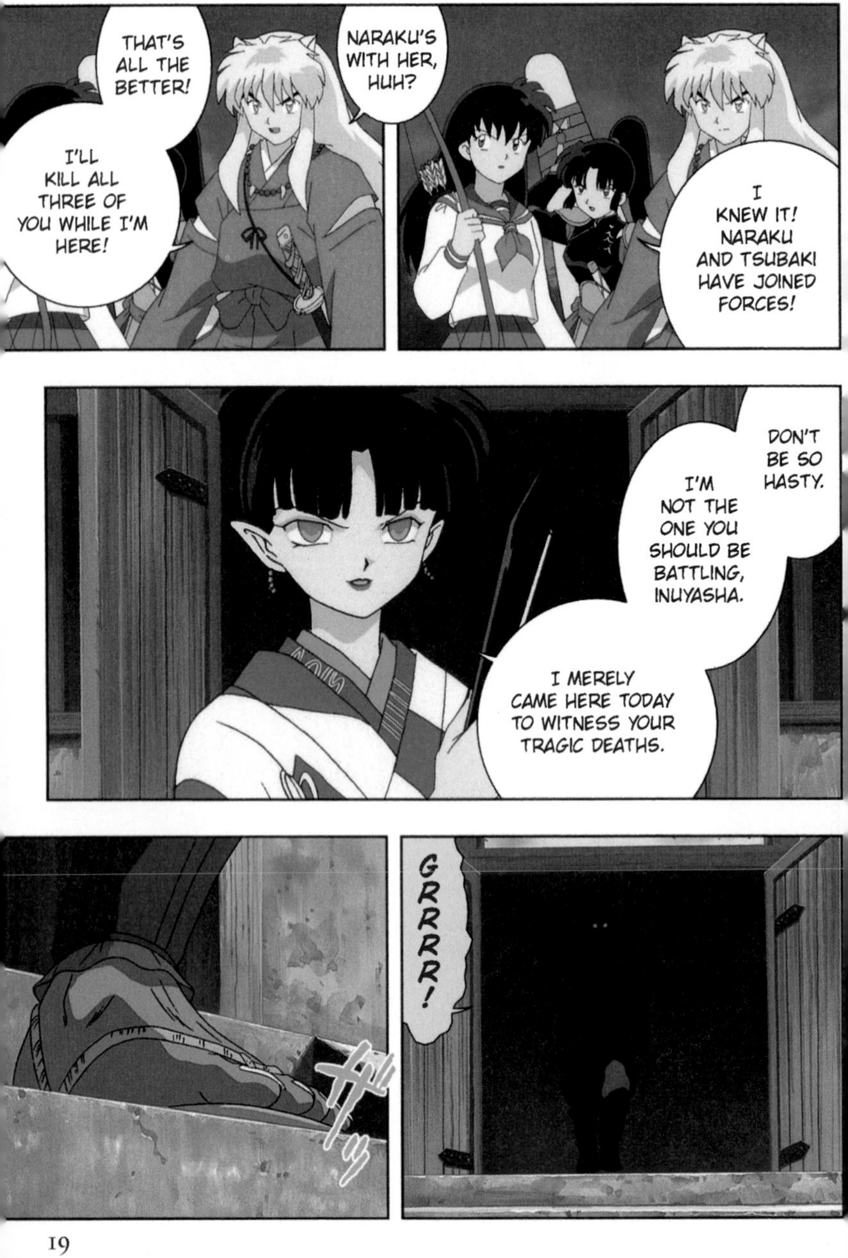
I KNEW IT! NARAKU AND TSUBAKI HAVE JOINED FORCES!
NARAKU'S WITH HER, HUH?
THAT'S ALL THE BETTER!
I'LL KILL ALL THREE OF YOU WHILE I'M HERE!
DON'T BE SO HASTY.
I'M NOT THE ONE YOU SHOULD BE BATTLING, INUYASHA.
I MERELY CAME HERE TODAY TO WITNESS YOUR TRAGIC DEATHS.
GRRRR!

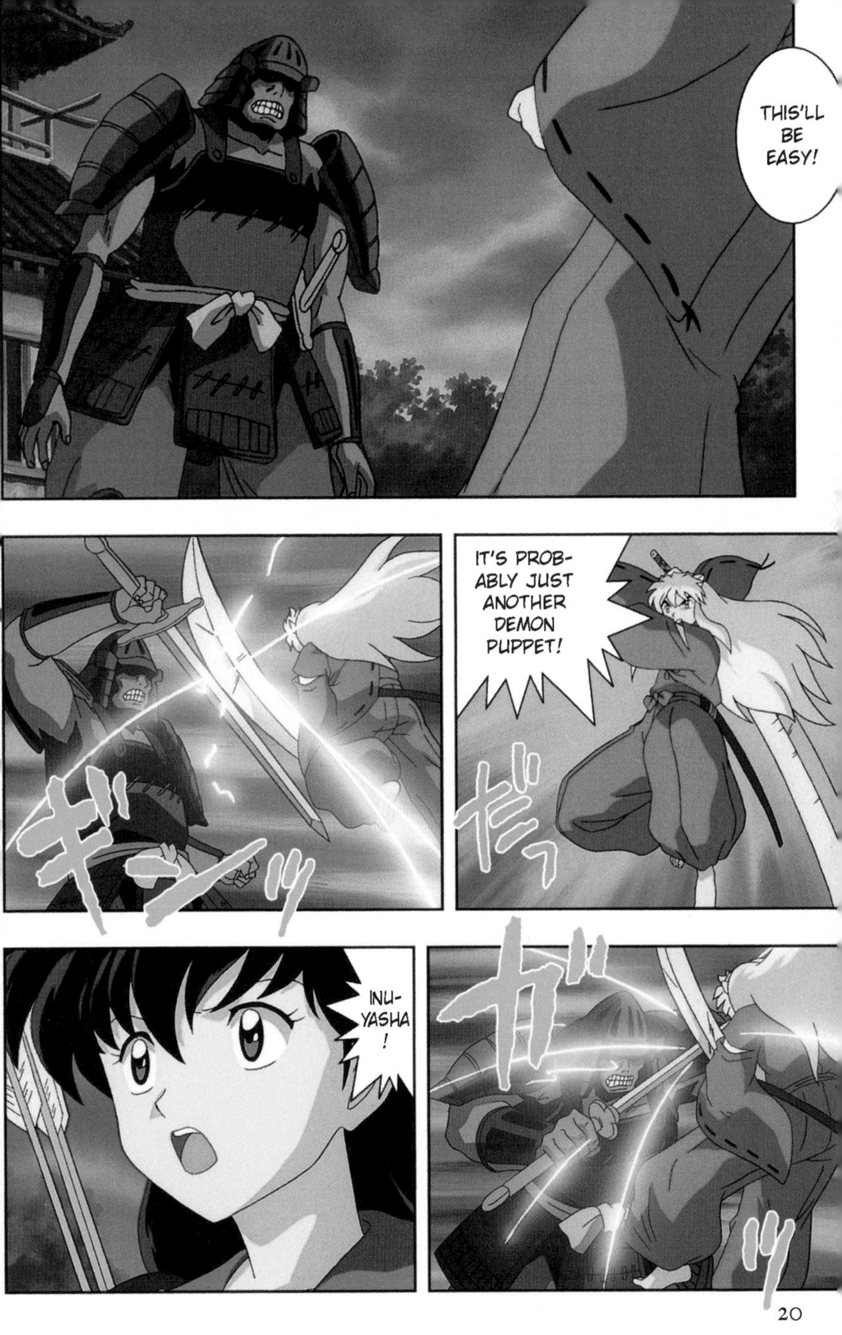
THIS'LL BE EASY!
IT'S PROB-ABLY JUST ANOTHER DEMON PUPPET!
だっ
ギンッ
ガッ
INU-YASHA!

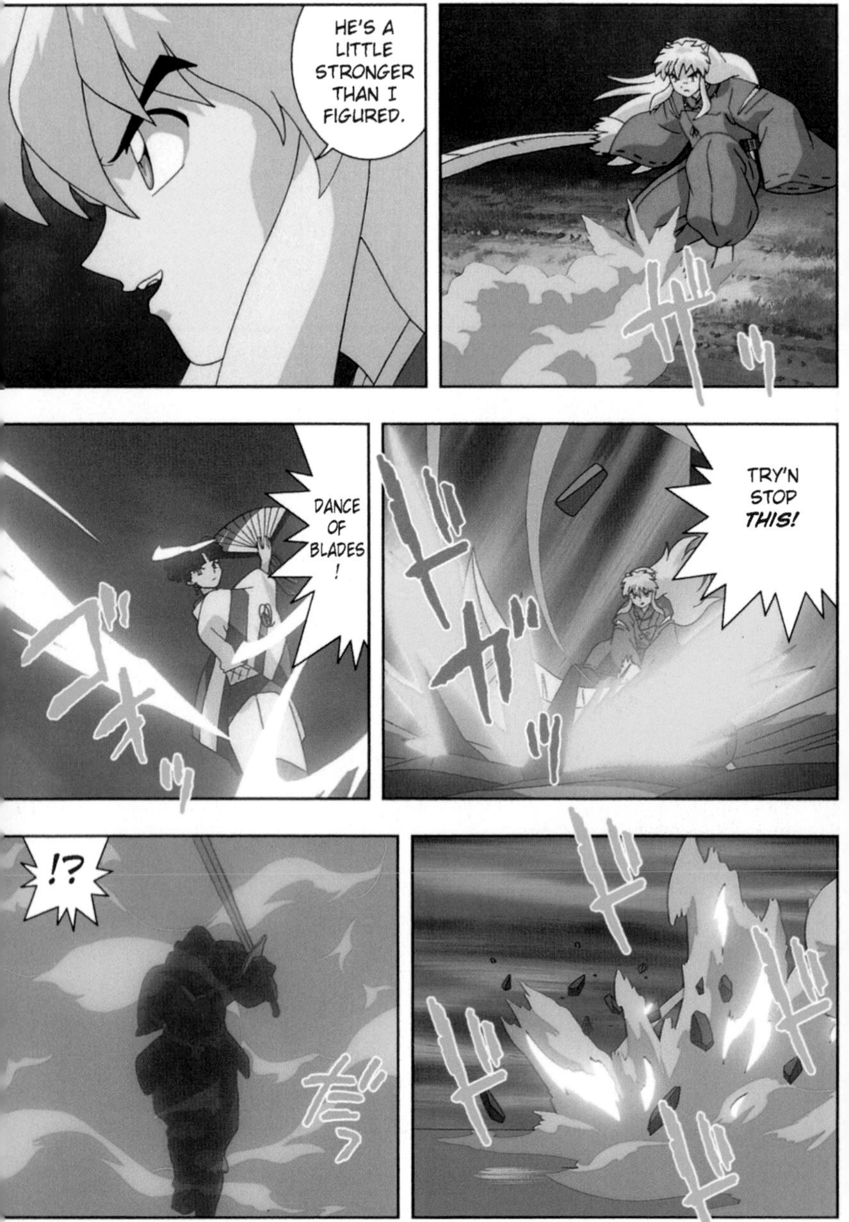
HE'S A LITTLE STRONGER THAN I FIGURED.
TRY'N STOP *THIS!*
DANCE OF BLADES!
!?

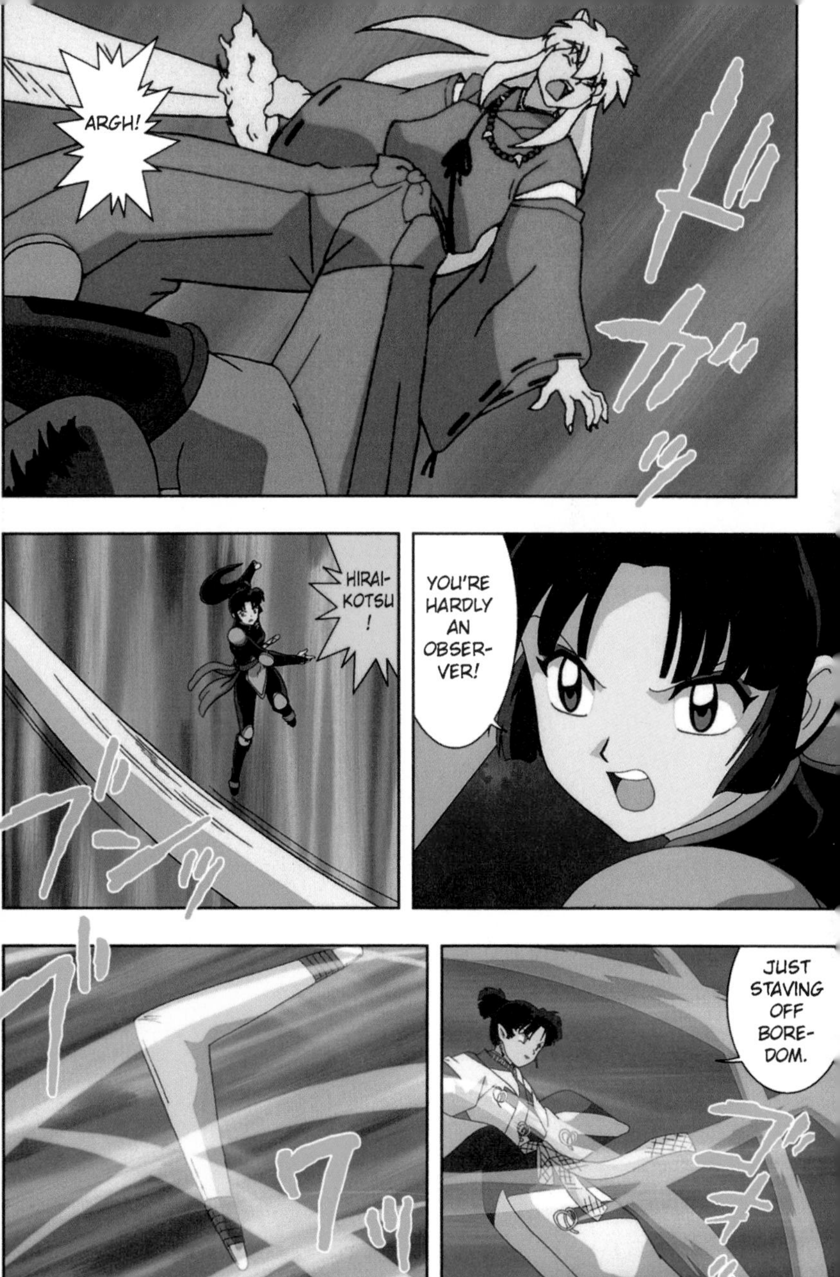
ARGH!
ドガッ
YOU'RE HARDLY AN OBSER-VER!
HIRAI-KOTSU!
ブーンッ
JUST STAVING OFF BORE-DOM.
ブワッ

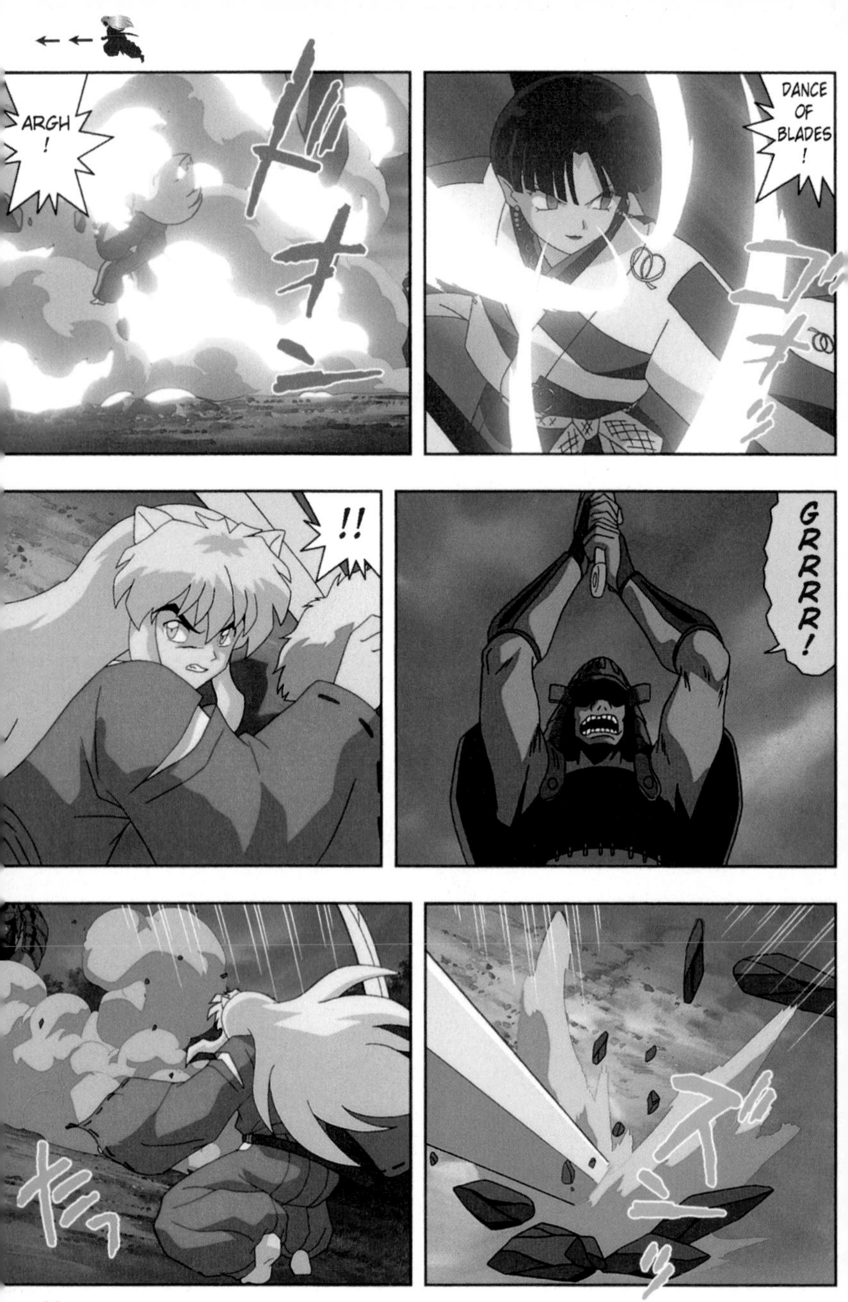
DANCE OF BLADES!
ARGH!
GRRRR!
!!

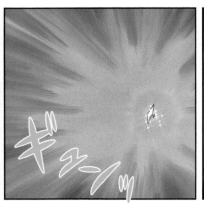

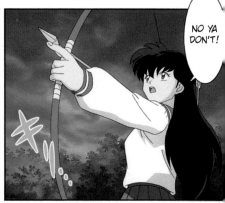

NO YA DON'T!

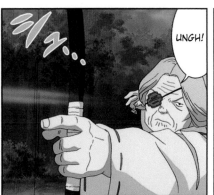

UNGH!

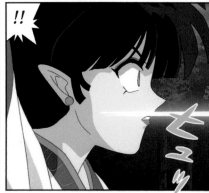

!!

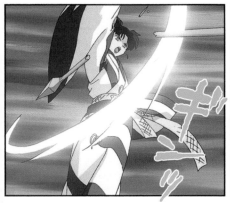

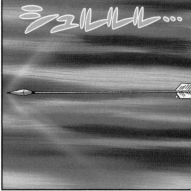

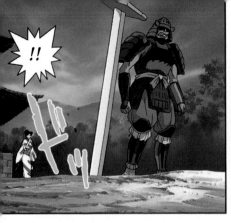

!!

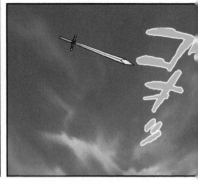

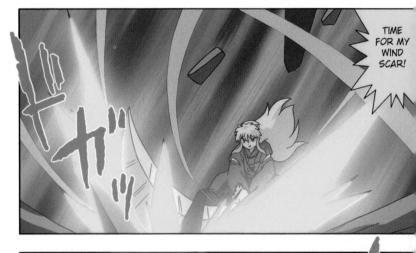

TIME FOR MY WIND SCAR!

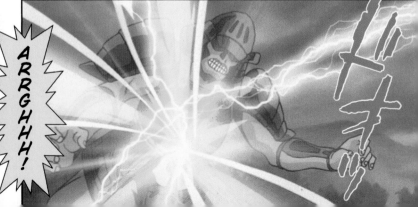

ARRGHHH!

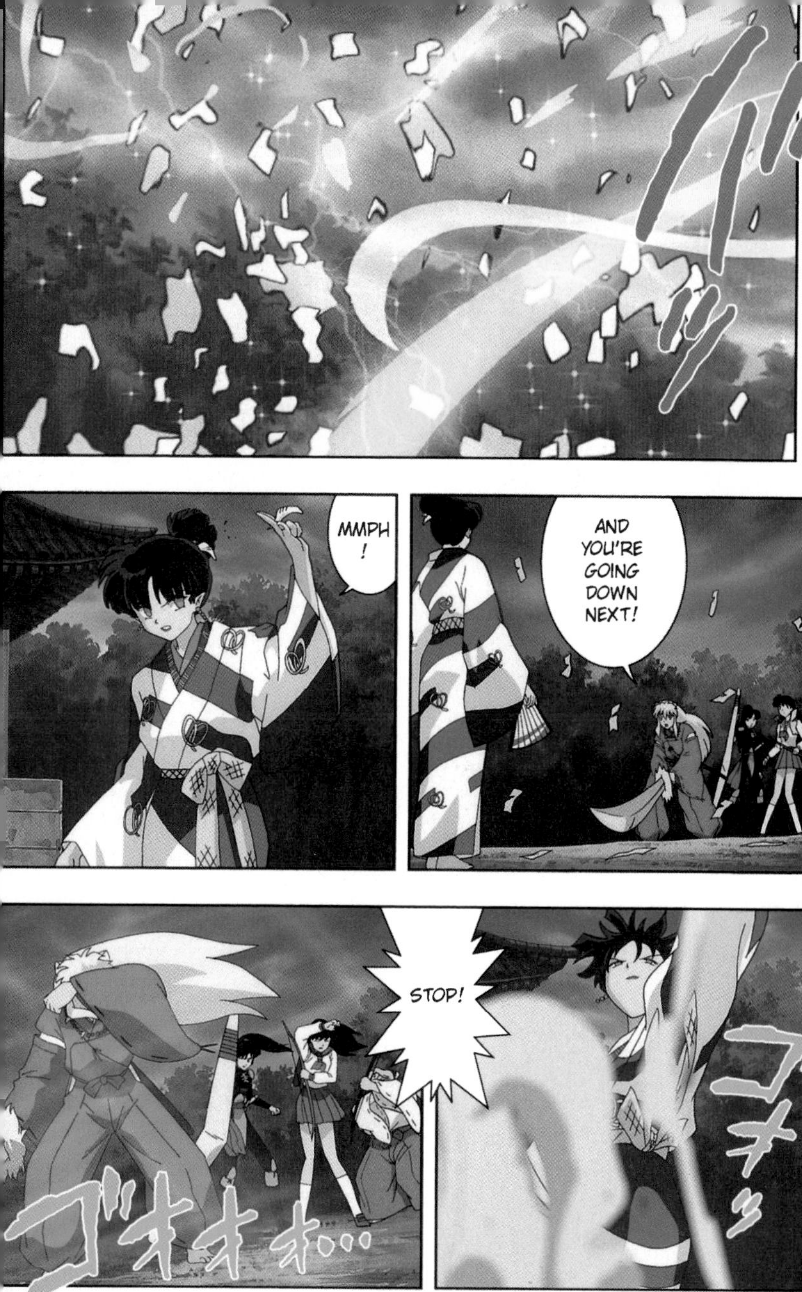
AND YOU'RE GOING DOWN NEXT!
MMPH!
STOP!

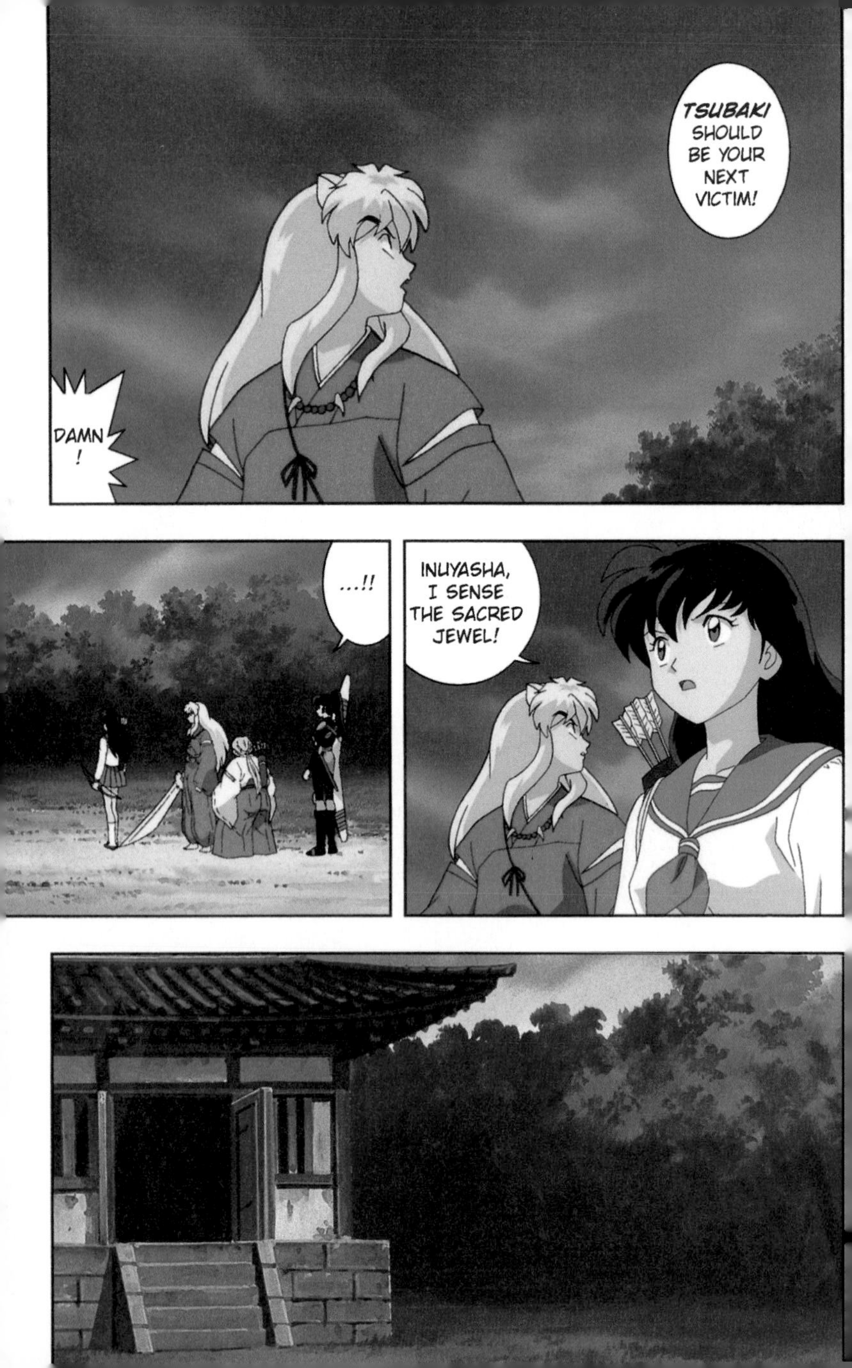
TSUBAKI SHOULD BE YOUR NEXT VICTIM!
DAMN!
INUYASHA, I SENSE THE SACRED JEWEL!
...!!

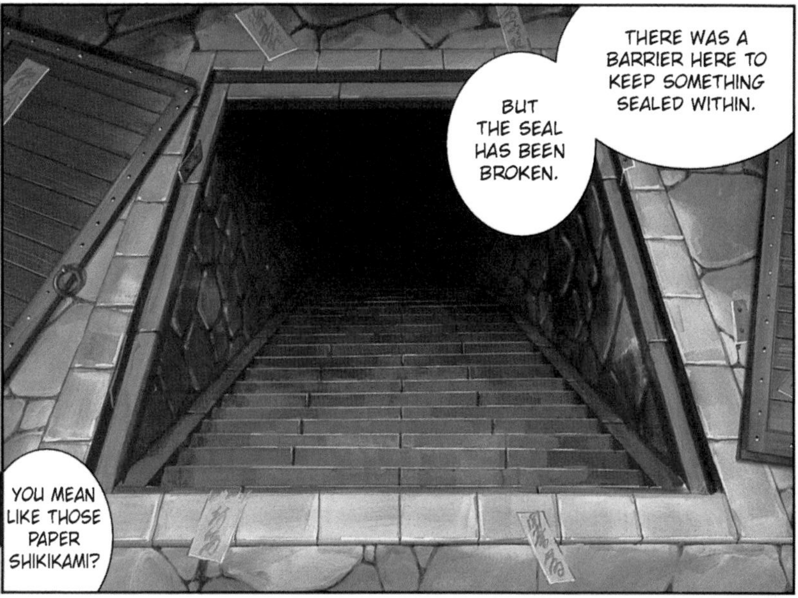
THERE WAS A BARRIER HERE TO KEEP SOMETHING SEALED WITHIN.
BUT THE SEAL HAS BEEN BROKEN.
YOU MEAN LIKE THOSE PAPER SHIKIKAMI?

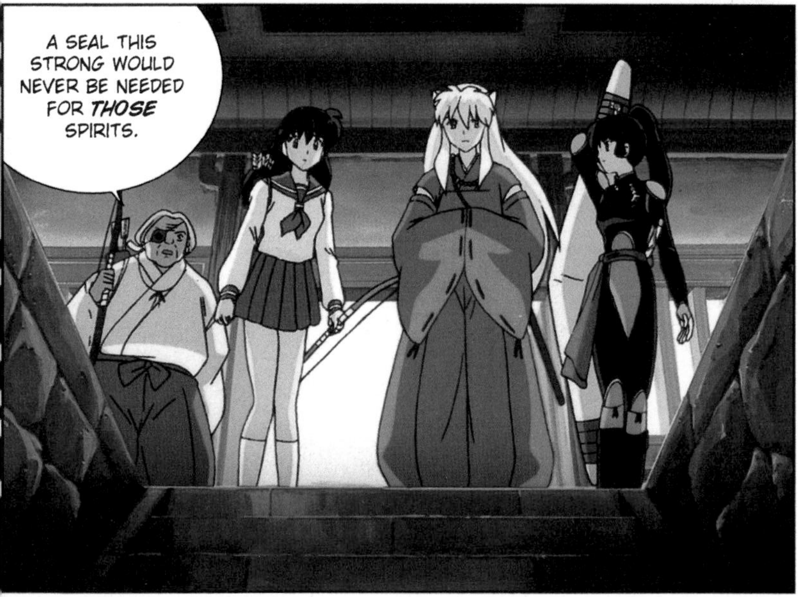
A SEAL THIS STRONG WOULD NEVER BE NEEDED FOR *THOSE* SPIRITS.

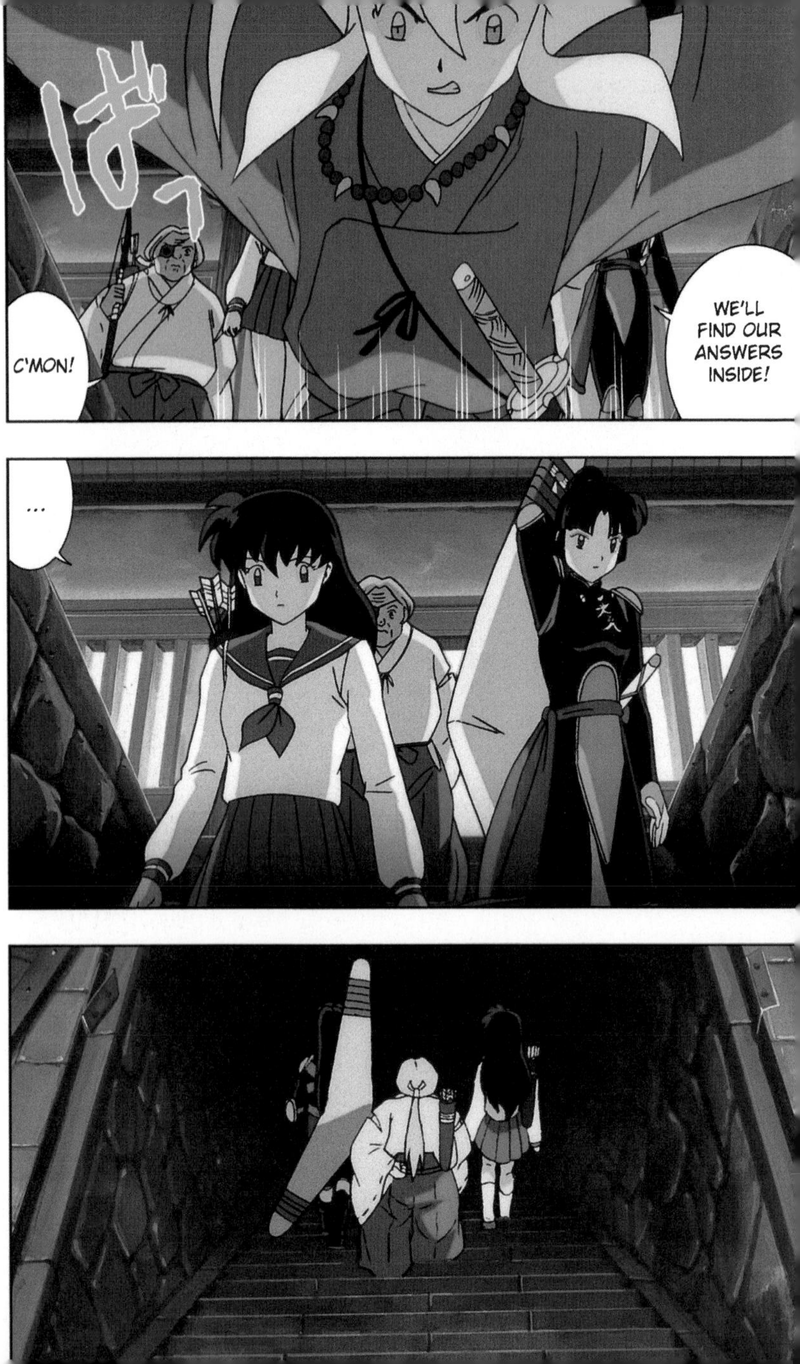
WE'LL FIND OUR ANSWERS INSIDE!
ぱっ
C'MON!
...

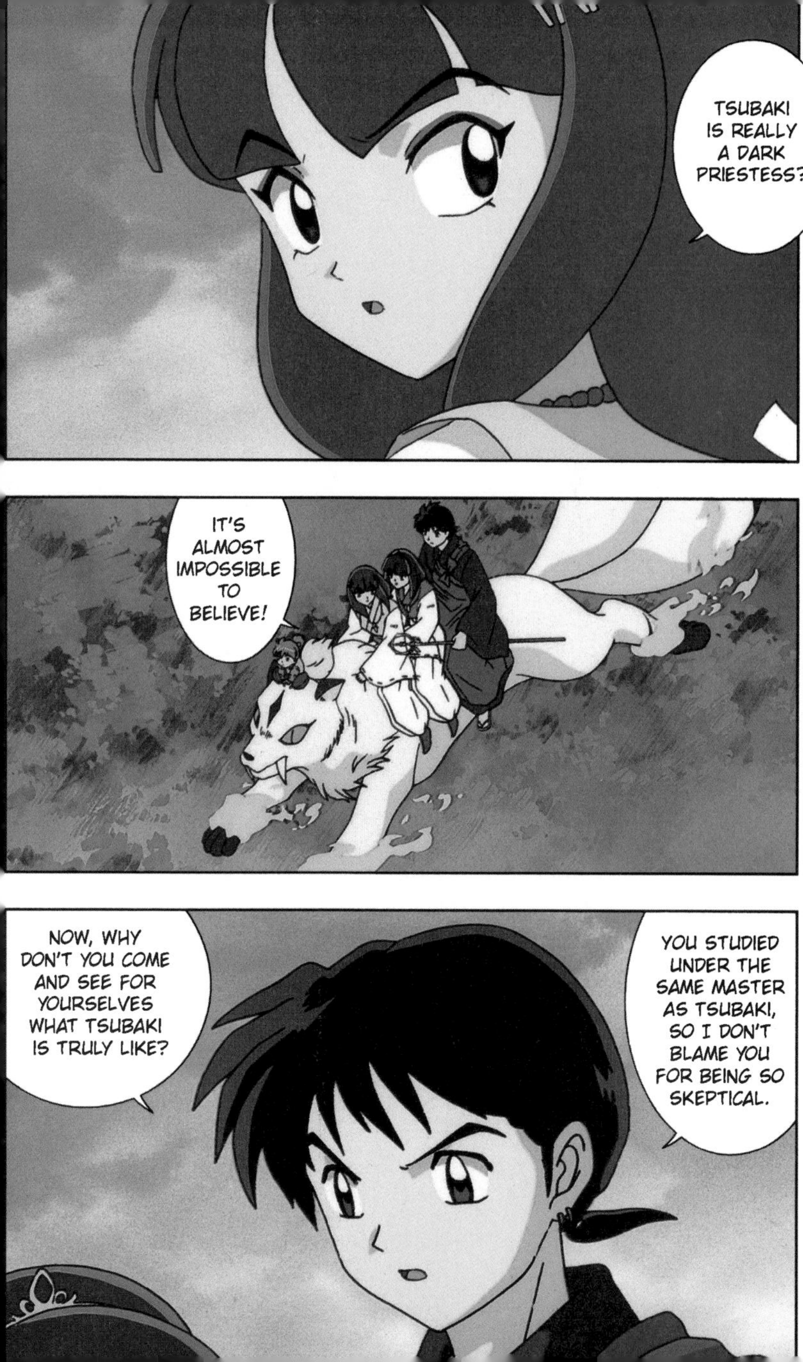
TSUBAKI IS REALLY A DARK PRIESTESS?
IT'S ALMOST IMPOSSIBLE TO BELIEVE!
YOU STUDIED UNDER THE SAME MASTER AS TSUBAKI, SO I DON'T BLAME YOU FOR BEING SO SKEPTICAL.
NOW, WHY DON'T YOU COME AND SEE FOR YOURSELVES WHAT TSUBAKI IS TRULY LIKE?

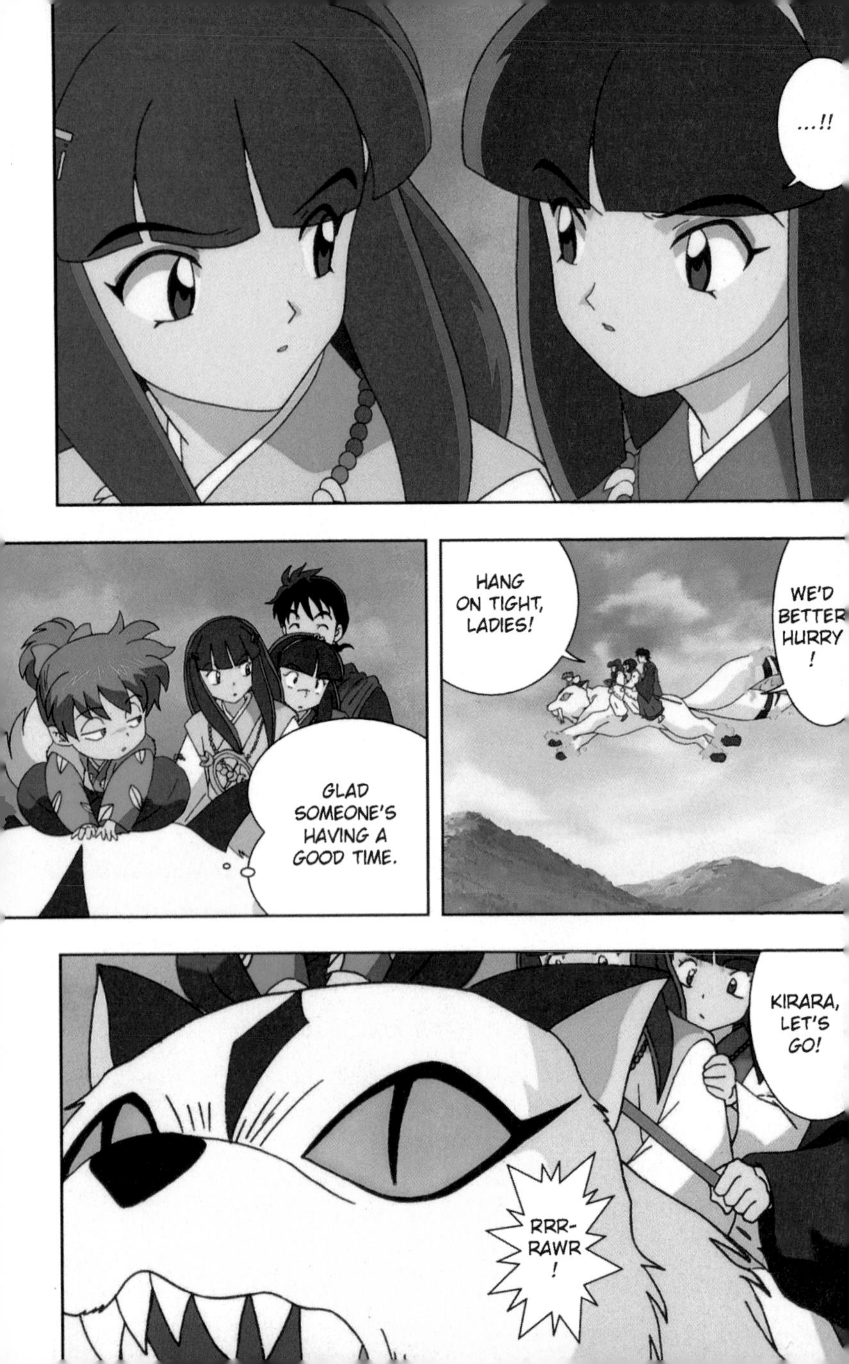
...!!
WE'D BETTER HURRY!
HANG ON TIGHT, LADIES!
GLAD SOMEONE'S HAVING A GOOD TIME.
KIRARA, LET'S GO!
RRR-RAWR!

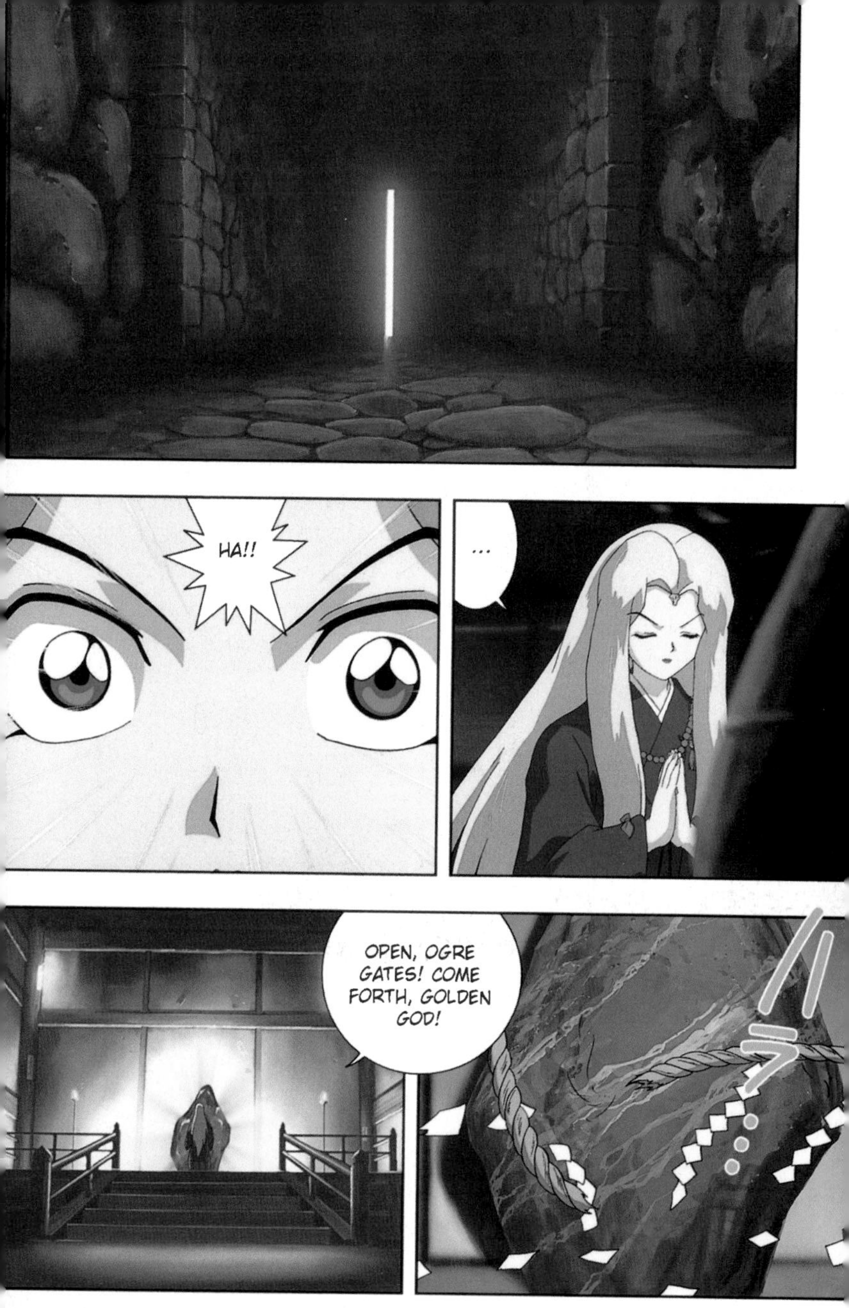
...
HA!!
ハラ
OPEN, OGRE GATES! COME FORTH, GOLDEN GOD!

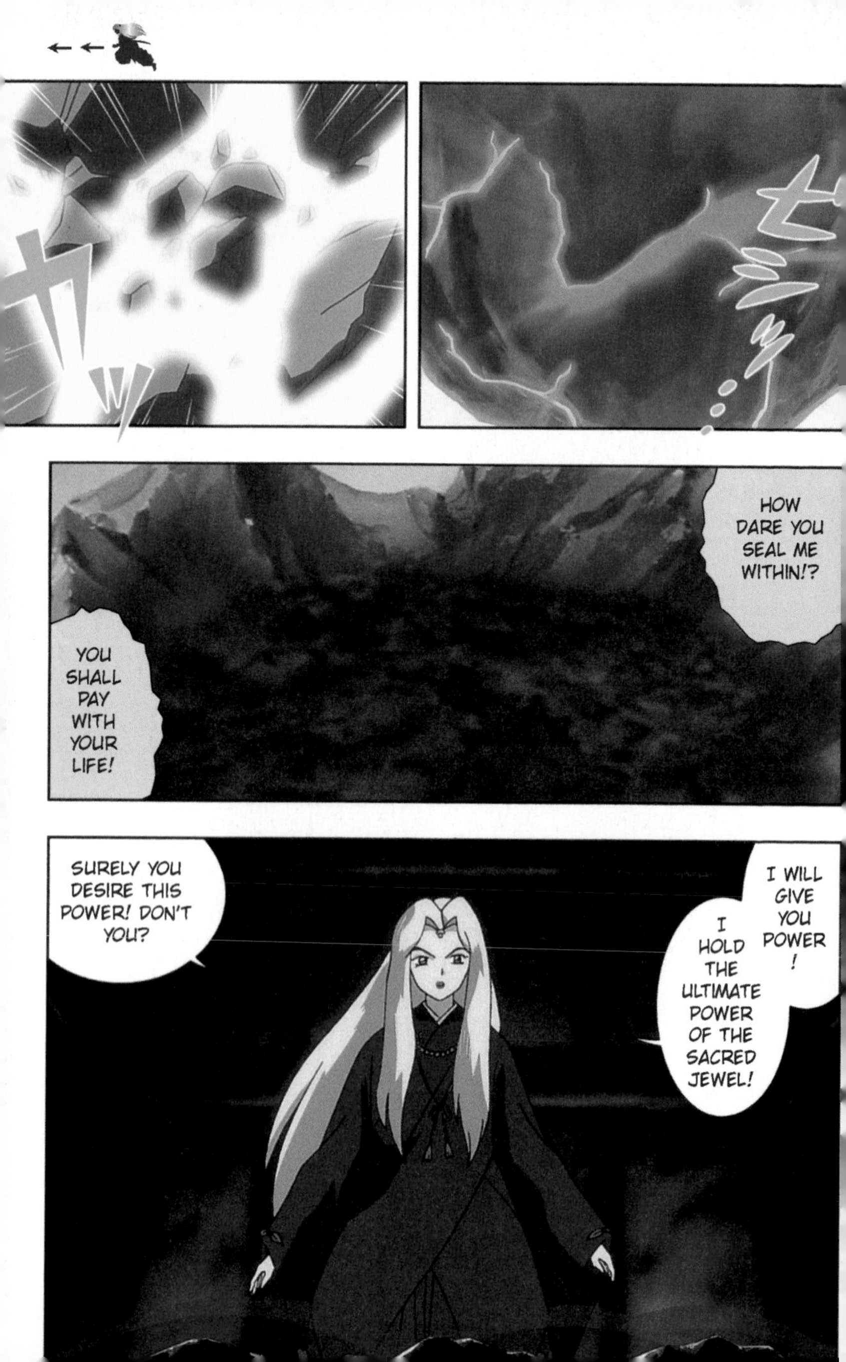
HOW DARE YOU SEAL ME WITHIN!?
YOU SHALL PAY WITH YOUR LIFE!
I WILL GIVE YOU POWER!
I HOLD THE ULTIMATE POWER OF THE SACRED JEWEL!
SURELY YOU DESIRE THIS POWER! DON'T YOU?

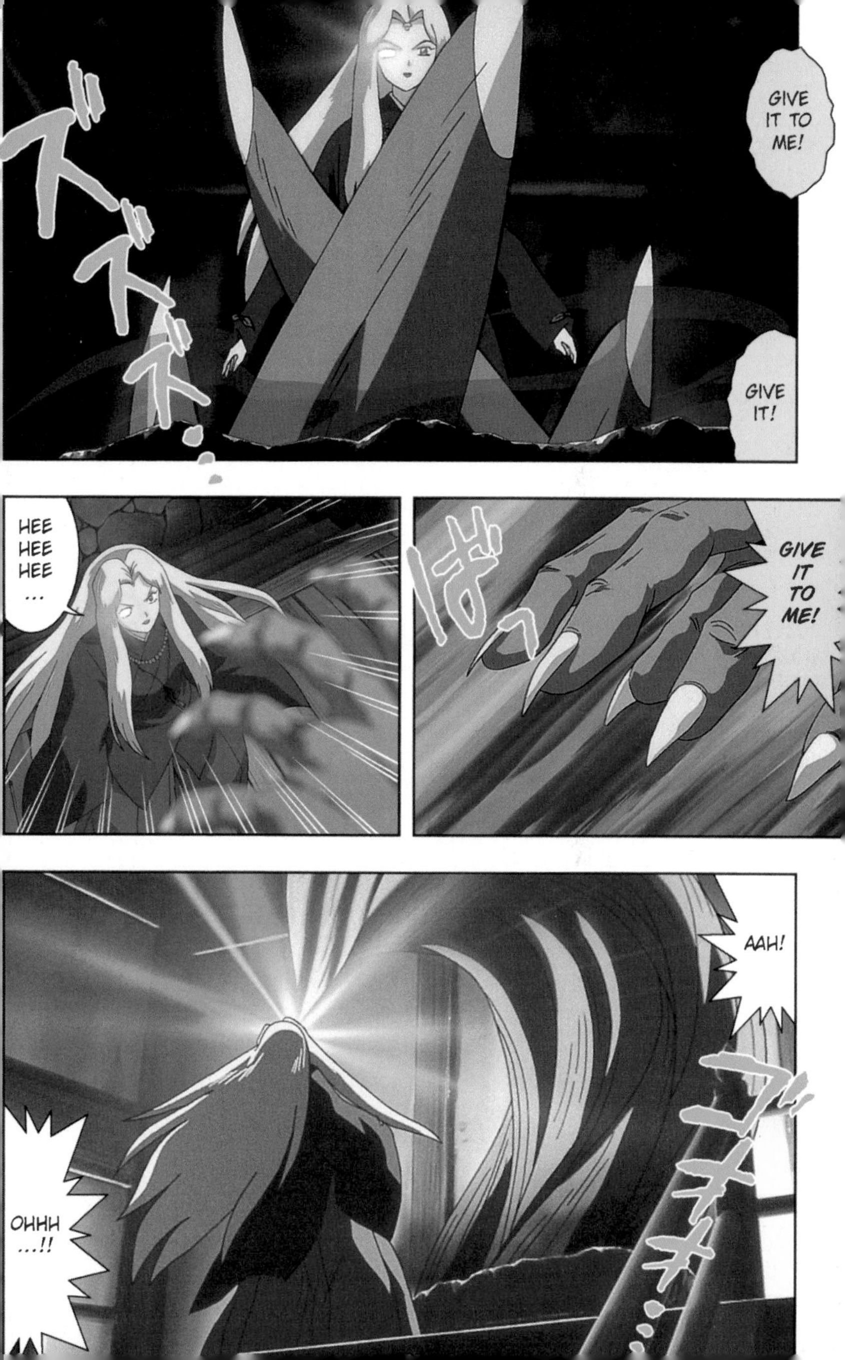
GIVE IT TO ME!
GIVE IT!
ズズズズ…
GIVE IT TO ME!
ばっ
HEE HEE HEE …
AAH!
ゴキキ…
OHHH …!!

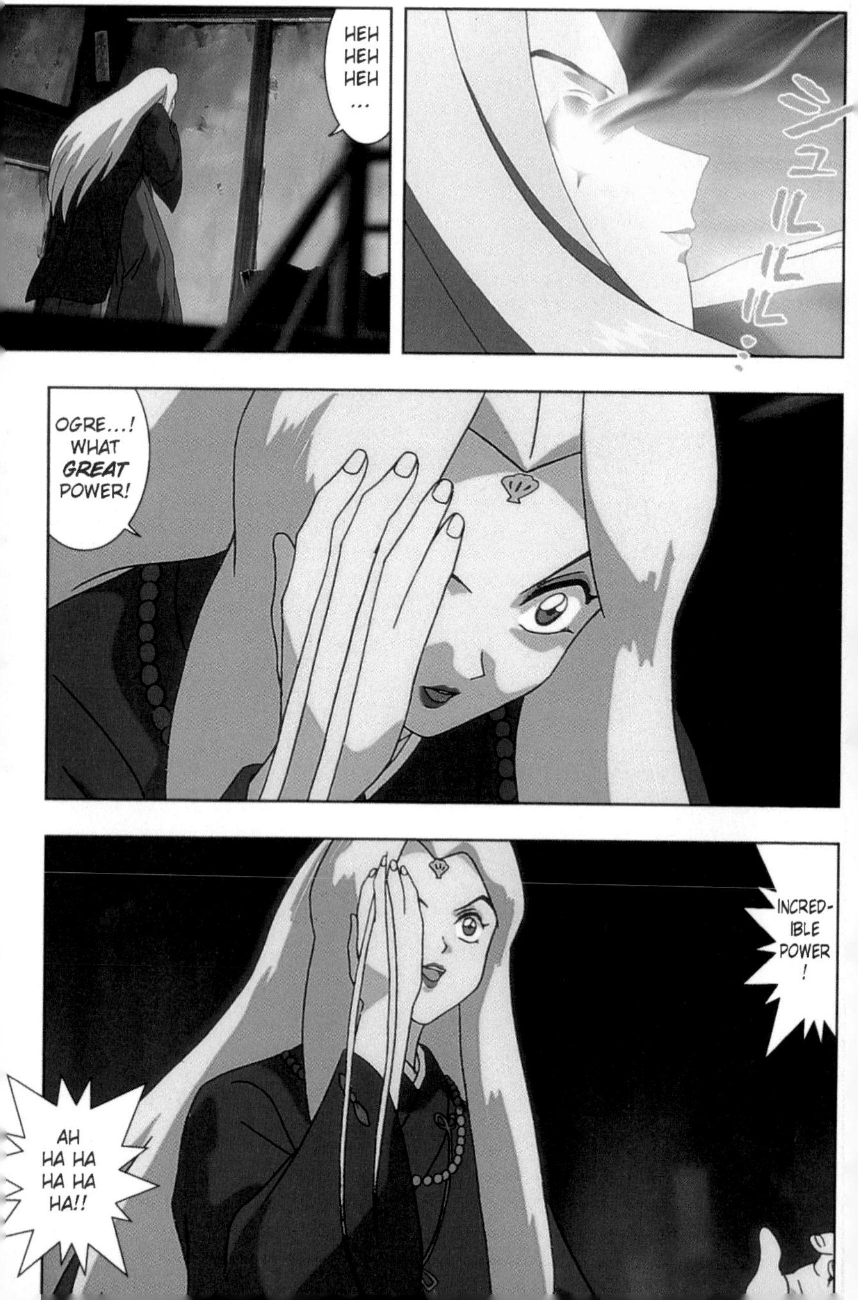
シュルルル…
HEH HEH HEH …
OGRE…! WHAT GREAT POWER!
INCRED-IBLE POWER!
AH HA HA HA HA HA!!

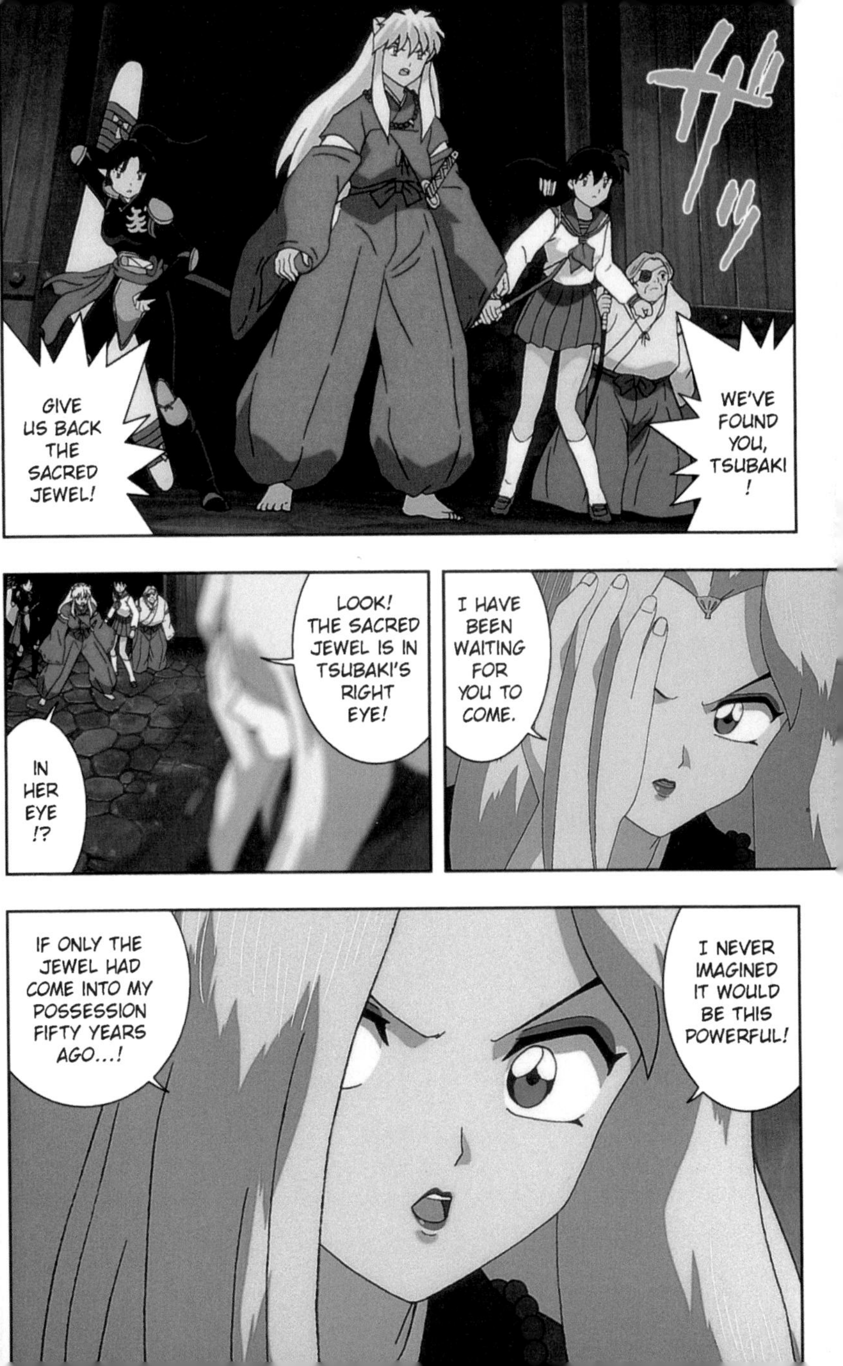
ザッ
WE'VE FOUND YOU, TSUBAKI!
GIVE US BACK THE SACRED JEWEL!
I HAVE BEEN WAITING FOR YOU TO COME.
LOOK! THE SACRED JEWEL IS IN TSUBAKI'S RIGHT EYE!
IN HER EYE!?
I NEVER IMAGINED IT WOULD BE THIS POWERFUL!
IF ONLY THE JEWEL HAD COME INTO MY POSSESSION FIFTY YEARS AGO...!

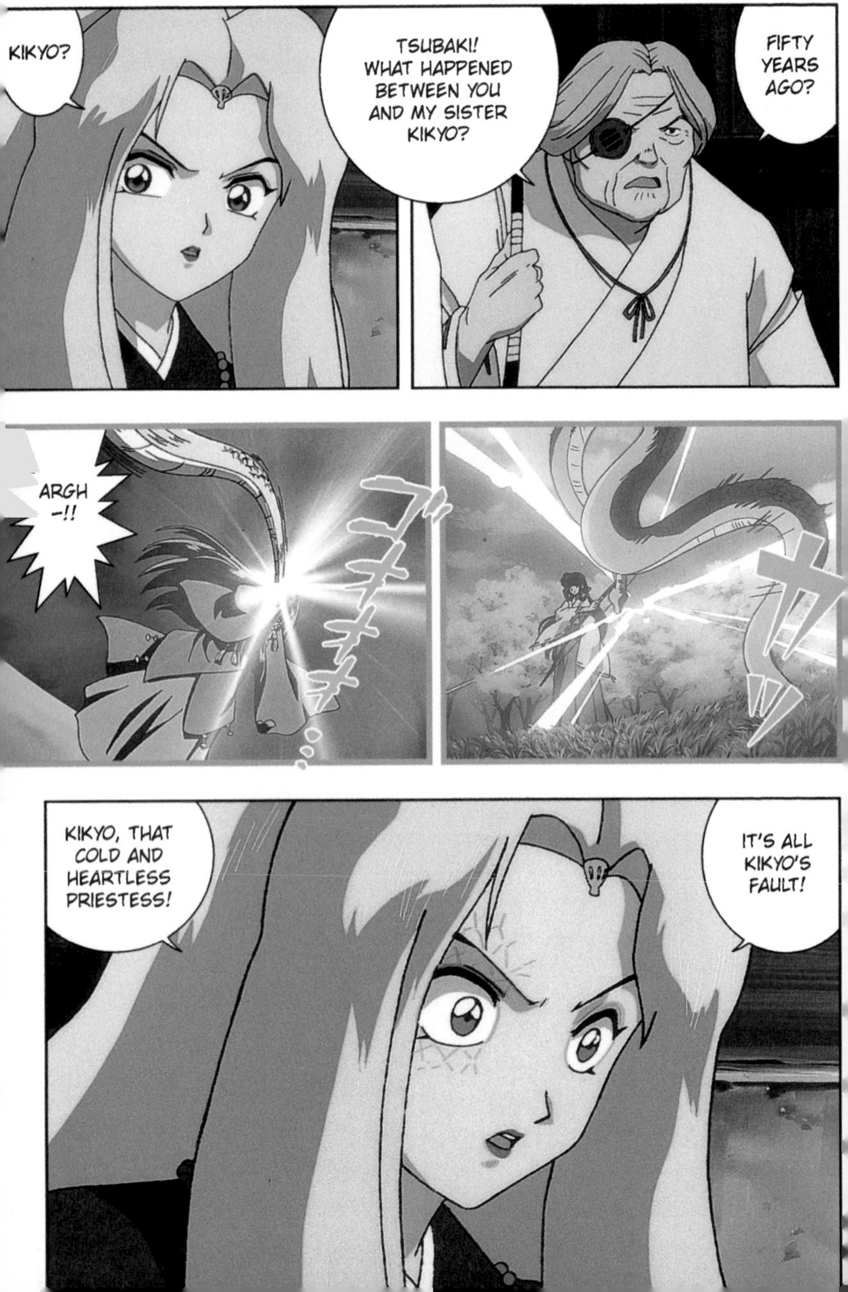
FIFTY YEARS AGO?
TSUBAKI! WHAT HAPPENED BETWEEN YOU AND MY SISTER KIKYO?
KIKYO?
ARGH -!!
IT'S ALL KIKYO'S FAULT!
KIKYO, THAT COLD AND HEARTLESS PRIESTESS!

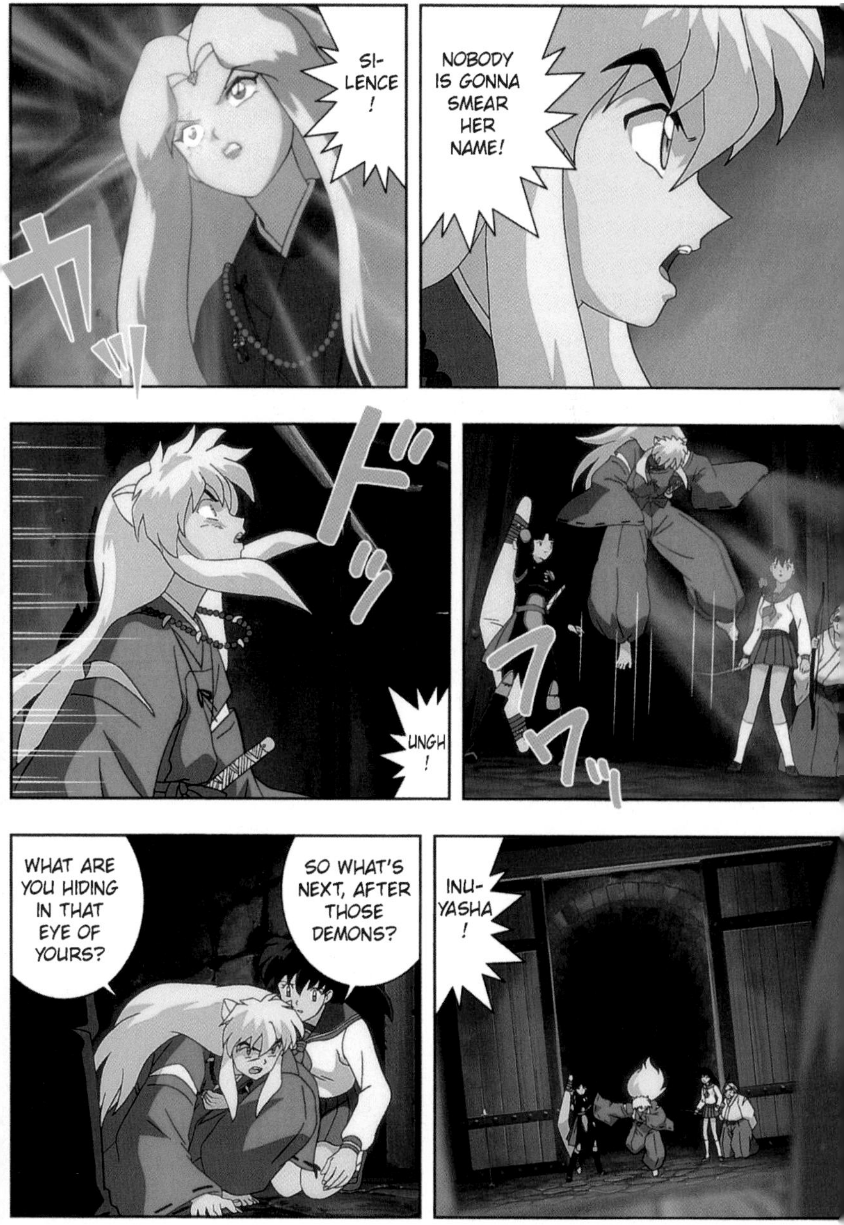
NOBODY IS GONNA SMEAR HER NAME!
SI-LENCE!
フワッ
ドッ
UNGH!
INU-YASHA!
SO WHAT'S NEXT, AFTER THOSE DEMONS?
WHAT ARE YOU HIDING IN THAT EYE OF YOURS?

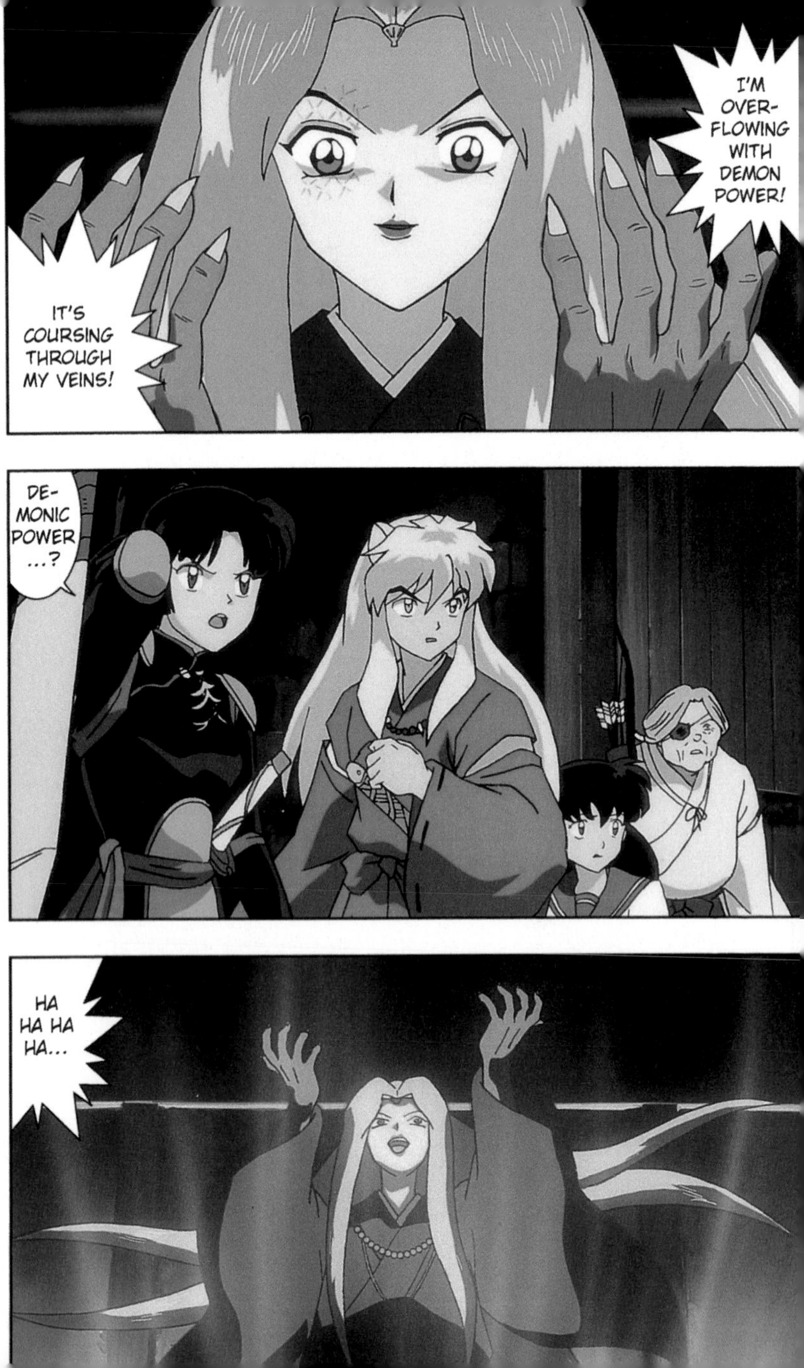
I'M OVER-FLOWING WITH DEMON POWER!
IT'S COURSING THROUGH MY VEINS!
DE-MONIC POWER ...?
HA HA HA HA...

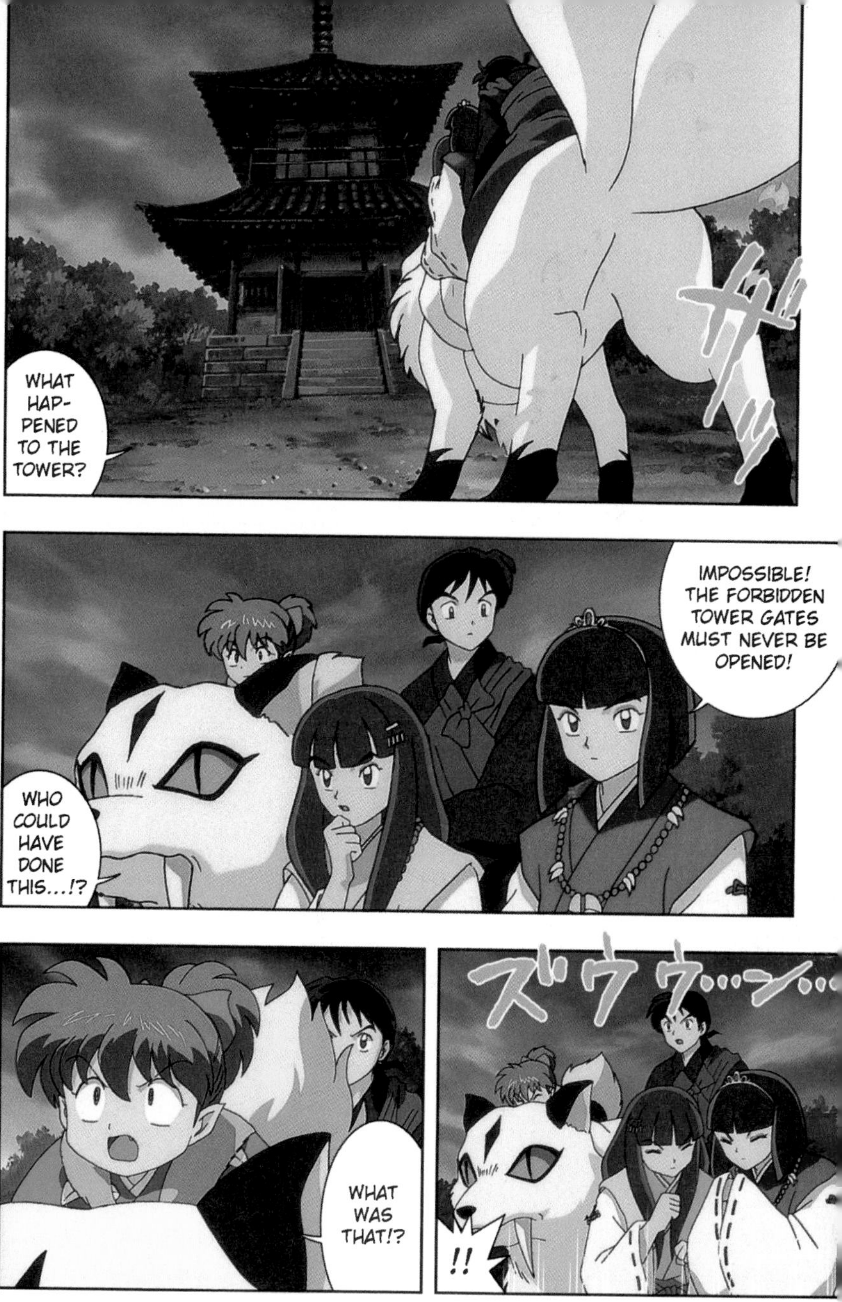
WHAT HAP-PENED TO THE TOWER?
IMPOSSIBLE! THE FORBIDDEN TOWER GATES MUST NEVER BE OPENED!
WHO COULD HAVE DONE THIS...!?
ズウウ…ン…
!!
WHAT WAS THAT!?

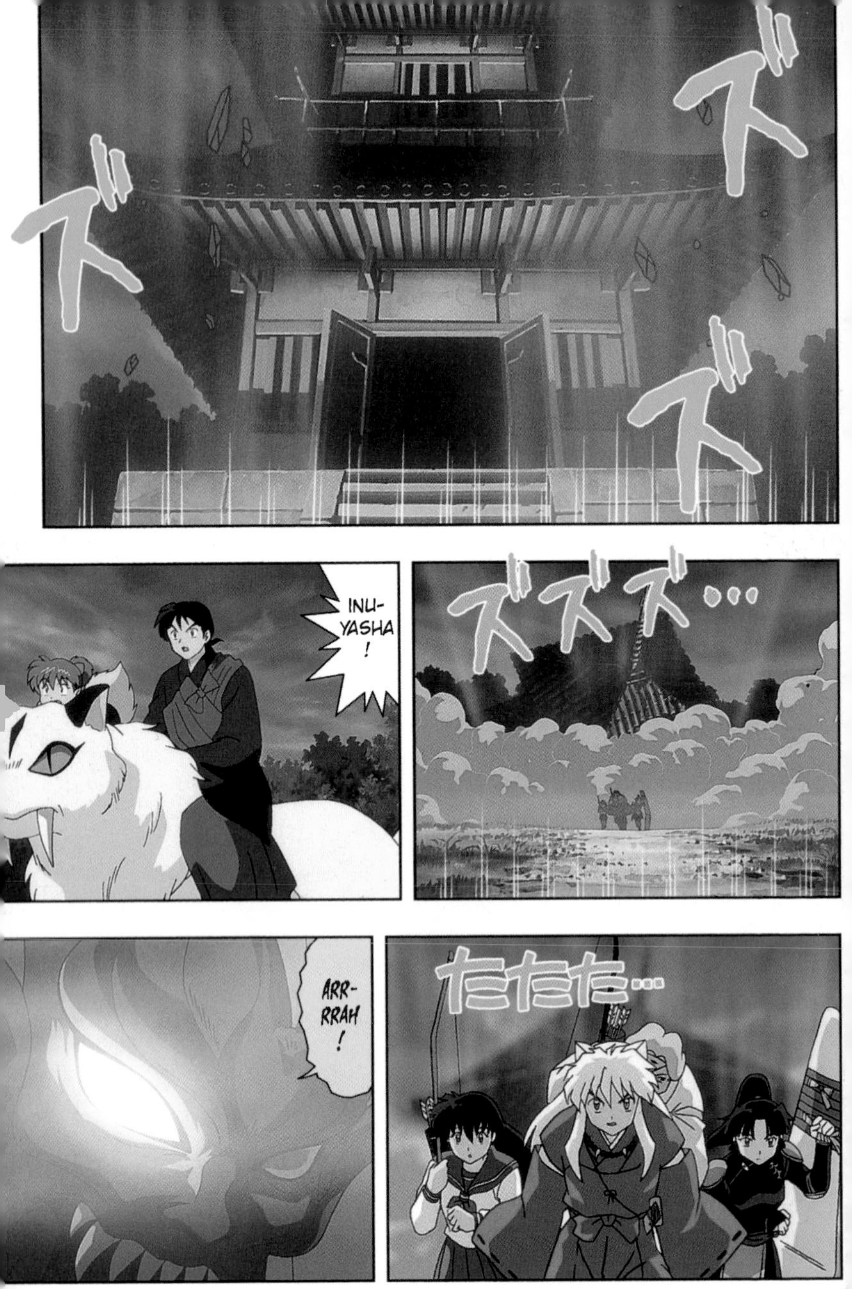
ズ
ズ
ズ
ズ
ズズズ…
INU-YASHA!
たたた…
ARR-RRAH!

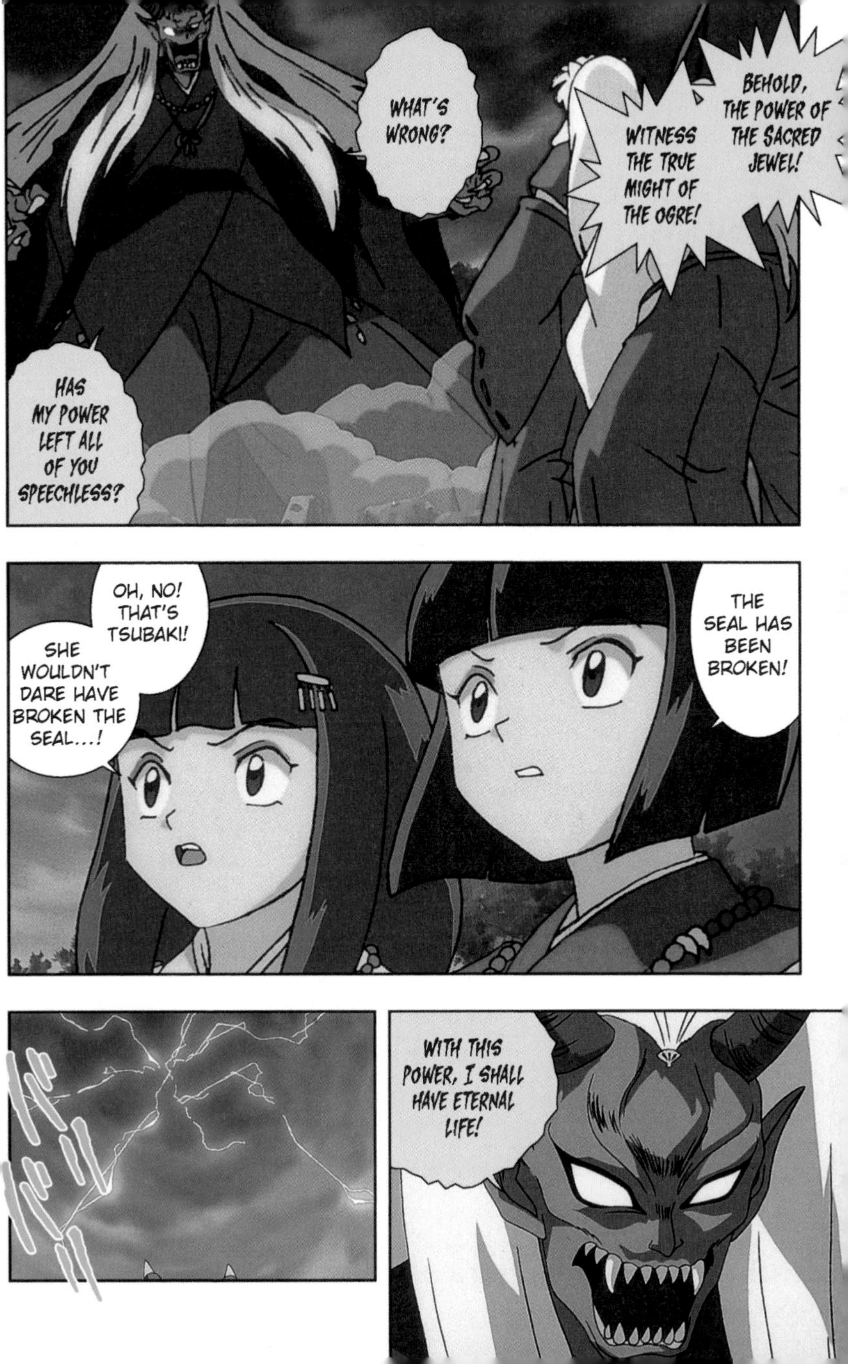

BEHOLD, THE POWER OF THE SACRED JEWEL!
WITNESS THE TRUE MIGHT OF THE OGRE!
WHAT'S WRONG?
HAS MY POWER LEFT ALL OF YOU SPEECHLESS?
THE SEAL HAS BEEN BROKEN!
OH, NO! THAT'S TSUBAKI!
SHE WOULDN'T DARE HAVE BROKEN THE SEAL...!
WITH THIS POWER, I SHALL HAVE ETERNAL LIFE!

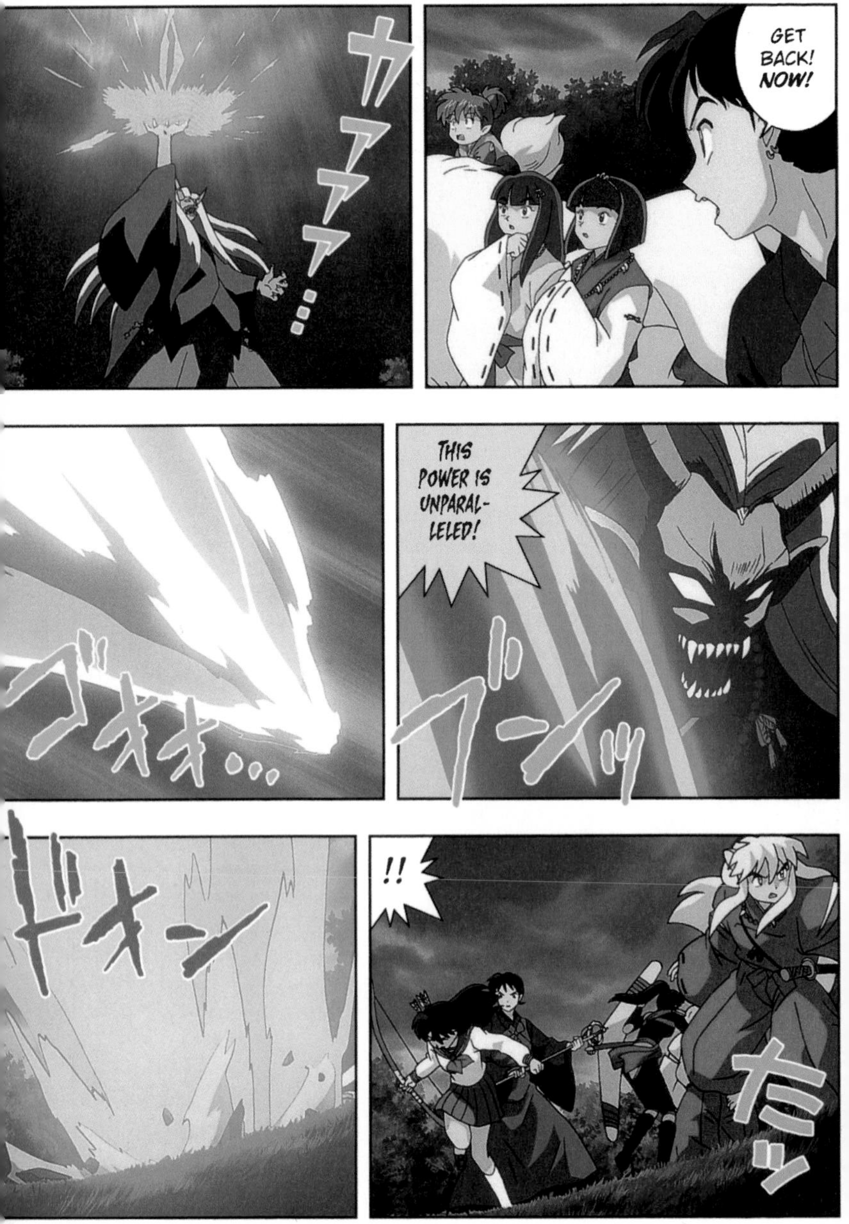
GET BACK! NOW!
カァァァ…
THIS POWER IS UNPARALLELED!
ブーンッ
ゴォォ…
!!
タッ
ドォーン

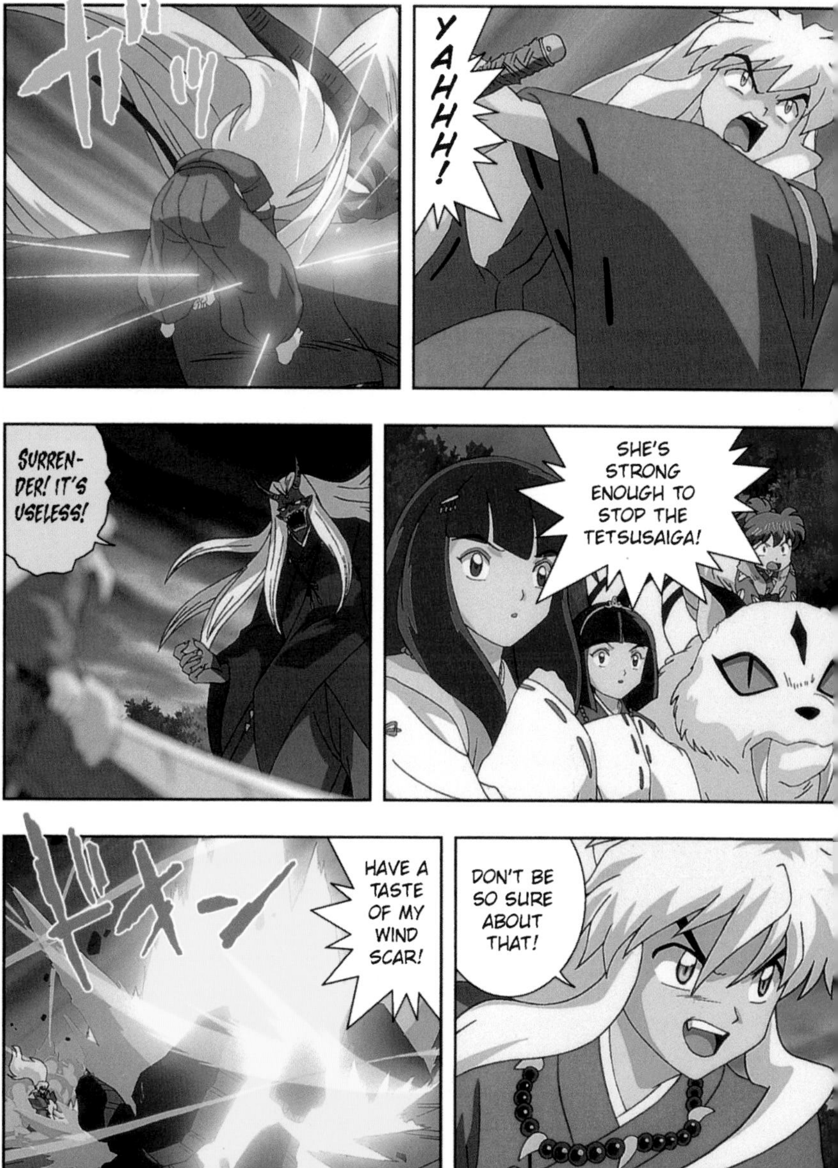
YAHHHH!
ガッ
SHE'S STRONG ENOUGH TO STOP THE TETSUSAIGA!
SURREN-DER! IT'S USELESS!
DON'T BE SO SURE ABOUT THAT!
HAVE A TASTE OF MY WIND SCAR!
ドオーン

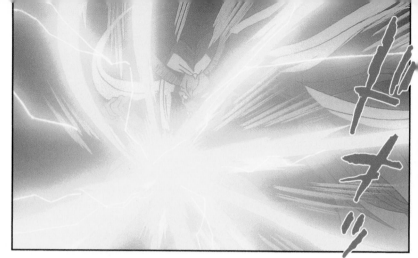

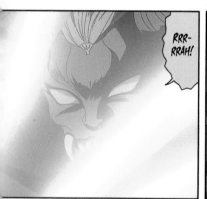

RRR-RRAH!

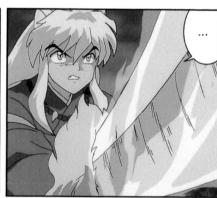

...

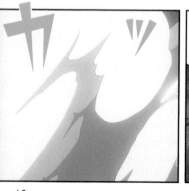

...!!

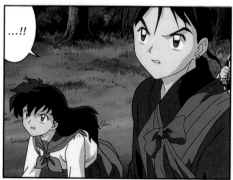

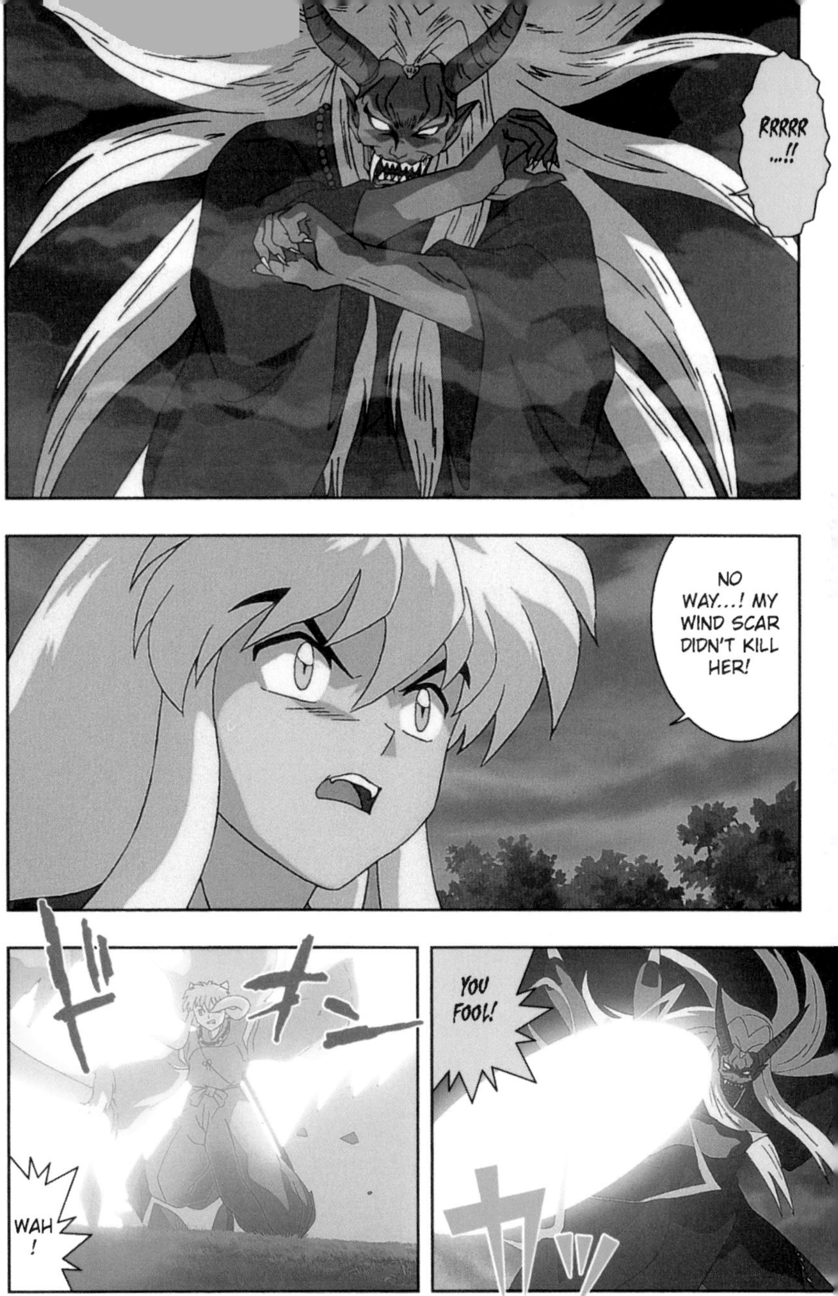
RRRRR ...!!
NO WAY...! MY WIND SCAR DIDN'T KILL HER!
YOU FOOL!
WAH !

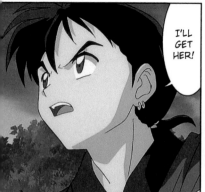

I'LL GET HER!

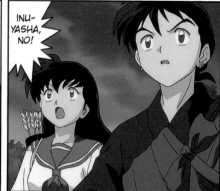

INU-YASHA, NO!

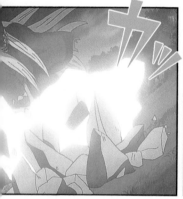

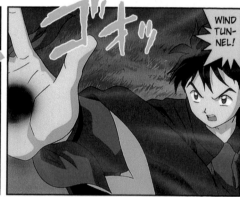

WIND TUN-NEL!

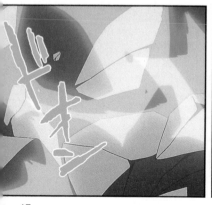

UGH!

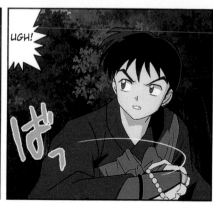

47

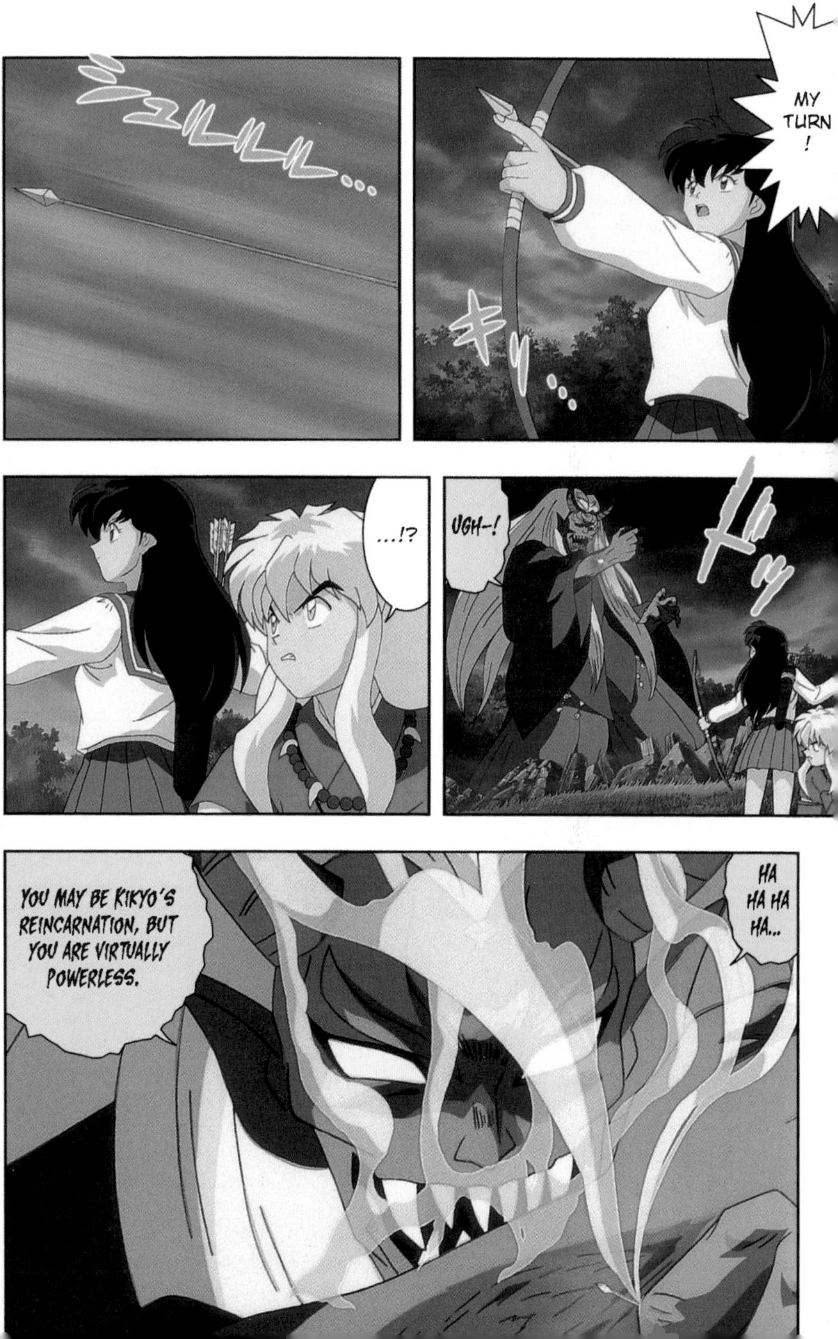
MY TURN!
キリ...
シュルルルル...
UGH-!
ドッ
...!?
HA HA HA HA...
YOU MAY BE KIKYO'S REINCARNATION, BUT YOU ARE VIRTUALLY POWERLESS.

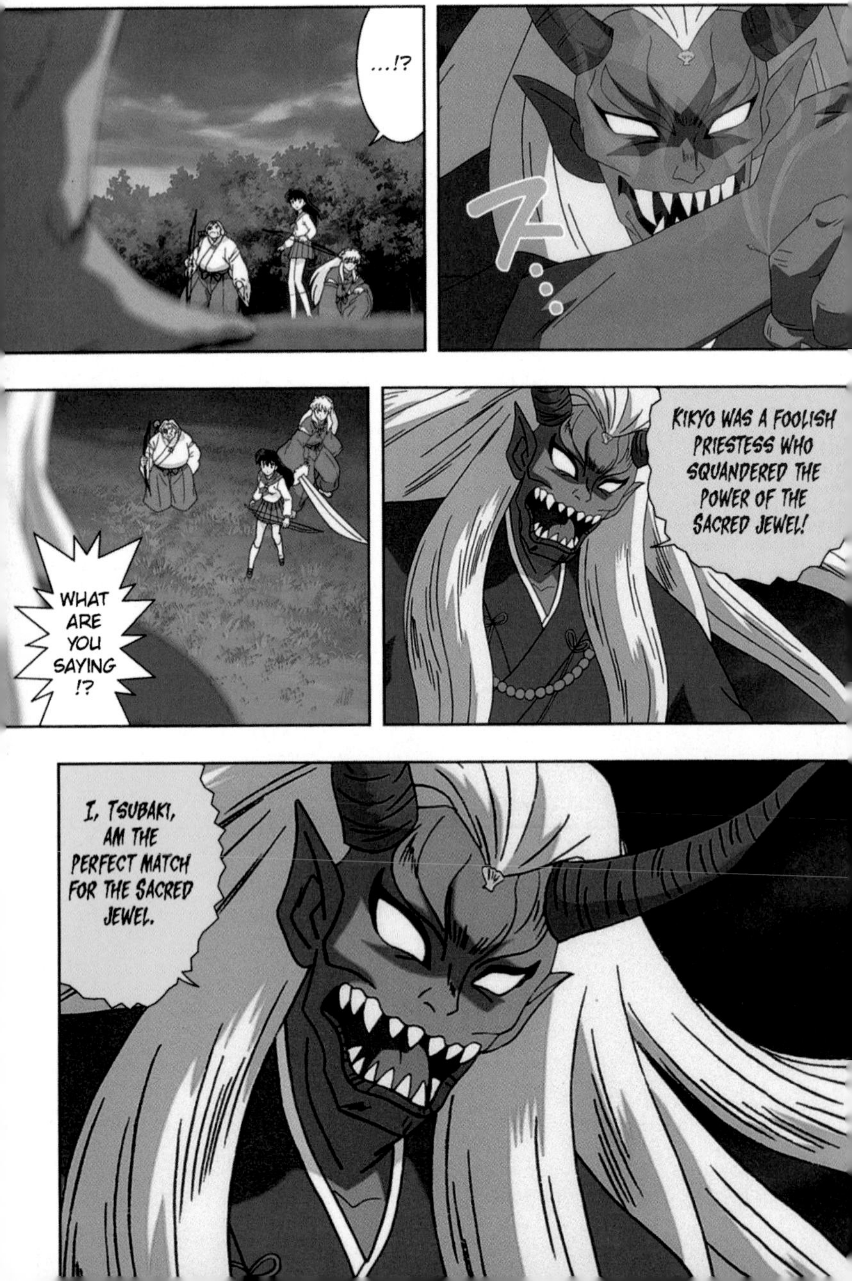
...!?
KIKYO WAS A FOOLISH PRIESTESS WHO SQUANDERED THE POWER OF THE SACRED JEWEL!
WHAT ARE YOU SAYING !?
I, TSUBAKI, AM THE PERFECT MATCH FOR THE SACRED JEWEL.

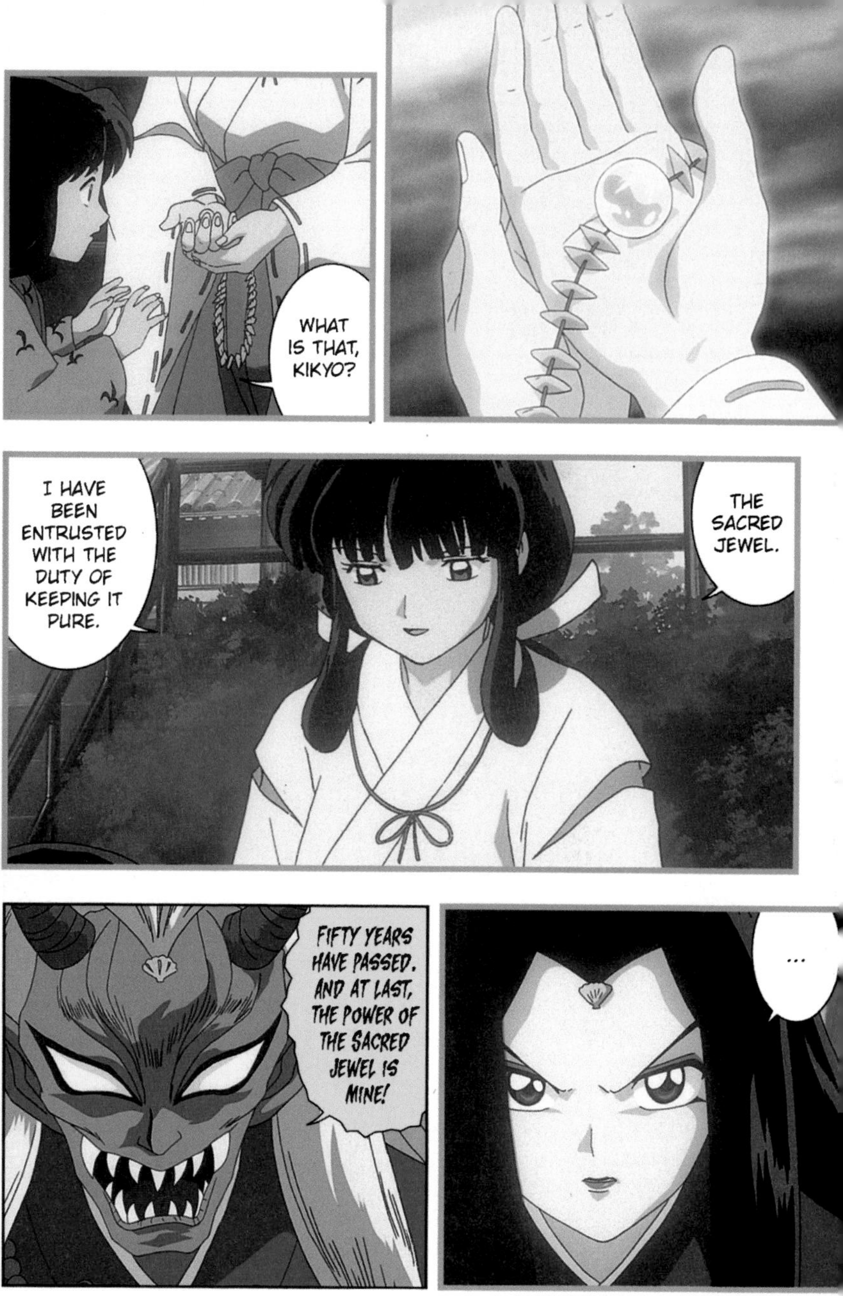
WHAT IS THAT, KIKYO?
THE SACRED JEWEL.
I HAVE BEEN ENTRUSTED WITH THE DUTY OF KEEPING IT PURE.
...
FIFTY YEARS HAVE PASSED. AND AT LAST, THE POWER OF THE SACRED JEWEL IS MINE!

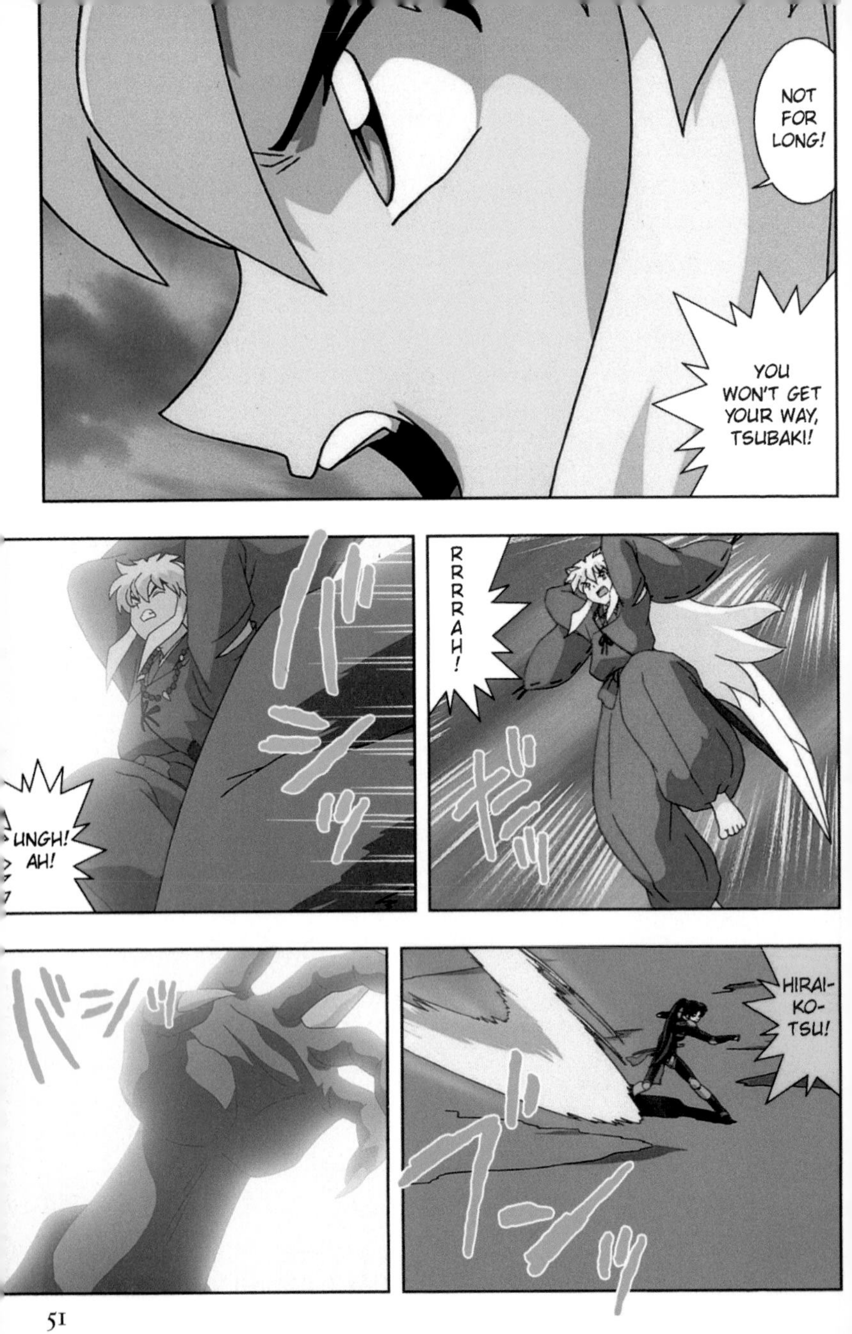
NOT FOR LONG!
YOU WON'T GET YOUR WAY, TSUBAKI!
RRRRAH!
ギッ
バシッ
UNGH! AH!
HIRAI-KOTSU!
バシッ

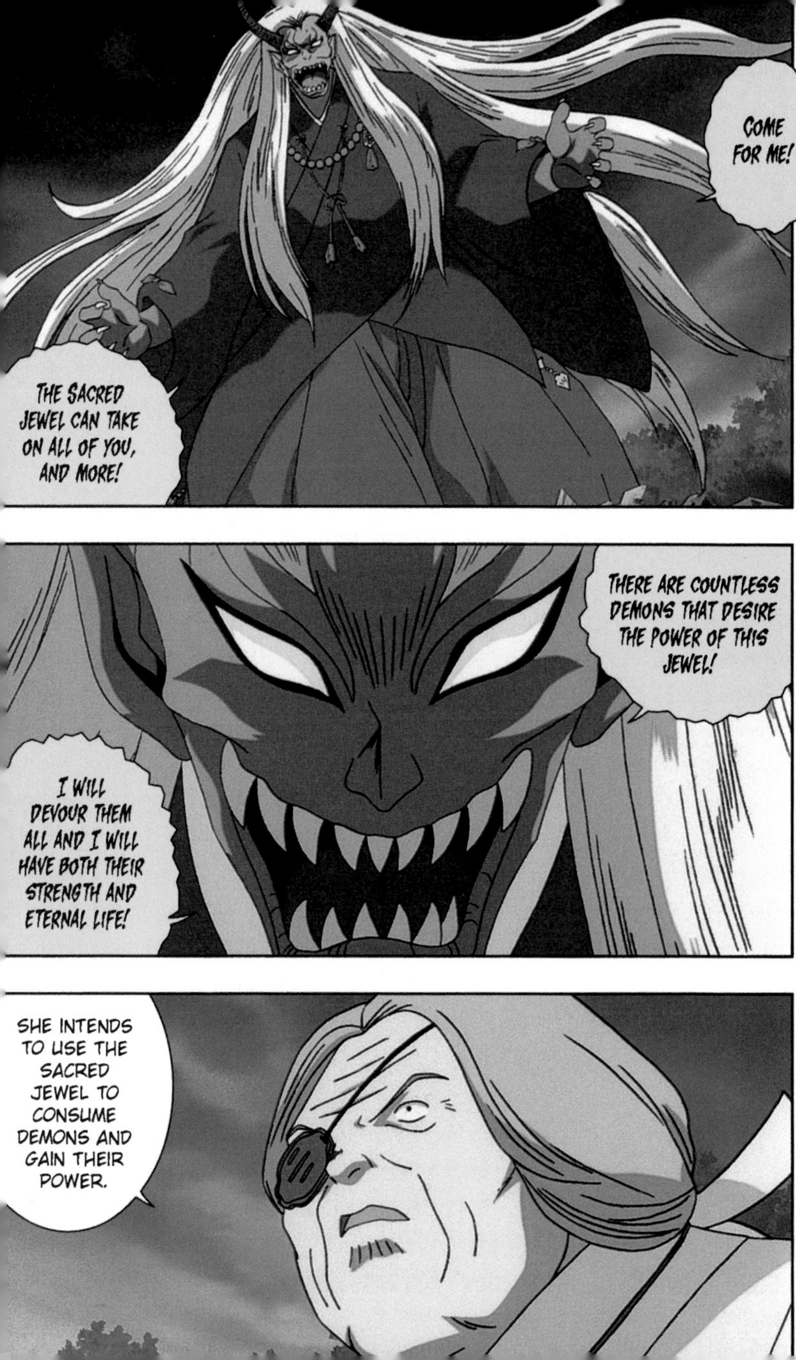
COME FOR ME!
THE SACRED JEWEL CAN TAKE ON ALL OF YOU, AND MORE!
THERE ARE COUNTLESS DEMONS THAT DESIRE THE POWER OF THIS JEWEL!
I WILL DEVOUR THEM ALL AND I WILL HAVE BOTH THEIR STRENGTH AND ETERNAL LIFE!
SHE INTENDS TO USE THE SACRED JEWEL TO CONSUME DEMONS AND GAIN THEIR POWER.

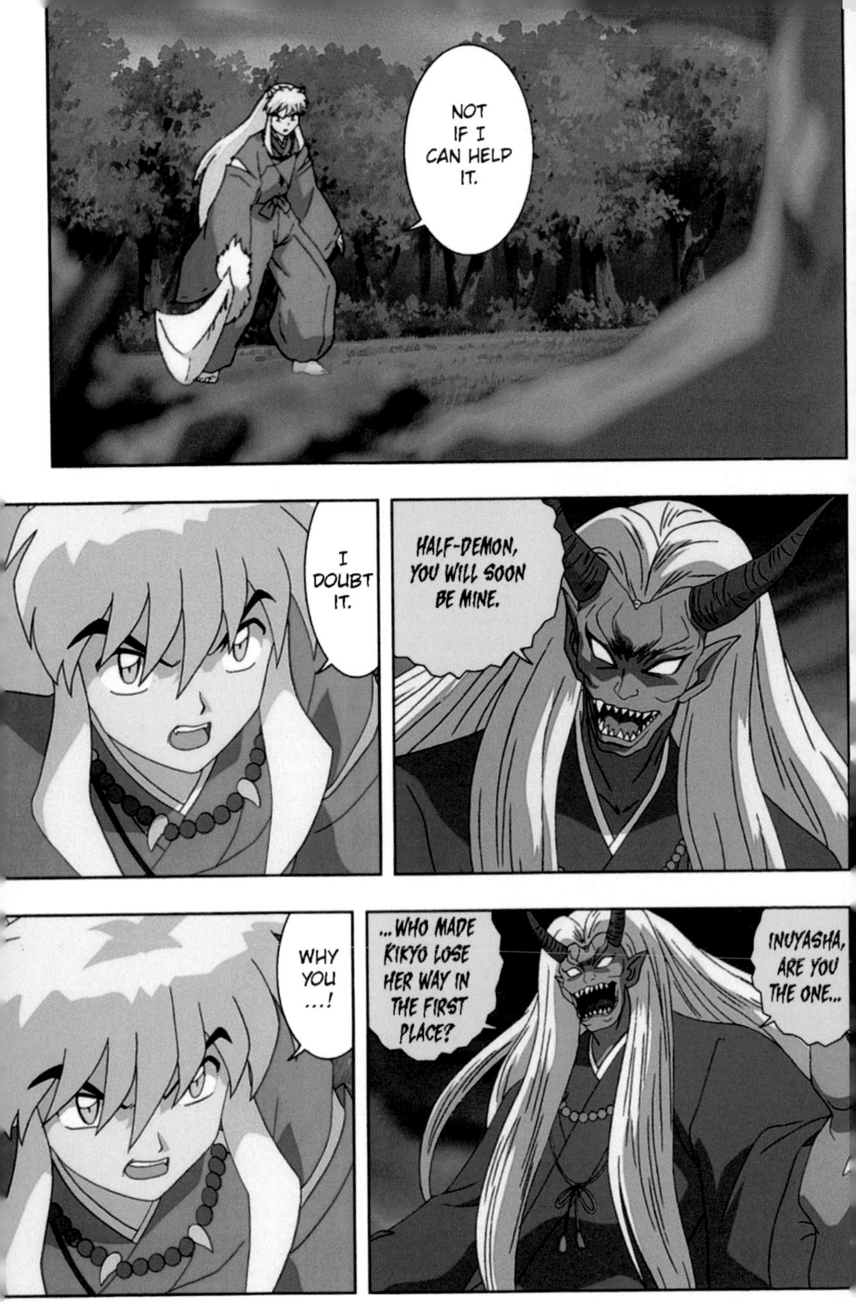
NOT IF I CAN HELP IT.
HALF-DEMON, YOU WILL SOON BE MINE.
I DOUBT IT.
INUYASHA, ARE YOU THE ONE...
...WHO MADE KIKYO LOSE HER WAY IN THE FIRST PLACE?
WHY YOU ...!

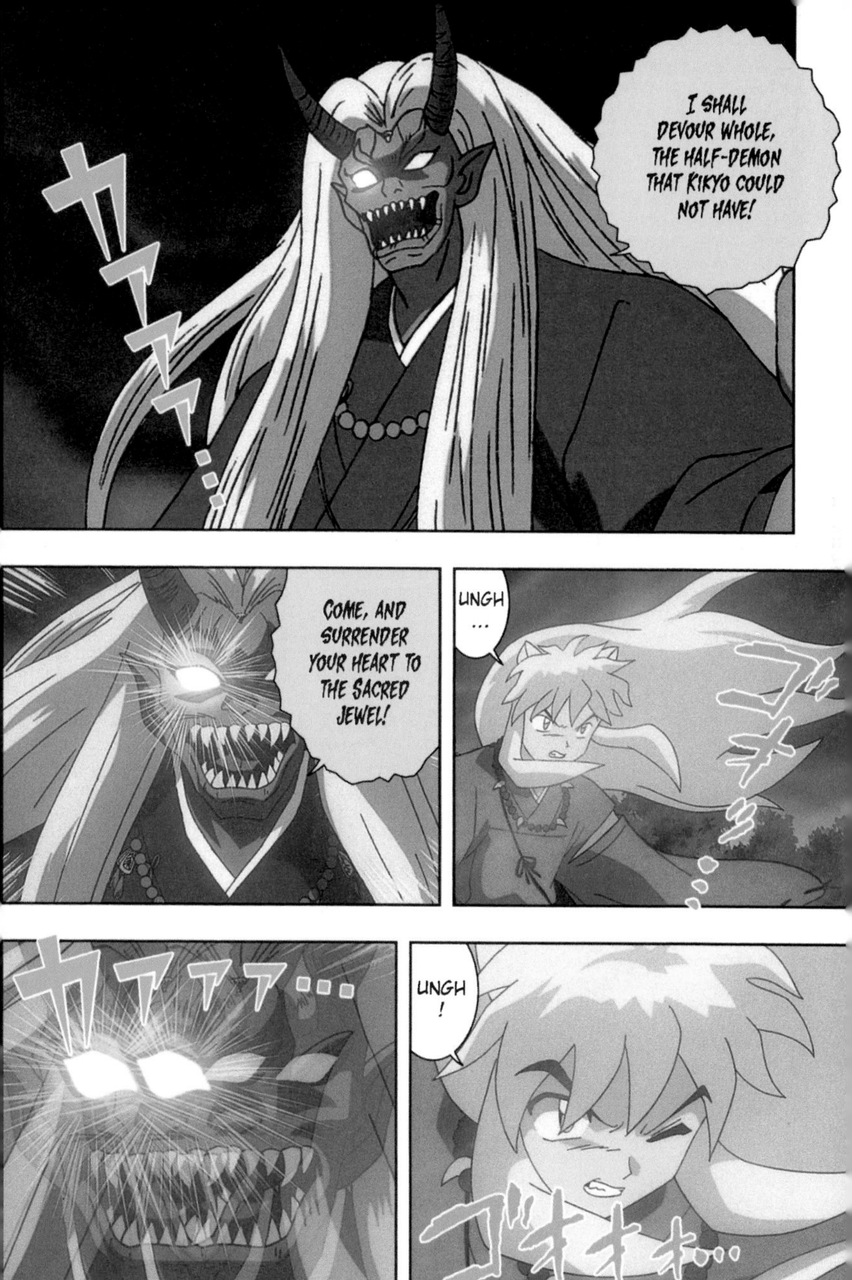
I SHALL DEVOUR WHOLE, THE HALF-DEMON THAT KIKYO COULD NOT HAVE!
カァァァ...
UNGH ...
ゴォォ...
COME, AND SURRENDER YOUR HEART TO THE SACRED JEWEL!
UNGH !
ゴオオオ...
カァァァ...

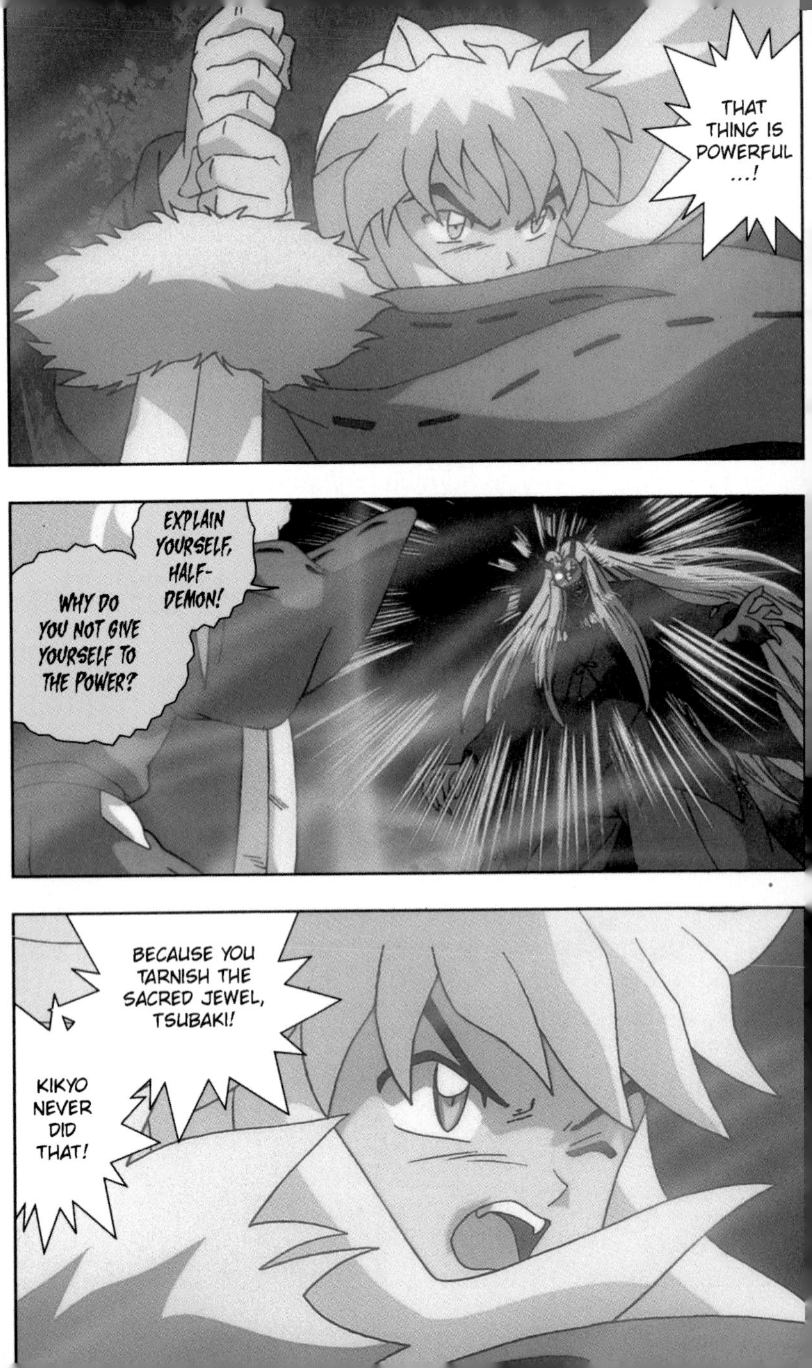
THAT THING IS POWERFUL ...!
EXPLAIN YOURSELF, HALF-DEMON!
WHY DO YOU NOT GIVE YOURSELF TO THE POWER?
BECAUSE YOU TARNISH THE SACRED JEWEL, TSUBAKI!
KIKYO NEVER DID THAT!

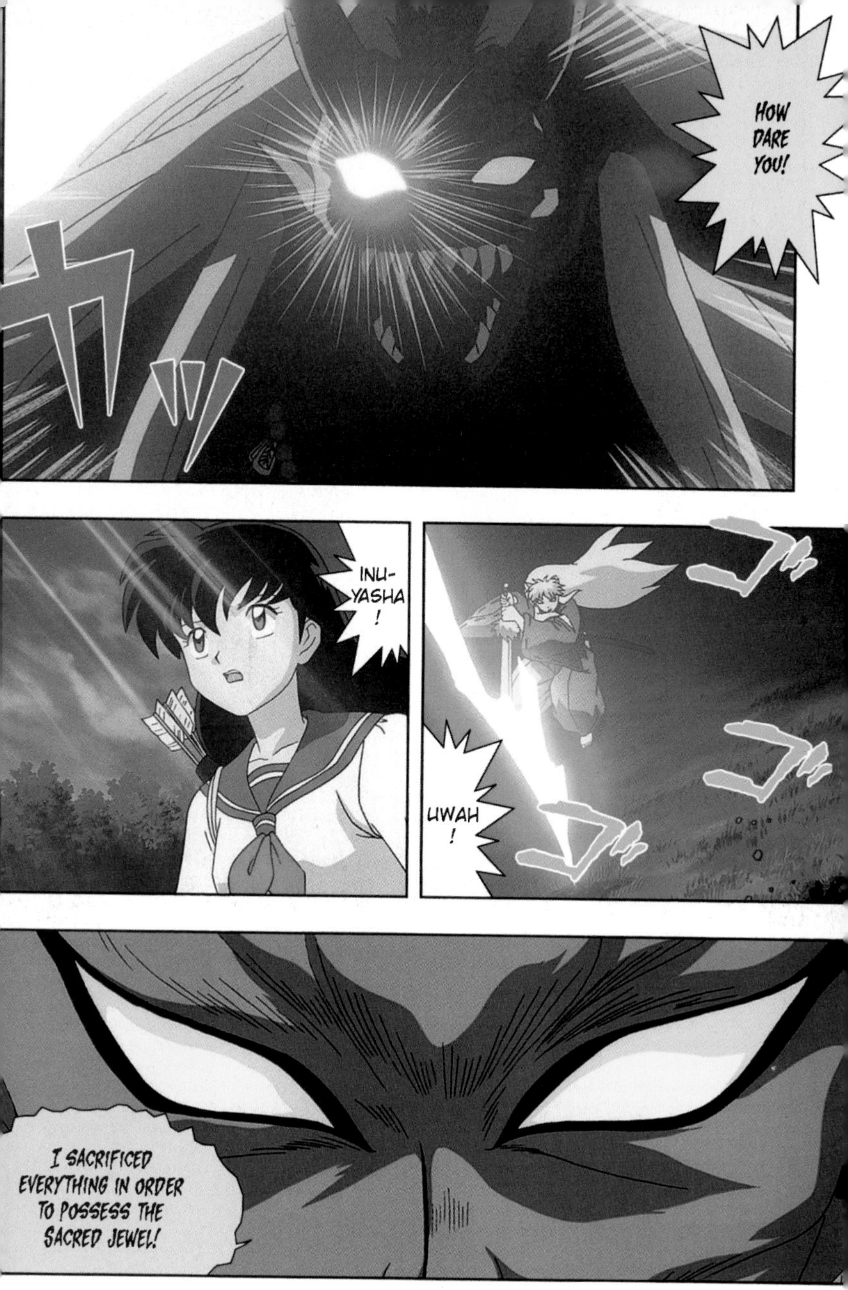
HOW DARE YOU!
カッ
ゴゴゴ
UWAH!
INU-YASHA!
I SACRIFICED EVERYTHING IN ORDER TO POSSESS THE SACRED JEWEL!

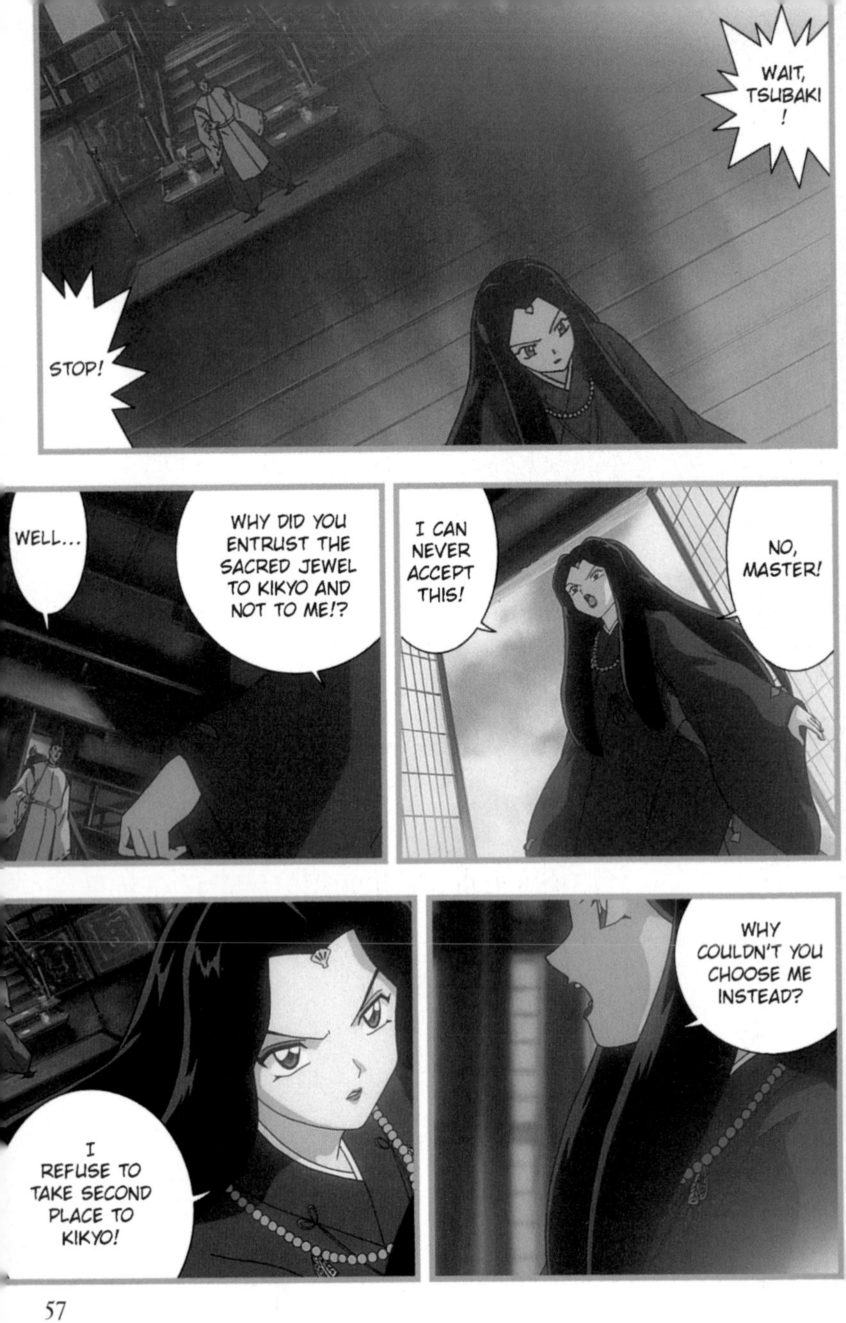
WAIT, TSUBAKI!
STOP!
NO, MASTER!
I CAN NEVER ACCEPT THIS!
WHY DID YOU ENTRUST THE SACRED JEWEL TO KIKYO AND NOT TO ME!?
WELL...
WHY COULDN'T YOU CHOOSE ME INSTEAD?
I REFUSE TO TAKE SECOND PLACE TO KIKYO!

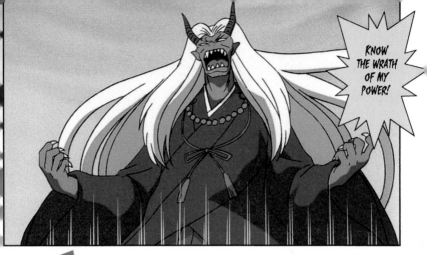

KNOW THE WRATH OF MY POWER!

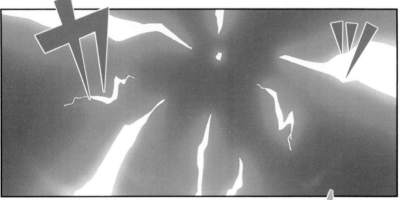

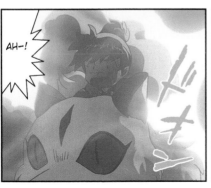

AH–!

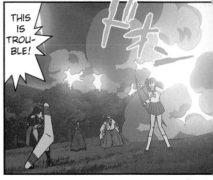

THIS IS TROU-BLE!

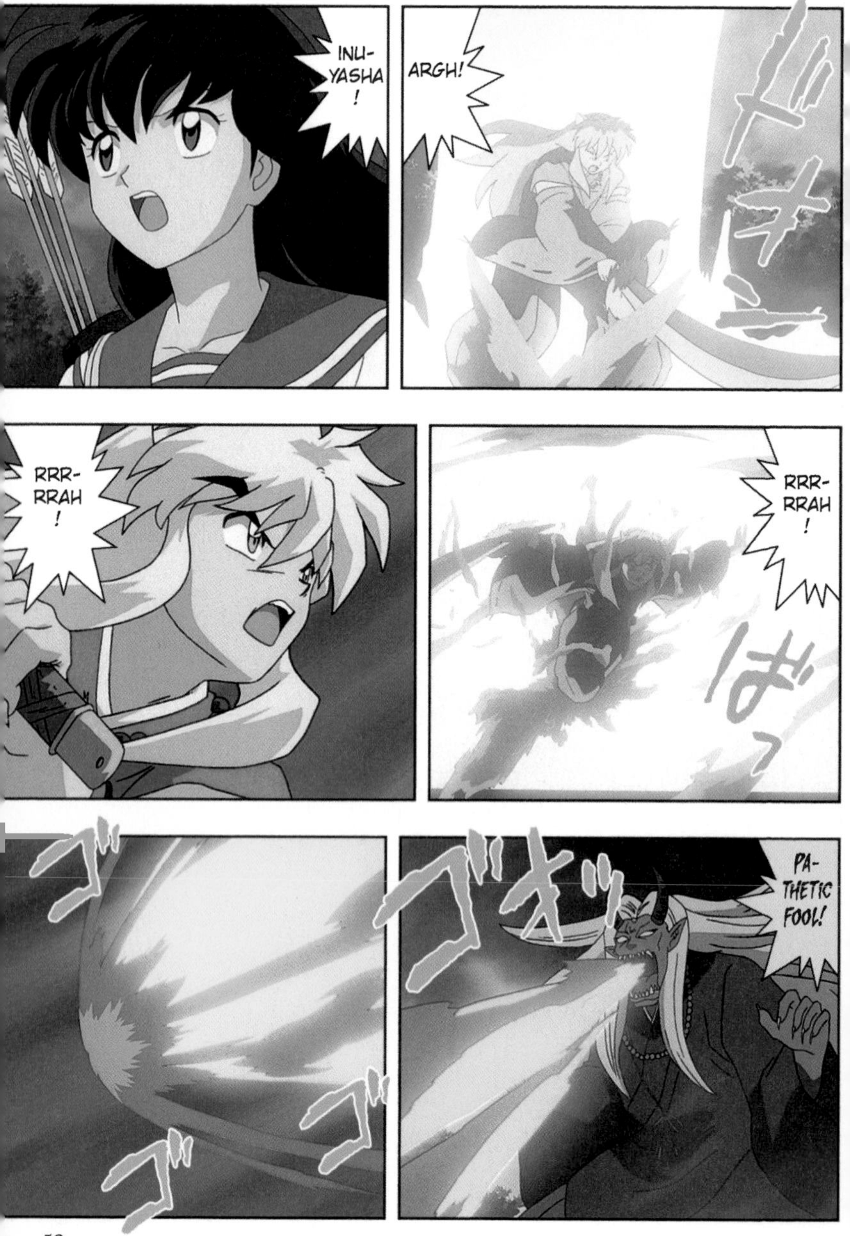
ARGH!
INU-YASHA!
RRR-RRAH!
RRR-RRAH!
PA-THETIC FOOL!

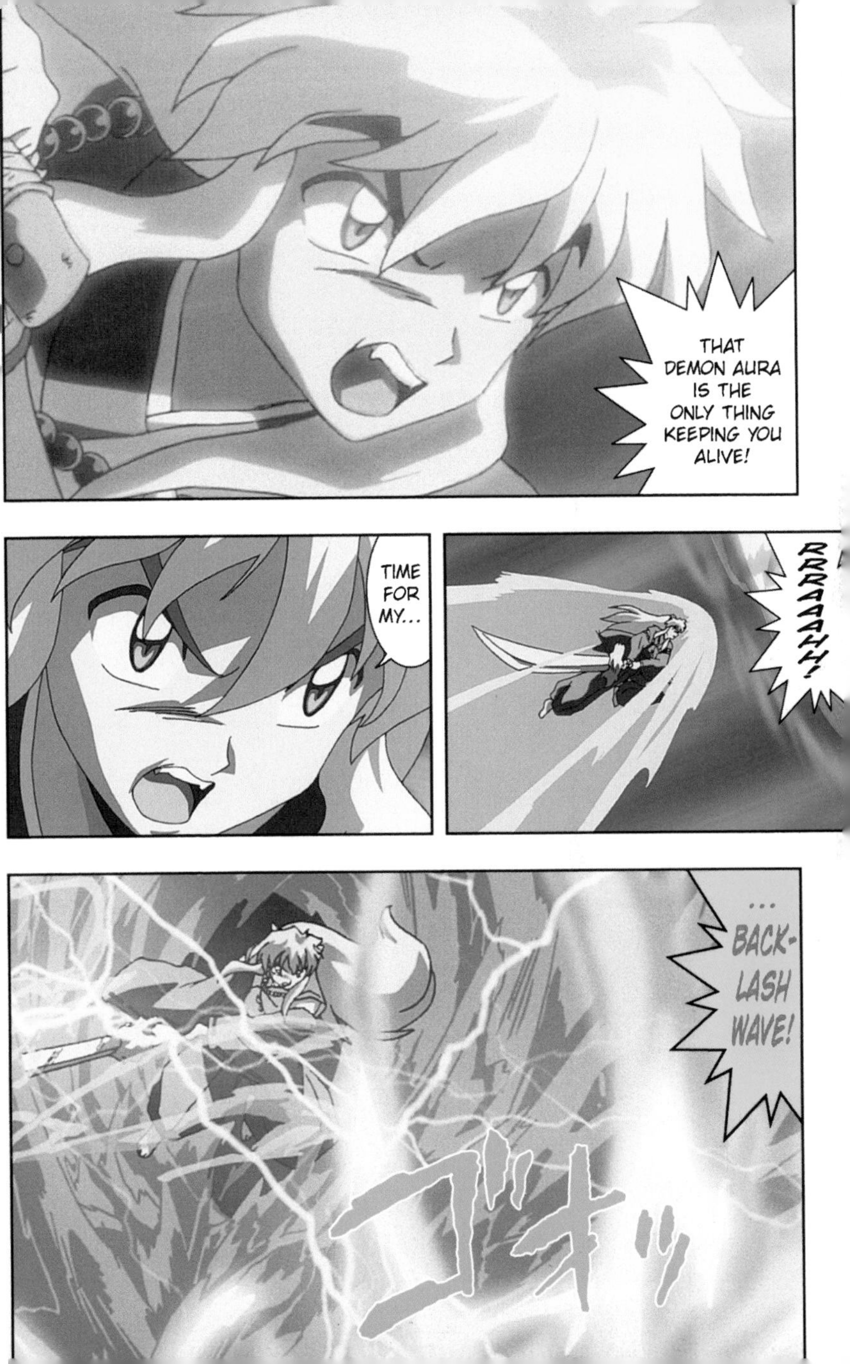
THAT DEMON AURA IS THE ONLY THING KEEPING YOU ALIVE!
RRRAAAHH!
TIME FOR MY...
...BACK-LASH WAVE!
ゴオッ

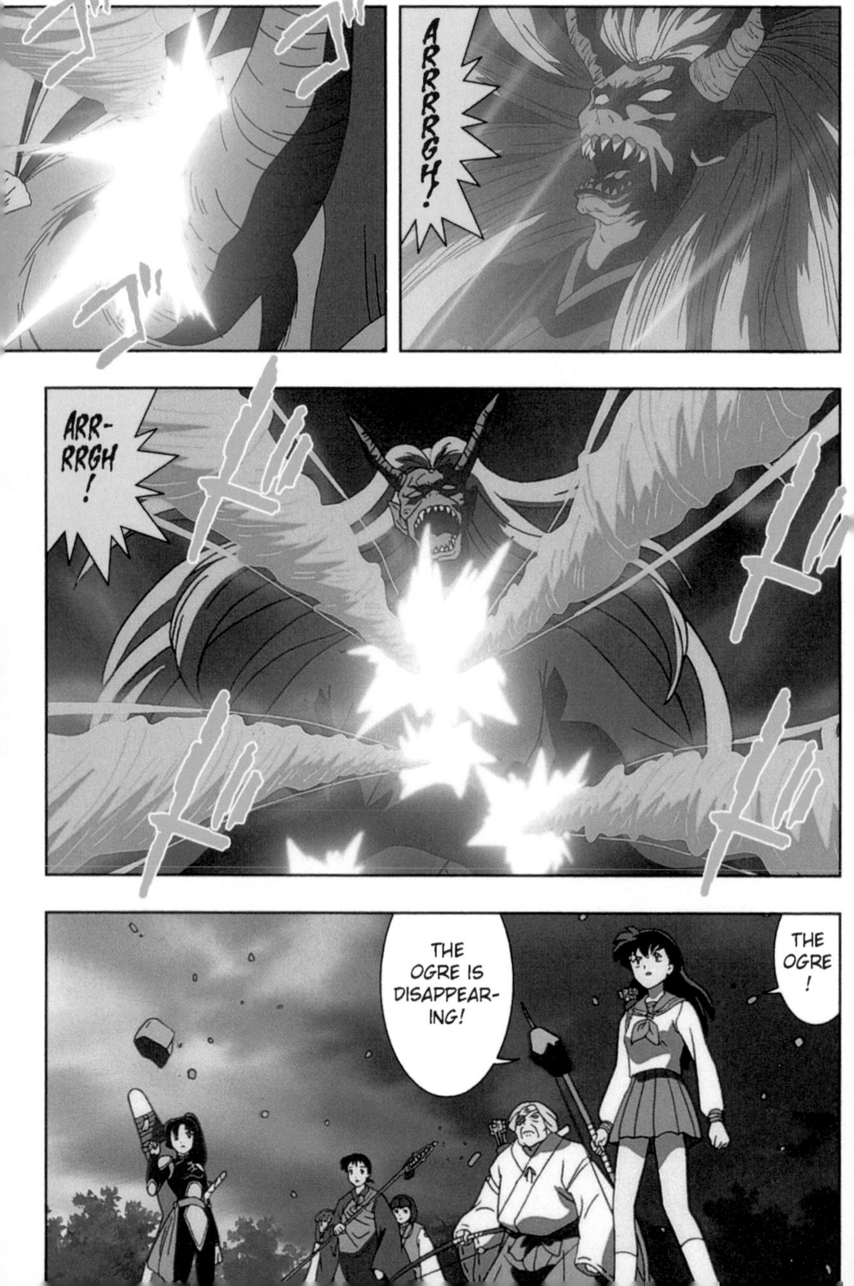
ARRRRGH!
ゴ
ゴ
ゴ
ARR-RRGH!
ド
ド
ド
ド
THE OGRE!
THE OGRE IS DISAPPEARING!

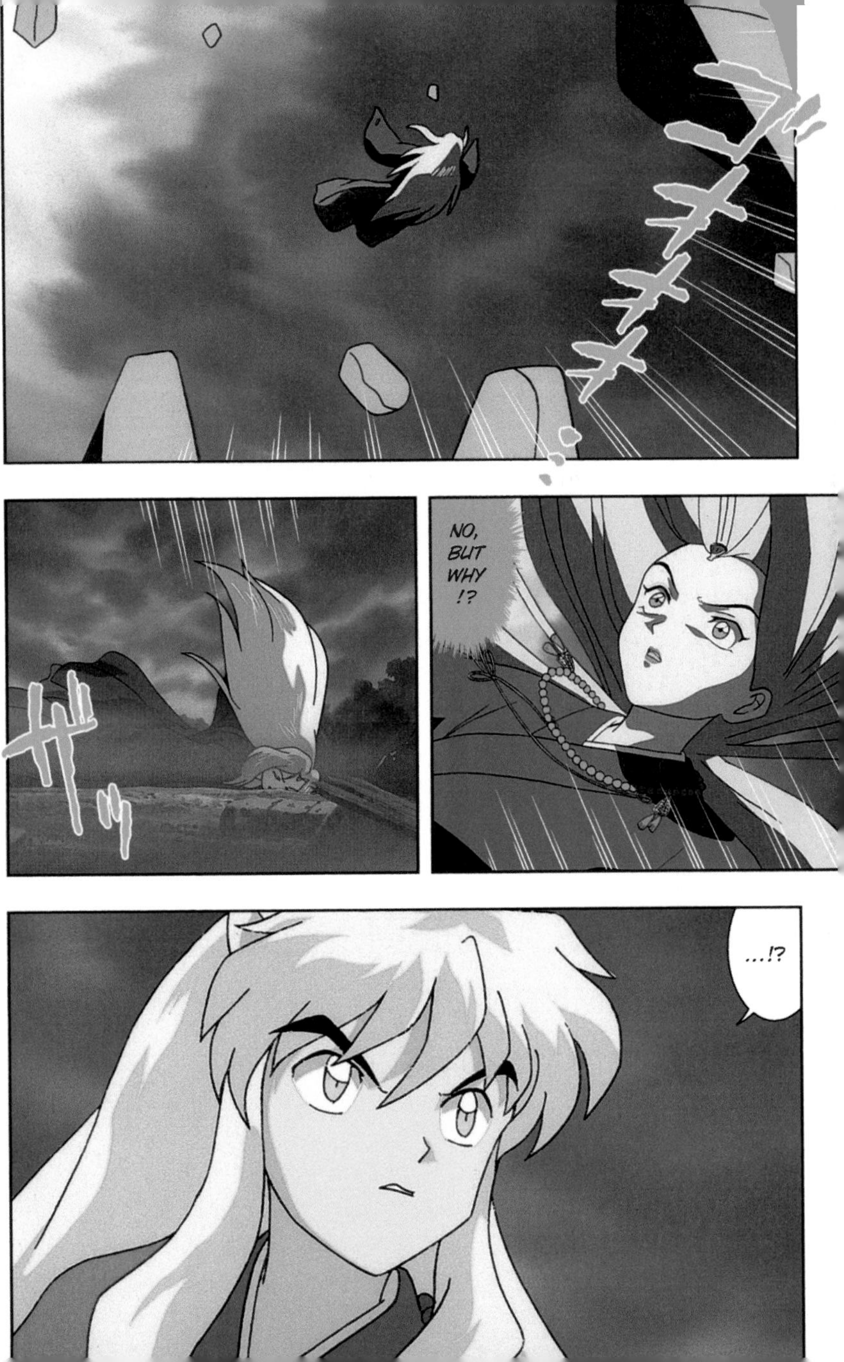
NO, BUT WHY !?
ザッ
...!?

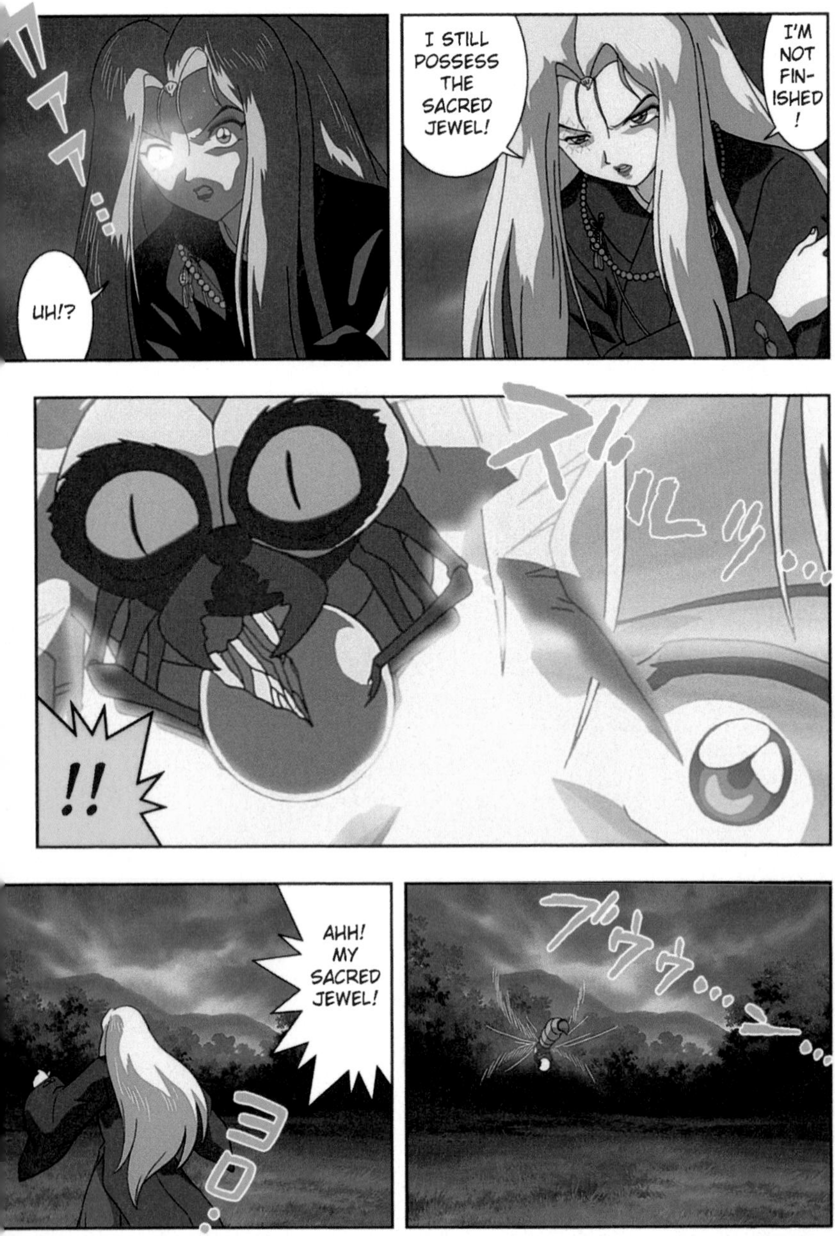
I'M NOT FIN-ISHED!
I STILL POSSESS THE SACRED JEWEL!
UH!?
ズルッ...
!!
ブウウ...ン...
AHH! MY SACRED JEWEL!
ヨロ...

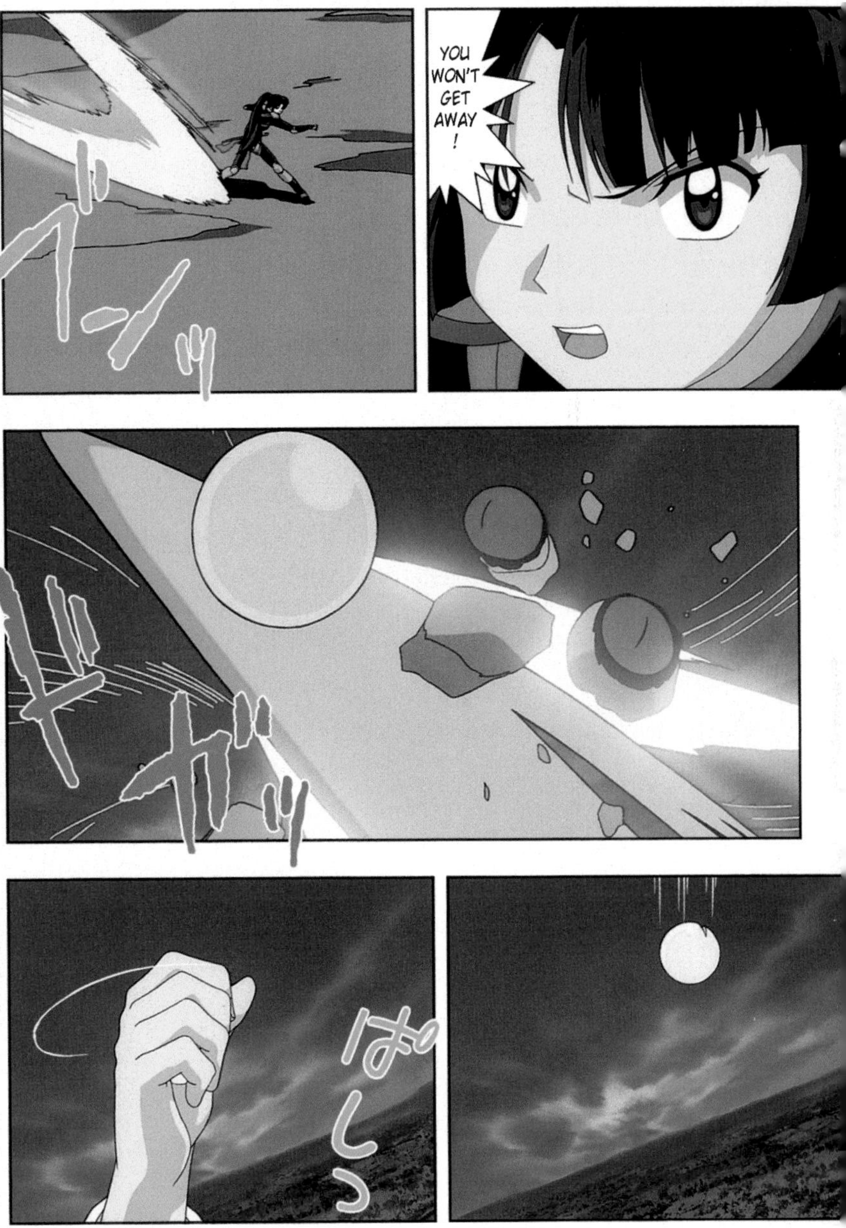
YOU WON'T GET AWAY!
ぱしっ

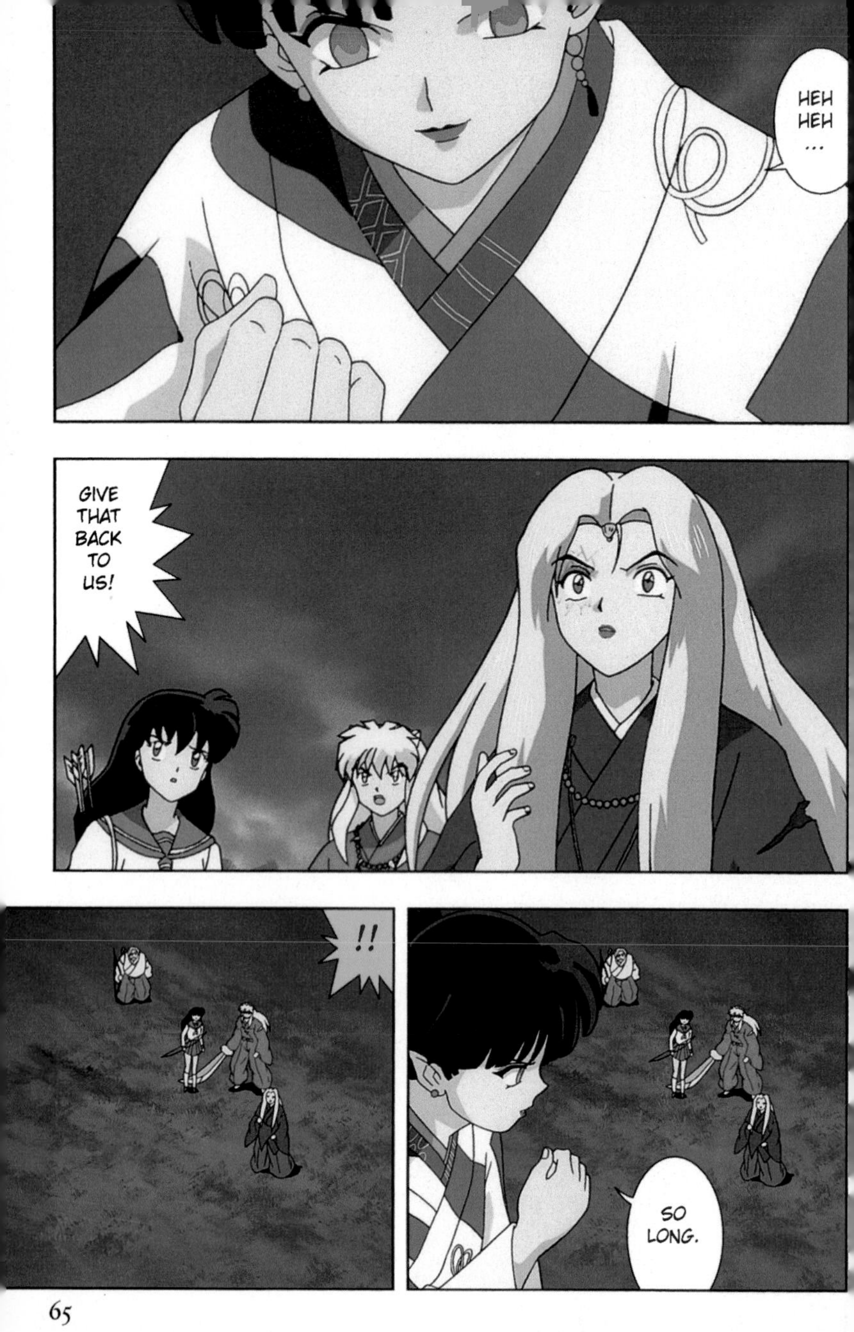
HEH HEH ...
GIVE THAT BACK TO US!
SO LONG.
!!

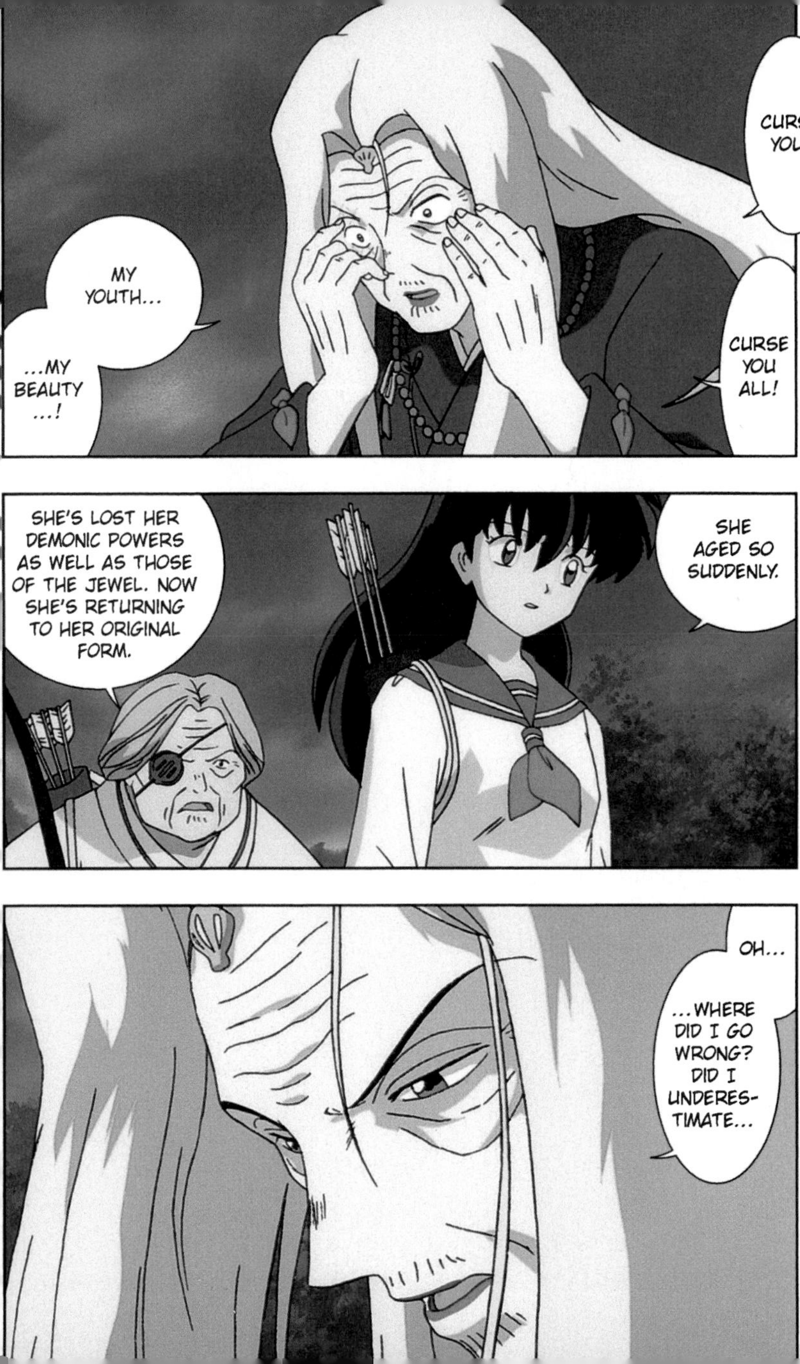
CURSE YOU!
CURSE YOU ALL!
MY YOUTH...
...MY BEAUTY ...!
SHE AGED SO SUDDENLY.
SHE'S LOST HER DEMONIC POWERS AS WELL AS THOSE OF THE JEWEL. NOW SHE'S RETURNING TO HER ORIGINAL FORM.
OH...
...WHERE DID I GO WRONG? DID I UNDERES-TIMATE...

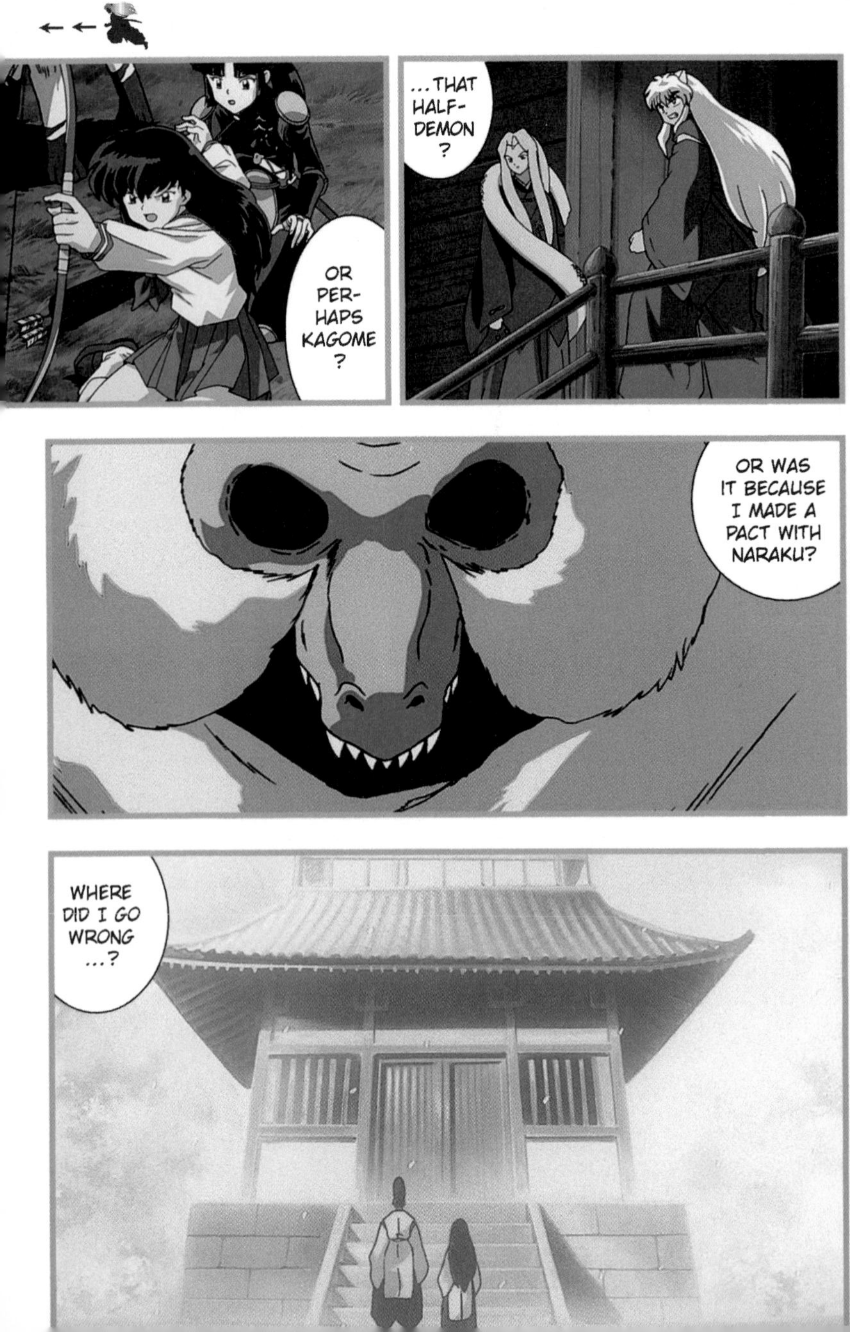
...THAT HALF-DEMON?
OR PER-HAPS KAGOME?
OR WAS IT BECAUSE I MADE A PACT WITH NARAKU?
WHERE DID I GO WRONG...?

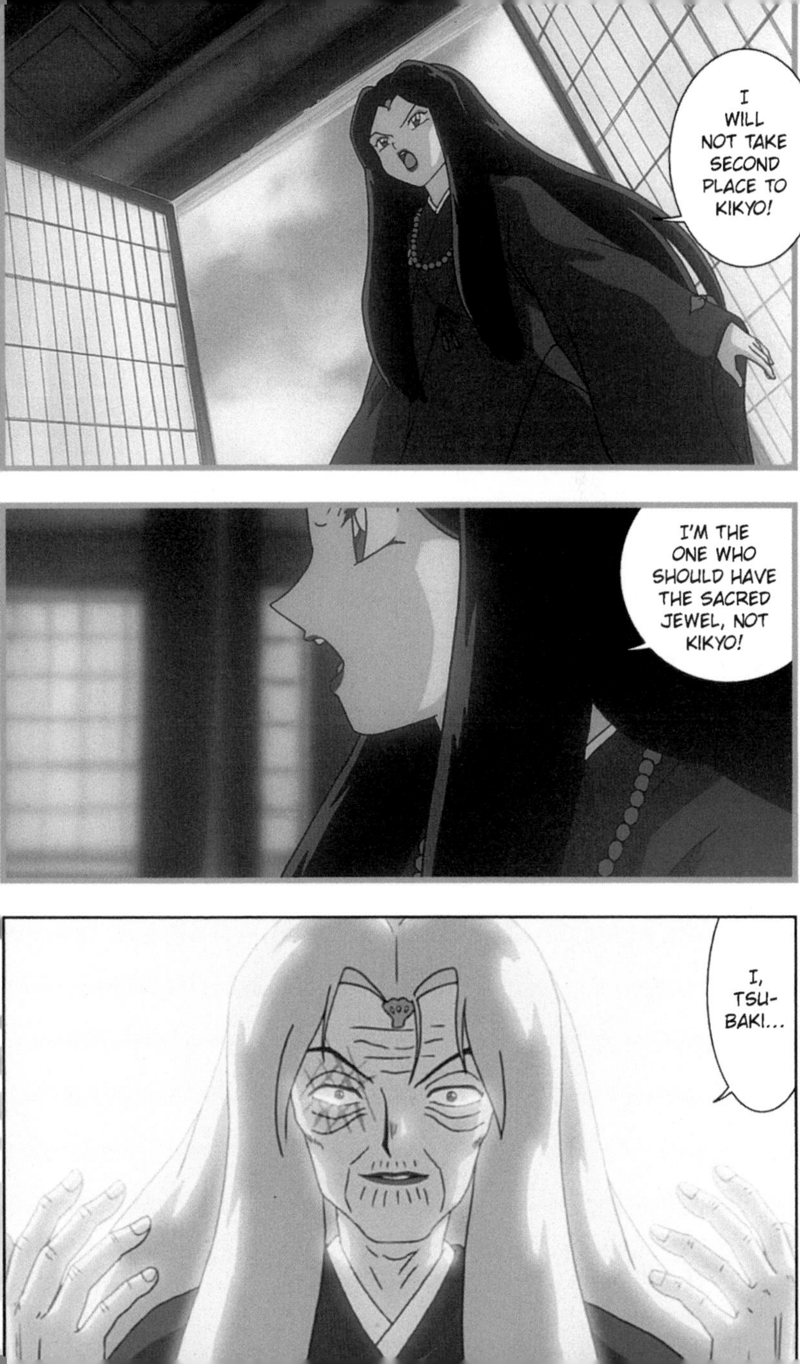
I WILL NOT TAKE SECOND PLACE TO KIKYO!
I'M THE ONE WHO SHOULD HAVE THE SACRED JEWEL, NOT KIKYO!
I, TSU-BAKI...

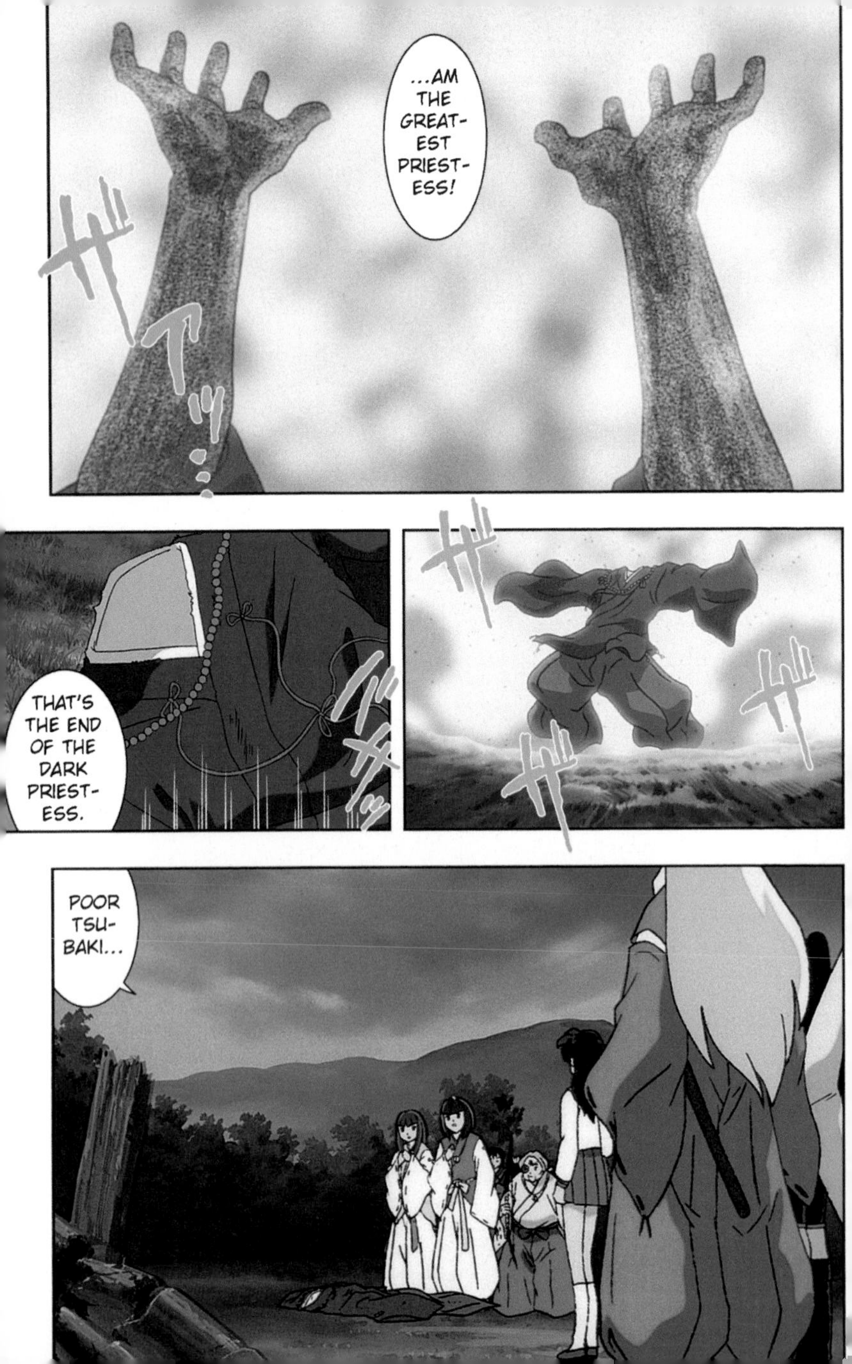
...AM THE GREAT-EST PRIEST-ESS!
THAT'S THE END OF THE DARK PRIEST-ESS.
POOR TSU-BAKI...

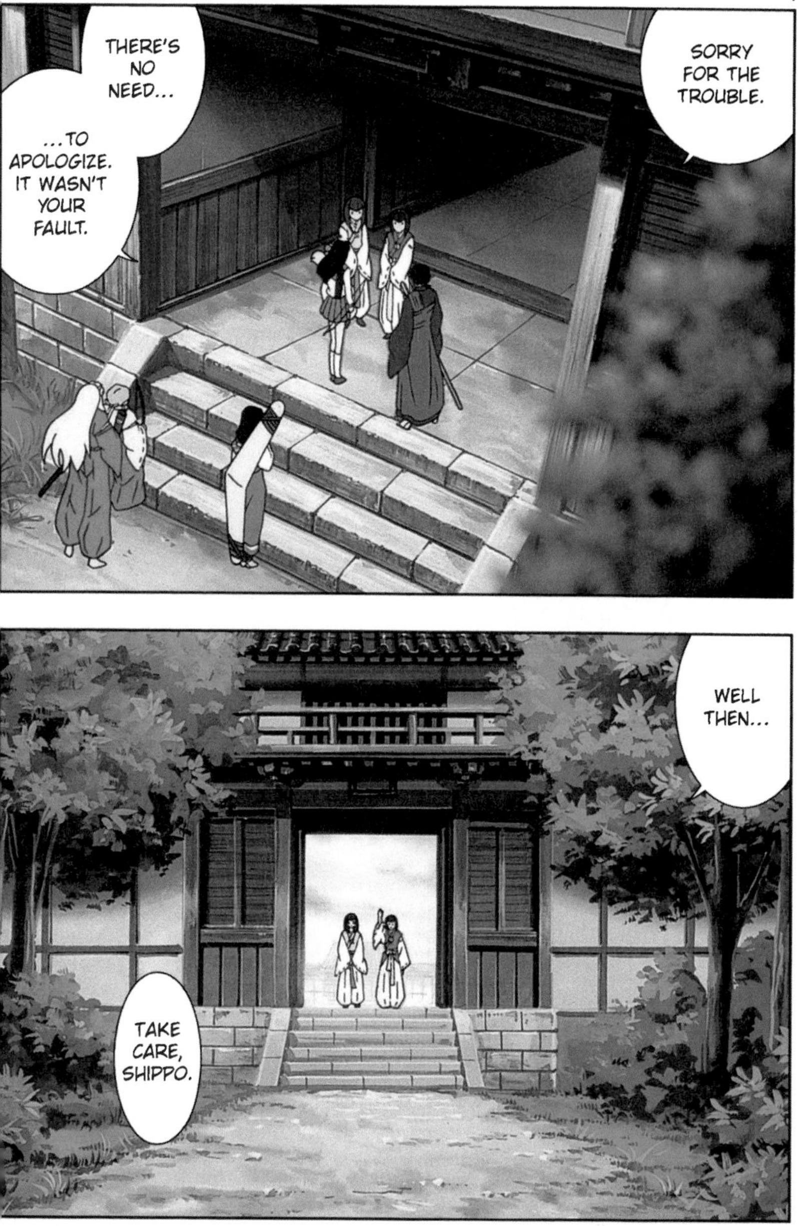
SORRY FOR THE TROUBLE.
THERE'S NO NEED...
...TO APOLOGIZE. IT WASN'T YOUR FAULT.
WELL THEN...
TAKE CARE, SHIPPO.

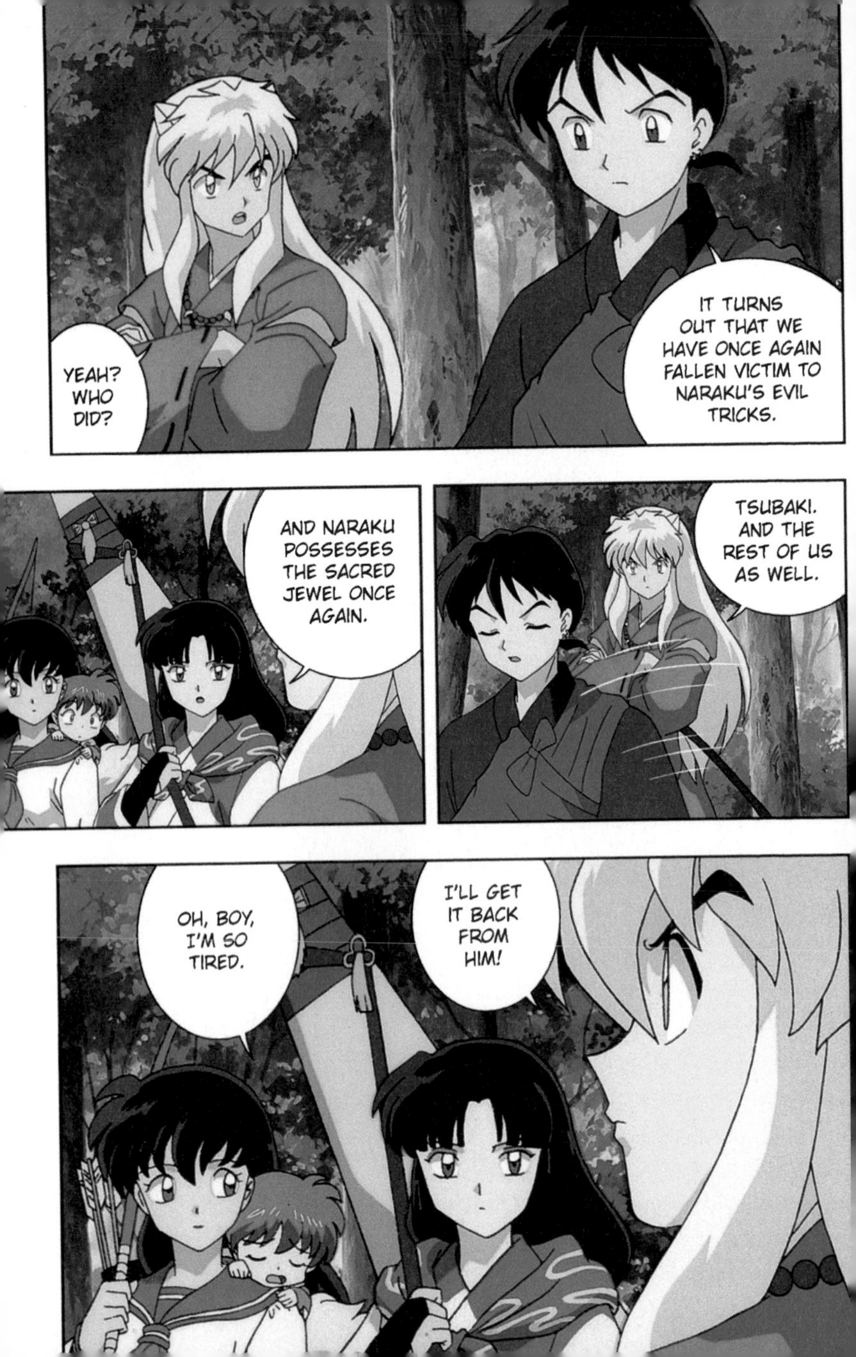
IT TURNS OUT THAT WE HAVE ONCE AGAIN FALLEN VICTIM TO NARAKU'S EVIL TRICKS.
YEAH? WHO DID?
TSUBAKI. AND THE REST OF US AS WELL.
AND NARAKU POSSESSES THE SACRED JEWEL ONCE AGAIN.
I'LL GET IT BACK FROM HIM!
OH, BOY, I'M SO TIRED.

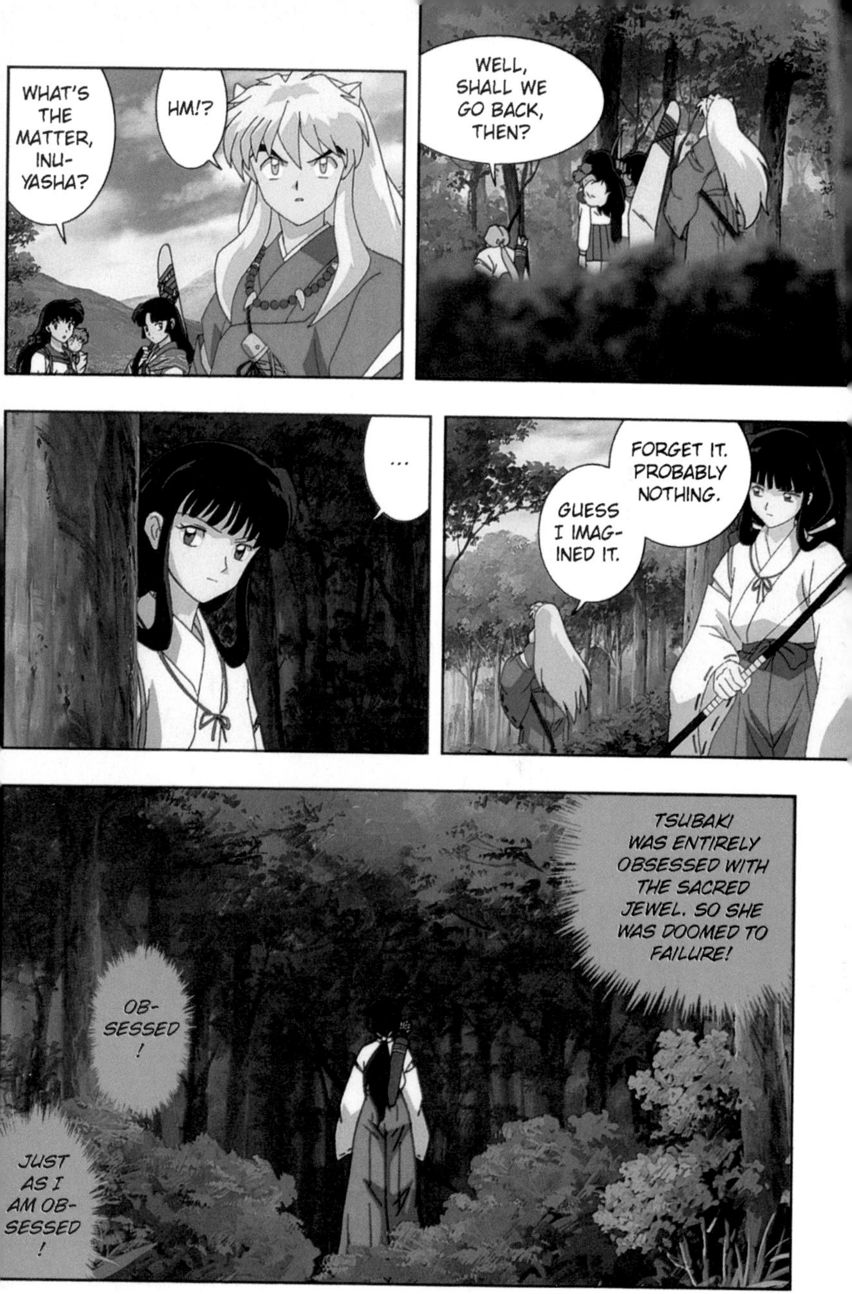
WELL, SHALL WE GO BACK, THEN?
HM!?
WHAT'S THE MATTER, INU-YASHA?
FORGET IT. PROBABLY NOTHING.
GUESS I IMAG-INED IT.
...
TSUBAKI WAS ENTIRELY OBSESSED WITH THE SACRED JEWEL. SO SHE WAS DOOMED TO FAILURE!
OB-SESSED!
JUST AS I AM OB-SESSED!

65 Farewell, Days of My Youth

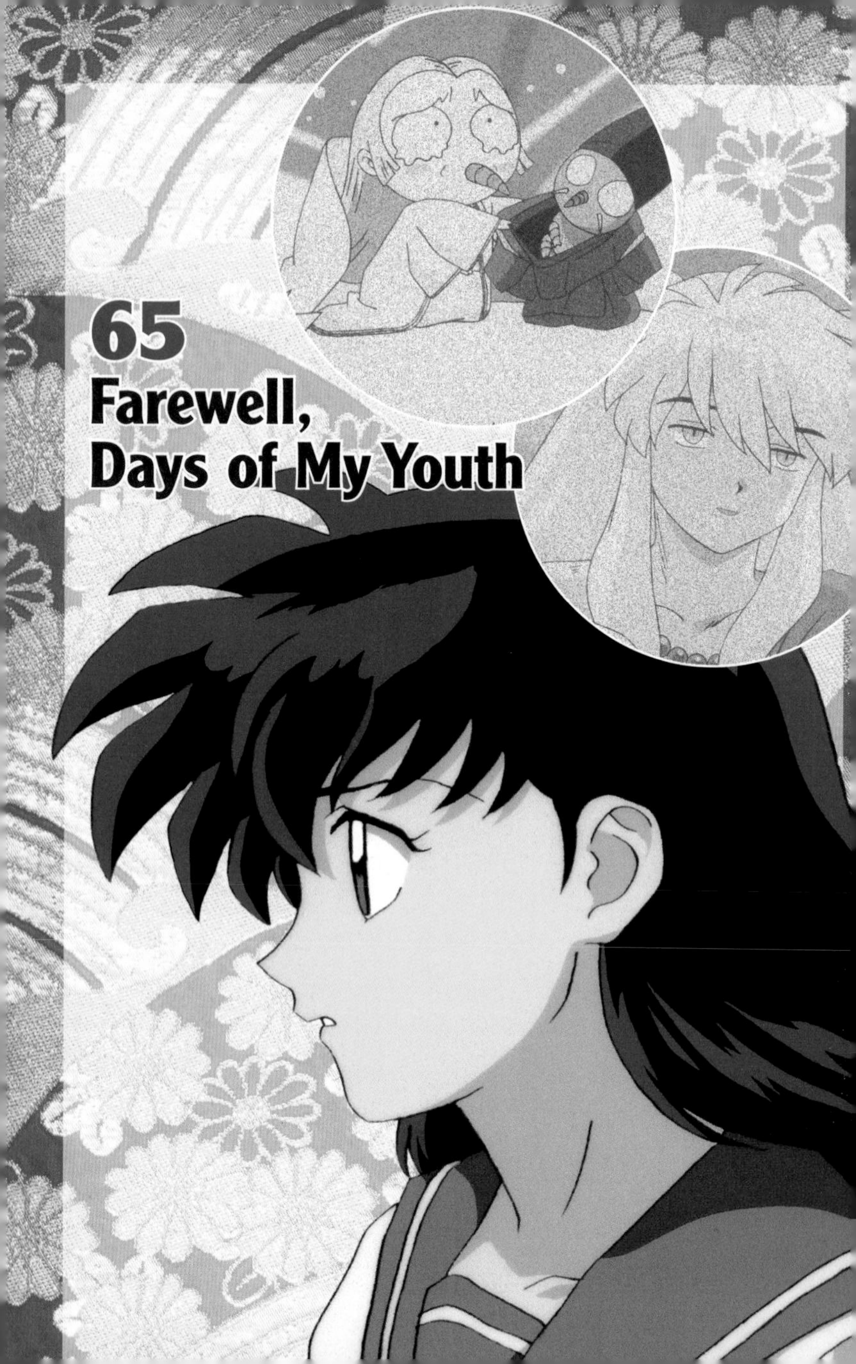

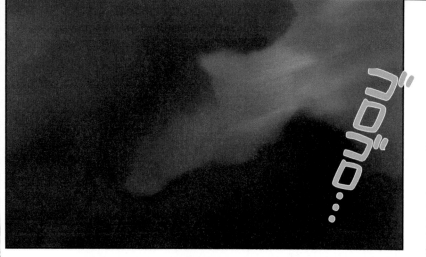

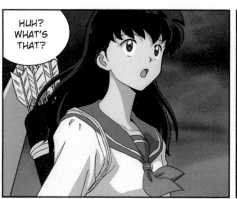

HUH?
WHAT'S
THAT?

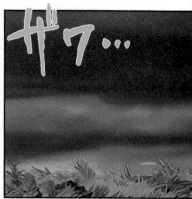

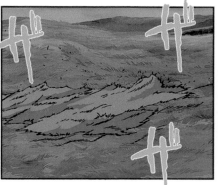

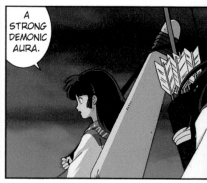

A
STRONG
DEMONIC
AURA.

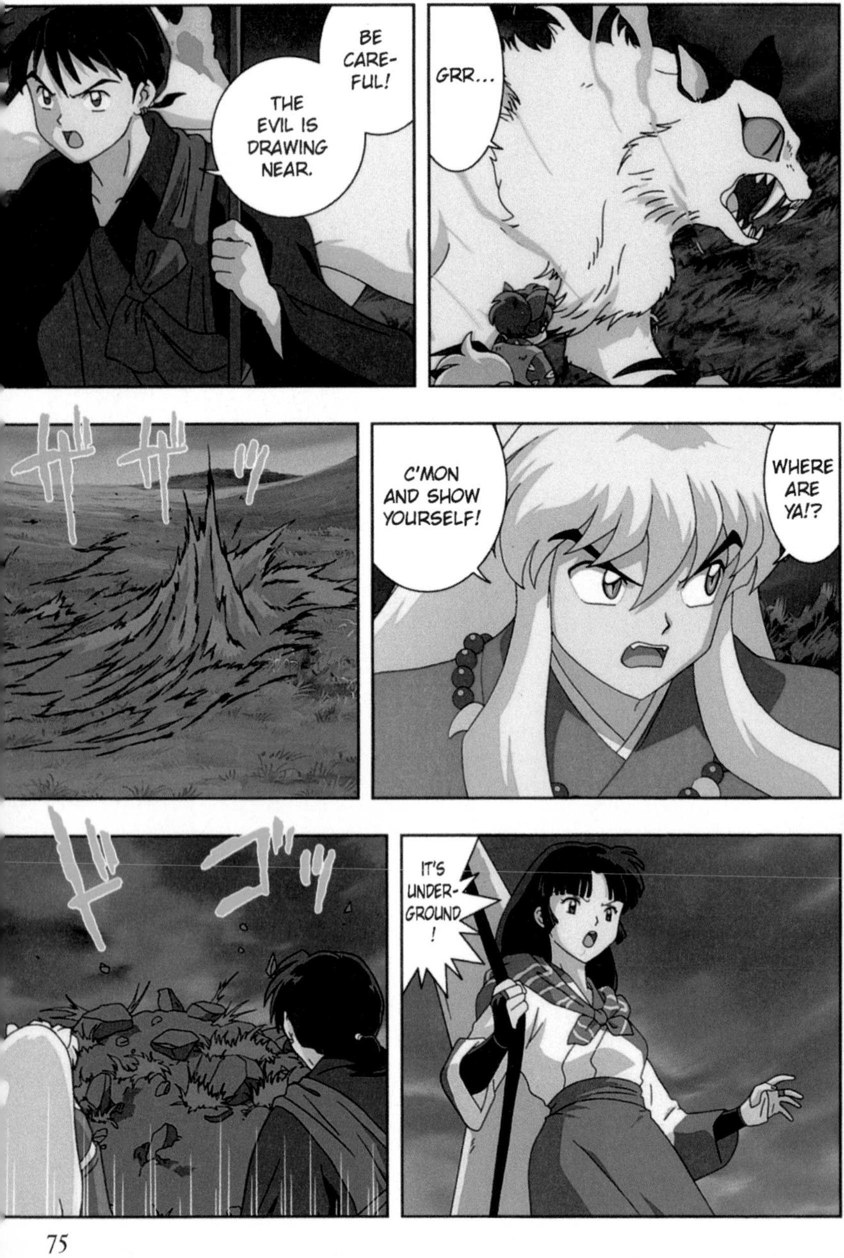
GRR...
BE CAREFUL!
THE EVIL IS DRAWING NEAR.
WHERE ARE YA!?
C'MON AND SHOW YOURSELF!
ザザッ
IT'S UNDERGROUND!
ドゴッ

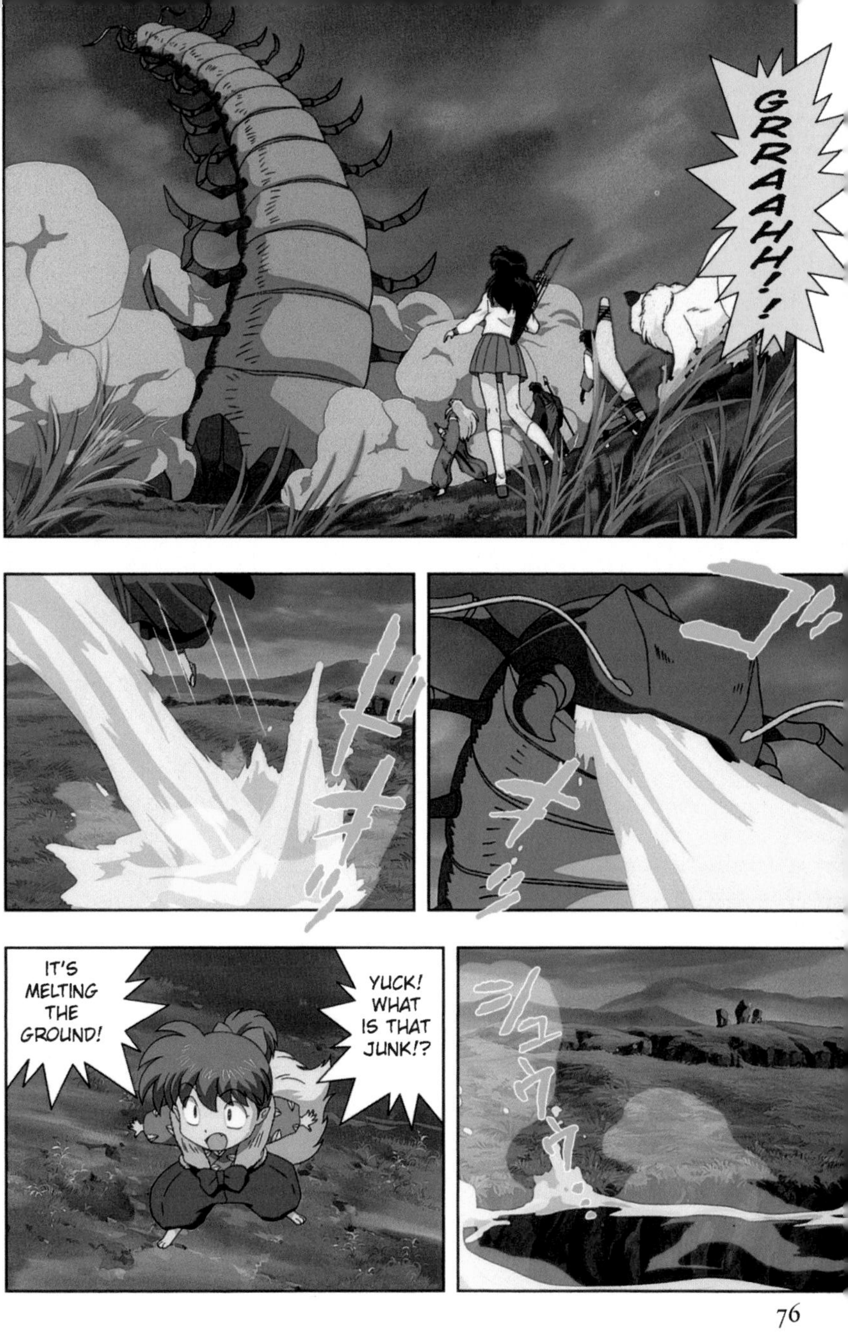
GRRAAHH!!
ゴ
メキッ
ドオッ
シュウウ
YUCK! WHAT IS THAT JUNK!?
IT'S MELTING THE GROUND!

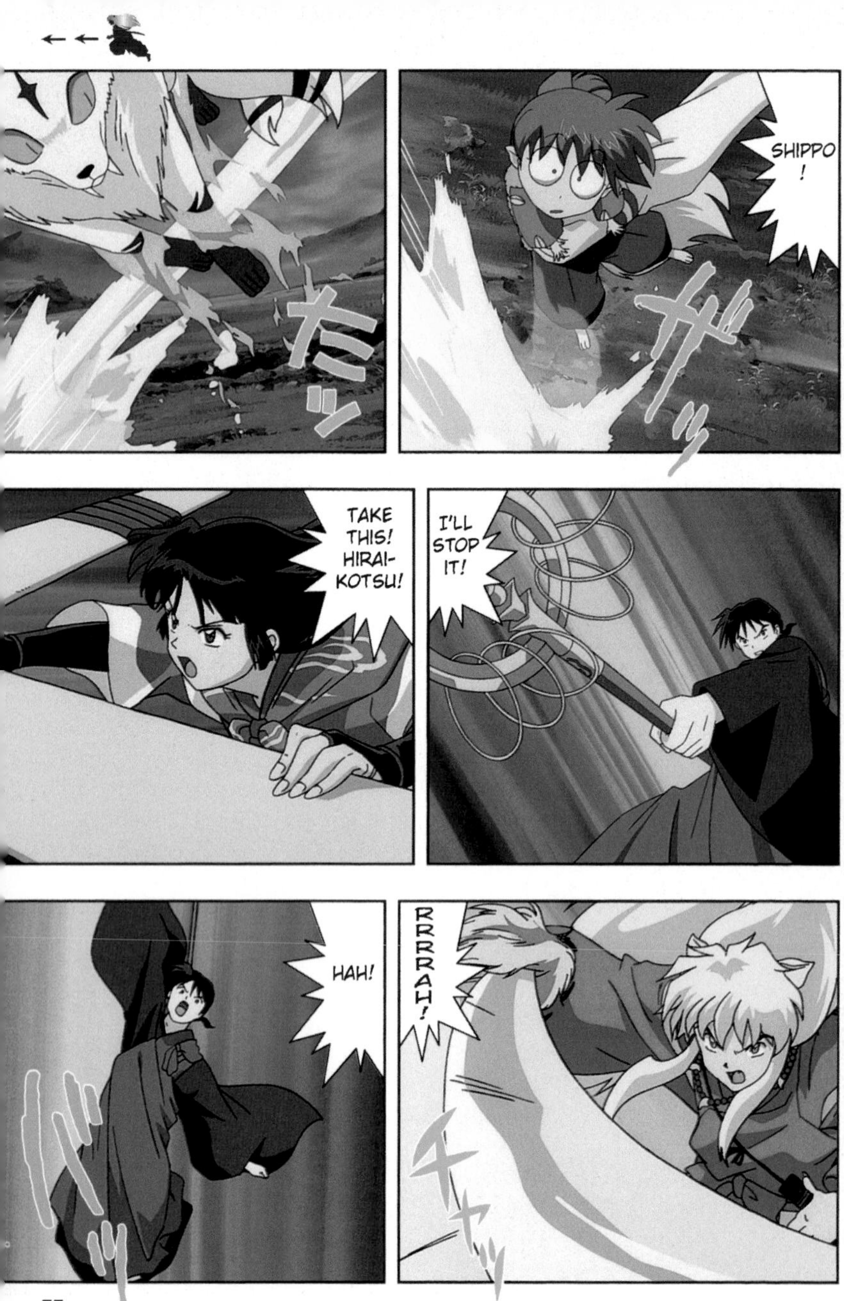
SHIPPO!
I'LL STOP IT!
TAKE THIS! HIRAI-KOTSU!
RRRRAH!
HAH!

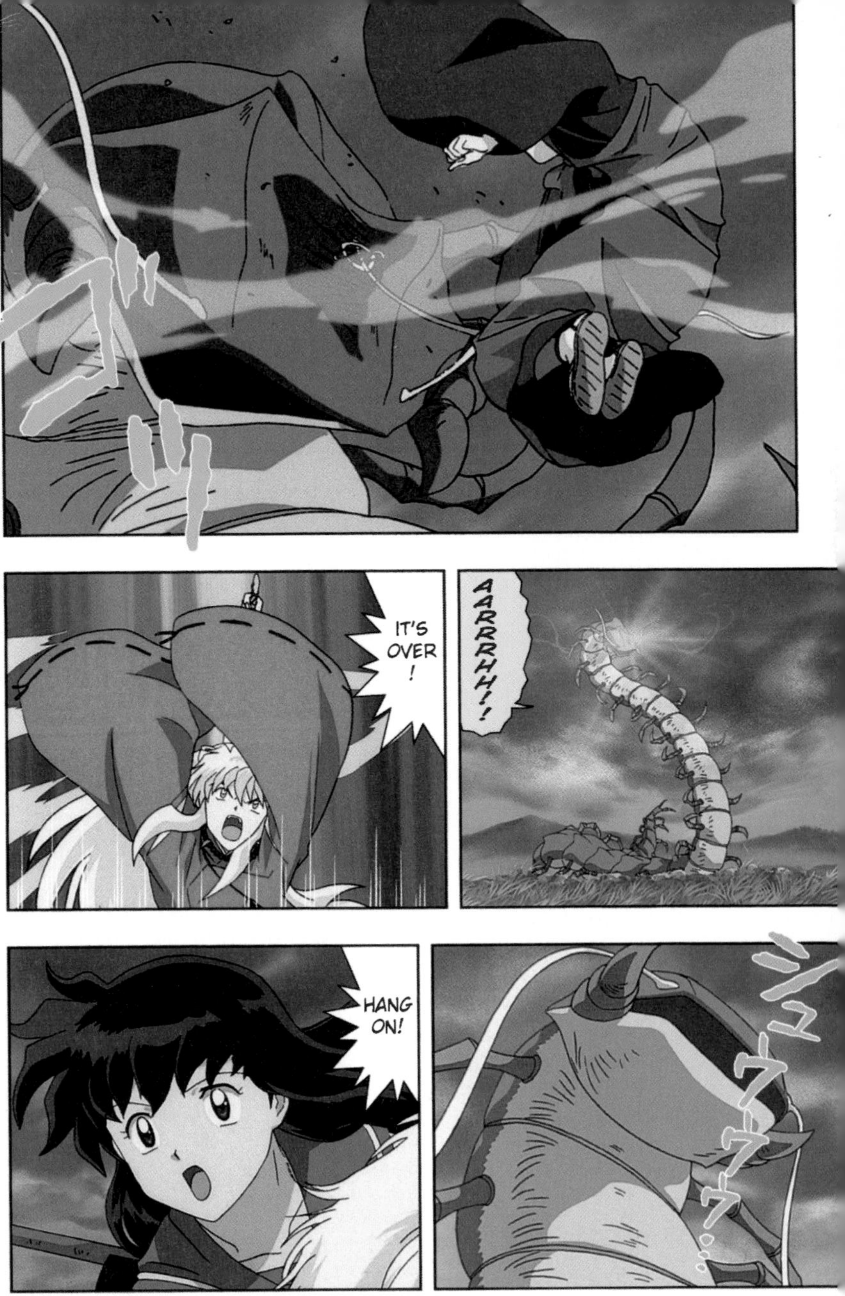
AARRRHH!!
IT'S OVER!
HANG ON!

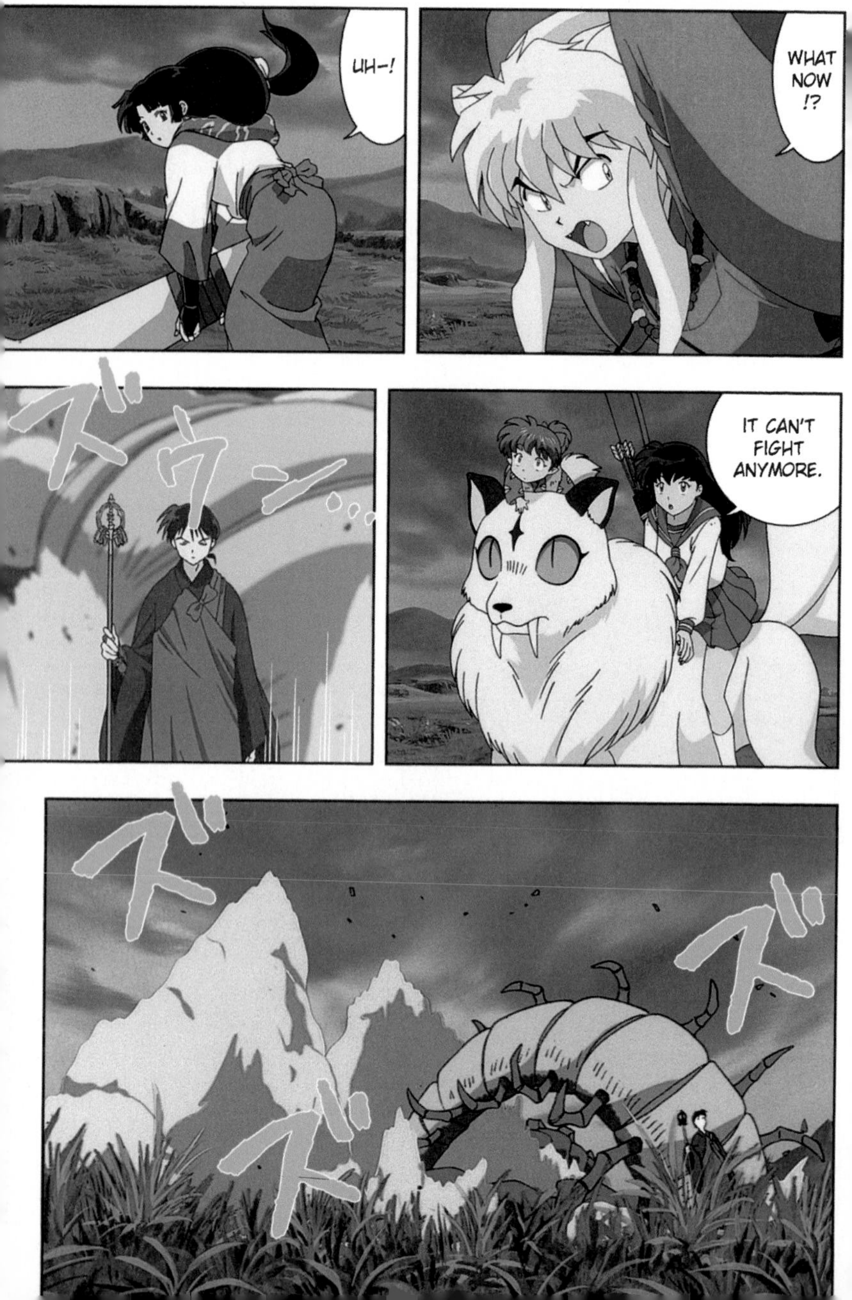
WHAT NOW !?
UH-!
IT CAN'T FIGHT ANYMORE.
ズウーン…
ズズズ

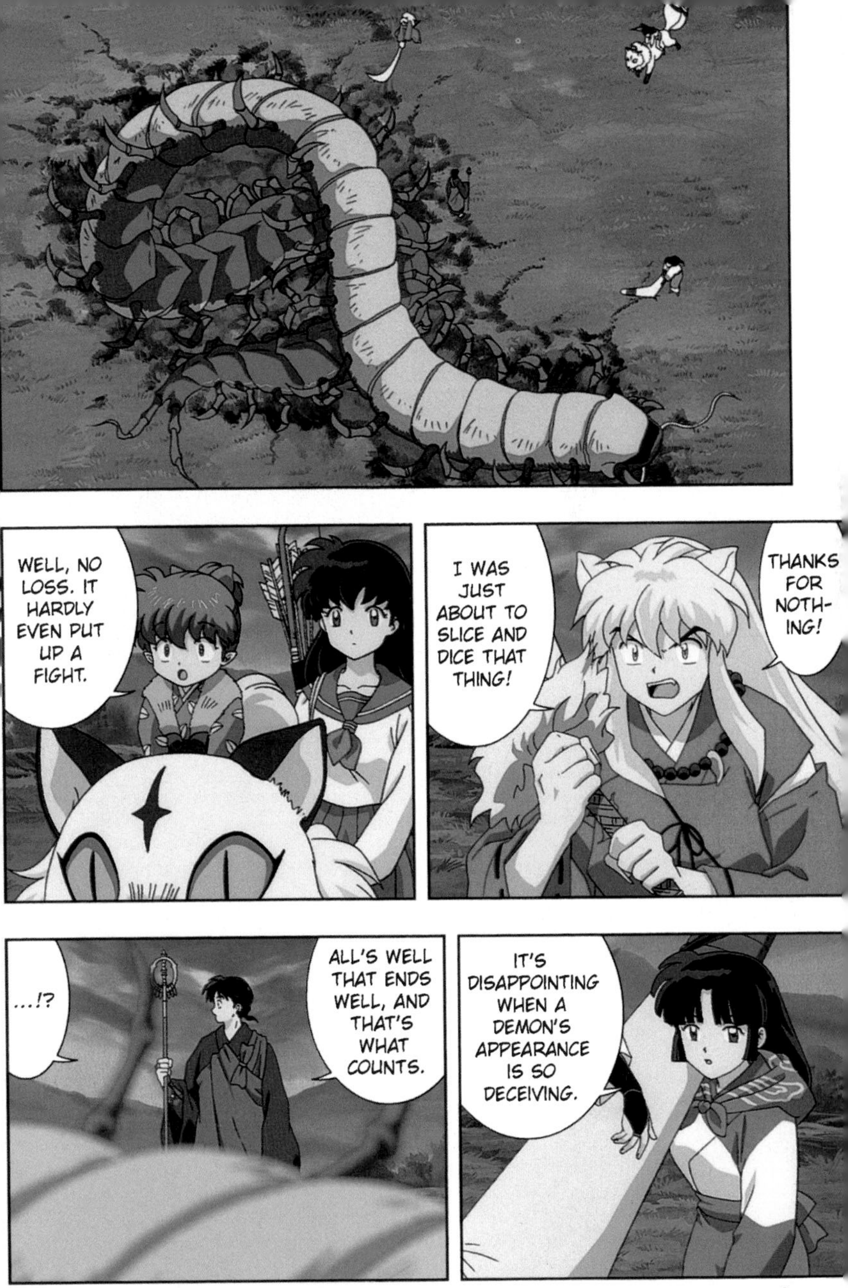
THANKS FOR NOTH-ING!
I WAS JUST ABOUT TO SLICE AND DICE THAT THING!
WELL, NO LOSS. IT HARDLY EVEN PUT UP A FIGHT.
IT'S DISAPPOINTING WHEN A DEMON'S APPEARANCE IS SO DECEIVING.
ALL'S WELL THAT ENDS WELL, AND THAT'S WHAT COUNTS.
...!?

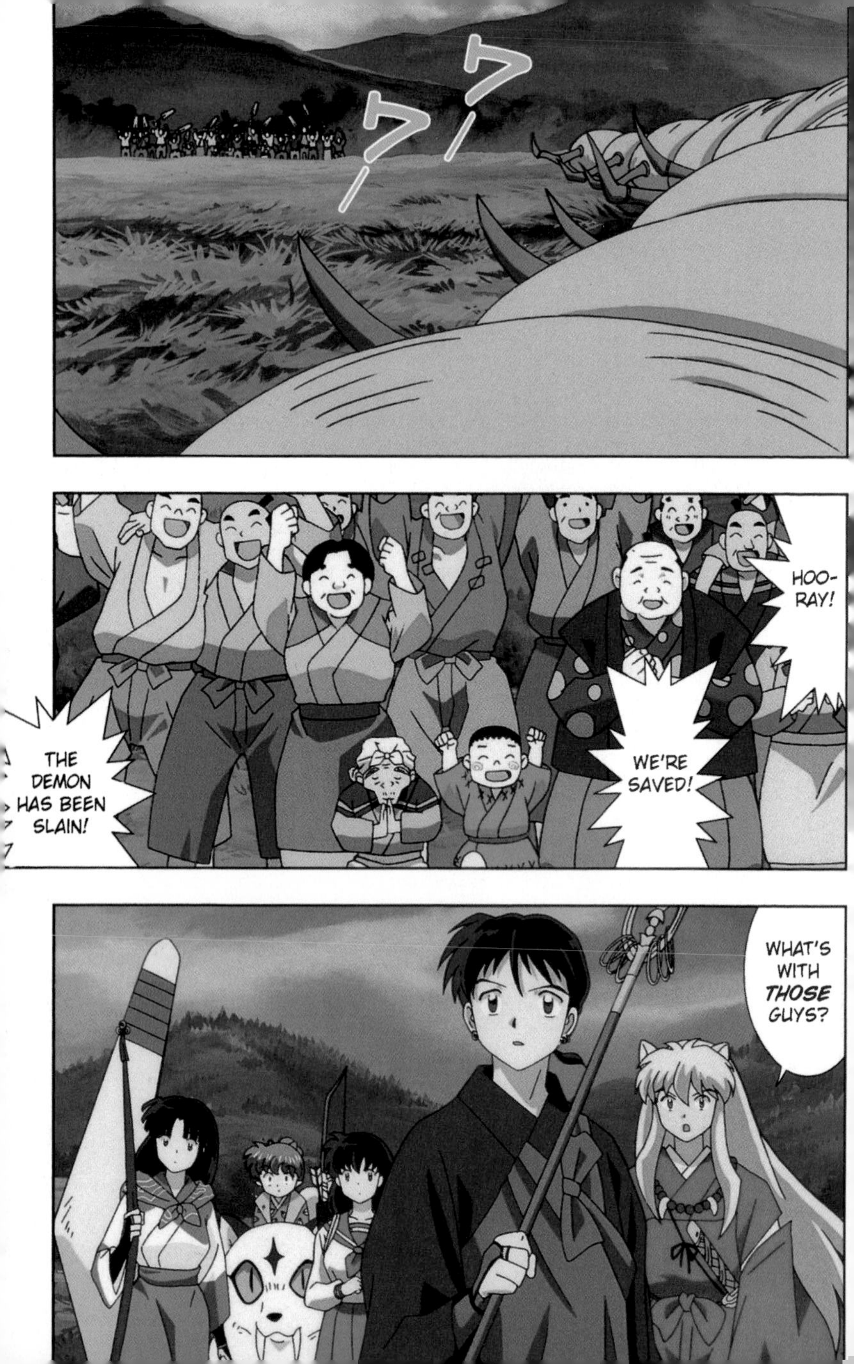

ワー
ワー
HOO-RAY!
WE'RE SAVED!
THE DEMON HAS BEEN SLAIN!
WHAT'S WITH *THOSE* GUYS?

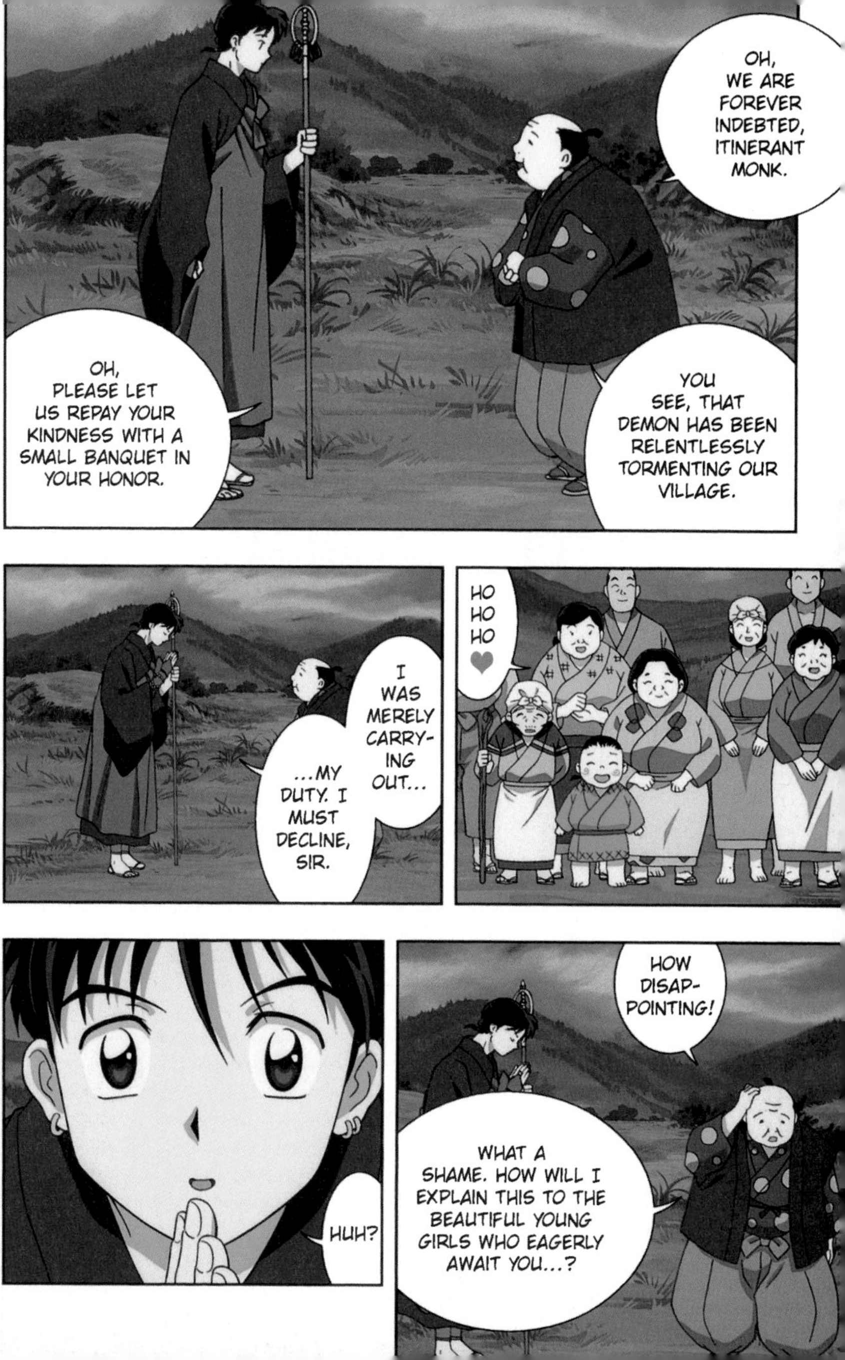
OH, WE ARE FOREVER INDEBTED, ITINERANT MONK.
YOU SEE, THAT DEMON HAS BEEN RELENTLESSLY TORMENTING OUR VILLAGE.
OH, PLEASE LET US REPAY YOUR KINDNESS WITH A SMALL BANQUET IN YOUR HONOR.
HO HO HO ♥
I WAS MERELY CARRY-ING OUT...
...MY DUTY. I MUST DECLINE, SIR.
HOW DISAP-POINTING!
WHAT A SHAME. HOW WILL I EXPLAIN THIS TO THE BEAUTIFUL YOUNG GIRLS WHO EAGERLY AWAIT YOU...?
HUH?

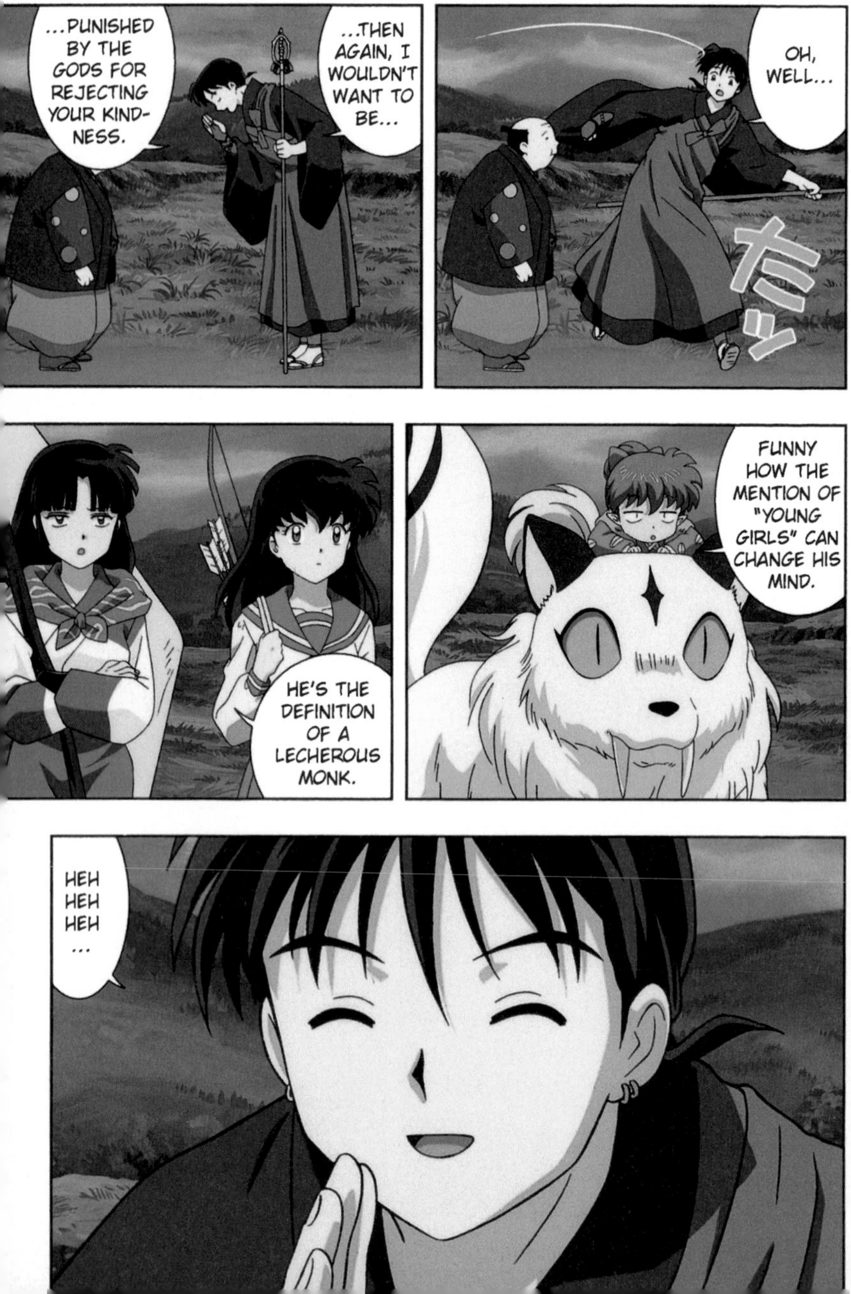
OH, WELL...
たミッ
...THEN AGAIN, I WOULDN'T WANT TO BE...
...PUNISHED BY THE GODS FOR REJECTING YOUR KINDNESS.
FUNNY HOW THE MENTION OF "YOUNG GIRLS" CAN CHANGE HIS MIND.
HE'S THE DEFINITION OF A LECHEROUS MONK.
HEH HEH HEH ...

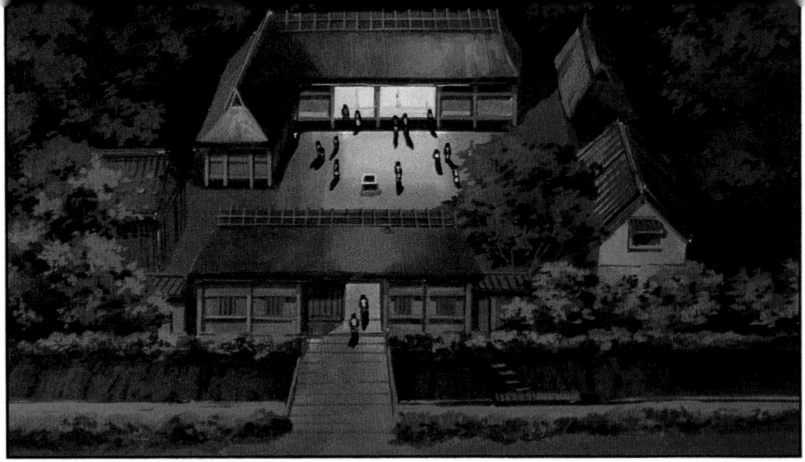

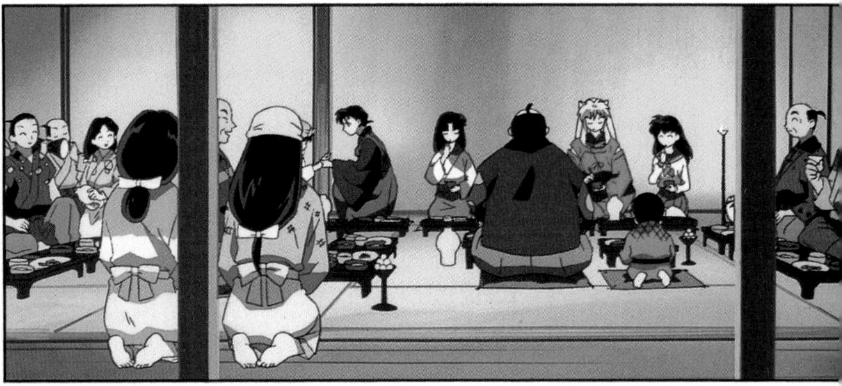

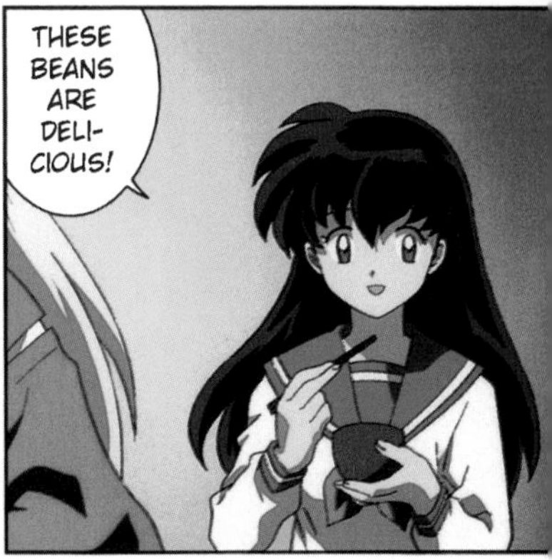
THESE BEANS ARE DELI-CIOUS!

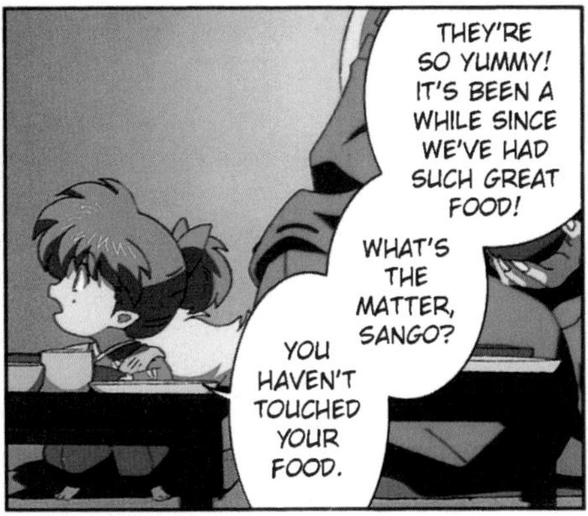
THEY'RE SO YUMMY! IT'S BEEN A WHILE SINCE WE'VE HAD SUCH GREAT FOOD!
WHAT'S THE MATTER, SANGO?
YOU HAVEN'T TOUCHED YOUR FOOD.

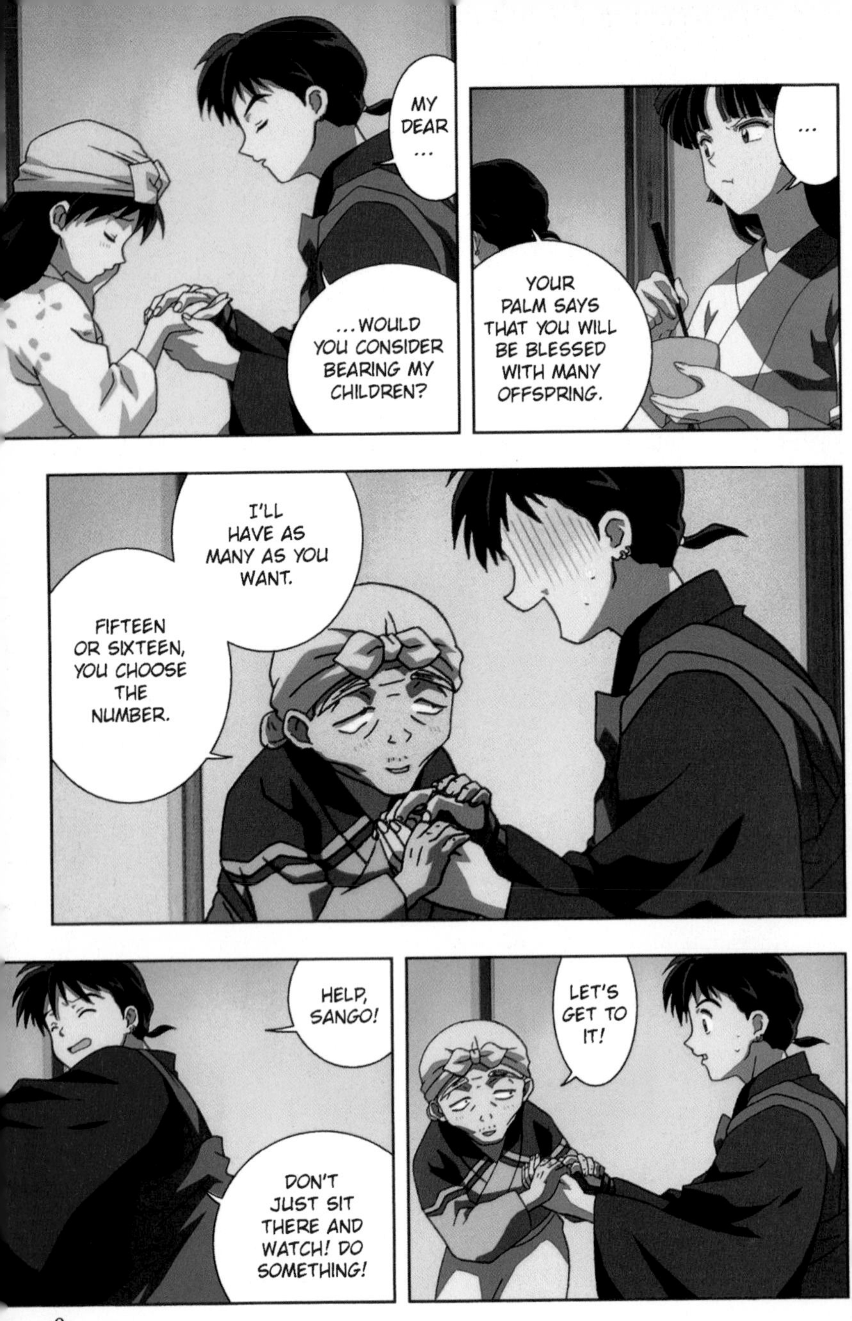
...
YOUR PALM SAYS THAT YOU WILL BE BLESSED WITH MANY OFFSPRING.
MY DEAR ...
...WOULD YOU CONSIDER BEARING MY CHILDREN?
I'LL HAVE AS MANY AS YOU WANT.
FIFTEEN OR SIXTEEN, YOU CHOOSE THE NUMBER.
LET'S GET TO IT!
HELP, SANGO!
DON'T JUST SIT THERE AND WATCH! DO SOMETHING!

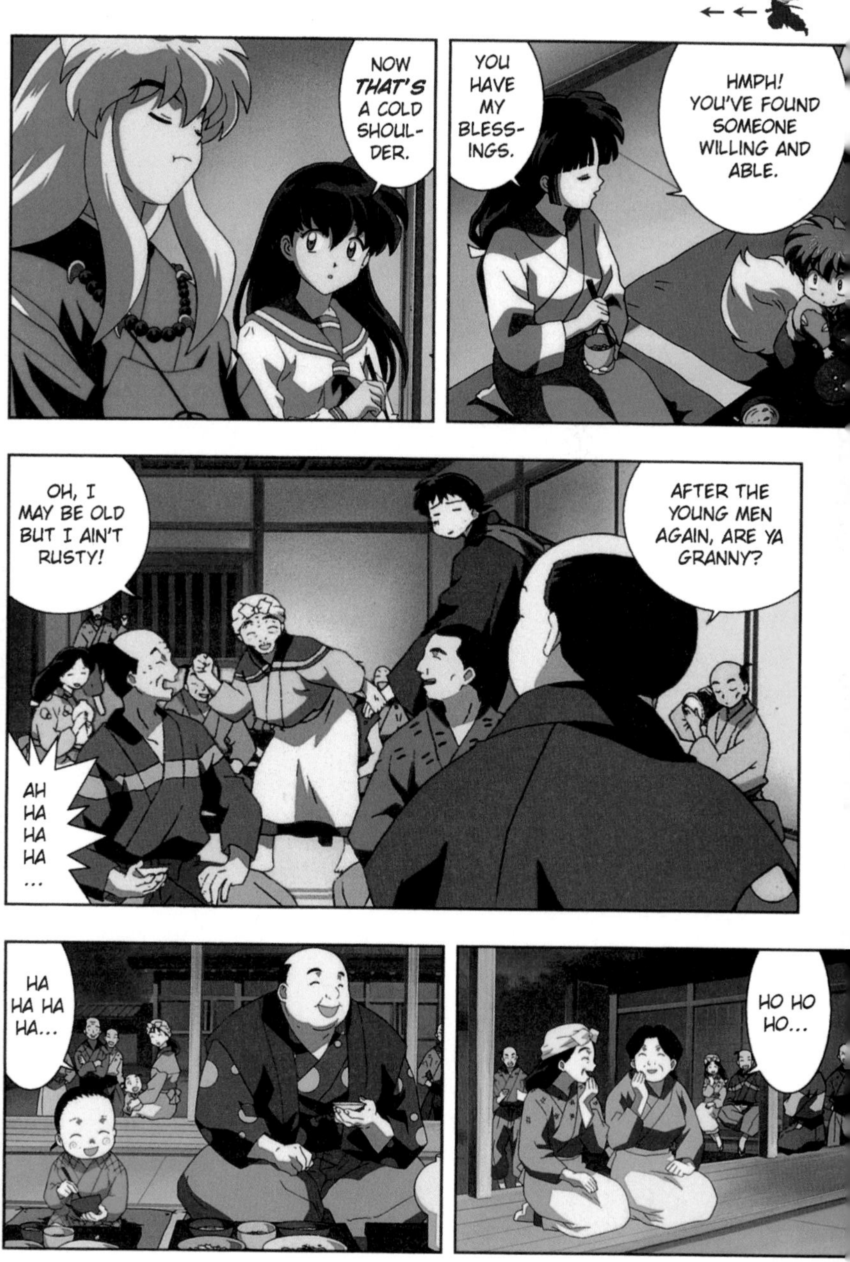
HMPH! YOU'VE FOUND SOMEONE WILLING AND ABLE.
YOU HAVE MY BLESS-INGS.
NOW *THAT'S* A COLD SHOUL-DER.
AFTER THE YOUNG MEN AGAIN, ARE YA GRANNY?
OH, I MAY BE OLD BUT I AIN'T RUSTY!
AH HA HA HA ...
HO HO HO...
HA HA HA HA...

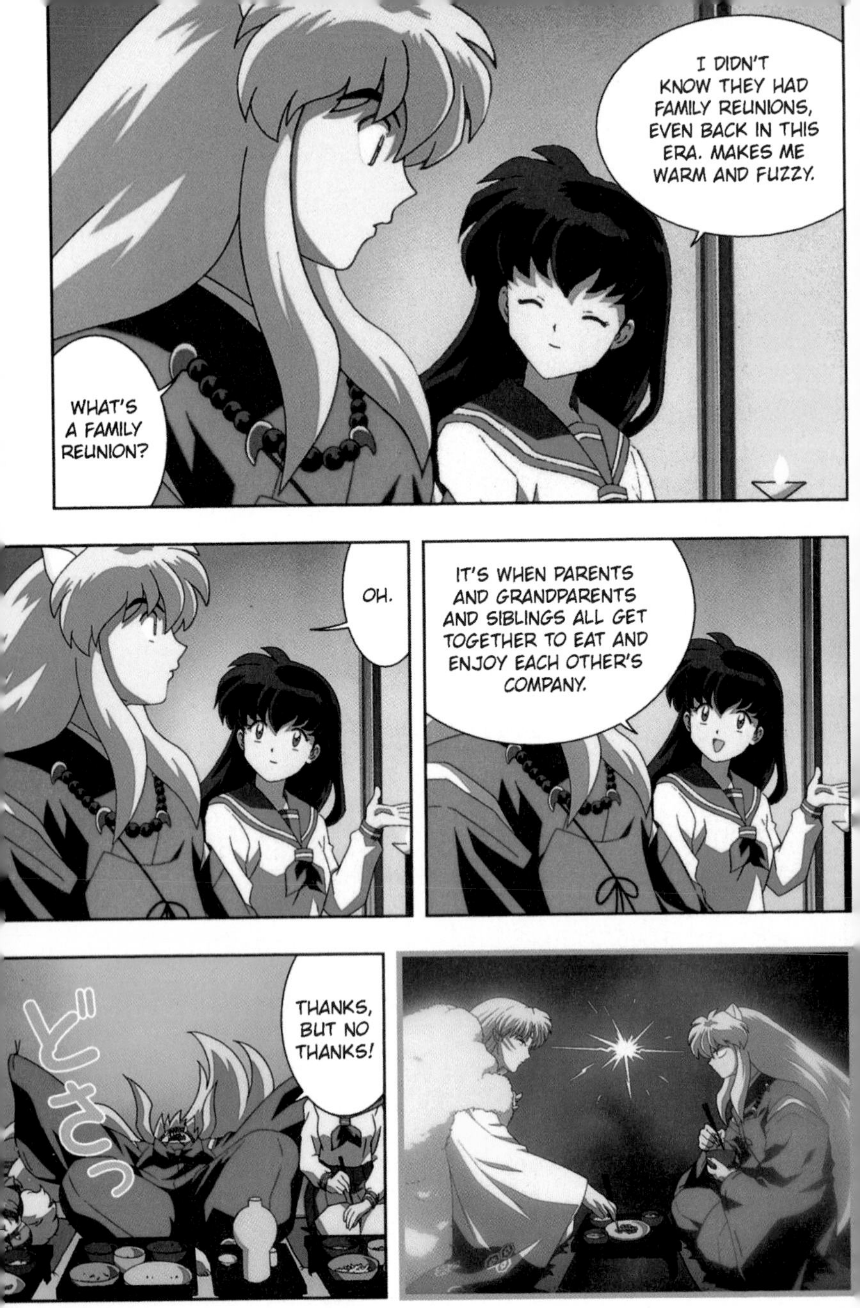
I DIDN'T KNOW THEY HAD FAMILY REUNIONS, EVEN BACK IN THIS ERA. MAKES ME WARM AND FUZZY.
WHAT'S A FAMILY REUNION?
IT'S WHEN PARENTS AND GRANDPARENTS AND SIBLINGS ALL GET TOGETHER TO EAT AND ENJOY EACH OTHER'S COMPANY.
OH.
THANKS, BUT NO THANKS!
どさっ

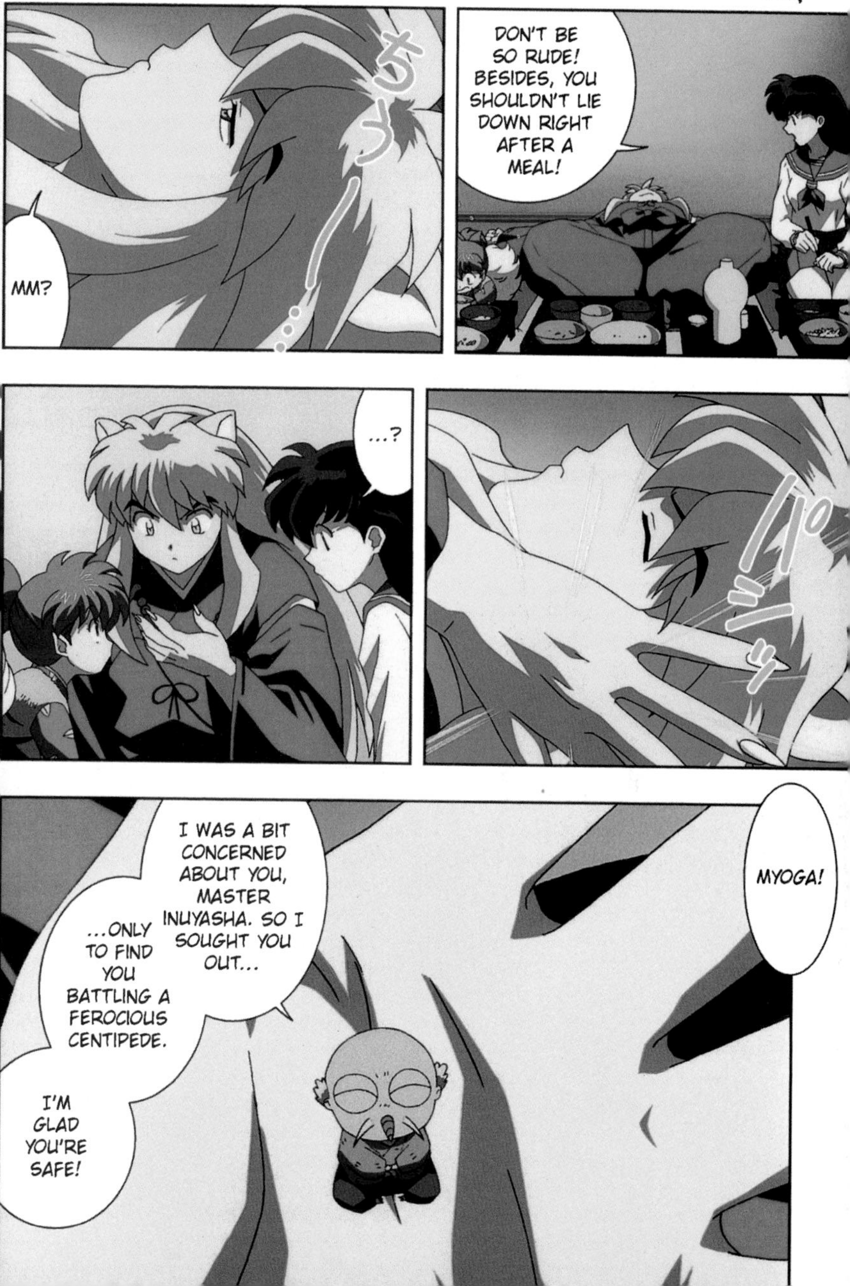
DON'T BE SO RUDE! BESIDES, YOU SHOULDN'T LIE DOWN RIGHT AFTER A MEAL!
MM?
...?
MYOGA!
I WAS A BIT CONCERNED ABOUT YOU, MASTER INUYASHA. SO I SOUGHT YOU OUT...
...ONLY TO FIND YOU BATTLING A FEROCIOUS CENTIPEDE.
I'M GLAD YOU'RE SAFE!

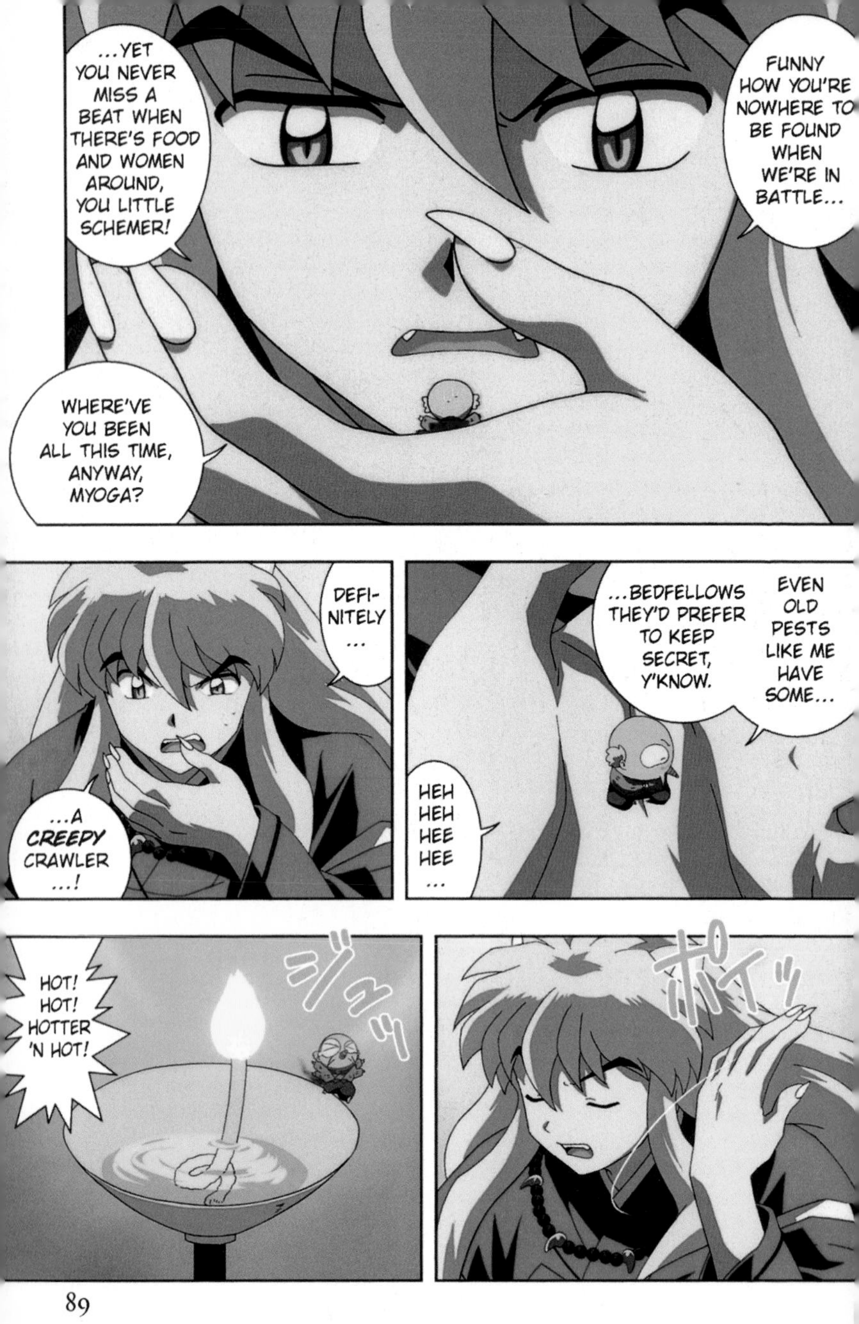
FUNNY HOW YOU'RE NOWHERE TO BE FOUND WHEN WE'RE IN BATTLE...
...YET YOU NEVER MISS A BEAT WHEN THERE'S FOOD AND WOMEN AROUND, YOU LITTLE SCHEMER!
WHERE'VE YOU BEEN ALL THIS TIME, ANYWAY, MYOGA?
EVEN OLD PESTS LIKE ME HAVE SOME...
...BEDFELLOWS THEY'D PREFER TO KEEP SECRET, Y'KNOW.
HEH HEH HEE HEE ...
DEFI-NITELY ...
...A *CREEPY* CRAWLER ...!
ポイッ
ジュッ
HOT! HOT! HOTTER 'N HOT!

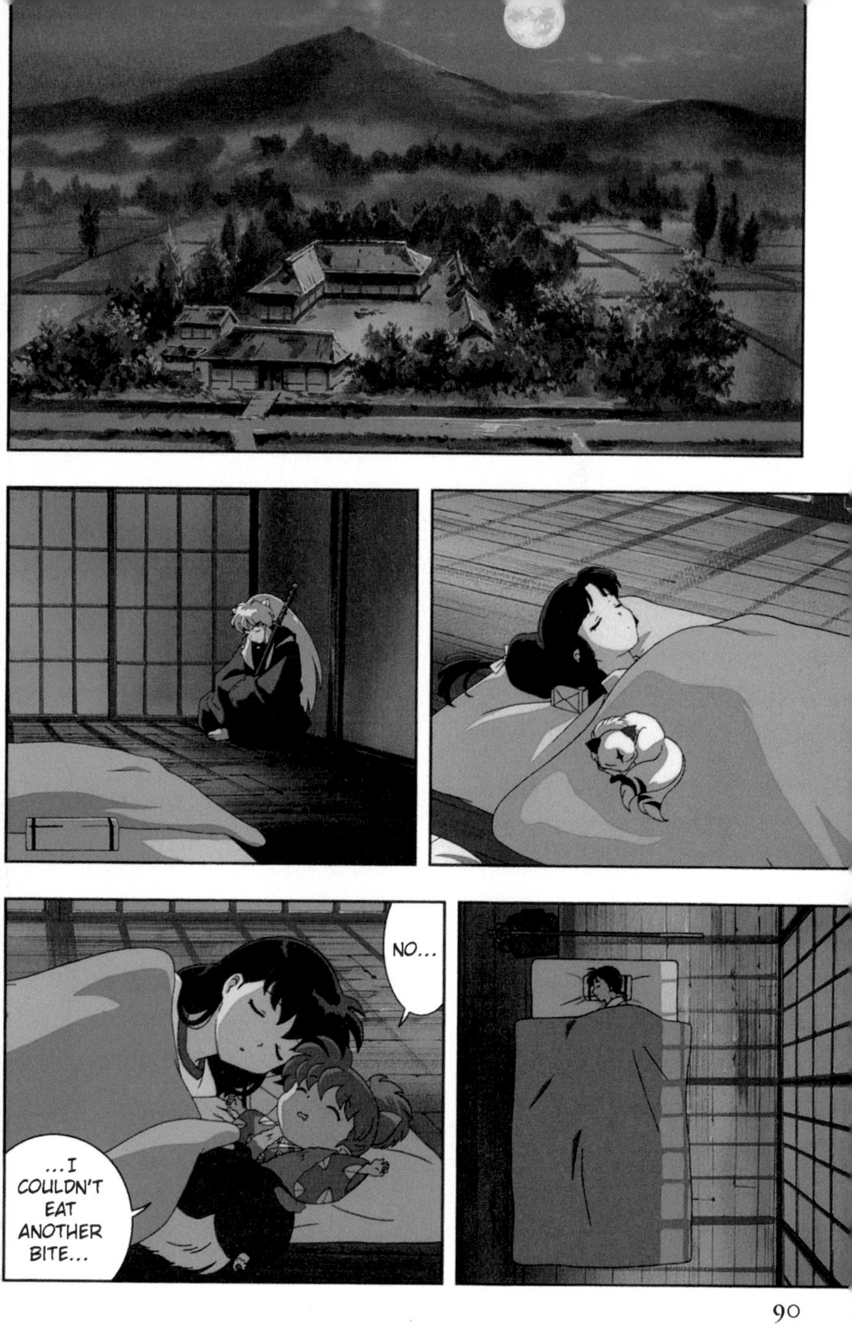
NO...
...I COULDN'T EAT ANOTHER BITE...

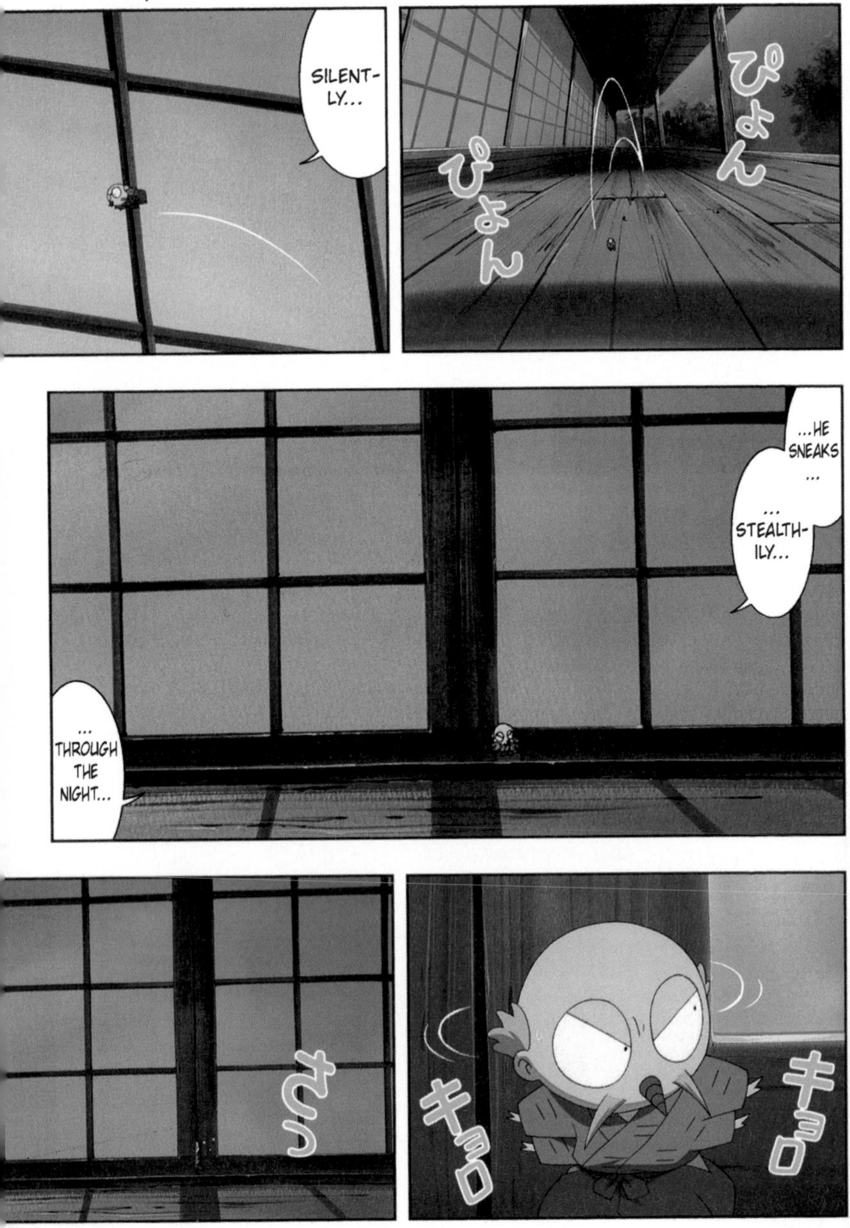
ぴょん
ぴょん
SILENT-LY…
…HE SNEAKS…
…STEALTH-ILY…
…THROUGH THE NIGHT…
キョロ
キョロ
さっ

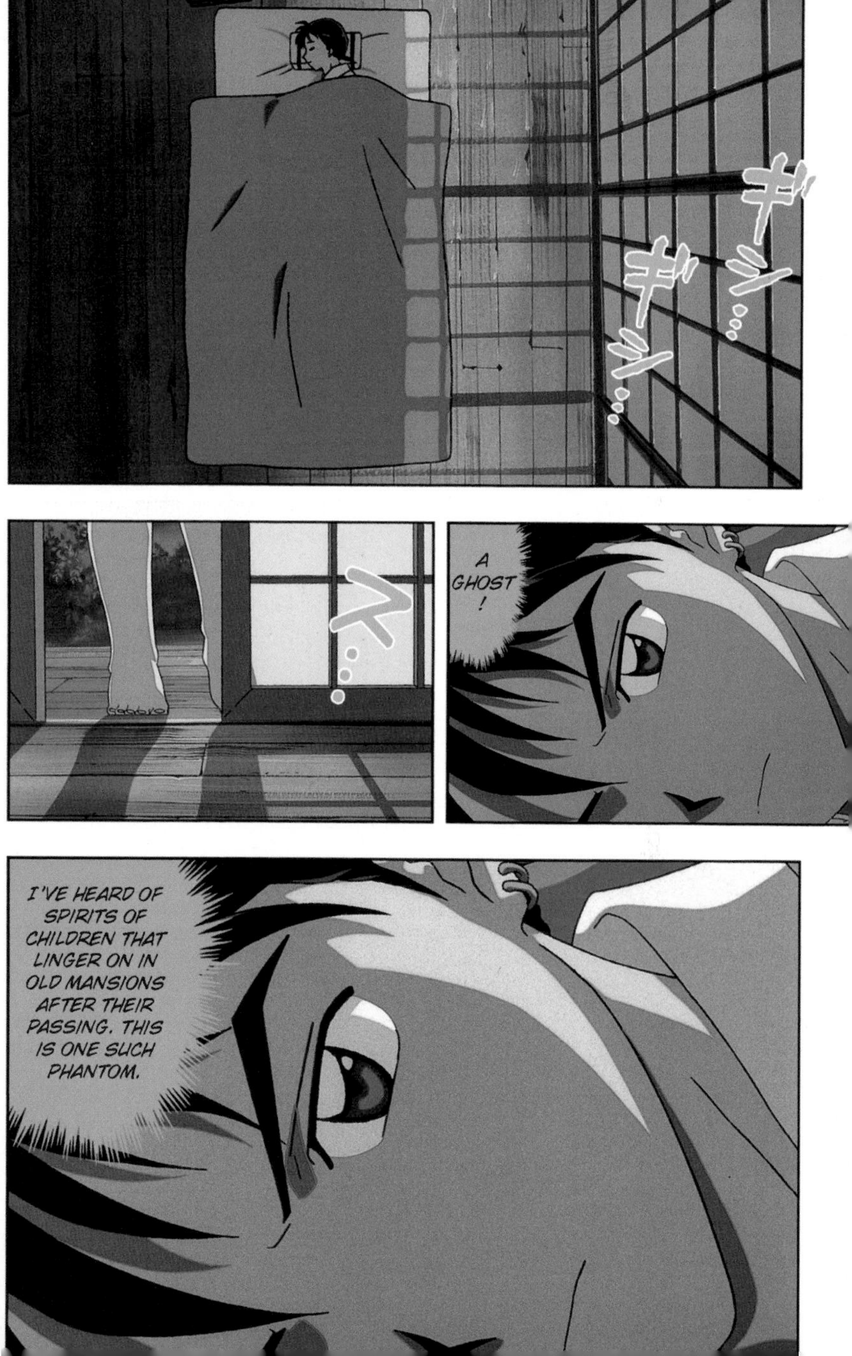
ギシ...
ギシ...
A GHOST!
ス...
I'VE HEARD OF SPIRITS OF CHILDREN THAT LINGER ON IN OLD MANSIONS AFTER THEIR PASSING. THIS IS ONE SUCH PHANTOM.

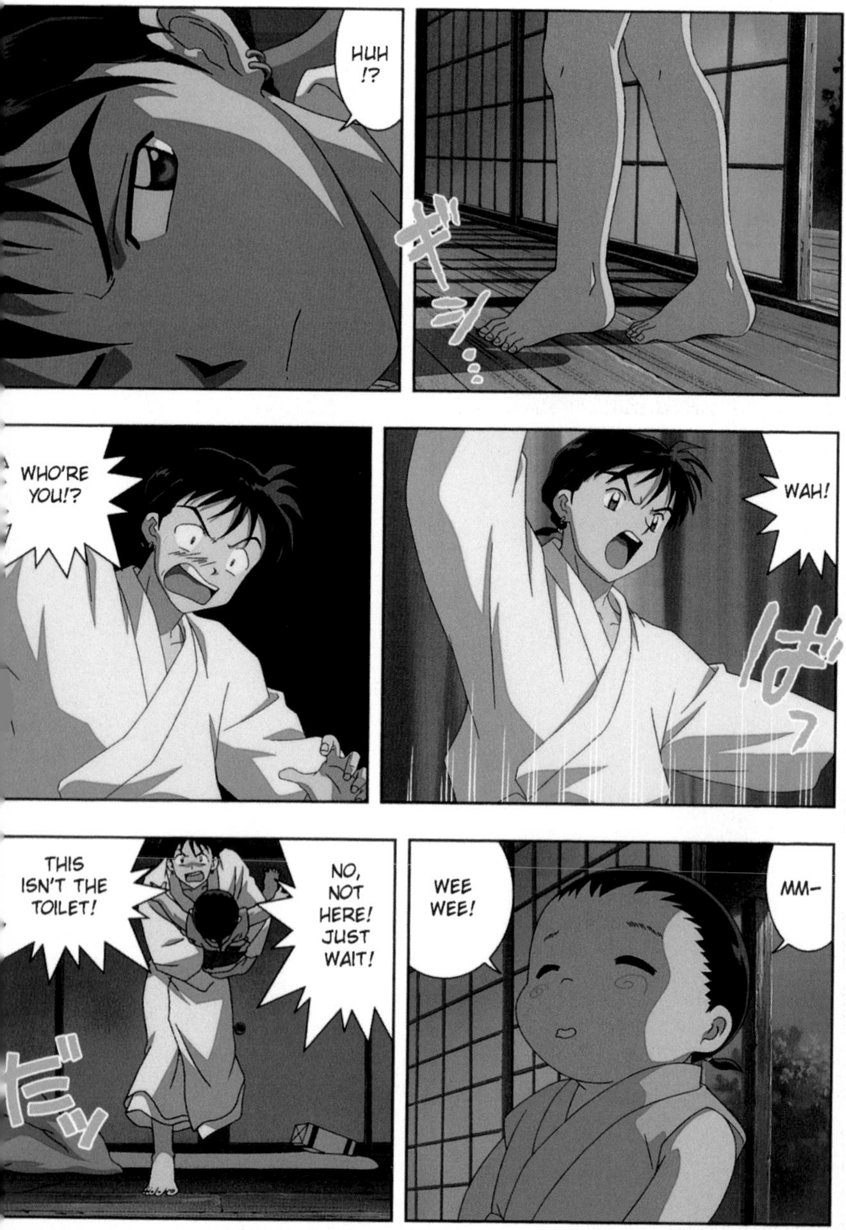
ギシ…
HUH !?
WAH!
ばっ
WHO'RE YOU!?
MM-
WEE WEE!
NO, NOT HERE! JUST WAIT!
THIS ISN'T THE TOILET!
だッ

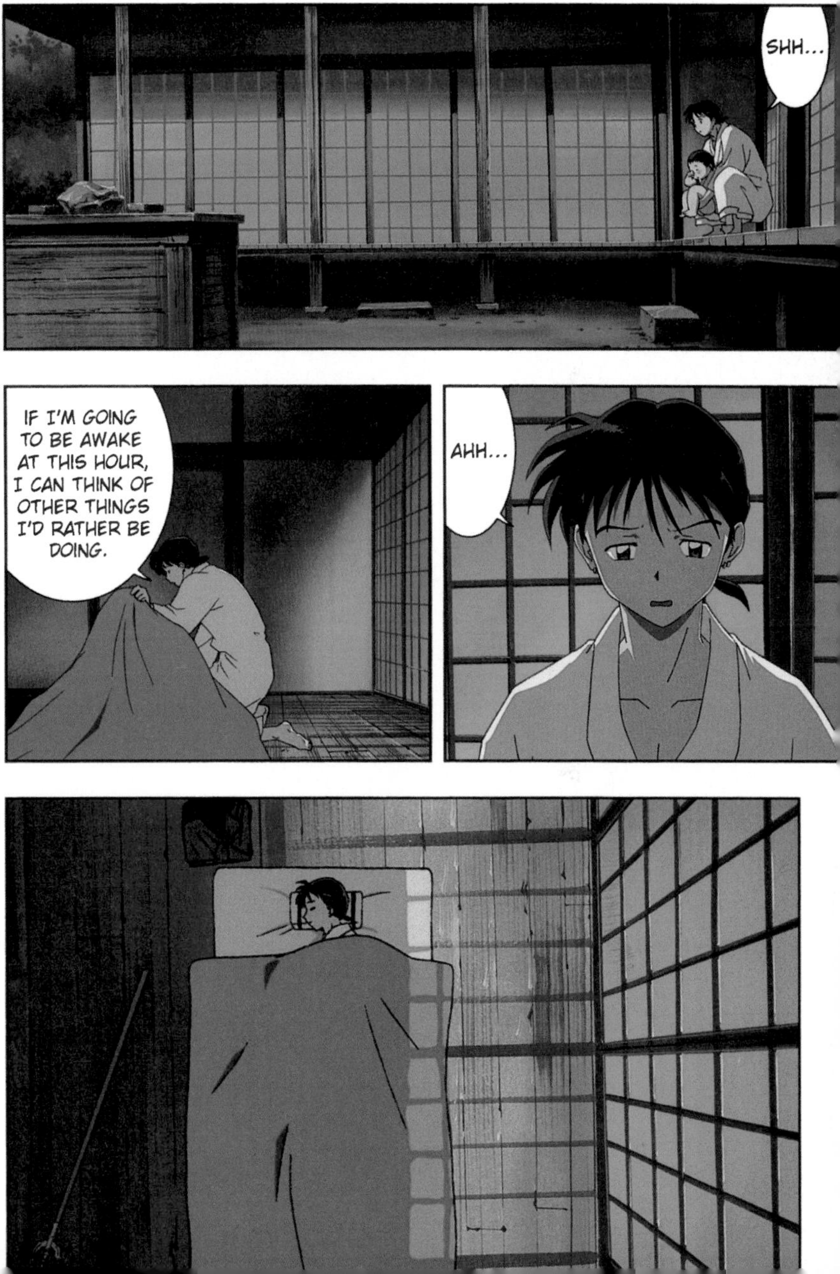
SHH...
AHH...
IF I'M GOING TO BE AWAKE AT THIS HOUR, I CAN THINK OF OTHER THINGS I'D RATHER BE DOING.

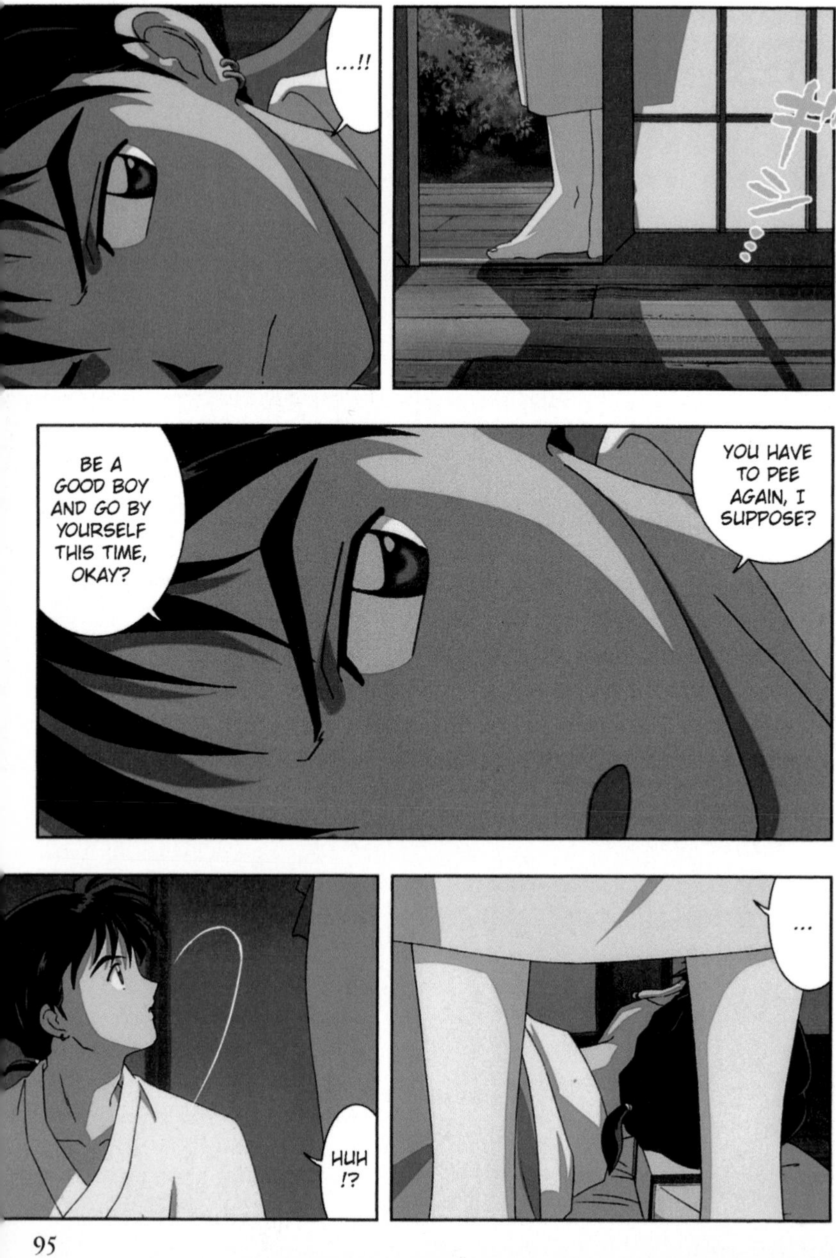
ギシ
...!!
YOU HAVE TO PEE AGAIN, I SUPPOSE?
BE A GOOD BOY AND GO BY YOURSELF THIS TIME, OKAY?
...
HUH !?

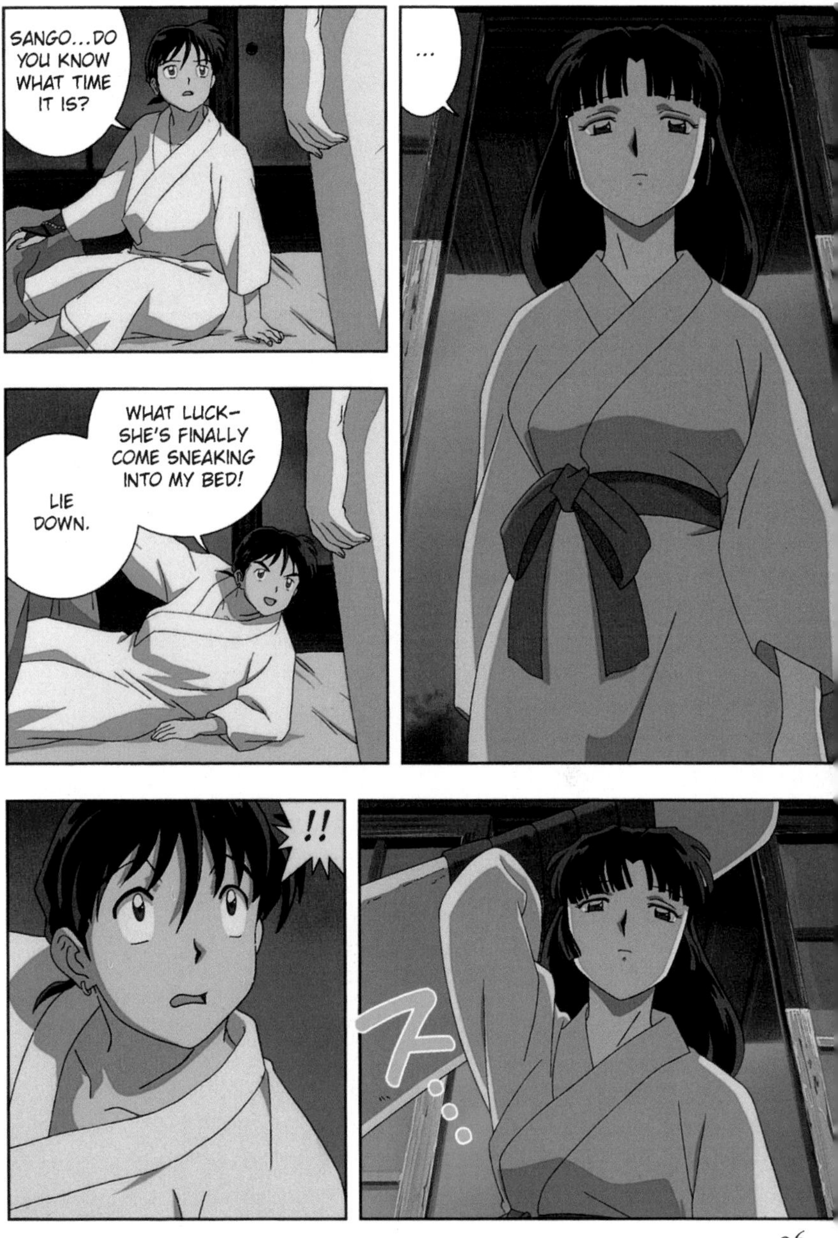
...
SANGO...DO YOU KNOW WHAT TIME IT IS?
WHAT LUCK—SHE'S FINALLY COME SNEAKING INTO MY BED!
LIE DOWN.
!!

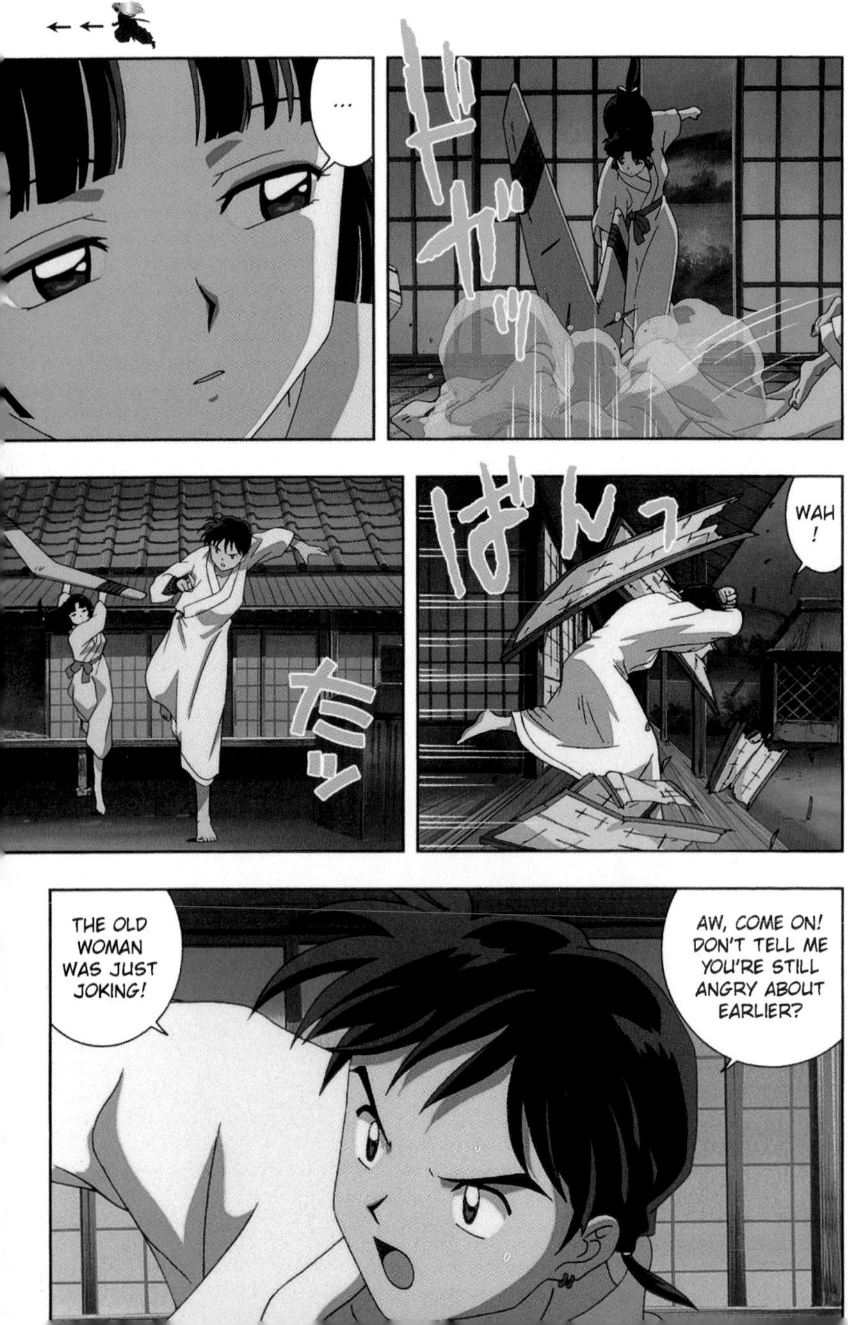
ドガッ
...
WAH!
ばんっ
タッ
AW, COME ON! DON'T TELL ME YOU'RE STILL ANGRY ABOUT EARLIER?
THE OLD WOMAN WAS JUST JOKING!

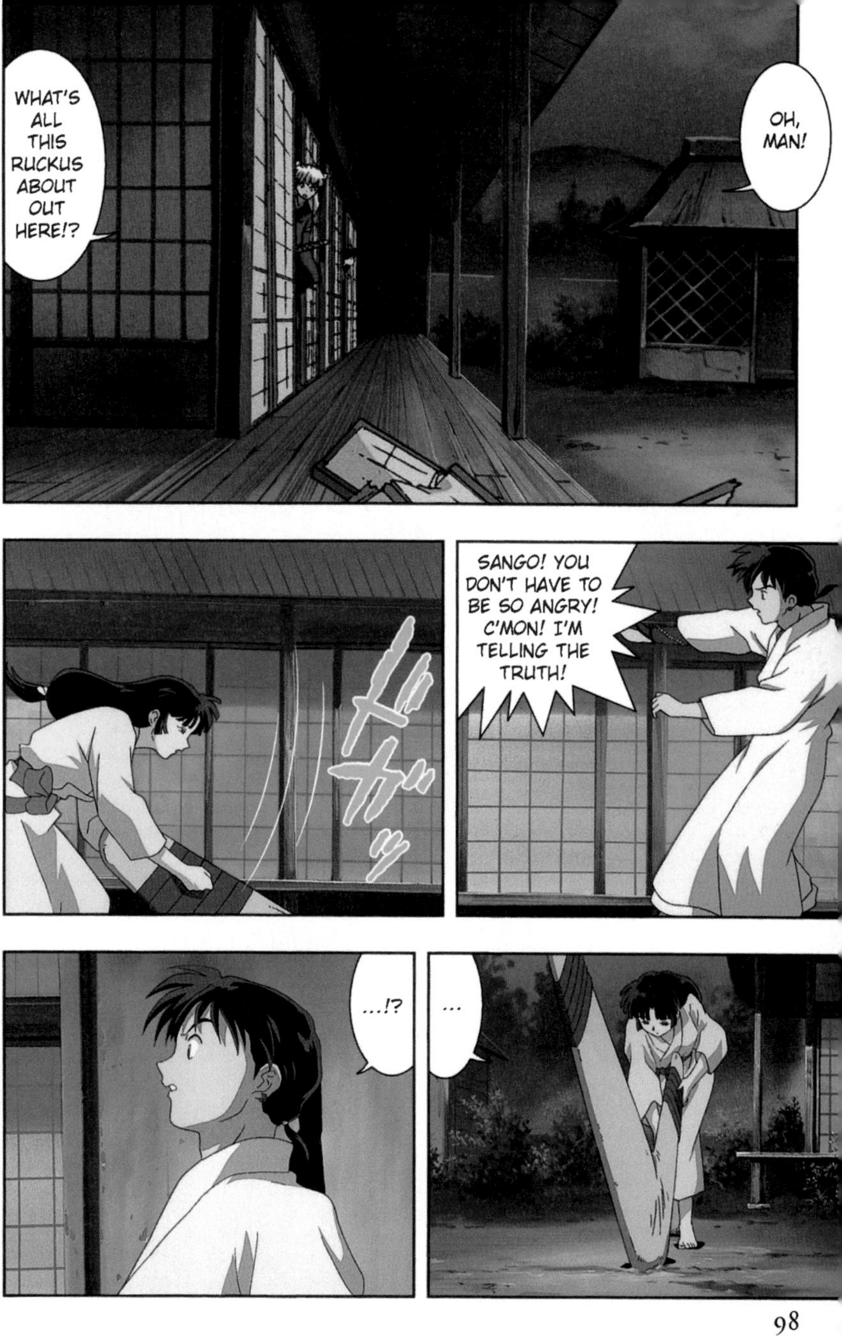
OH, MAN!
WHAT'S ALL THIS RUCKUS ABOUT OUT HERE!?
SANGO! YOU DON'T HAVE TO BE SO ANGRY! C'MON! I'M TELLING THE TRUTH!
...
...!?

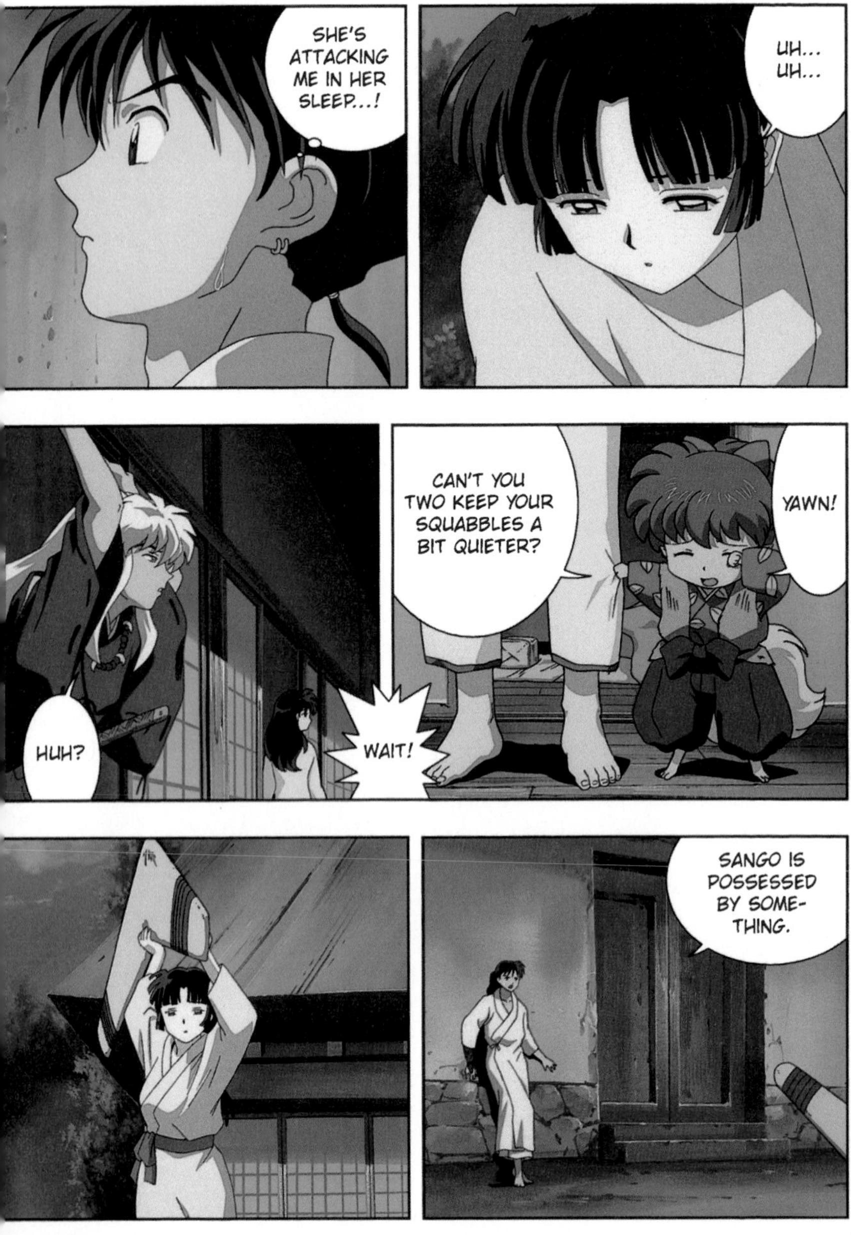
UH... UH...
SHE'S ATTACKING ME IN HER SLEEP...!
YAWN!
CAN'T YOU TWO KEEP YOUR SQUABBLES A BIT QUIETER?
WAIT!
HUH?
SANGO IS POSSESSED BY SOME-THING.

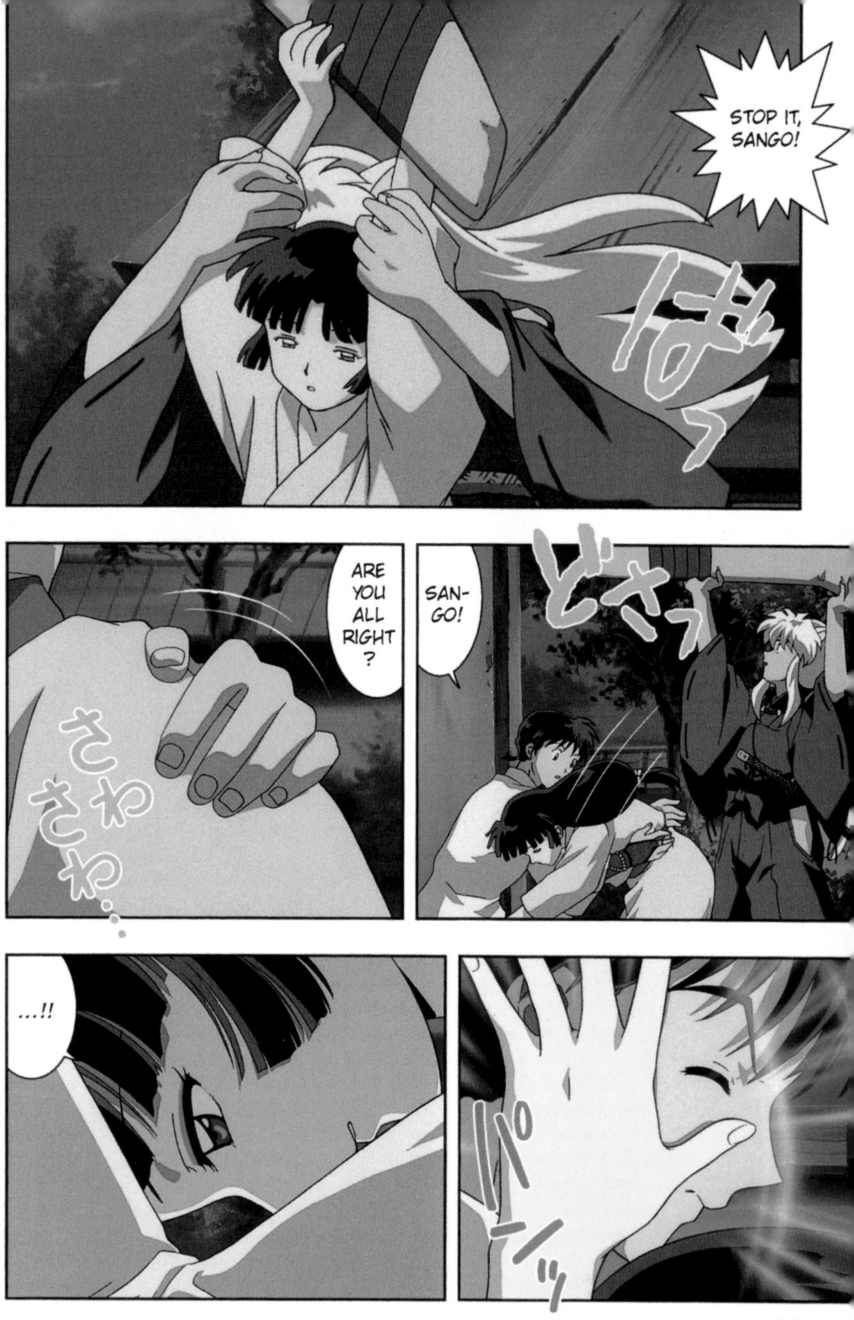
STOP IT, SANGO!
ばっ
どさっ
SAN-GO!
ARE YOU ALL RIGHT?
さわさわ...
パンッ
...!!

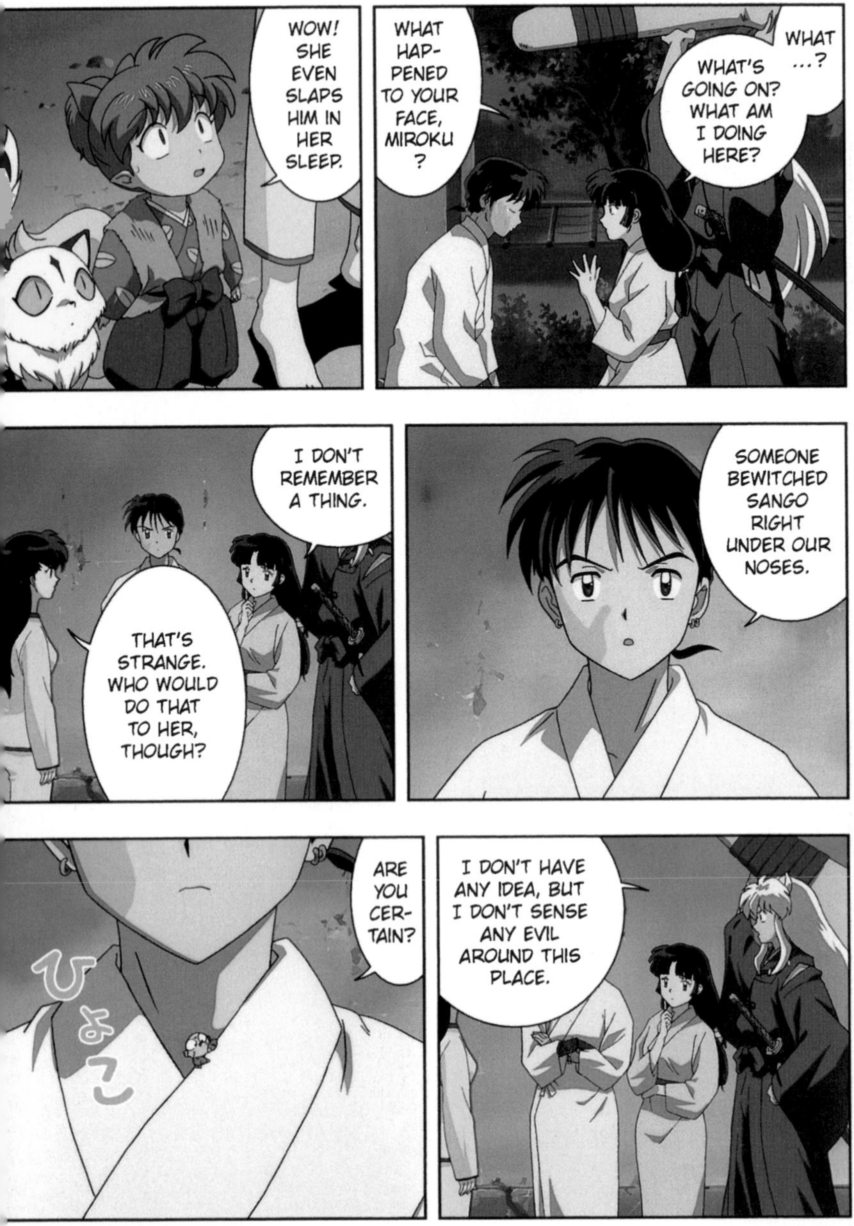
WHAT ...?
WHAT'S GOING ON? WHAT AM I DOING HERE?
WHAT HAP-PENED TO YOUR FACE, MIROKU?
WOW! SHE EVEN SLAPS HIM IN HER SLEEP.
SOMEONE BEWITCHED SANGO RIGHT UNDER OUR NOSES.
I DON'T REMEMBER A THING.
THAT'S STRANGE. WHO WOULD DO THAT TO HER, THOUGH?
I DON'T HAVE ANY IDEA, BUT I DON'T SENSE ANY EVIL AROUND THIS PLACE.
ARE YOU CER-TAIN?
ひょこ

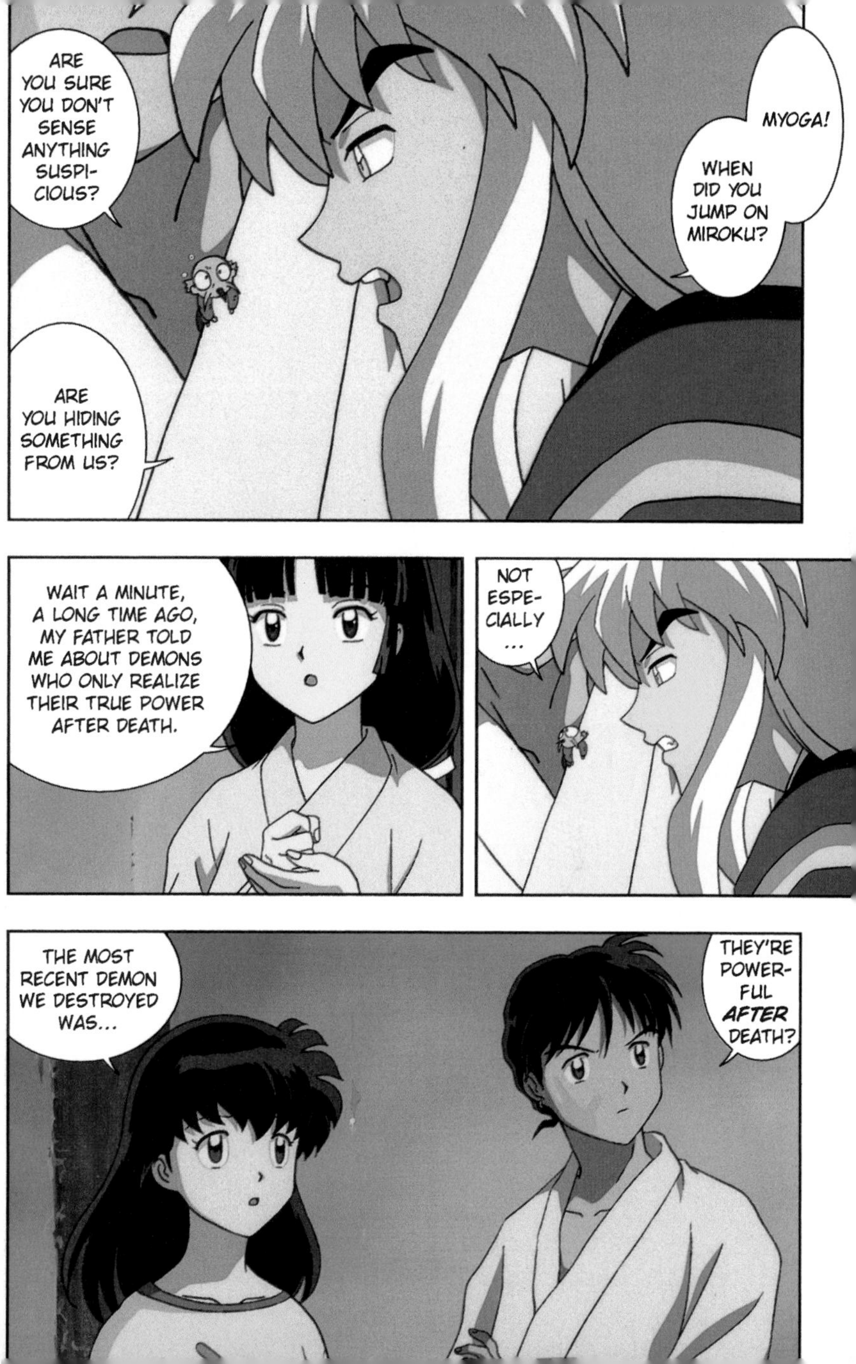
MYOGA!
WHEN DID YOU JUMP ON MIROKU?
ARE YOU SURE YOU DON'T SENSE ANYTHING SUSPICIOUS?
ARE YOU HIDING SOMETHING FROM US?
NOT ESPECIALLY...
WAIT A MINUTE, A LONG TIME AGO, MY FATHER TOLD ME ABOUT DEMONS WHO ONLY REALIZE THEIR TRUE POWER AFTER DEATH.
THEY'RE POWERFUL *AFTER* DEATH?
THE MOST RECENT DEMON WE DESTROYED WAS...

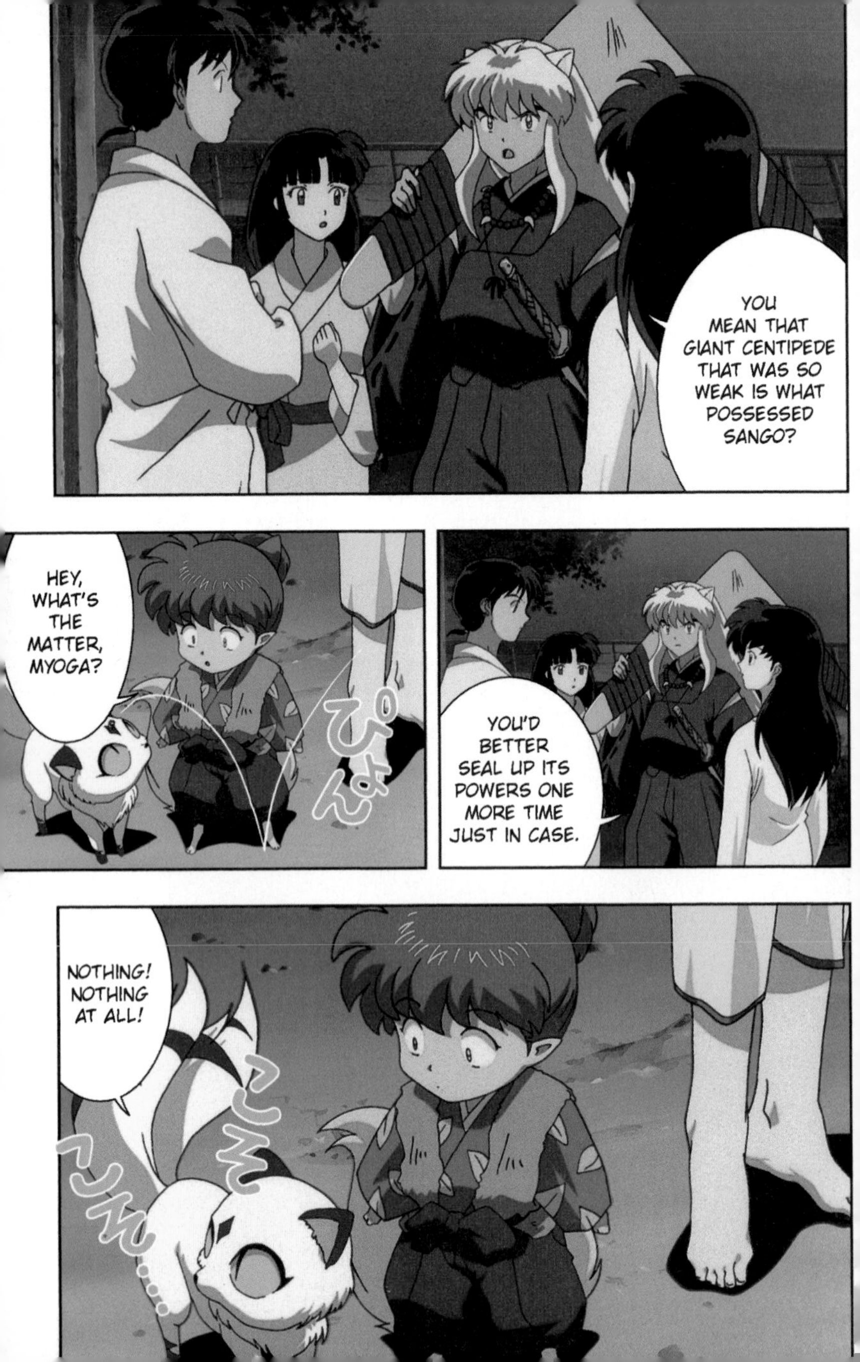
YOU MEAN THAT GIANT CENTIPEDE THAT WAS SO WEAK IS WHAT POSSESSED SANGO?
YOU'D BETTER SEAL UP ITS POWERS ONE MORE TIME JUST IN CASE.
HEY, WHAT'S THE MATTER, MYOGA?
ぴょん
NOTHING! NOTHING AT ALL!

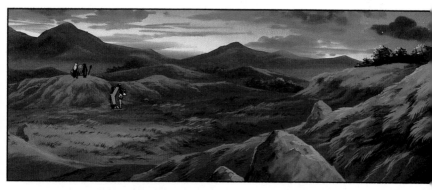

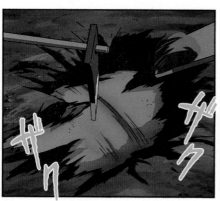

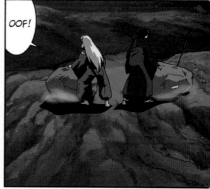

OOF!

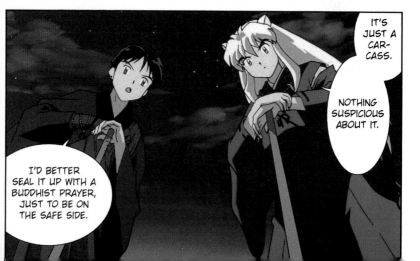

IT'S JUST A CAR- CASS.

NOTHING SUSPICIOUS ABOUT IT.

I'D BETTER SEAL IT UP WITH A BUDDHIST PRAYER, JUST TO BE ON THE SAFE SIDE.

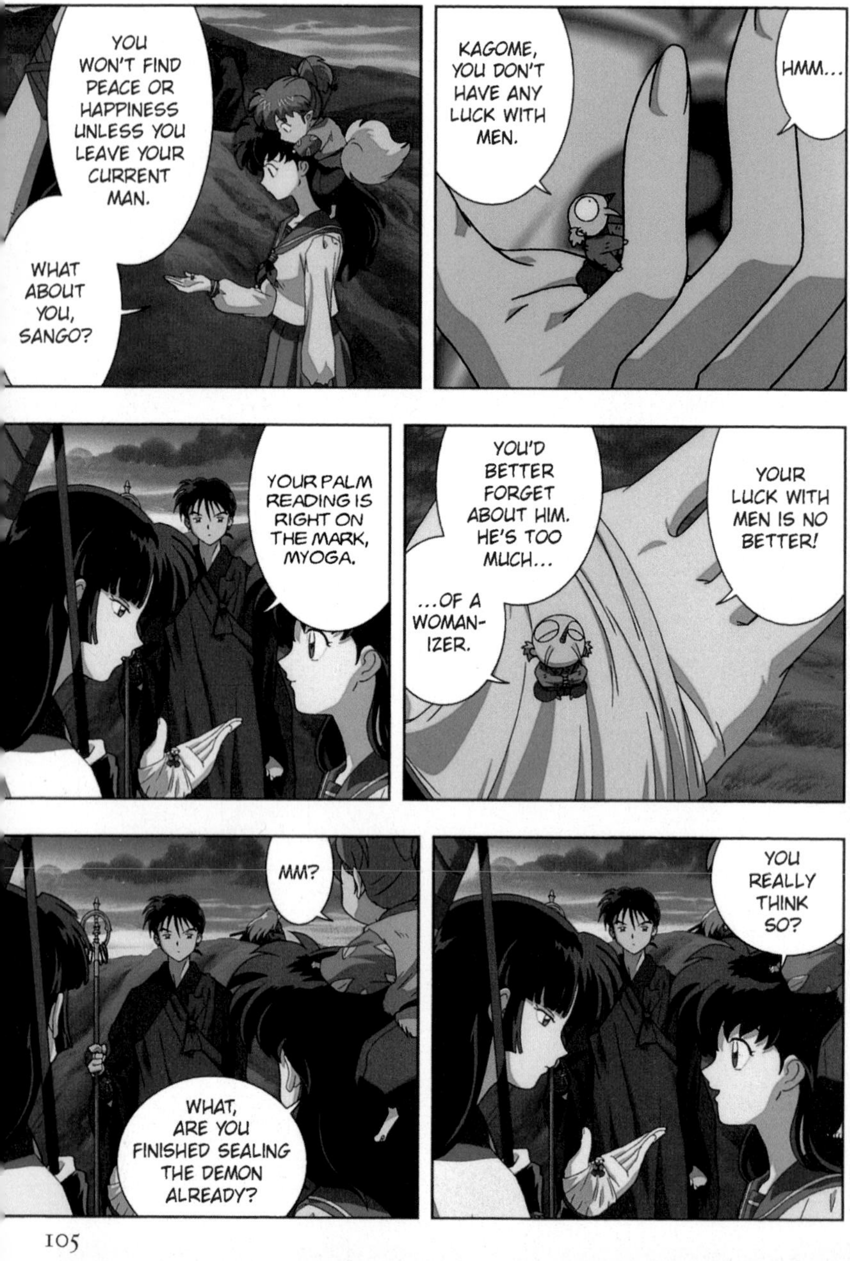
HMM...
KAGOME, YOU DON'T HAVE ANY LUCK WITH MEN.
YOU WON'T FIND PEACE OR HAPPINESS UNLESS YOU LEAVE YOUR CURRENT MAN.
WHAT ABOUT YOU, SANGO?
YOUR LUCK WITH MEN IS NO BETTER!
YOU'D BETTER FORGET ABOUT HIM. HE'S TOO MUCH...
...OF A WOMAN-IZER.
YOUR PALM READING IS RIGHT ON THE MARK, MYOGA.
YOU REALLY THINK SO?
MM?
WHAT, ARE YOU FINISHED SEALING THE DEMON ALREADY?

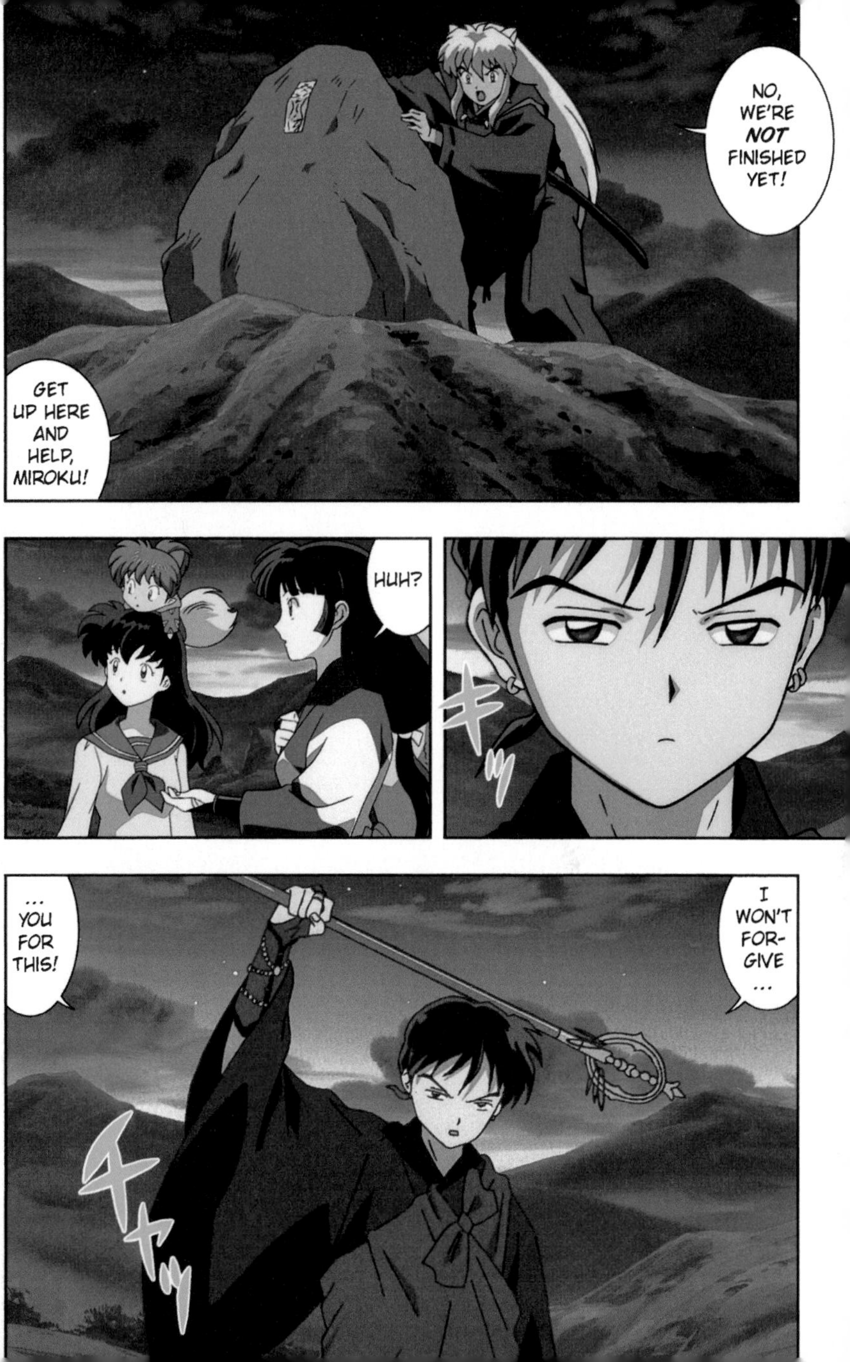
NO, WE'RE **NOT** FINISHED YET!
GET UP HERE AND HELP, MIROKU!
HUH?
I WON'T FOR-GIVE ...
... YOU FOR THIS!

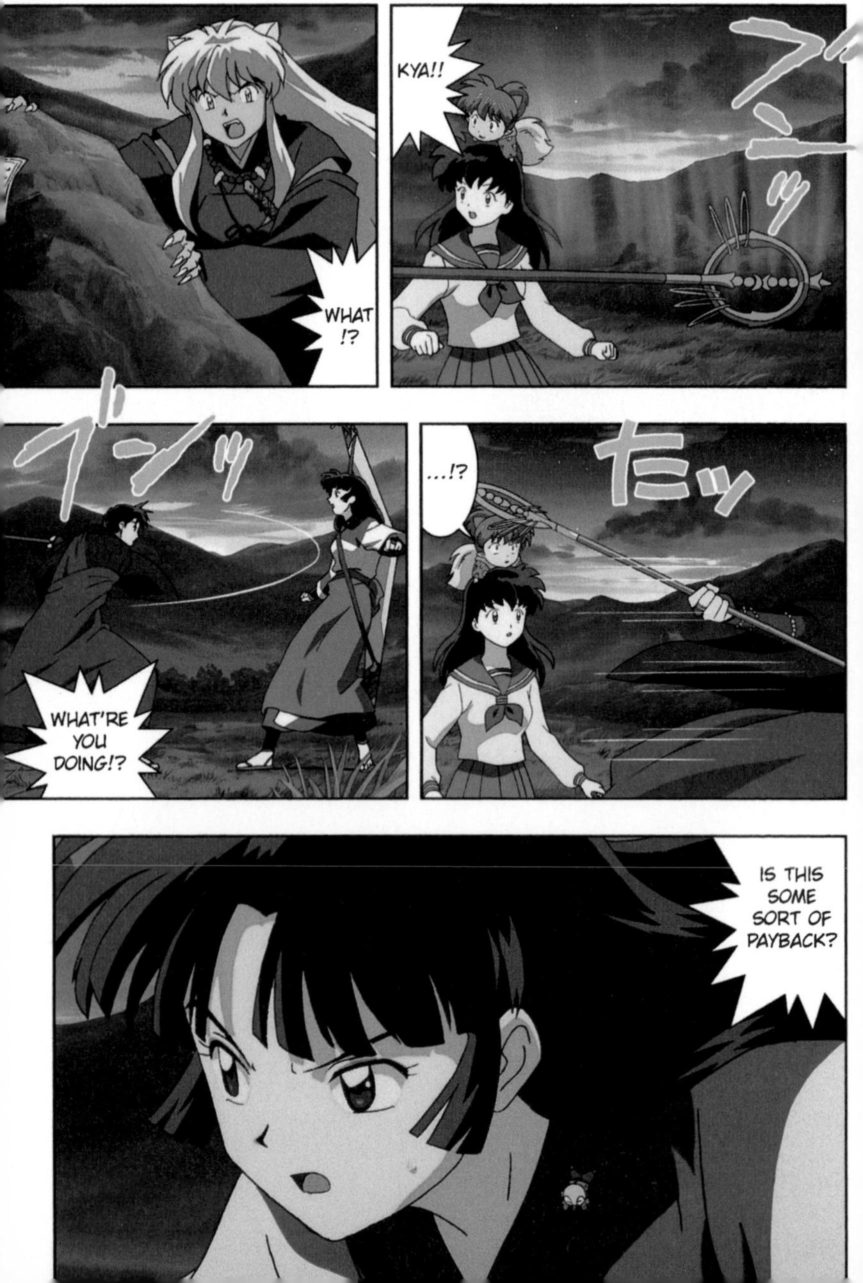
KYA!!
WHAT !?
...!?
WHAT'RE YOU DOING!?
IS THIS SOME SORT OF PAYBACK?

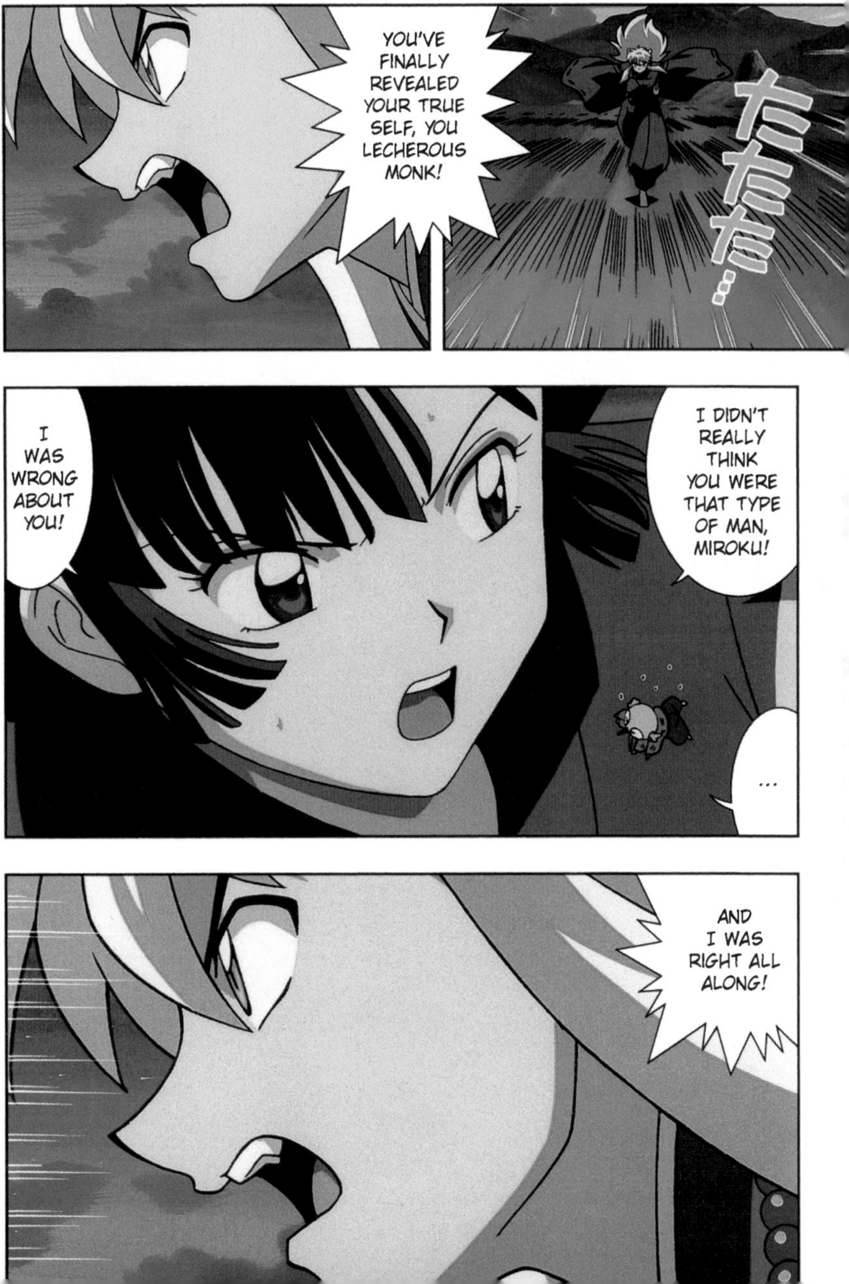
たたた…
YOU'VE FINALLY REVEALED YOUR TRUE SELF, YOU LECHEROUS MONK!
I DIDN'T REALLY THINK YOU WERE THAT TYPE OF MAN, MIROKU!
I WAS WRONG ABOUT YOU!
...
AND I WAS RIGHT ALL ALONG!

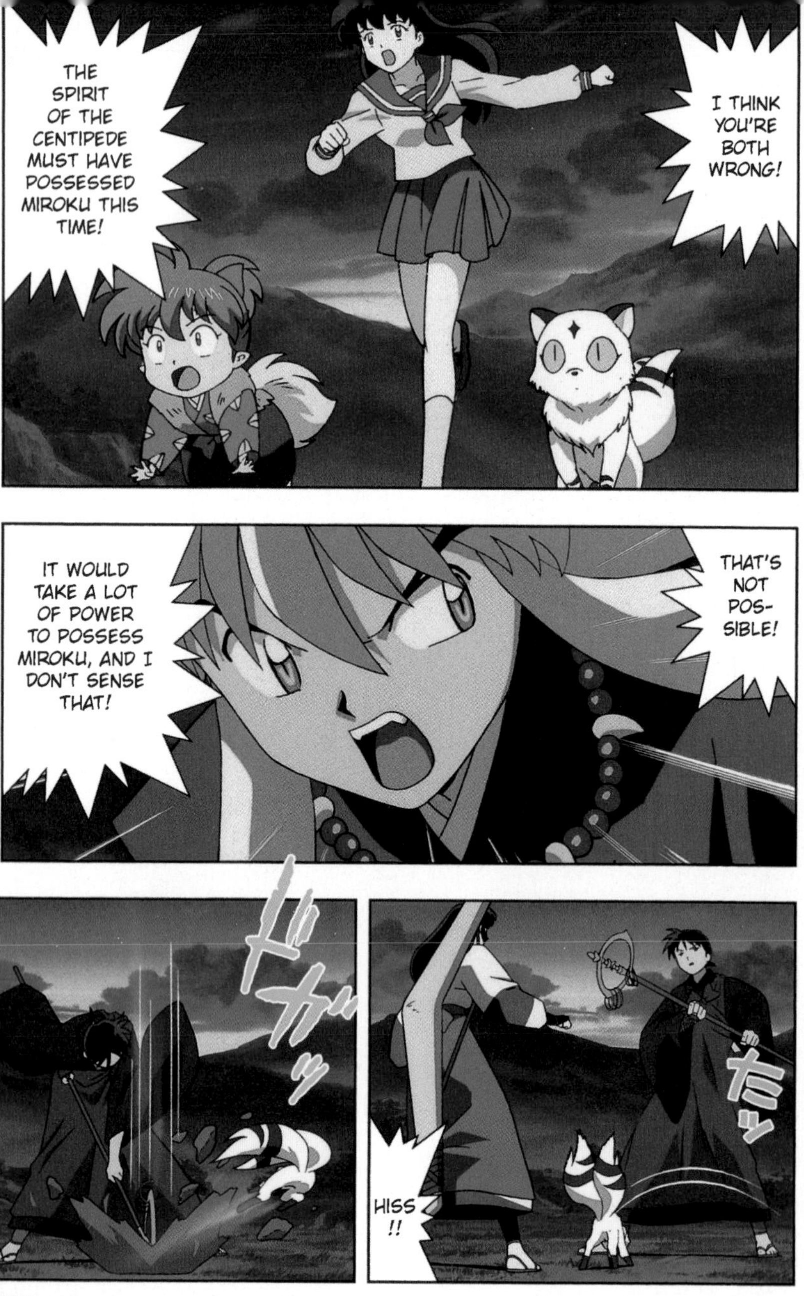
I THINK YOU'RE BOTH WRONG!
THE SPIRIT OF THE CENTIPEDE MUST HAVE POSSESSED MIROKU THIS TIME!
THAT'S NOT POS-SIBLE!
IT WOULD TAKE A LOT OF POWER TO POSSESS MIROKU, AND I DON'T SENSE THAT!
たッ
HISS !!
ドガッ

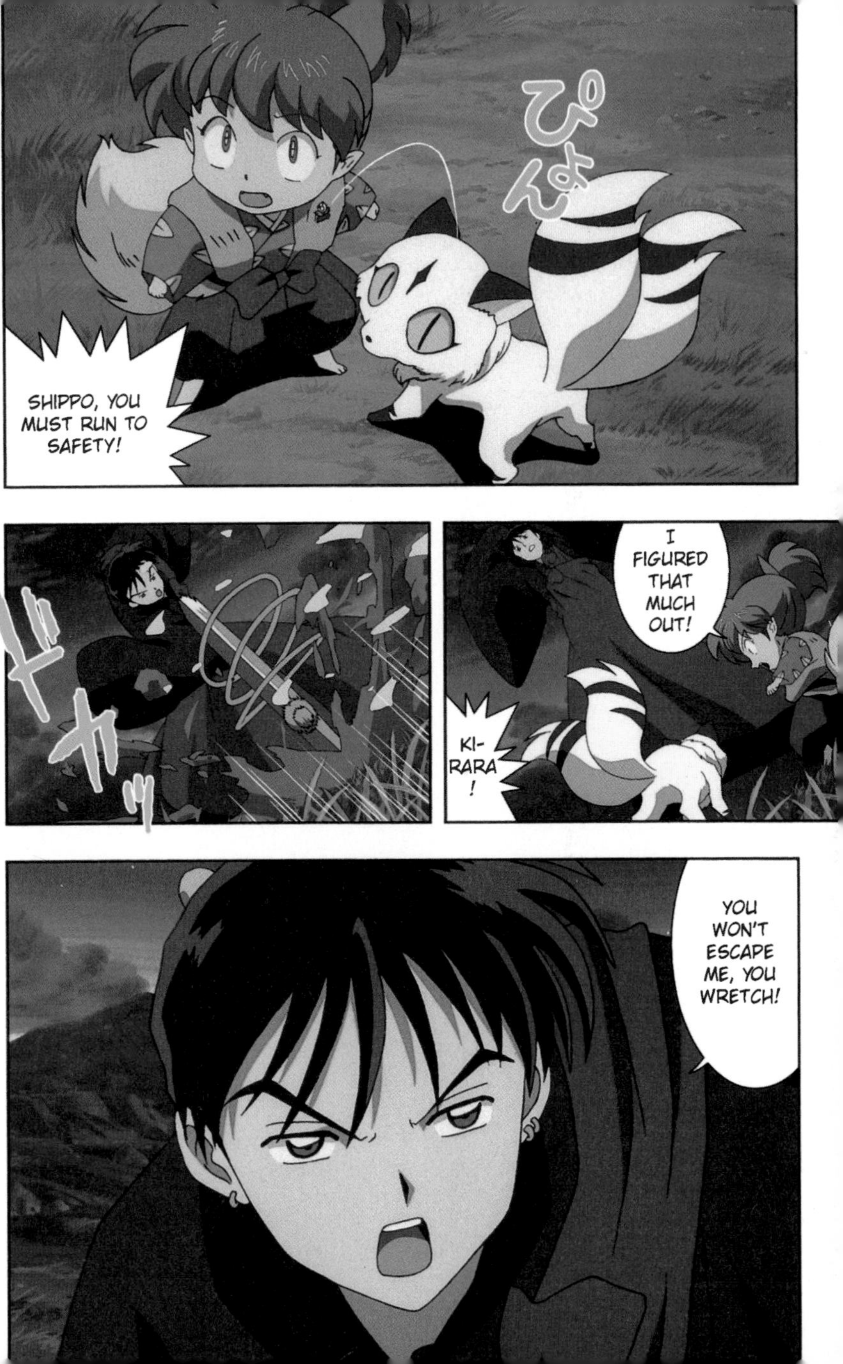
ぴょん
SHIPPO, YOU MUST RUN TO SAFETY!
I FIGURED THAT MUCH OUT!
KI-RARA!
YOU WON'T ESCAPE ME, YOU WRETCH!

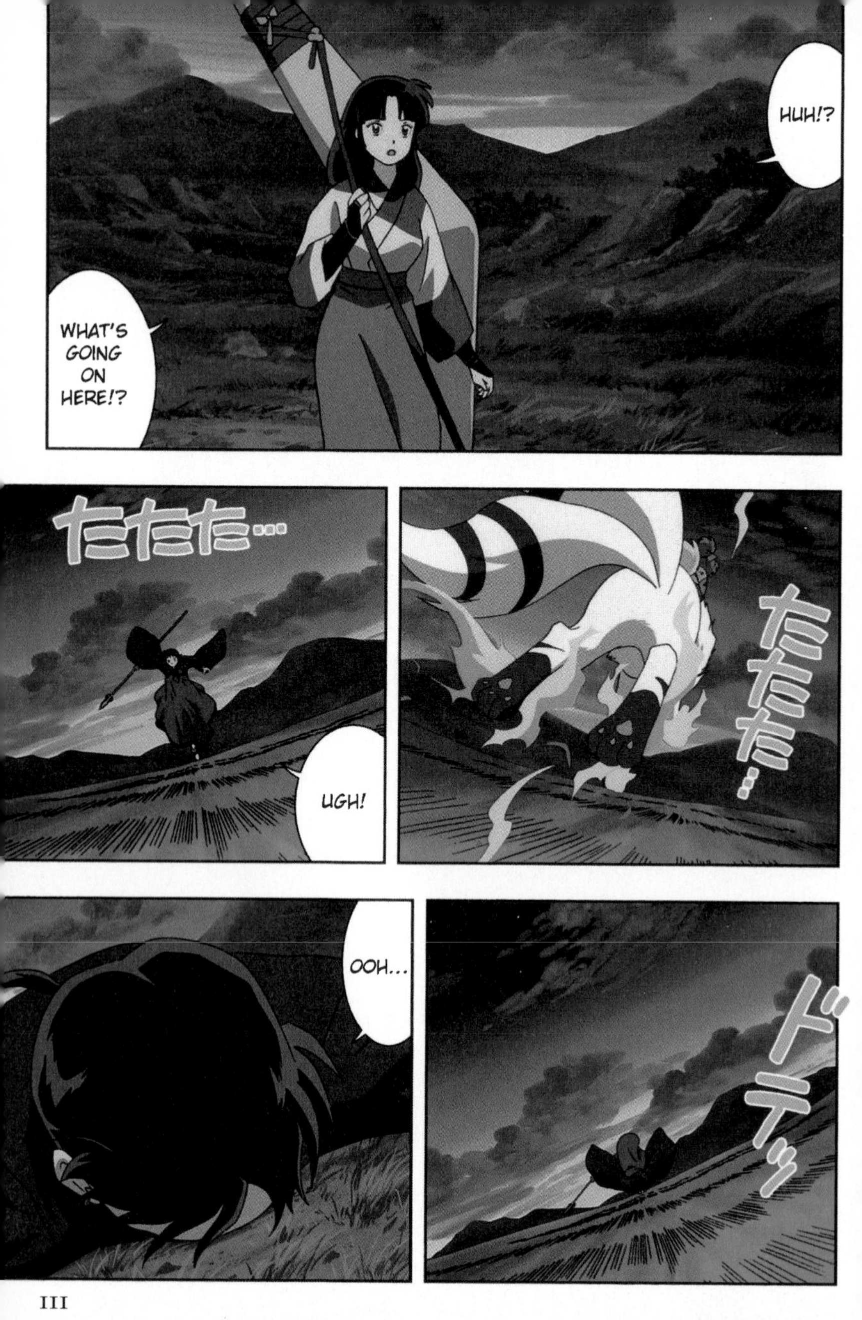
HUH!?
WHAT'S GOING ON HERE!?
たたた…
たたた…
UGH!
ドテッ
OOH...

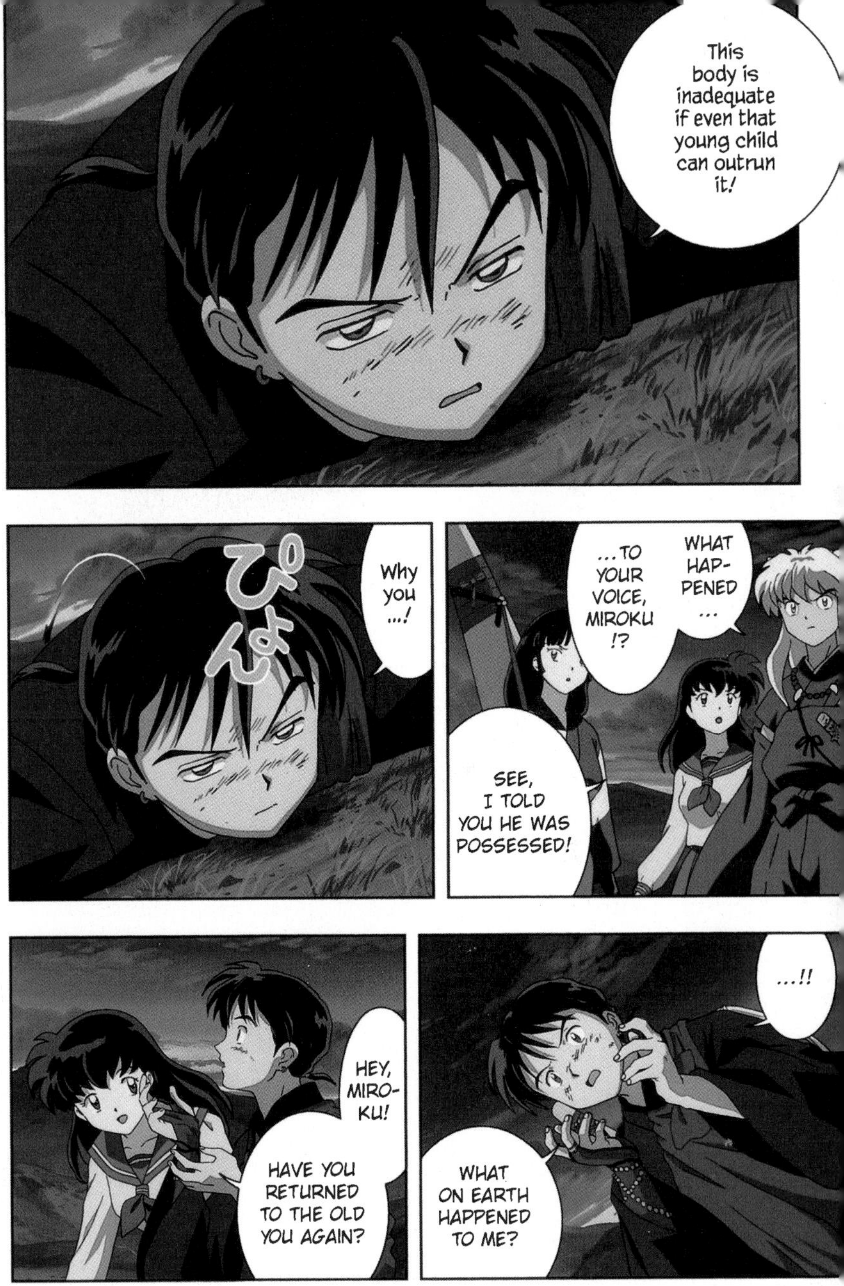
This body is inadequate if even that young child can outrun it!
WHAT HAP-PENED ...
...TO YOUR VOICE, MIROKU !?
SEE, I TOLD YOU HE WAS POSSESSED!
ぴょん
Why you ...!
...!!
WHAT ON EARTH HAPPENED TO ME?
HEY, MIRO-KU!
HAVE YOU RETURNED TO THE OLD YOU AGAIN?

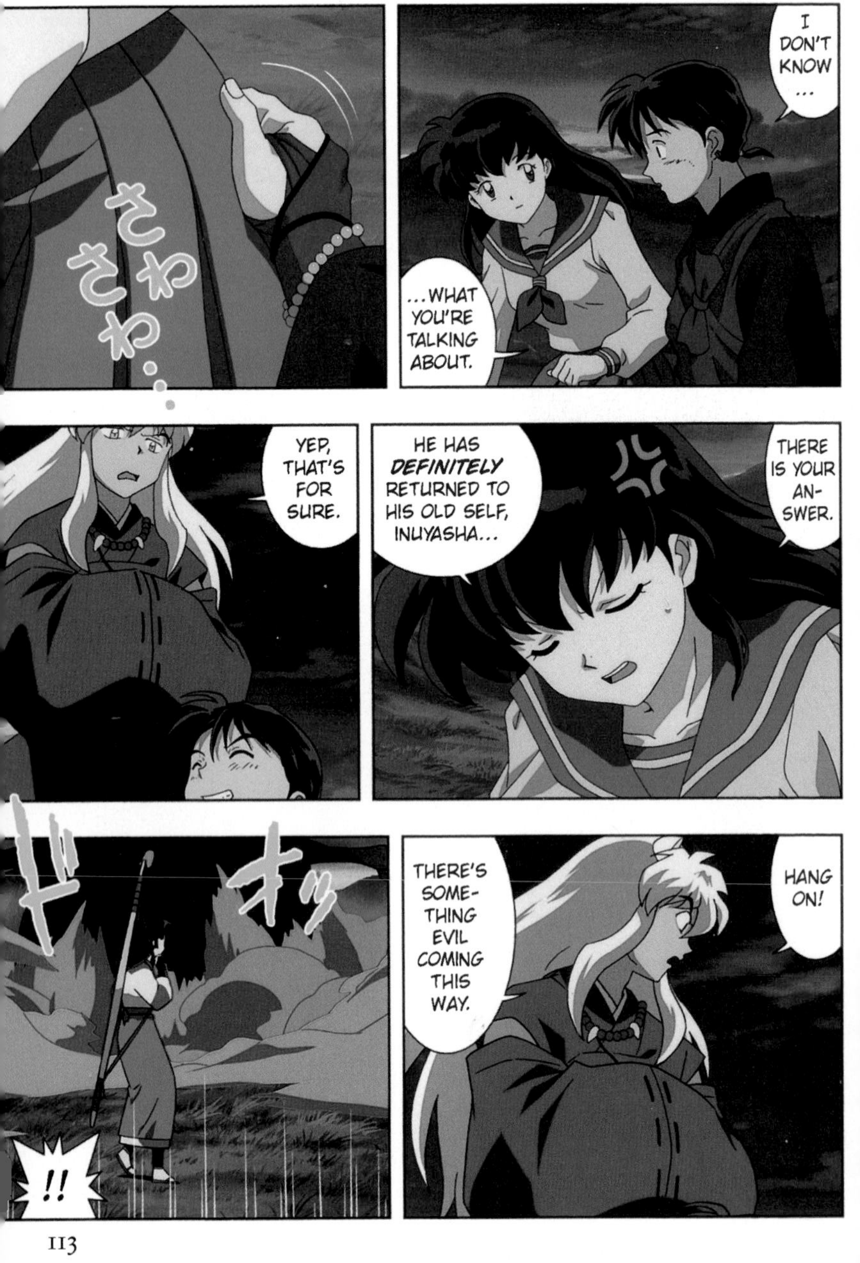
I DON'T KNOW ...
...WHAT YOU'RE TALKING ABOUT.
さわさわ...
THERE IS YOUR AN-SWER.
HE HAS *DEFINITELY* RETURNED TO HIS OLD SELF, INUYASHA...
YEP, THAT'S FOR SURE.
HANG ON!
THERE'S SOME-THING EVIL COMING THIS WAY.
ドオッ
!!

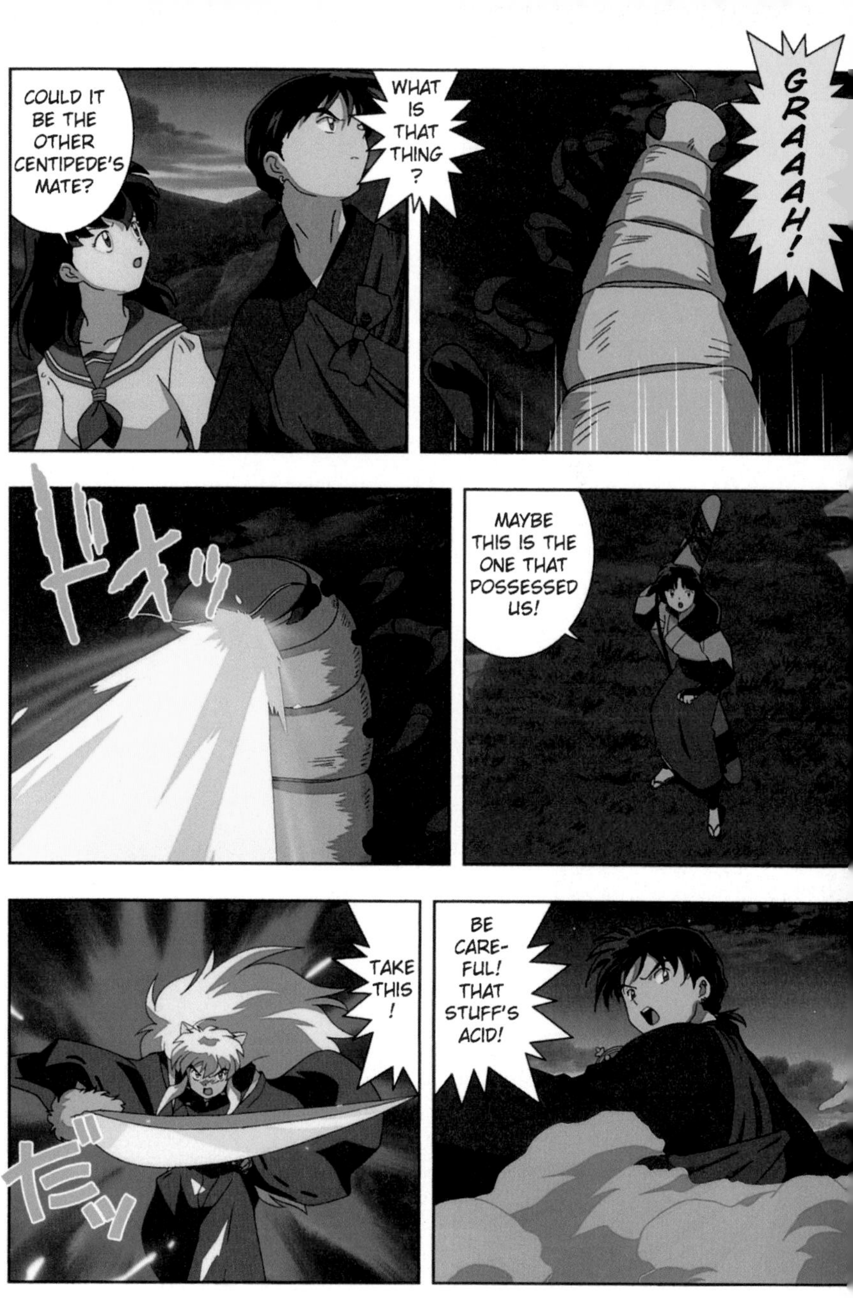
GRAAAAH!
WHAT IS THAT THING?
COULD IT BE THE OTHER CENTIPEDE'S MATE?
MAYBE THIS IS THE ONE THAT POSSESSED US!
ドォッ
BE CAREFUL! THAT STUFF'S ACID!
TAKE THIS!
ガッ

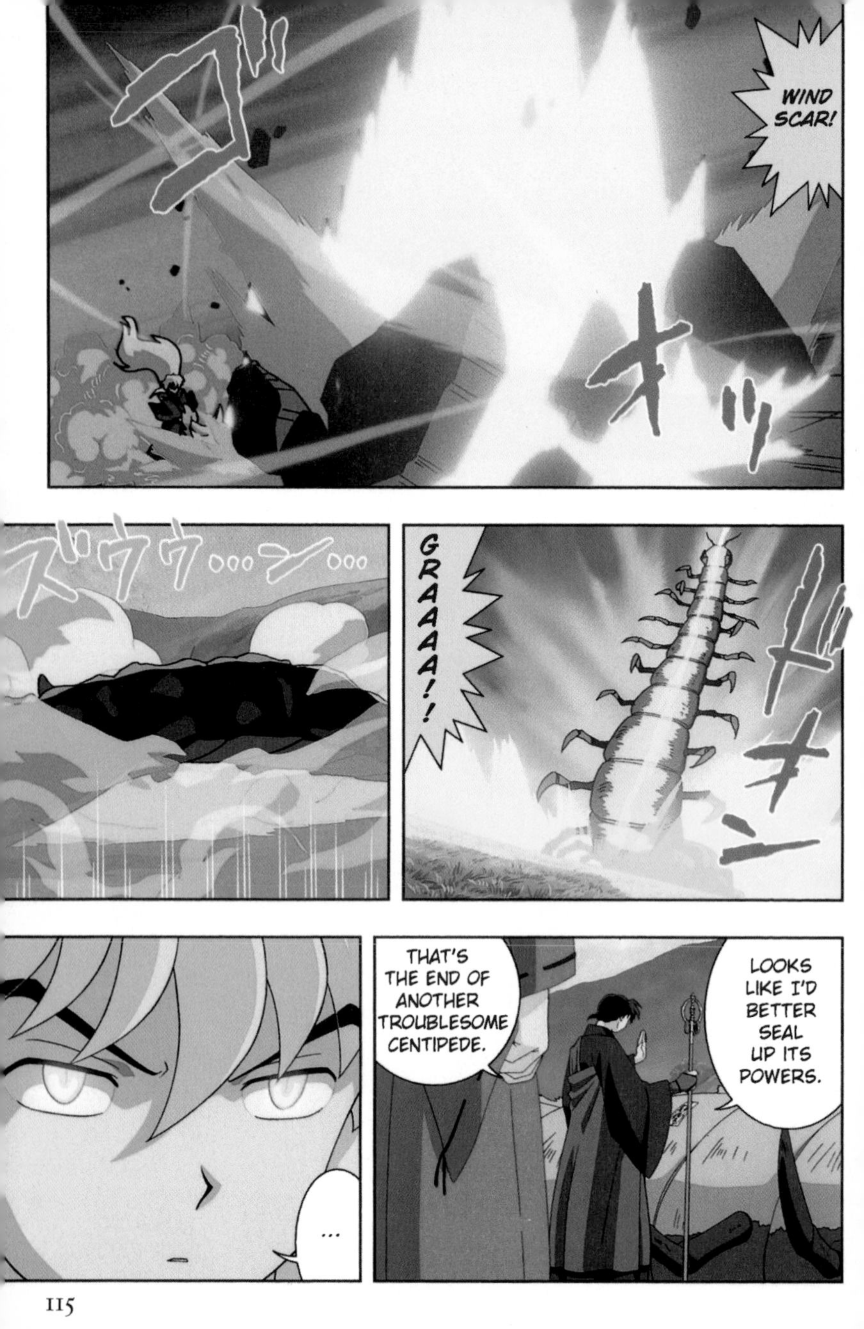
WIND SCAR!
GRAAAAA!!
LOOKS LIKE I'D BETTER SEAL UP ITS POWERS.
THAT'S THE END OF ANOTHER TROUBLESOME CENTIPEDE.
...

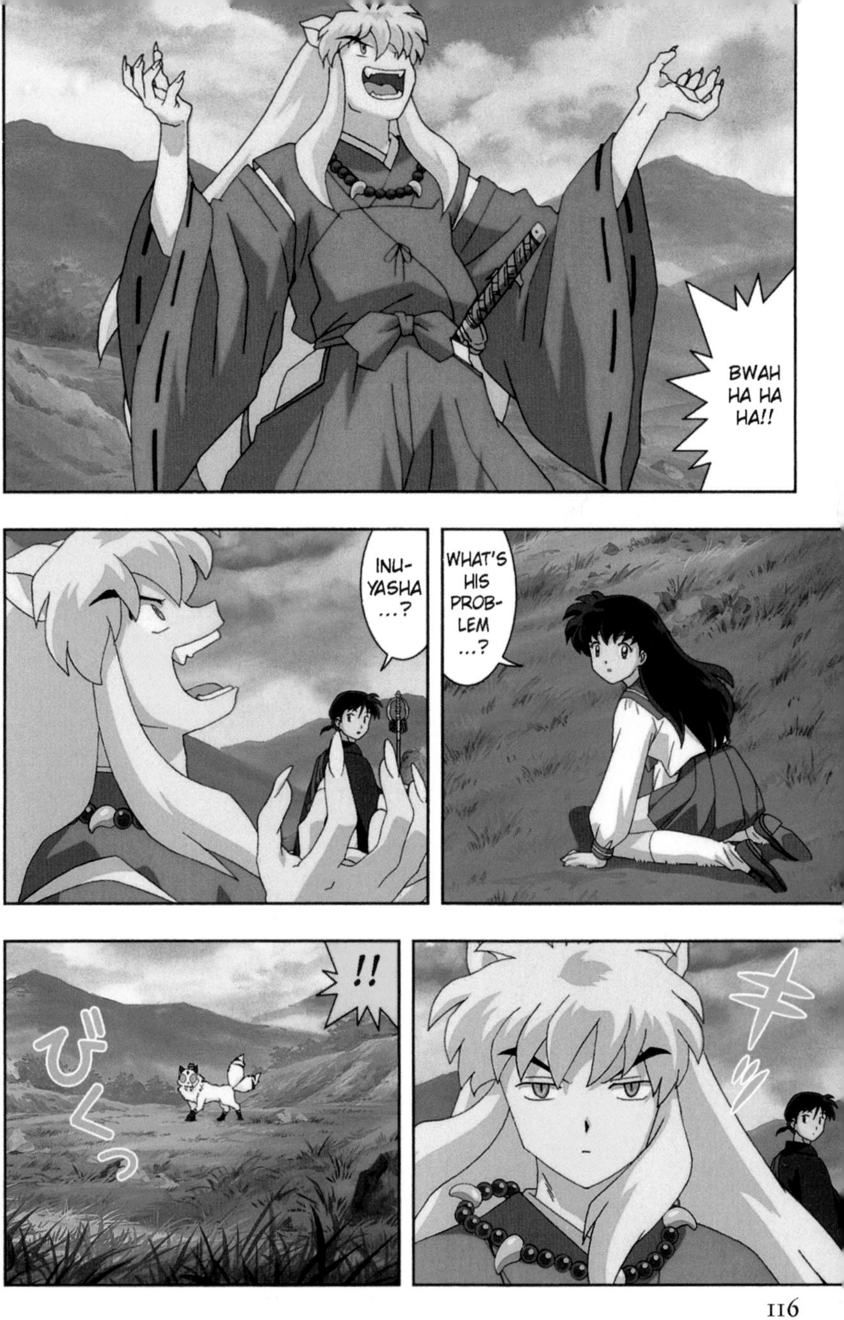
BWAH HA HA HA!!
WHAT'S HIS PROB-LEM ...?
INU-YASHA ...?
キッ
!!
びくっ

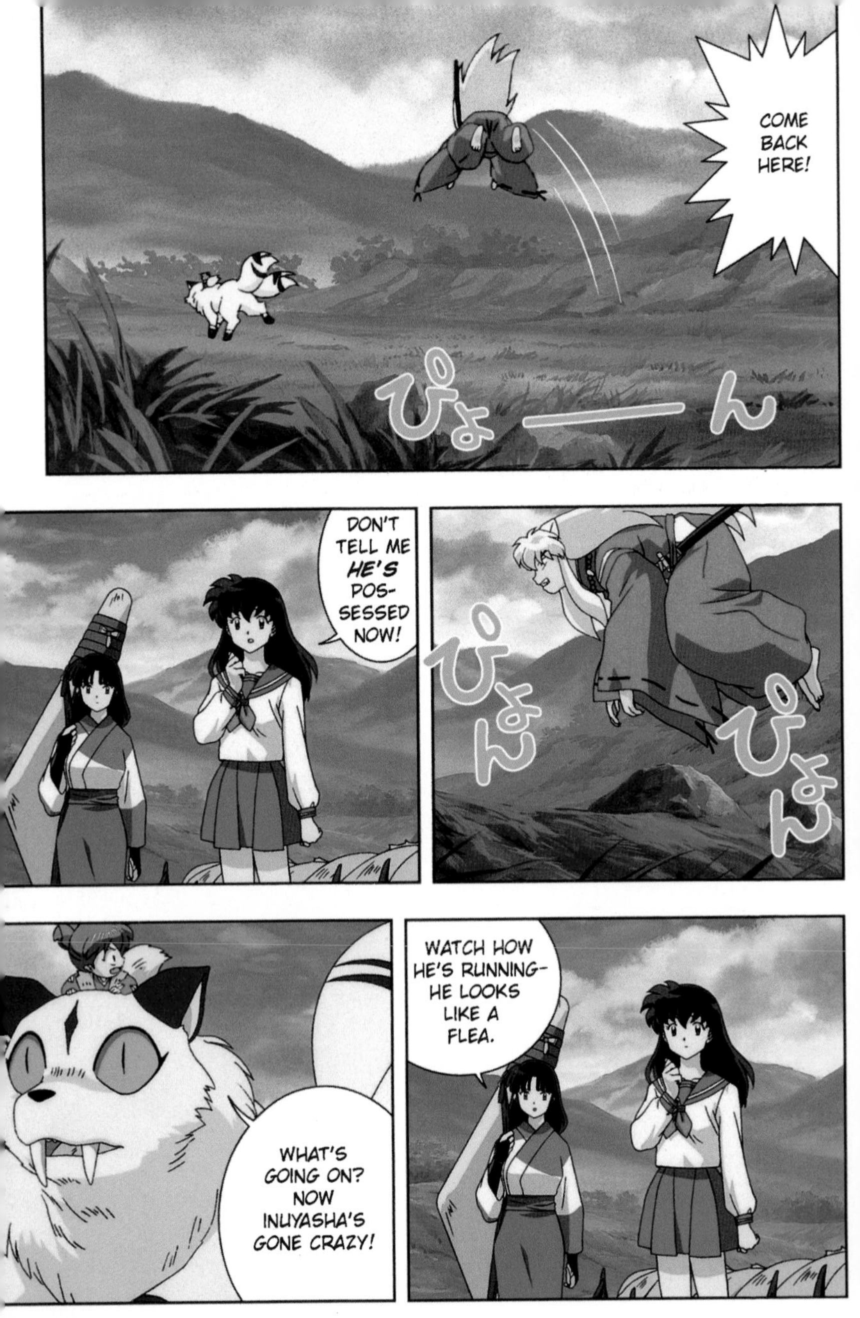
COME BACK HERE!
ぴょ——ん
ぴょん
ぴょん
DON'T TELL ME ***HE'S*** POS-SESSED NOW!
WATCH HOW HE'S RUNNING-HE LOOKS LIKE A FLEA.
WHAT'S GOING ON? NOW INUYASHA'S GONE CRAZY!

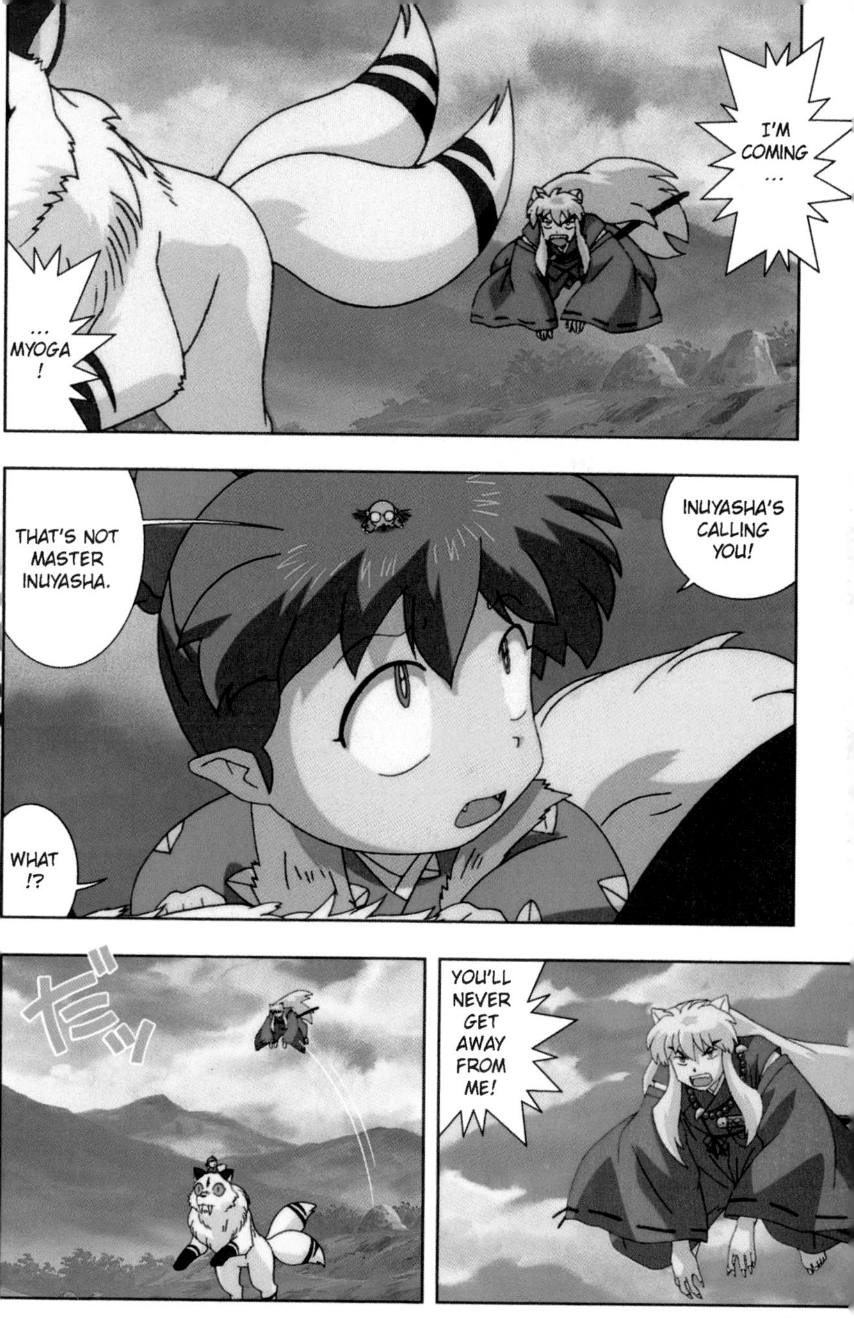
I'M COMING ...
... MYOGA !
INUYASHA'S CALLING YOU!
THAT'S NOT MASTER INUYASHA.
WHAT !?
YOU'LL NEVER GET AWAY FROM ME!
ダッ

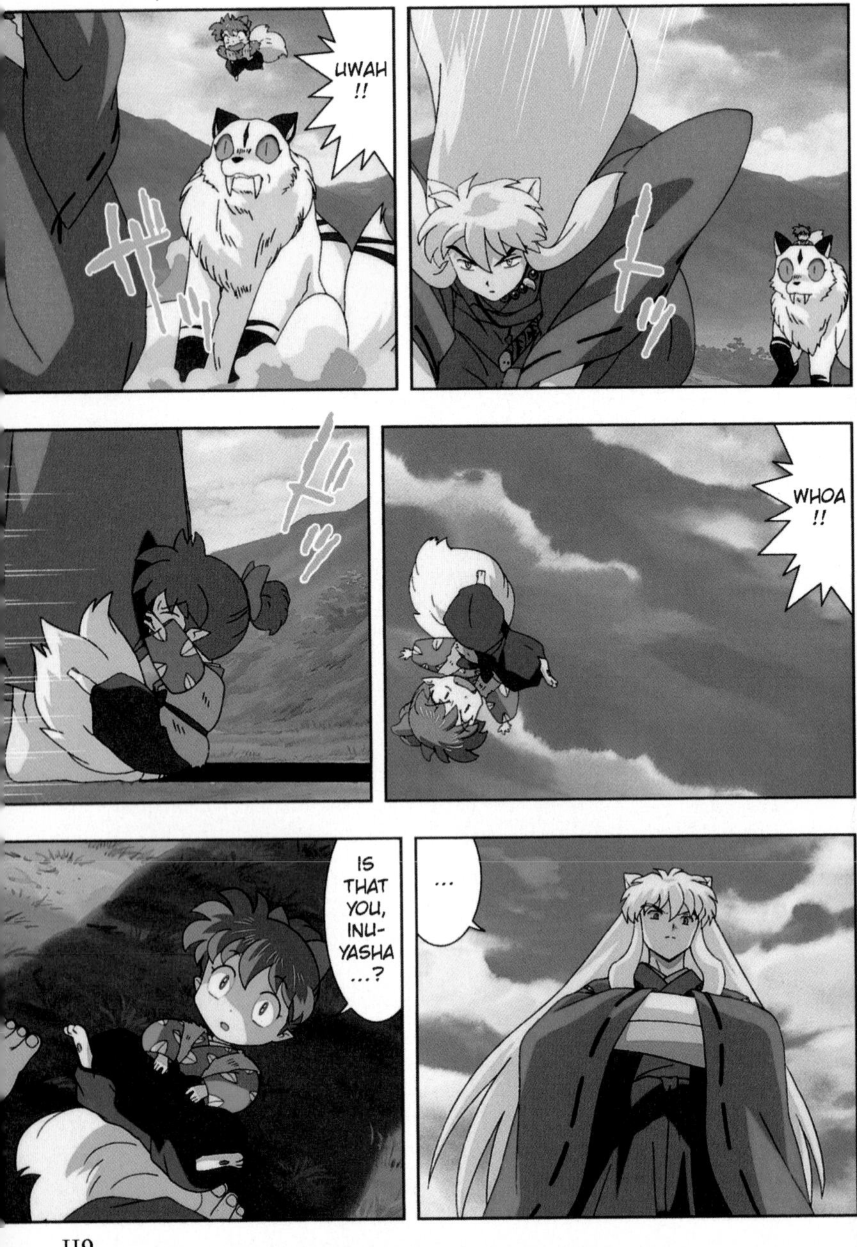
UWAH !!
WHOA !!
...
IS THAT YOU, INU-YASHA ...?

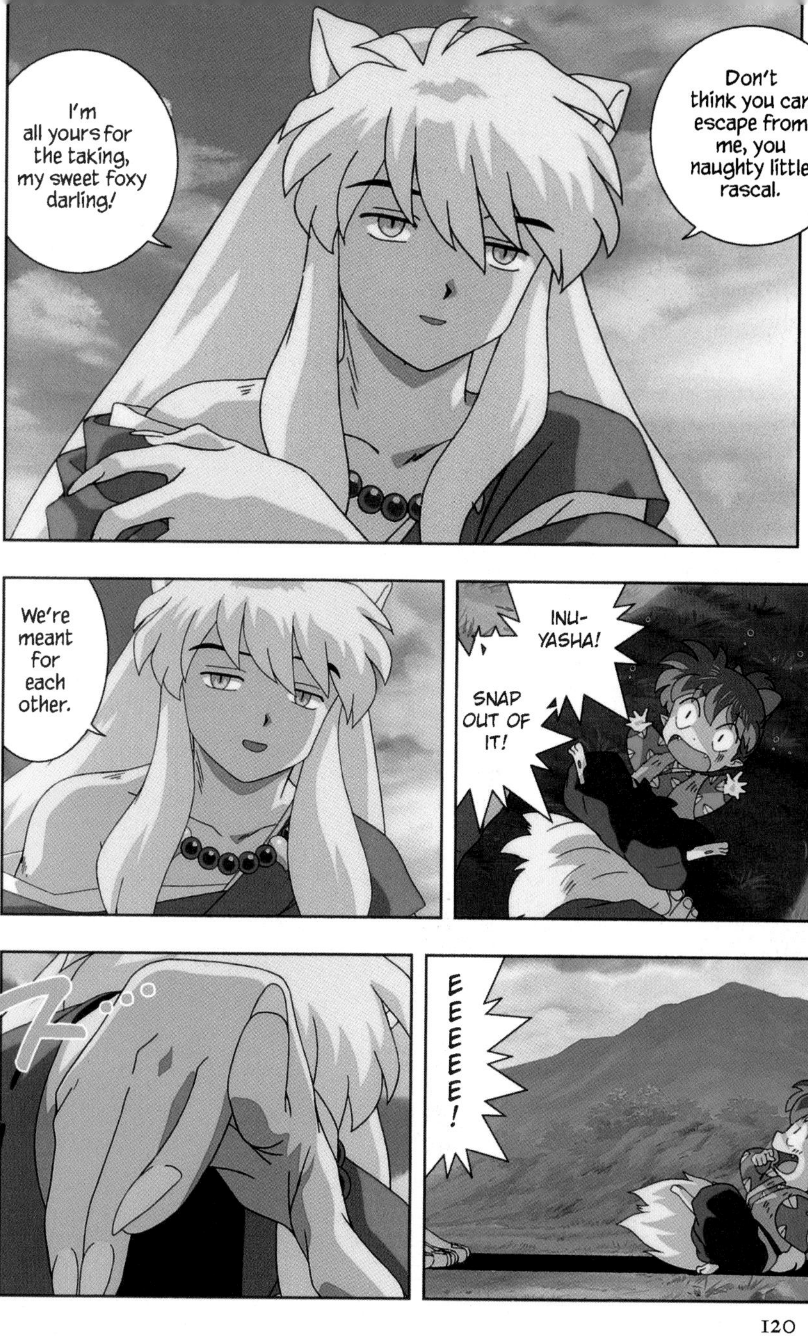
Don't think you can escape from me, you naughty little rascal.
I'm all yours for the taking, my sweet foxy darling!
INU-YASHA!
SNAP OUT OF IT!
We're meant for each other.
EEEEEE!

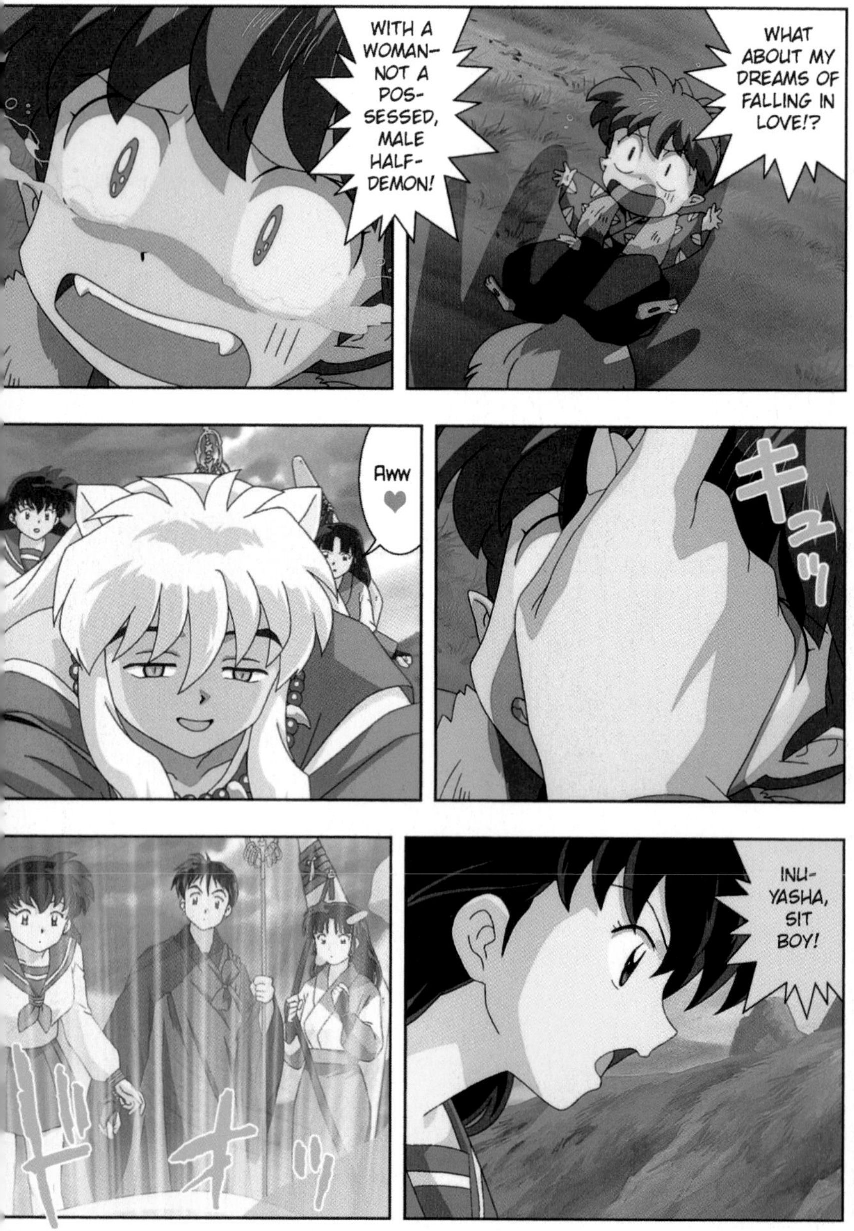
WHAT ABOUT MY DREAMS OF FALLING IN LOVE!?
WITH A WOMAN-NOT A POS-SESSED, MALE HALF-DEMON!
キュッ
Aww ♥
INU-YASHA, SIT BOY!
ドオッ

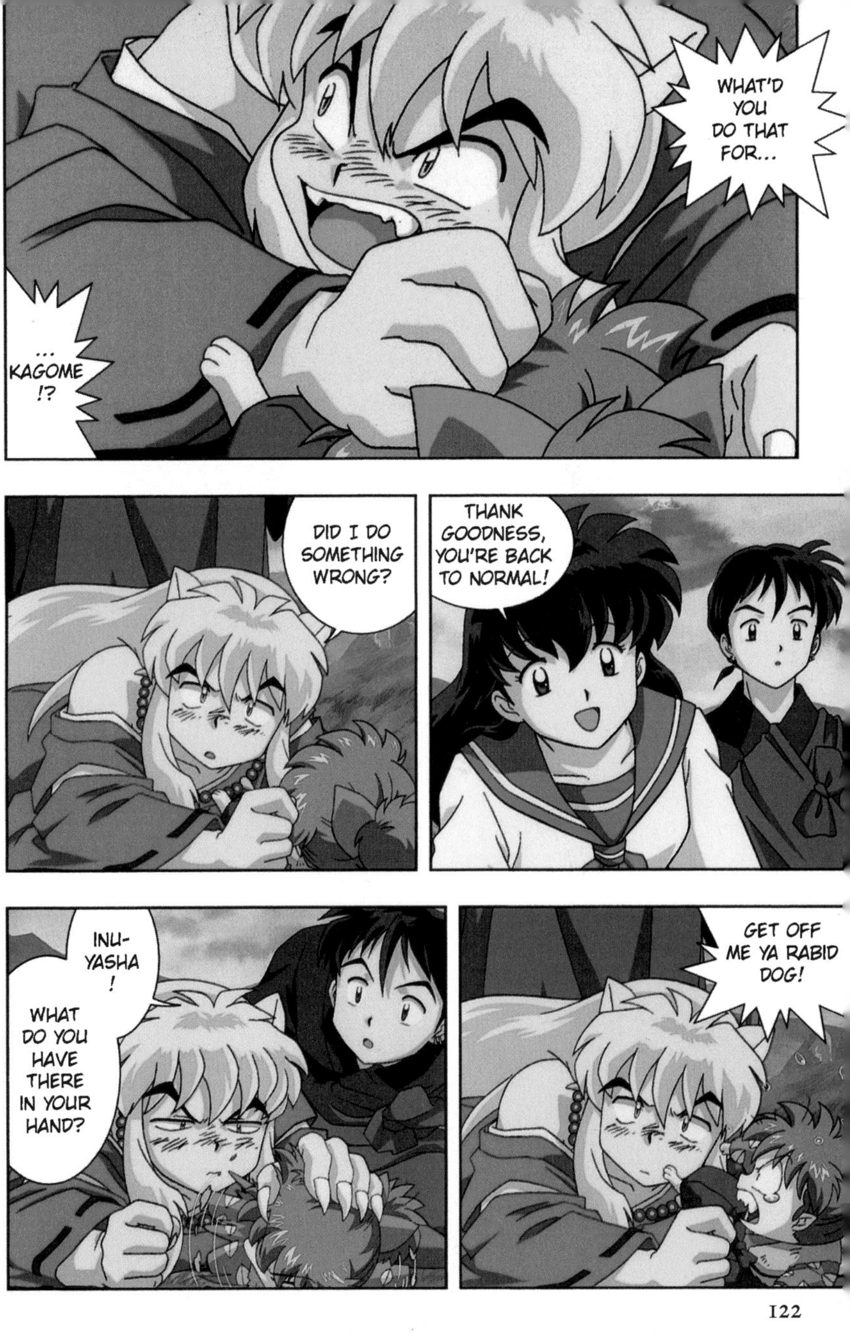
WHAT'D YOU DO THAT FOR...
...KAGOME!?
THANK GOODNESS, YOU'RE BACK TO NORMAL!
DID I DO SOMETHING WRONG?
GET OFF ME YA RABID DOG!
INU-YASHA!
WHAT DO YOU HAVE THERE IN YOUR HAND?

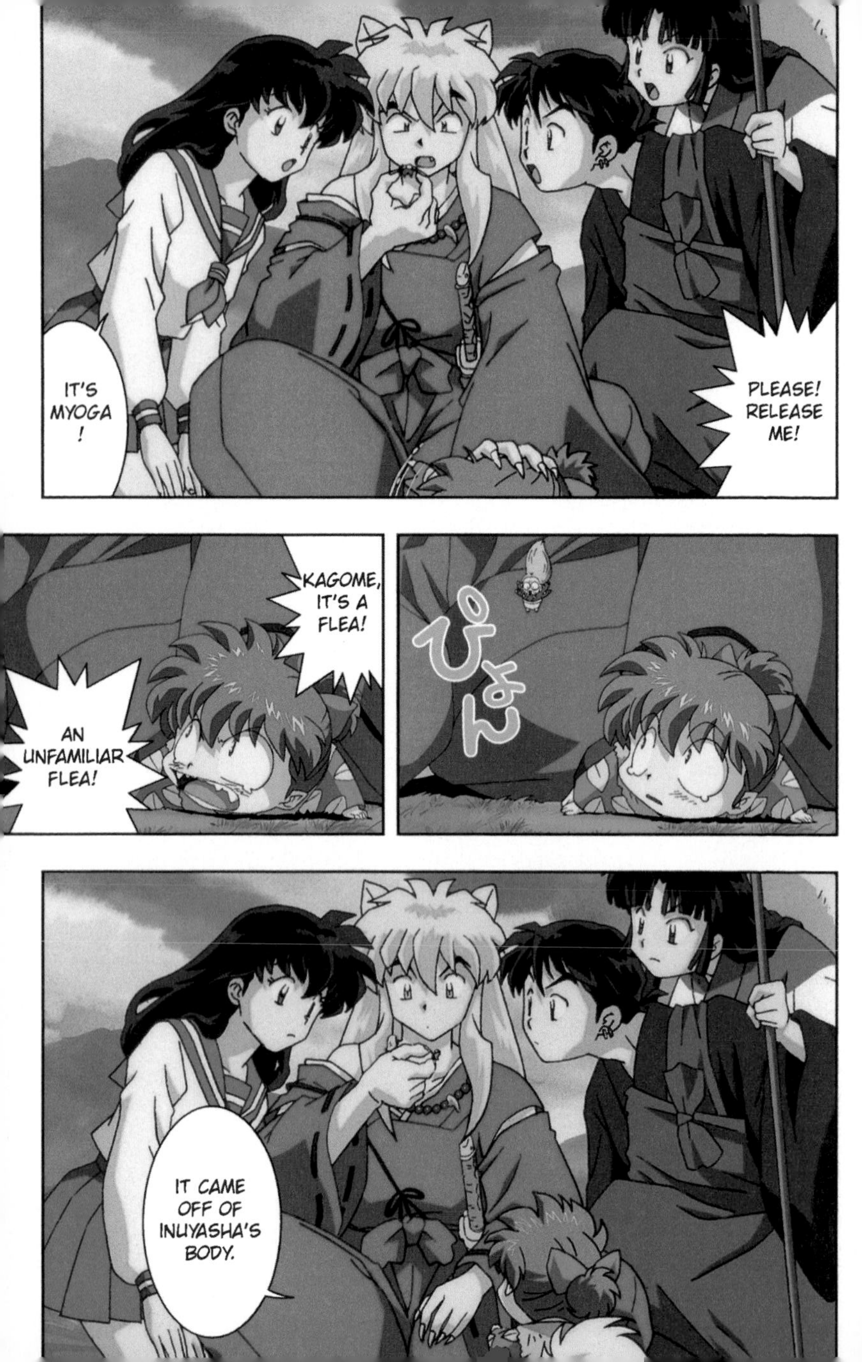
PLEASE! RELEASE ME!
IT'S MYOGA!
ぴょん
KAGOME, IT'S A FLEA!
AN UNFAMILIAR FLEA!
IT CAME OFF OF INUYASHA'S BODY.

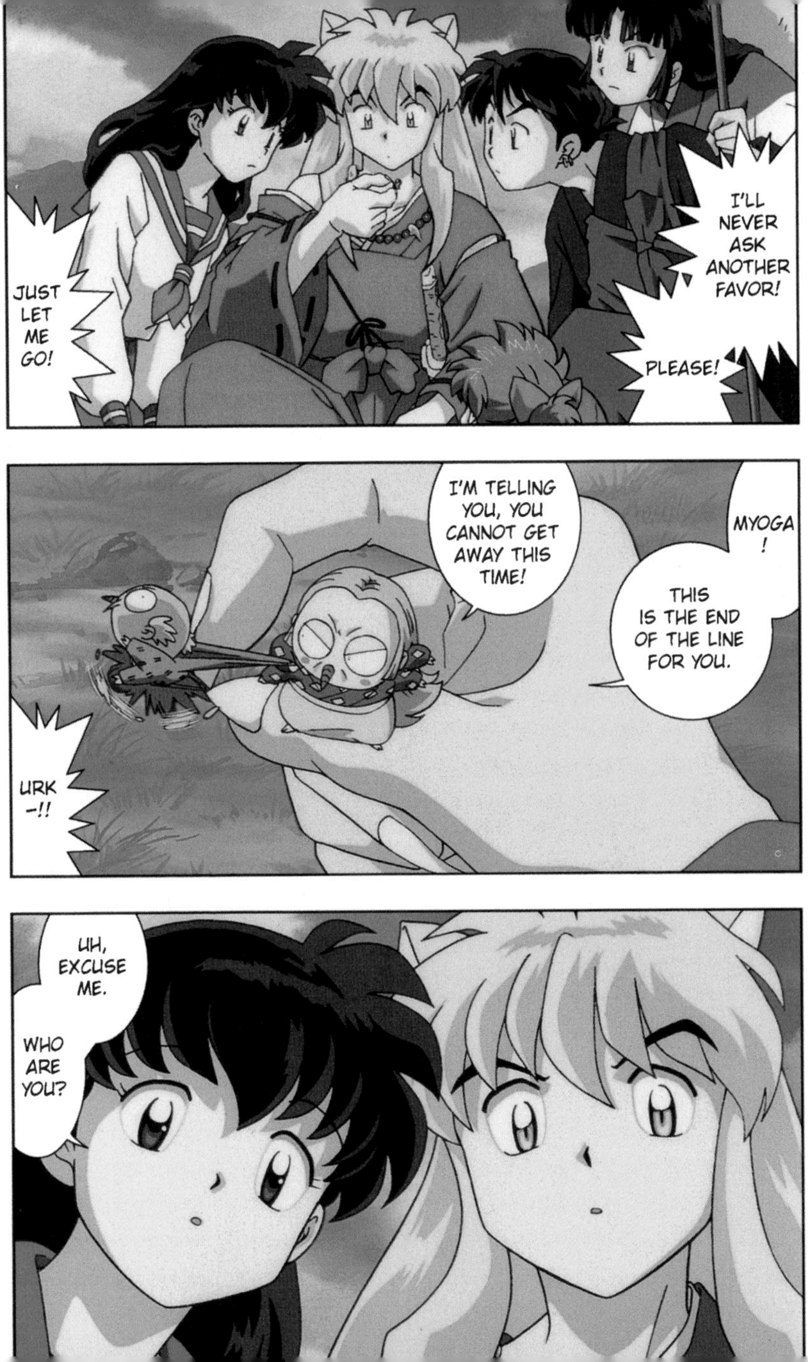
I'LL NEVER ASK ANOTHER FAVOR!
PLEASE!
JUST LET ME GO!
MYOGA!
THIS IS THE END OF THE LINE FOR YOU.
I'M TELLING YOU, YOU CANNOT GET AWAY THIS TIME!
URK—!!
UH, EXCUSE ME.
WHO ARE YOU?

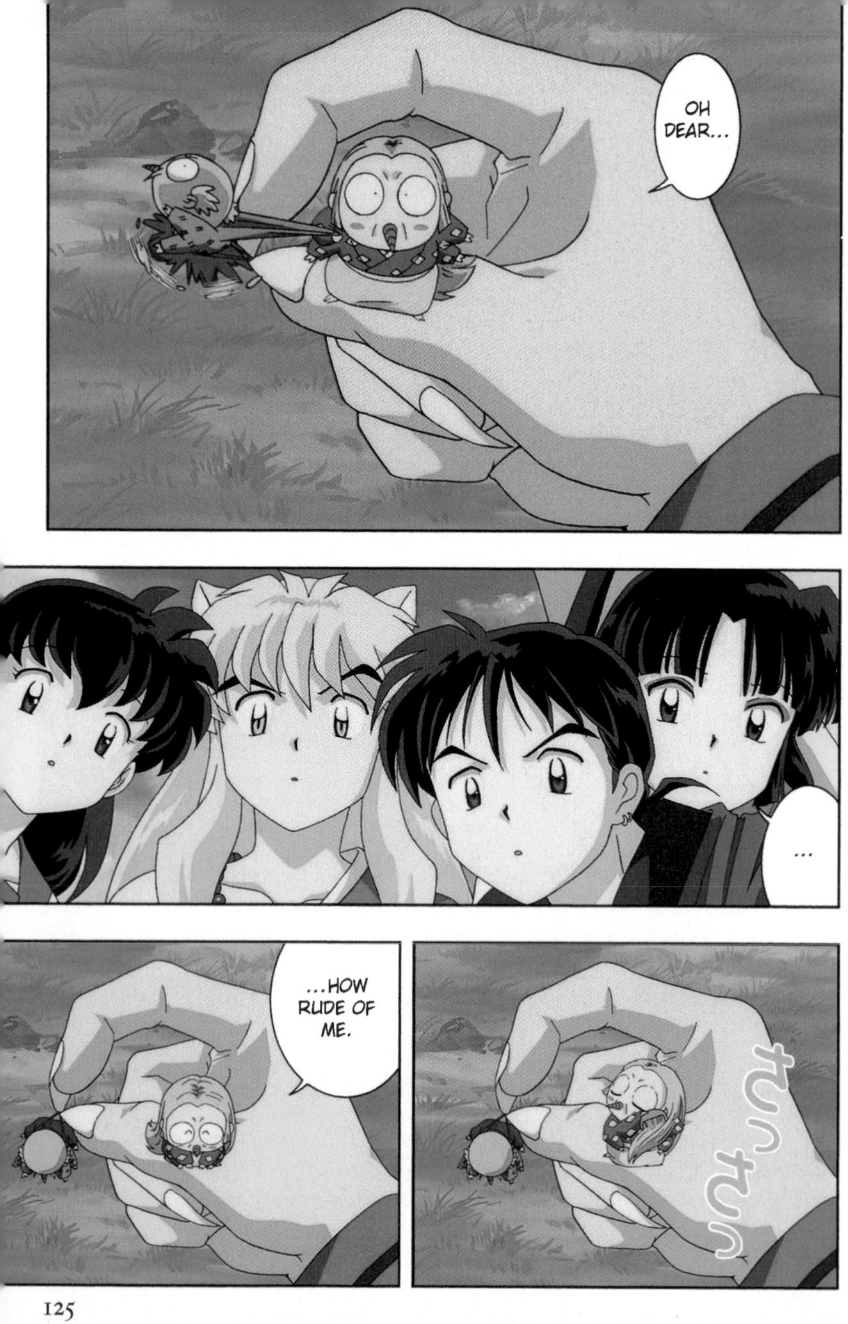
OH DEAR...
...
さっさっ
...HOW RUDE OF ME.

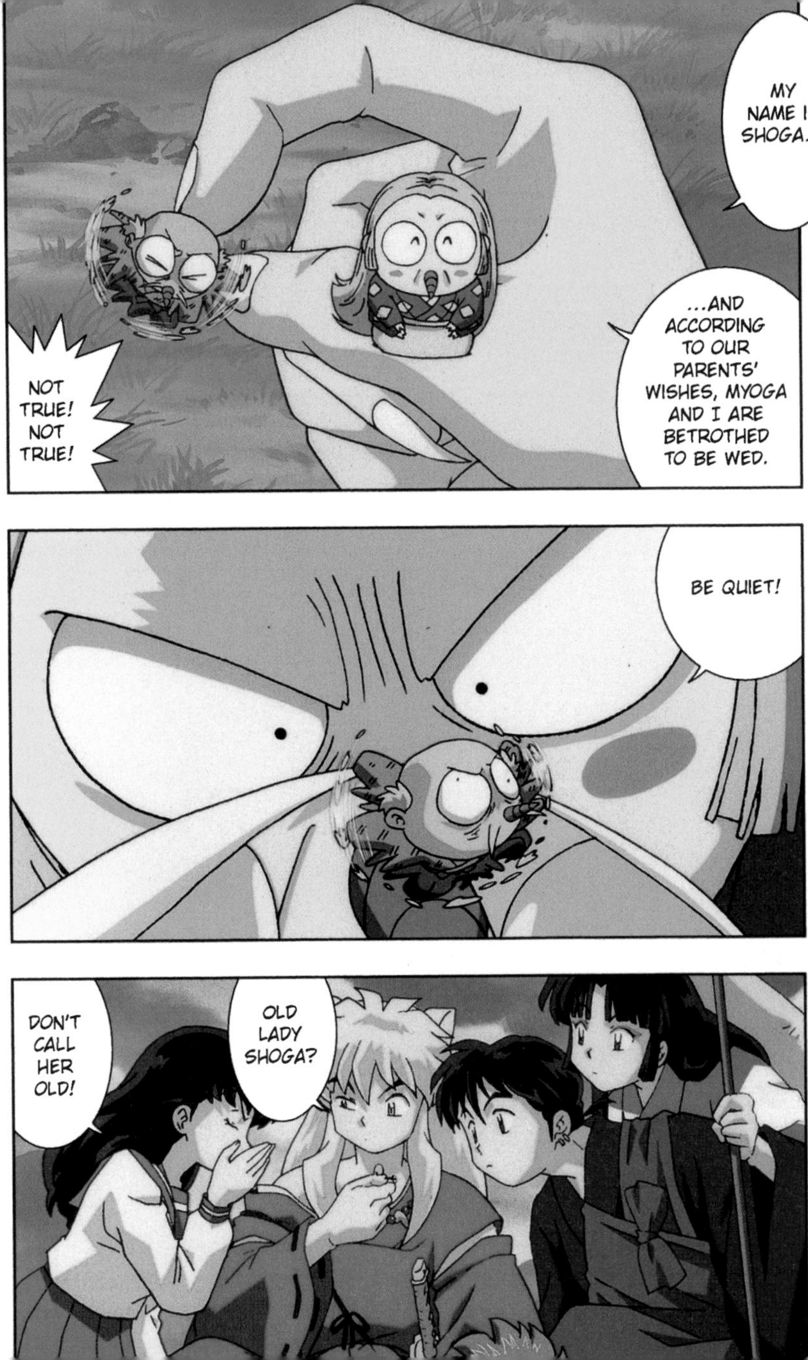
MY NAME IS SHOGA...
...AND ACCORDING TO OUR PARENTS' WISHES, MYOGA AND I ARE BETROTHED TO BE WED.
NOT TRUE! NOT TRUE!
BE QUIET!
OLD LADY SHOGA?
DON'T CALL HER OLD!

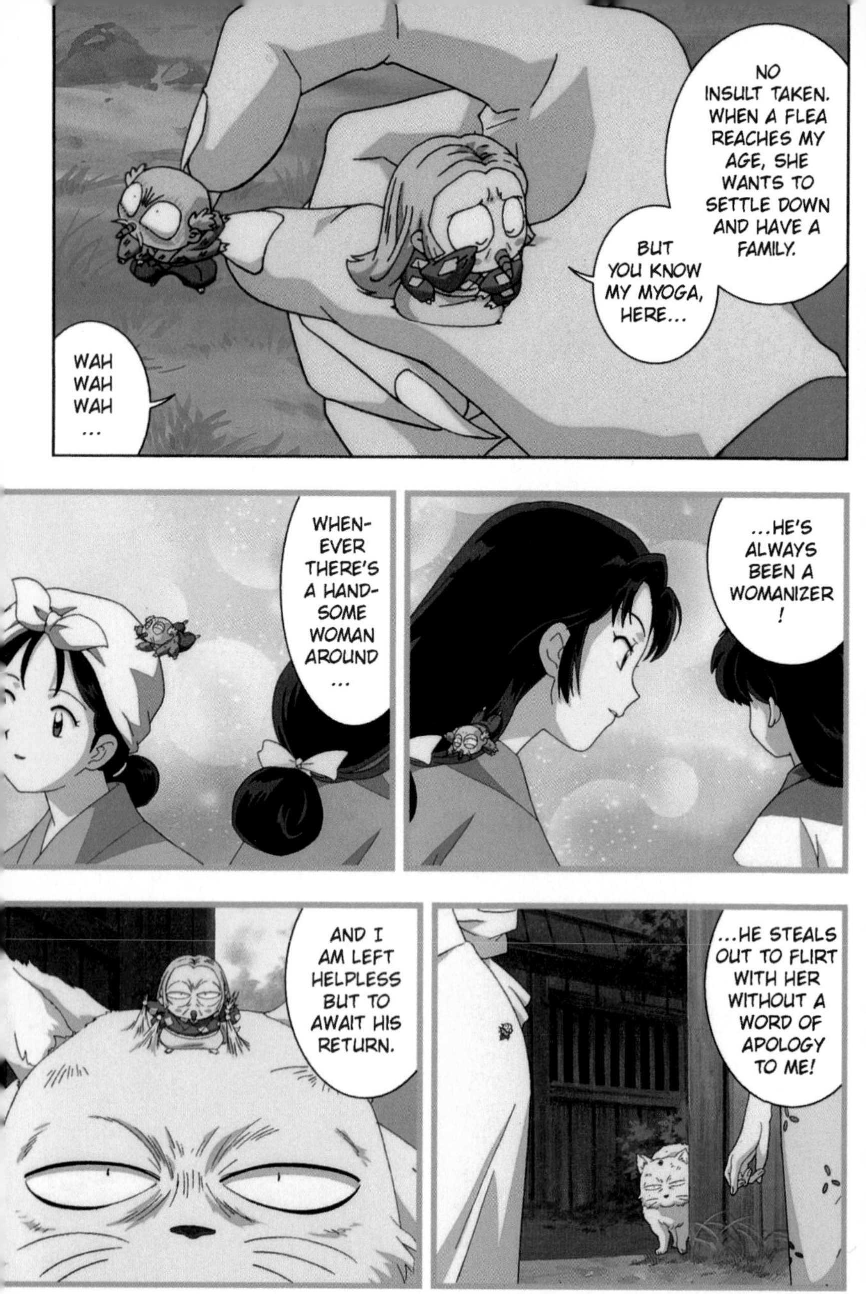
NO INSULT TAKEN. WHEN A FLEA REACHES MY AGE, SHE WANTS TO SETTLE DOWN AND HAVE A FAMILY.
BUT YOU KNOW MY MYOGA, HERE...
WAH WAH WAH ...
...HE'S ALWAYS BEEN A WOMANIZER!
WHEN-EVER THERE'S A HAND-SOME WOMAN AROUND...
...HE STEALS OUT TO FLIRT WITH HER WITHOUT A WORD OF APOLOGY TO ME!
AND I AM LEFT HELPLESS BUT TO AWAIT HIS RETURN.

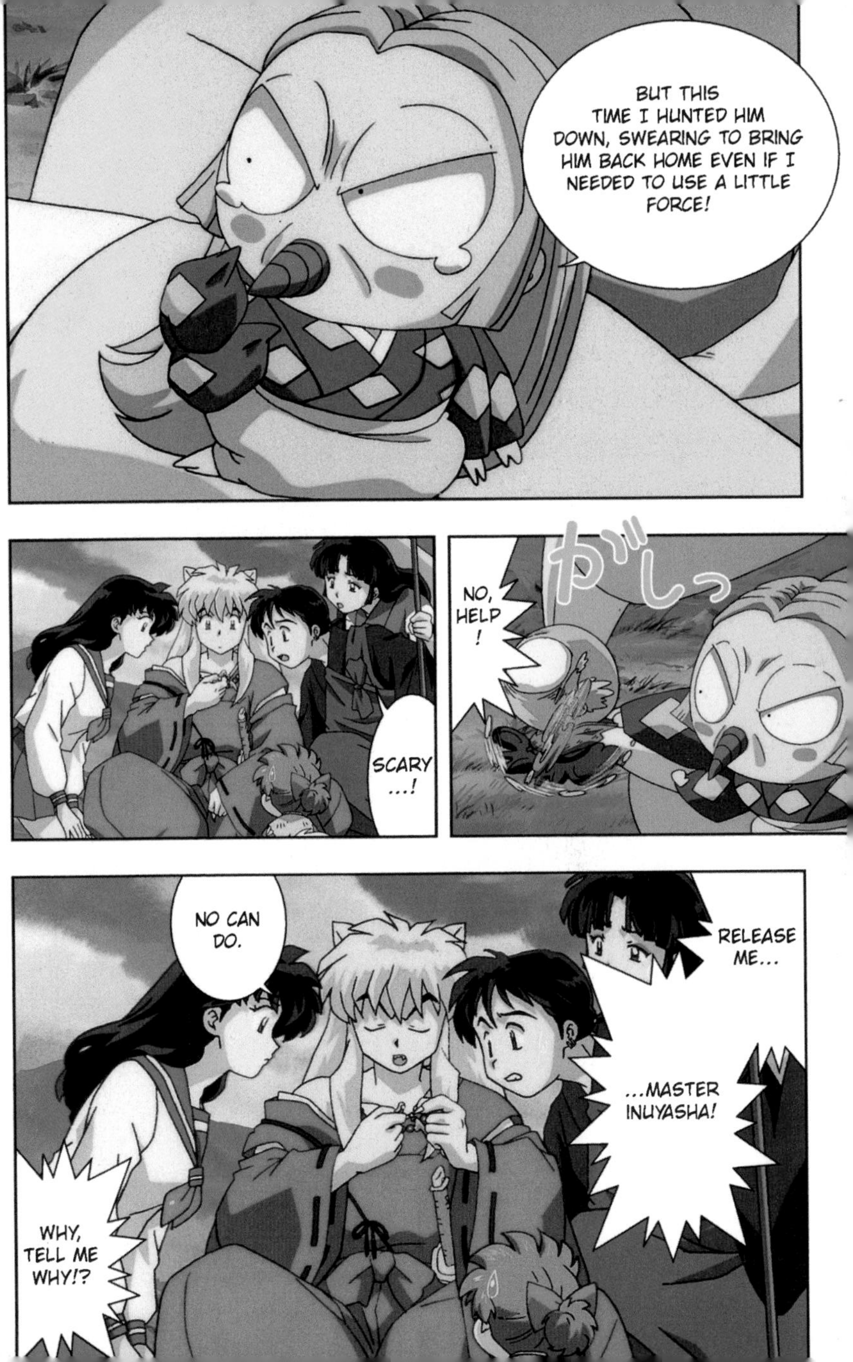
BUT THIS TIME I HUNTED HIM DOWN, SWEARING TO BRING HIM BACK HOME EVEN IF I NEEDED TO USE A LITTLE FORCE!
がしっ
NO, HELP!
SCARY...!
RELEASE ME...
...MASTER INUYASHA!
NO CAN DO.
WHY, TELL ME WHY!?

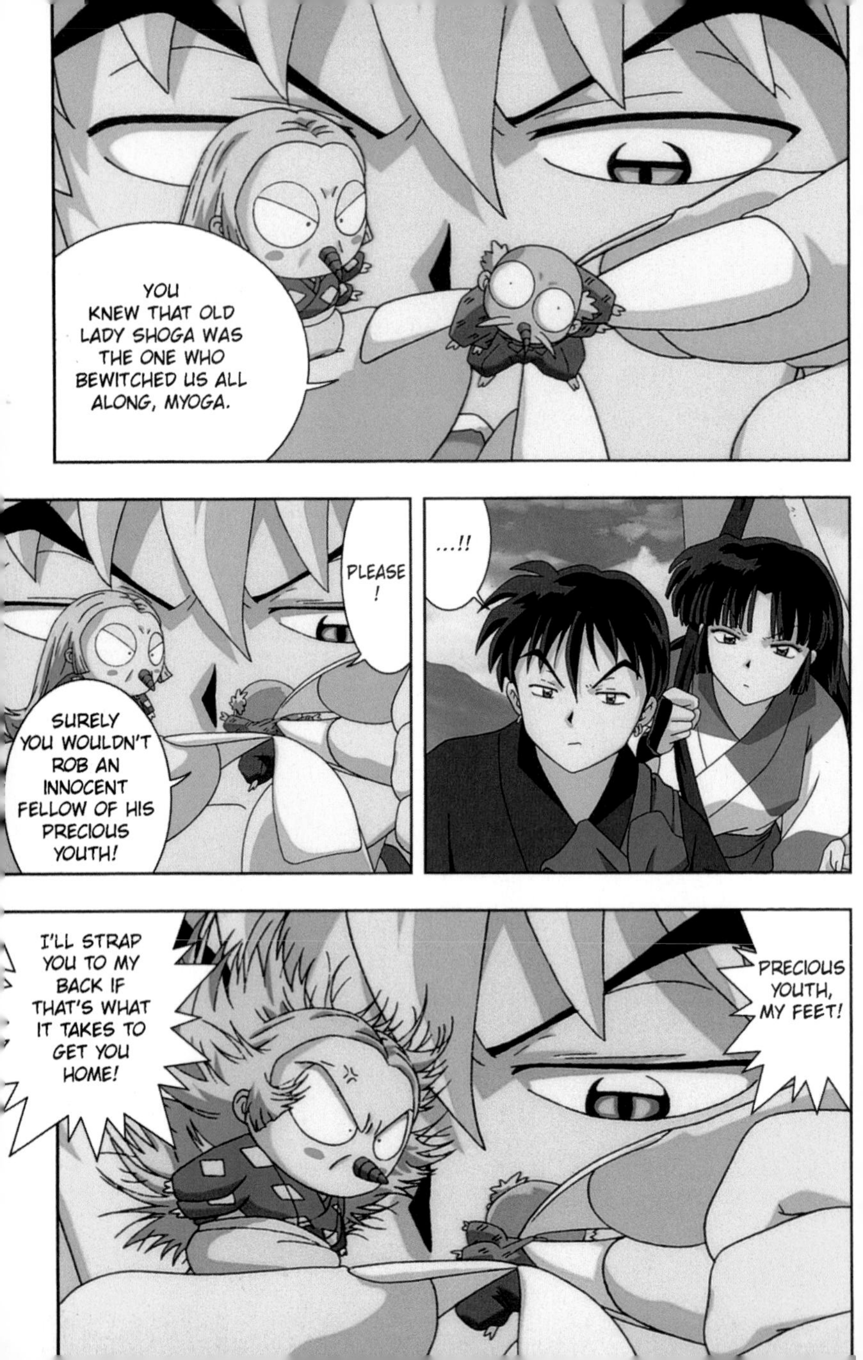
YOU KNEW THAT OLD LADY SHOGA WAS THE ONE WHO BEWITCHED US ALL ALONG, MYOGA.
...!!
PLEASE!
SURELY YOU WOULDN'T ROB AN INNOCENT FELLOW OF HIS PRECIOUS YOUTH!
PRECIOUS YOUTH, MY FEET!
I'LL STRAP YOU TO MY BACK IF THAT'S WHAT IT TAKES TO GET YOU HOME!

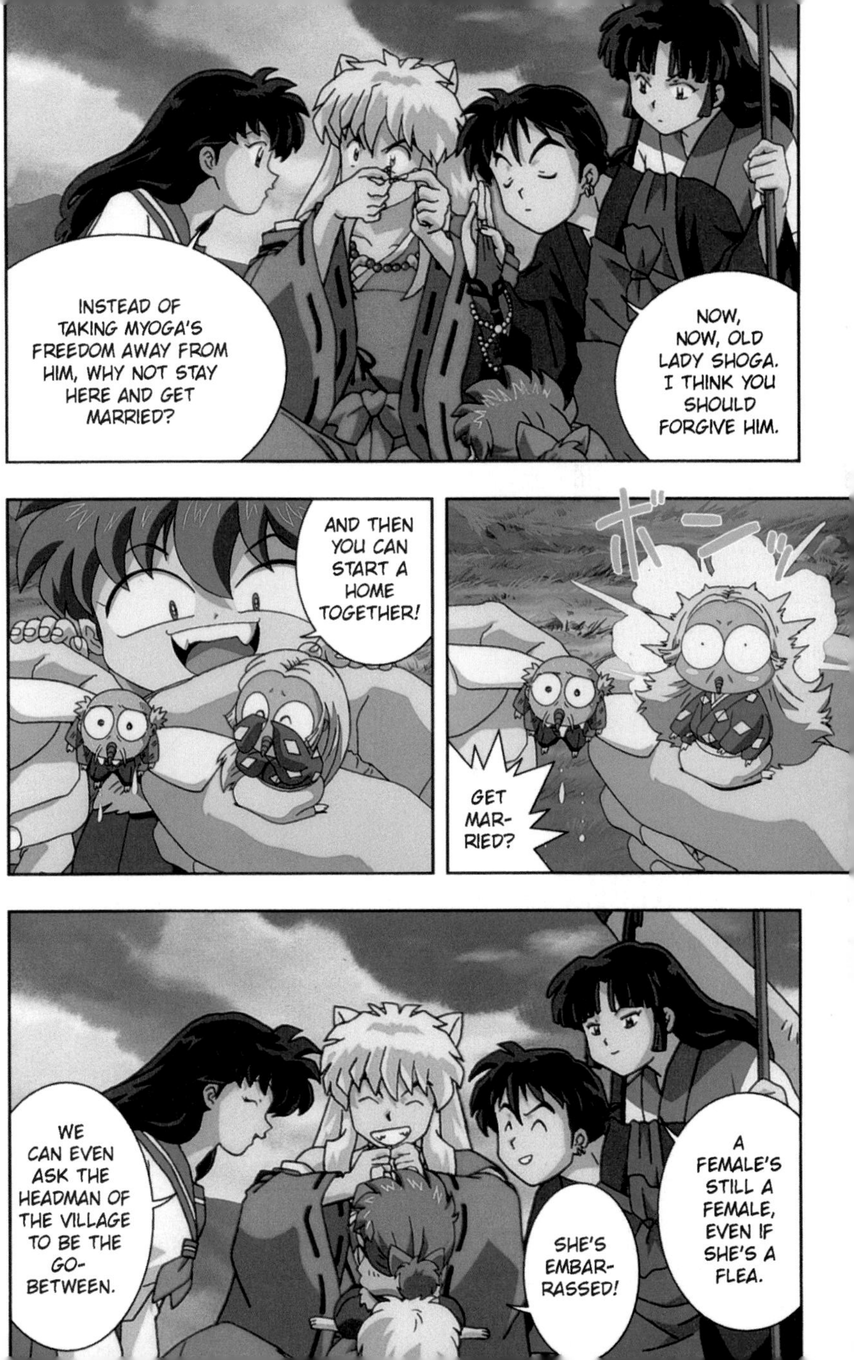
NOW, NOW, OLD LADY SHOGA. I THINK YOU SHOULD FORGIVE HIM.
INSTEAD OF TAKING MYOGA'S FREEDOM AWAY FROM HIM, WHY NOT STAY HERE AND GET MARRIED?
ボーッ
GET MAR-RIED?
AND THEN YOU CAN START A HOME TOGETHER!
A FEMALE'S STILL A FEMALE, EVEN IF SHE'S A FLEA.
SHE'S EMBAR-RASSED!
WE CAN EVEN ASK THE HEADMAN OF THE VILLAGE TO BE THE GO-BETWEEN.

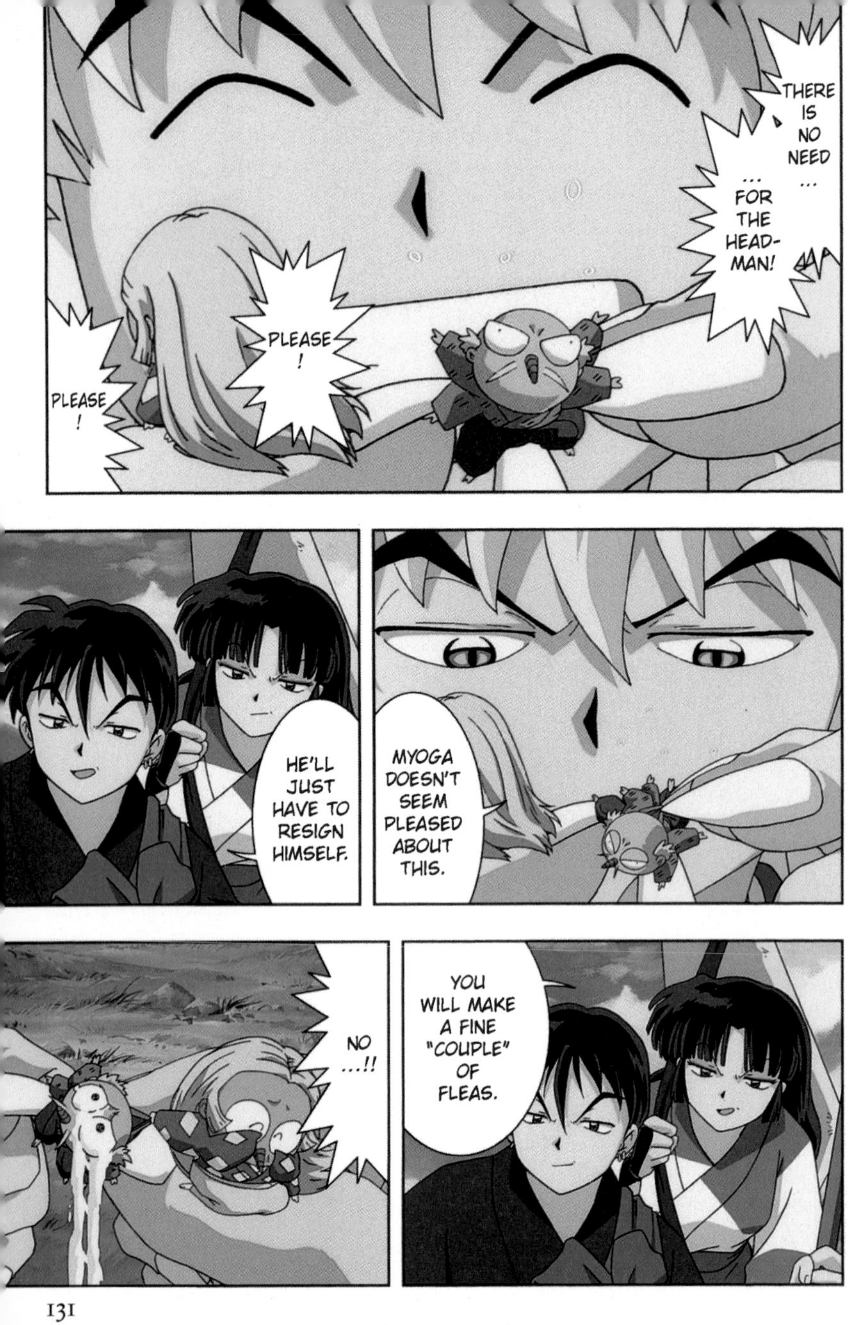
THERE IS NO NEED ... FOR THE HEAD-MAN!
PLEASE!
PLEASE!
MYOGA DOESN'T SEEM PLEASED ABOUT THIS.
HE'LL JUST HAVE TO RESIGN HIMSELF.
YOU WILL MAKE A FINE "COUPLE" OF FLEAS.
NO ...!!

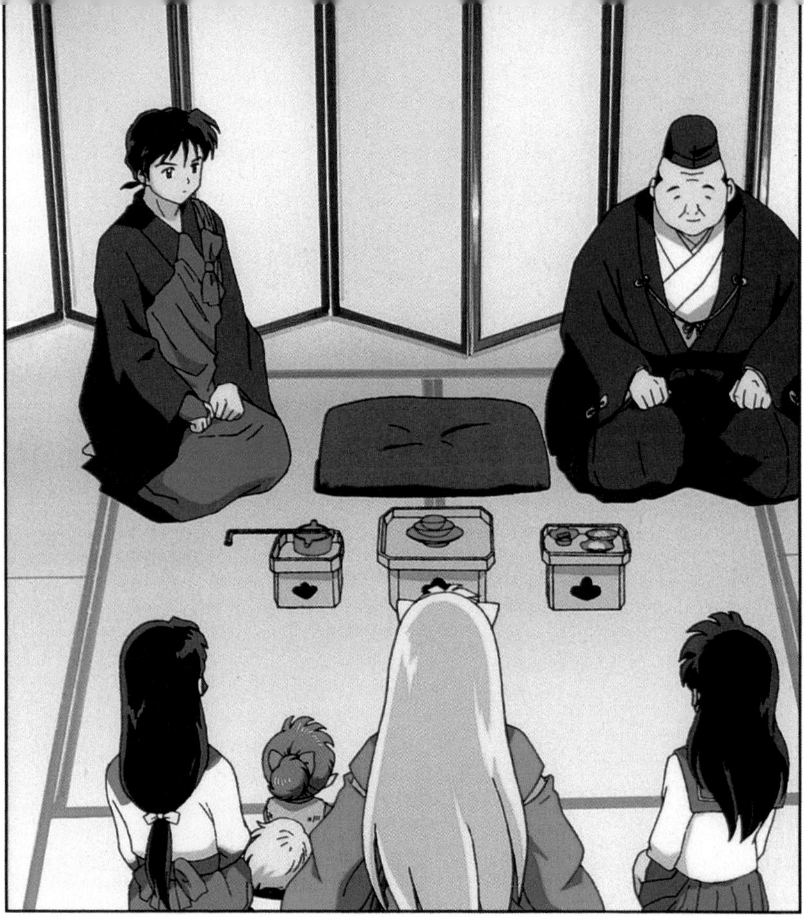

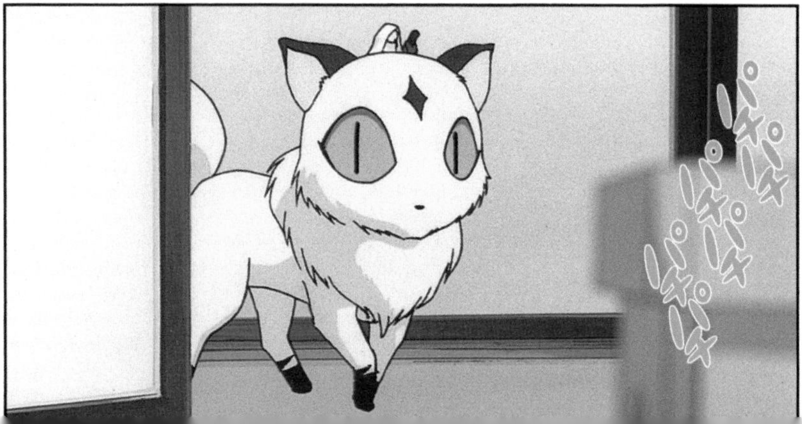
パォパォ
パォパォ
パォパォ

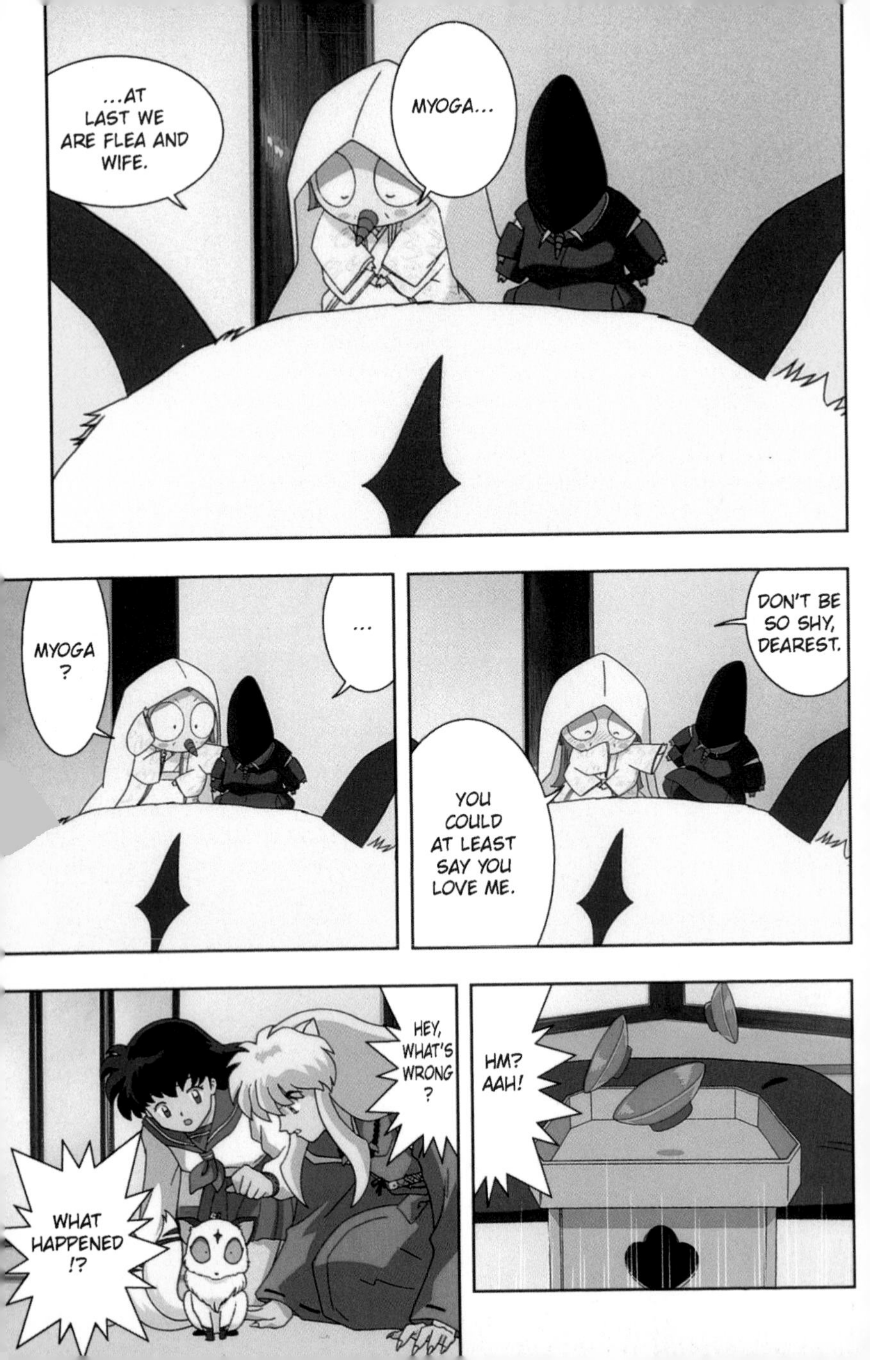
MYOGA...
...AT LAST WE ARE FLEA AND WIFE.
DON'T BE SO SHY, DEAREST.
YOU COULD AT LEAST SAY YOU LOVE ME.
...
MYOGA ?
HM? AAH!
HEY, WHAT'S WRONG ?
WHAT HAPPENED !?

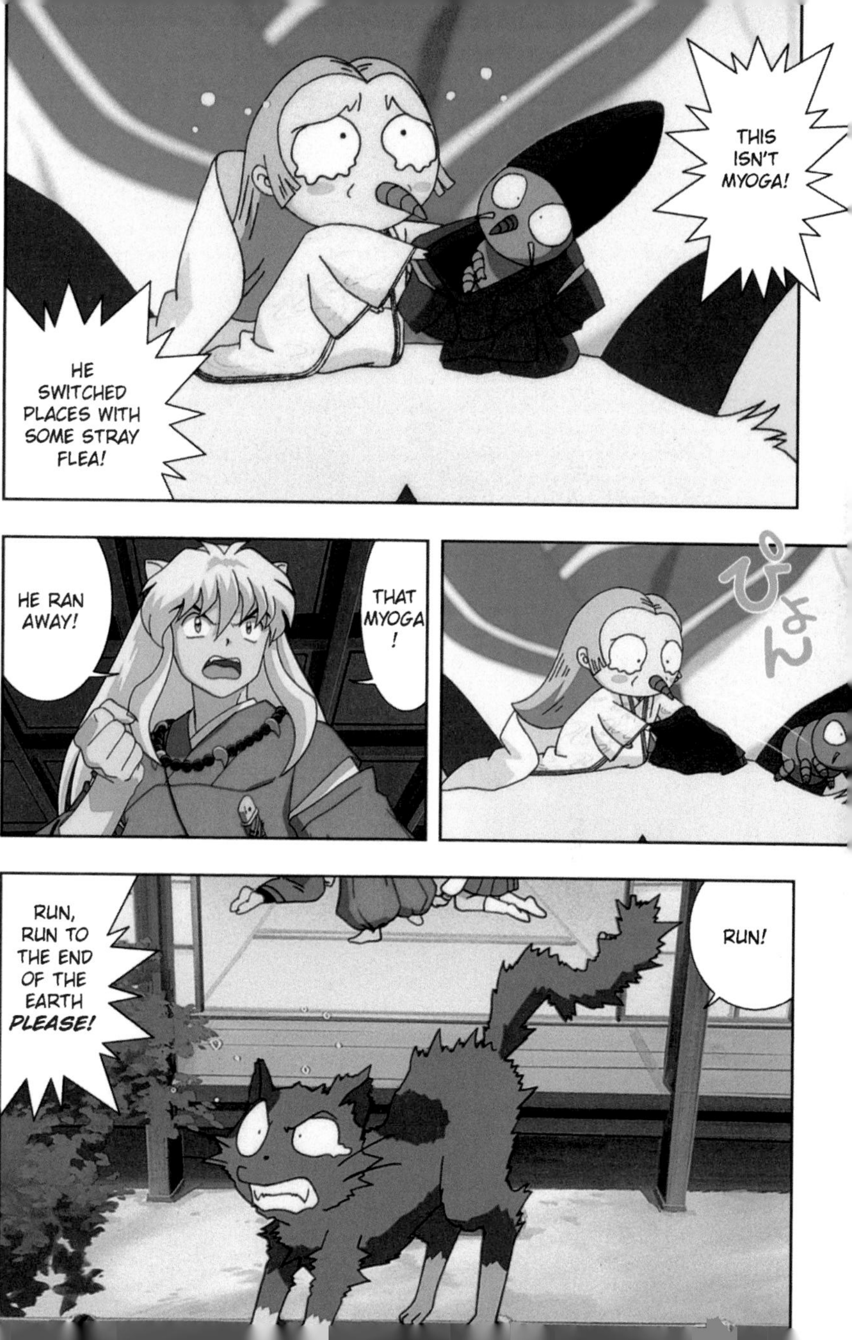
THIS ISN'T MYOGA!
HE SWITCHED PLACES WITH SOME STRAY FLEA!
ぴょん
THAT MYOGA!
HE RAN AWAY!
RUN!
RUN, RUN TO THE END OF THE EARTH **PLEASE!**

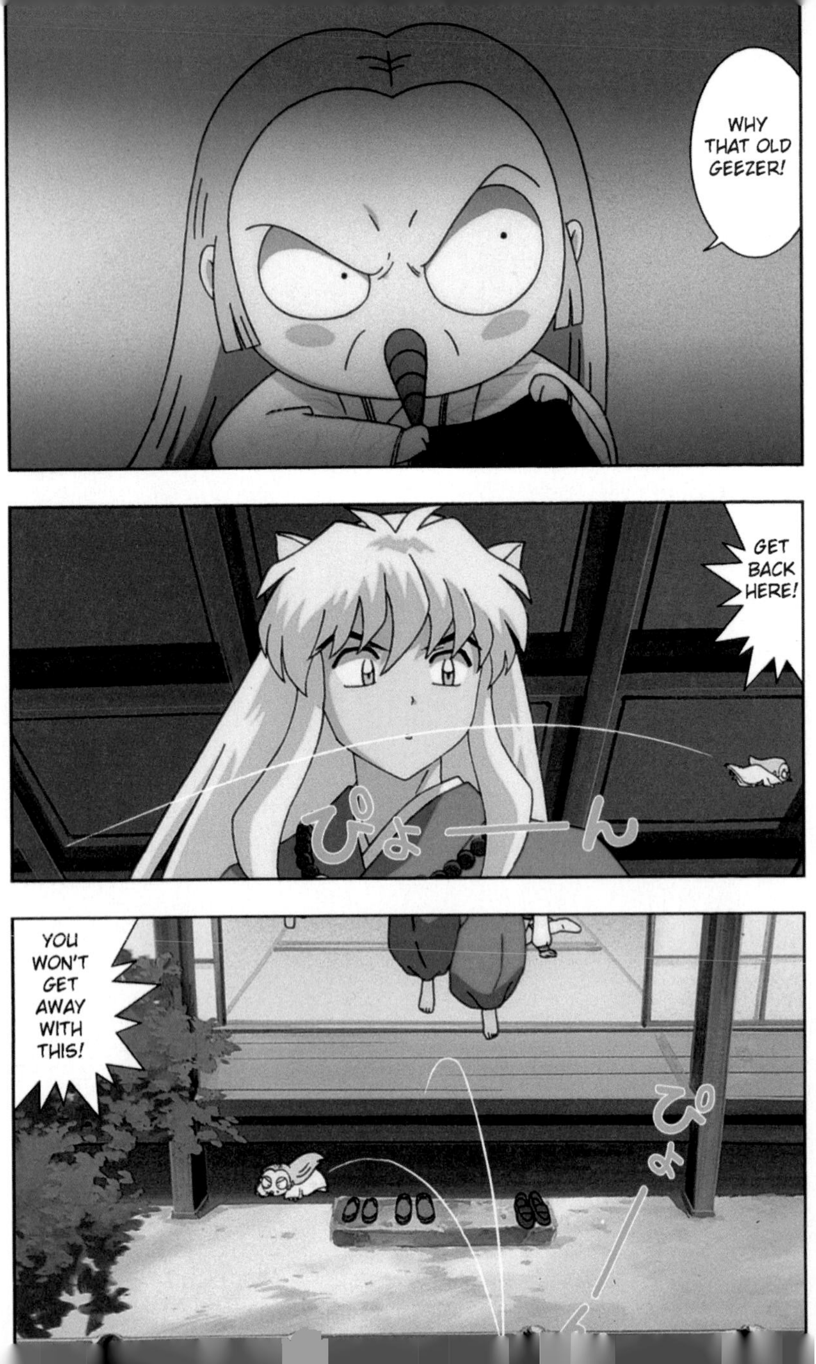
WHY THAT OLD GEEZER!
GET BACK HERE!
ぴょーーん
YOU WON'T GET AWAY WITH THIS!
ぴょー

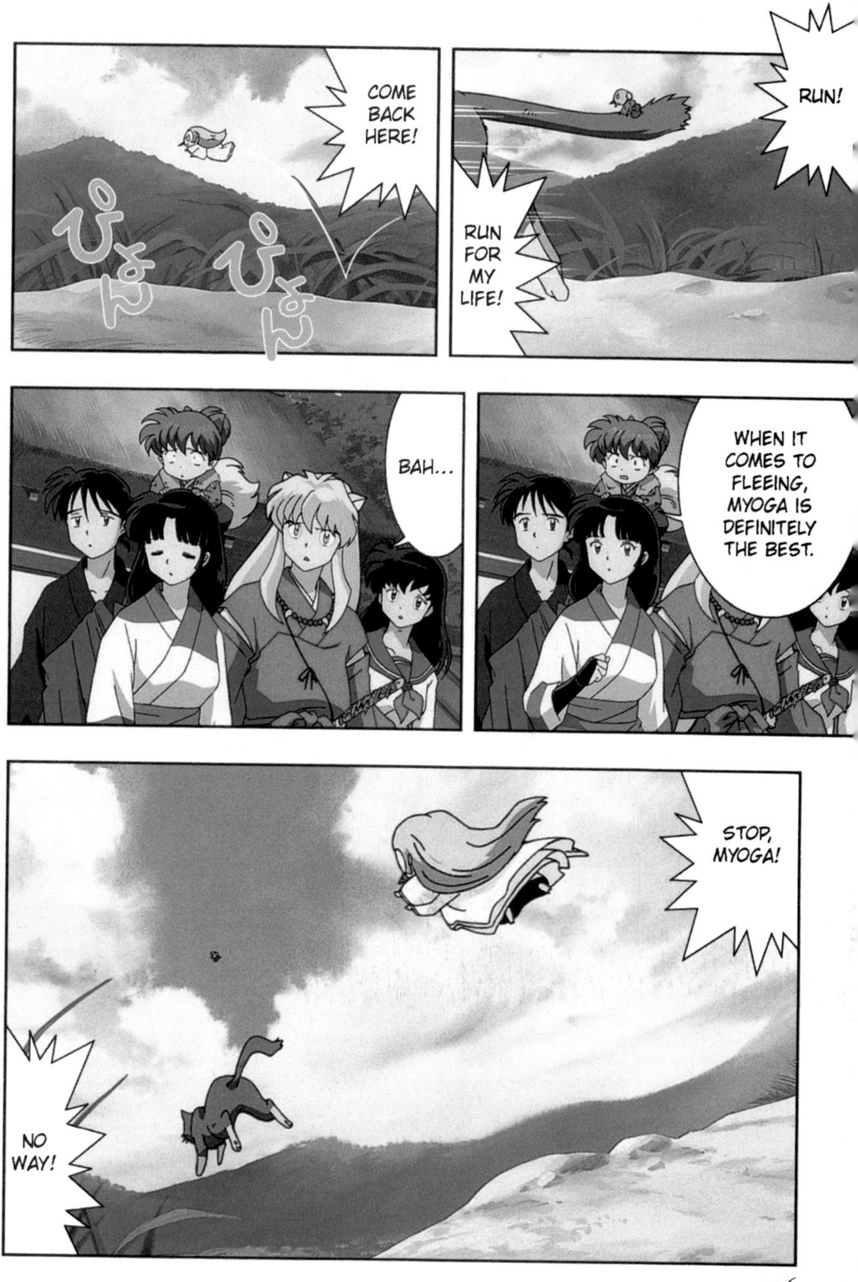
RUN!
RUN FOR MY LIFE!
COME BACK HERE!
ぴょん
ぴょん
WHEN IT COMES TO FLEEING, MYOGA IS DEFINITELY THE BEST.
BAH...
STOP, MYOGA!
NO WAY!

66 Naraku's Barrier–Kagura's Decision

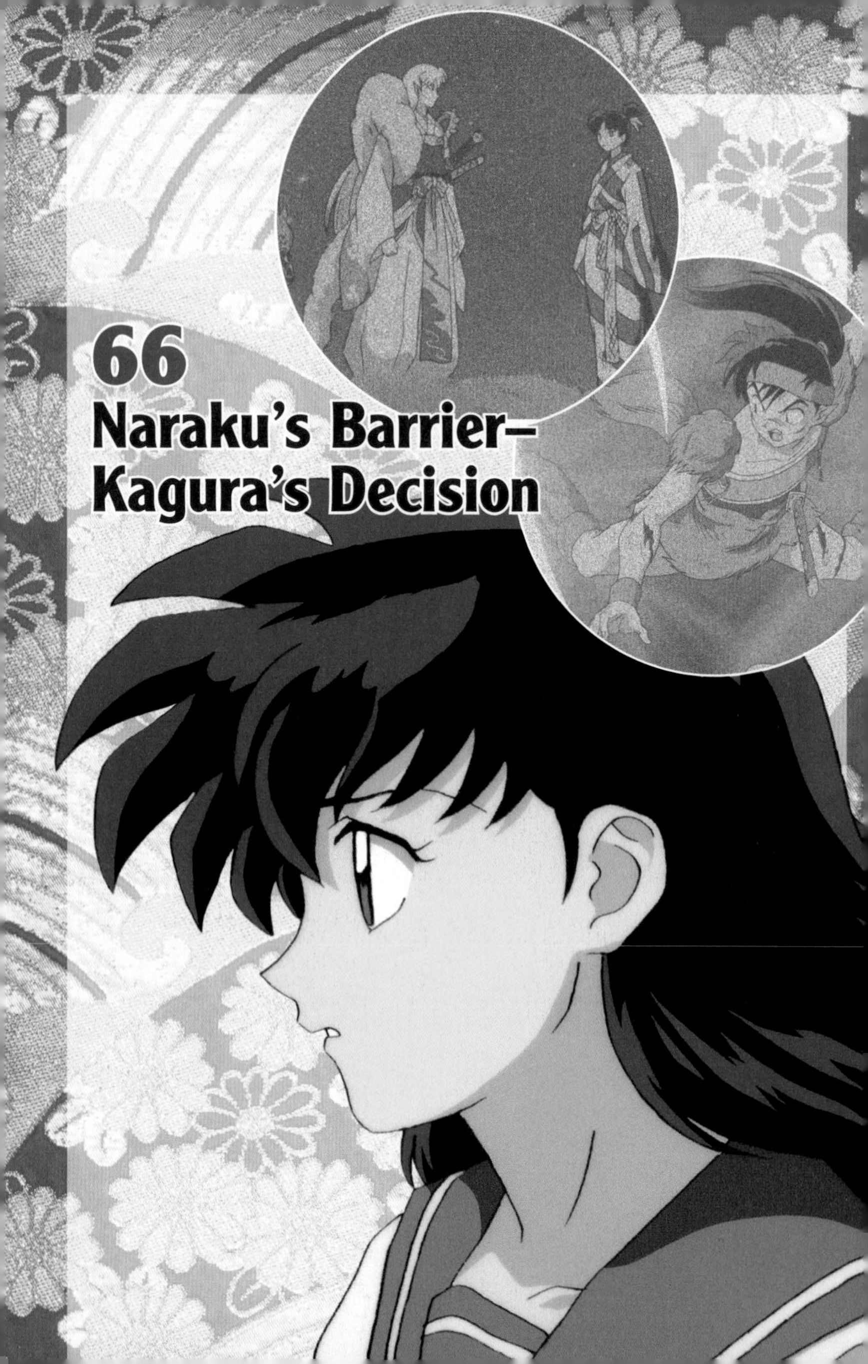

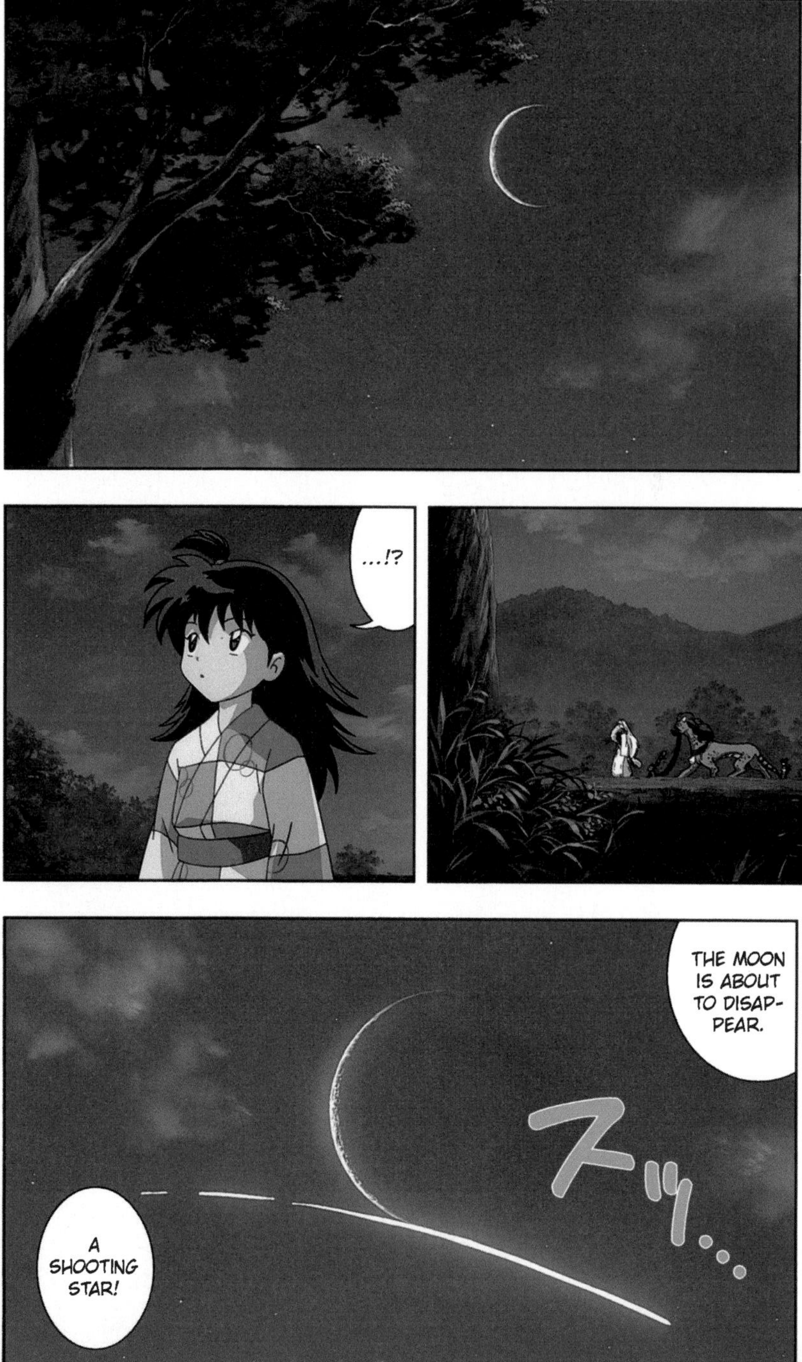
...!?
THE MOON IS ABOUT TO DISAP-PEAR.
スッ...
A SHOOTING STAR!

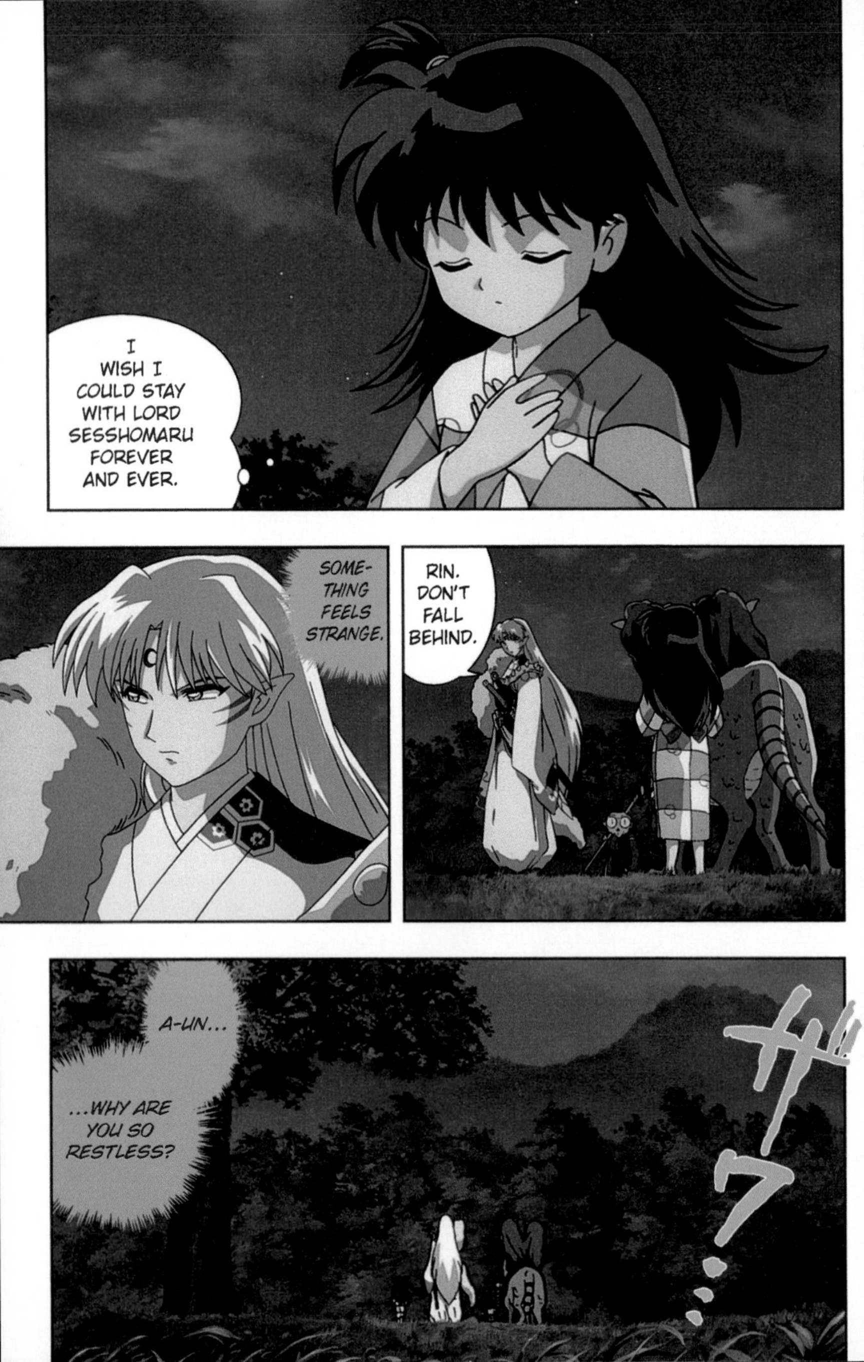
I WISH I COULD STAY WITH LORD SESSHOMARU FOREVER AND EVER.
RIN. DON'T FALL BEHIND.
SOME-THING FEELS STRANGE.
A-UN...
...WHY ARE YOU SO RESTLESS?
ザワ…

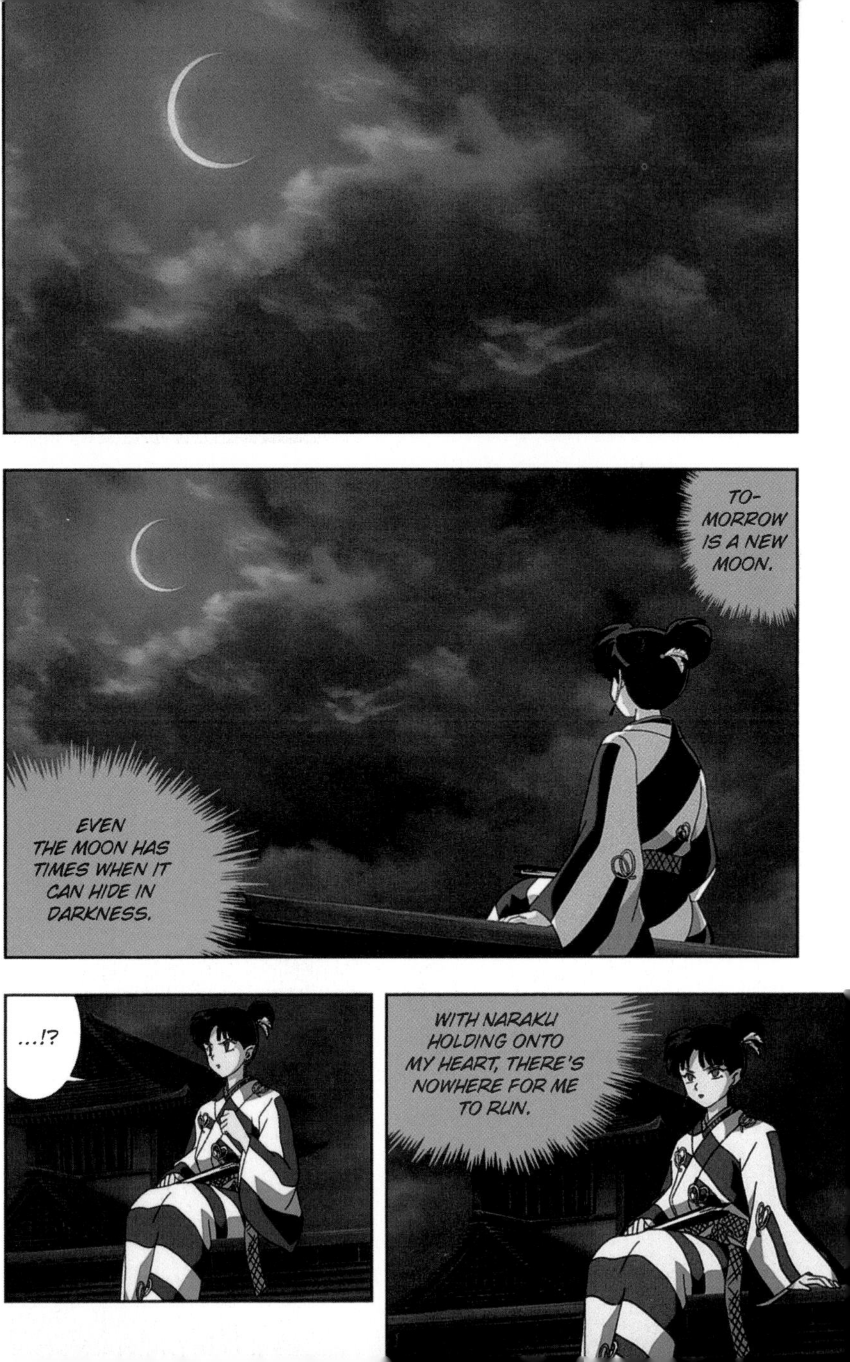
TO-MORROW IS A NEW MOON.
EVEN THE MOON HAS TIMES WHEN IT CAN HIDE IN DARKNESS.
WITH NARAKU HOLDING ONTO MY HEART, THERE'S NOWHERE FOR ME TO RUN.
...!?

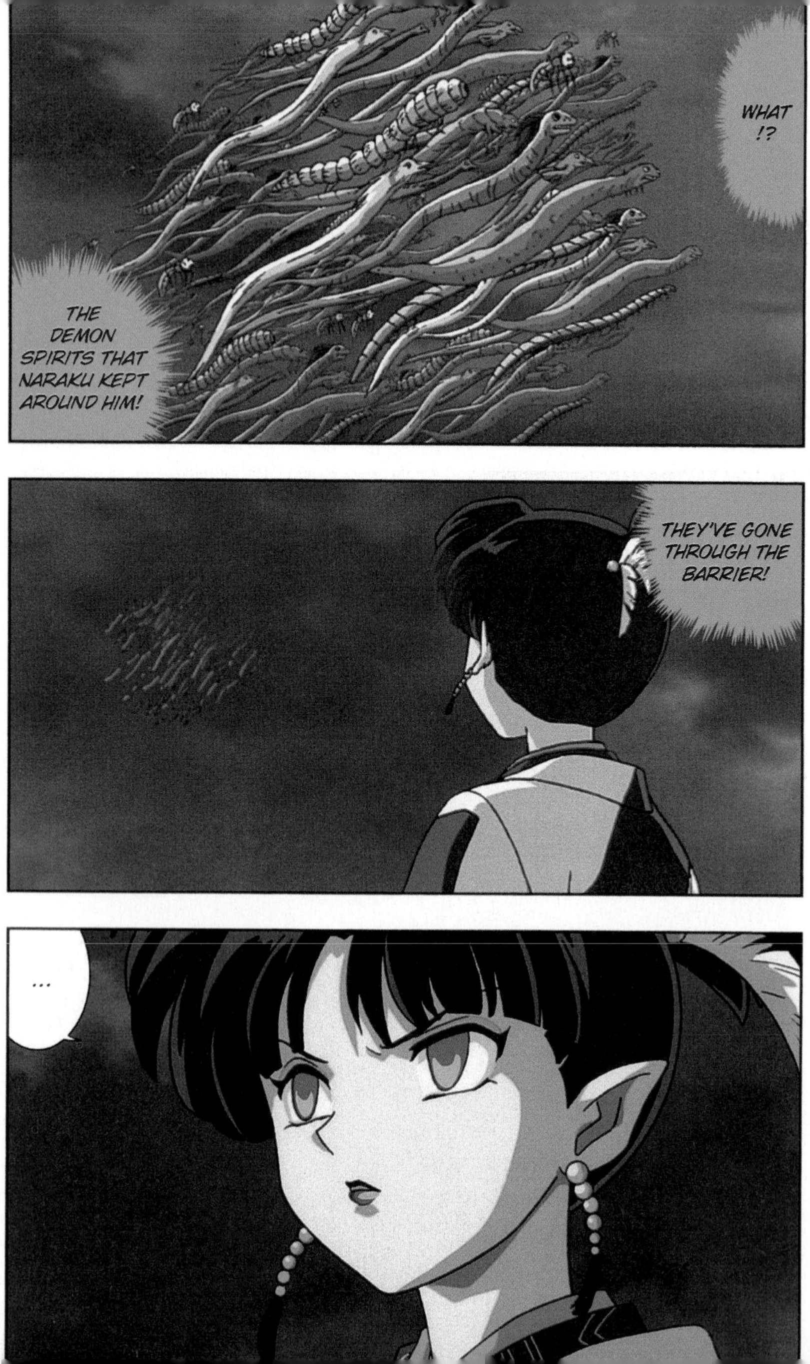
WHAT !?
THE DEMON SPIRITS THAT NARAKU KEPT AROUND HIM!
THEY'VE GONE THROUGH THE BARRIER!
...

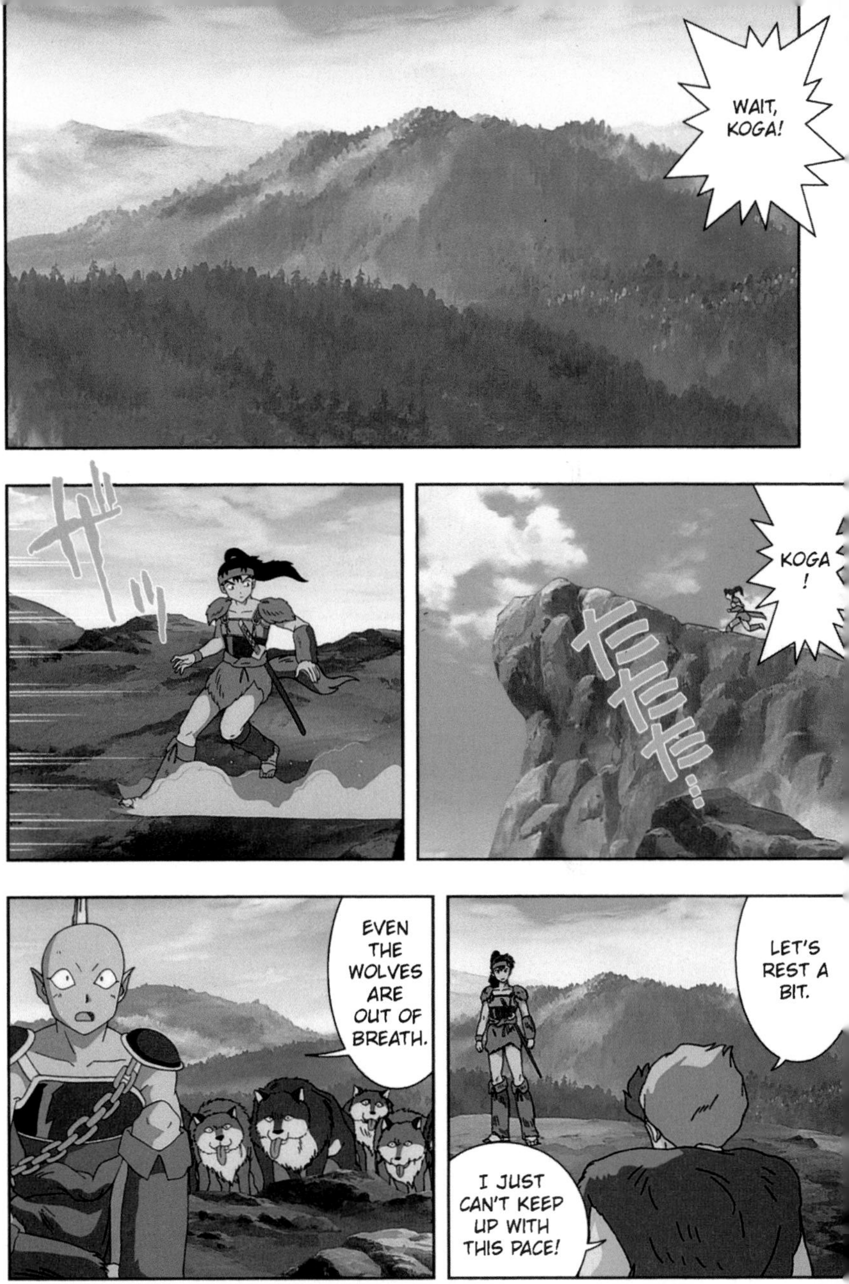
WAIT, KOGA!
KOGA!
たたた…
ザッ
LET'S REST A BIT.
I JUST CAN'T KEEP UP WITH THIS PACE!
EVEN THE WOLVES ARE OUT OF BREATH.

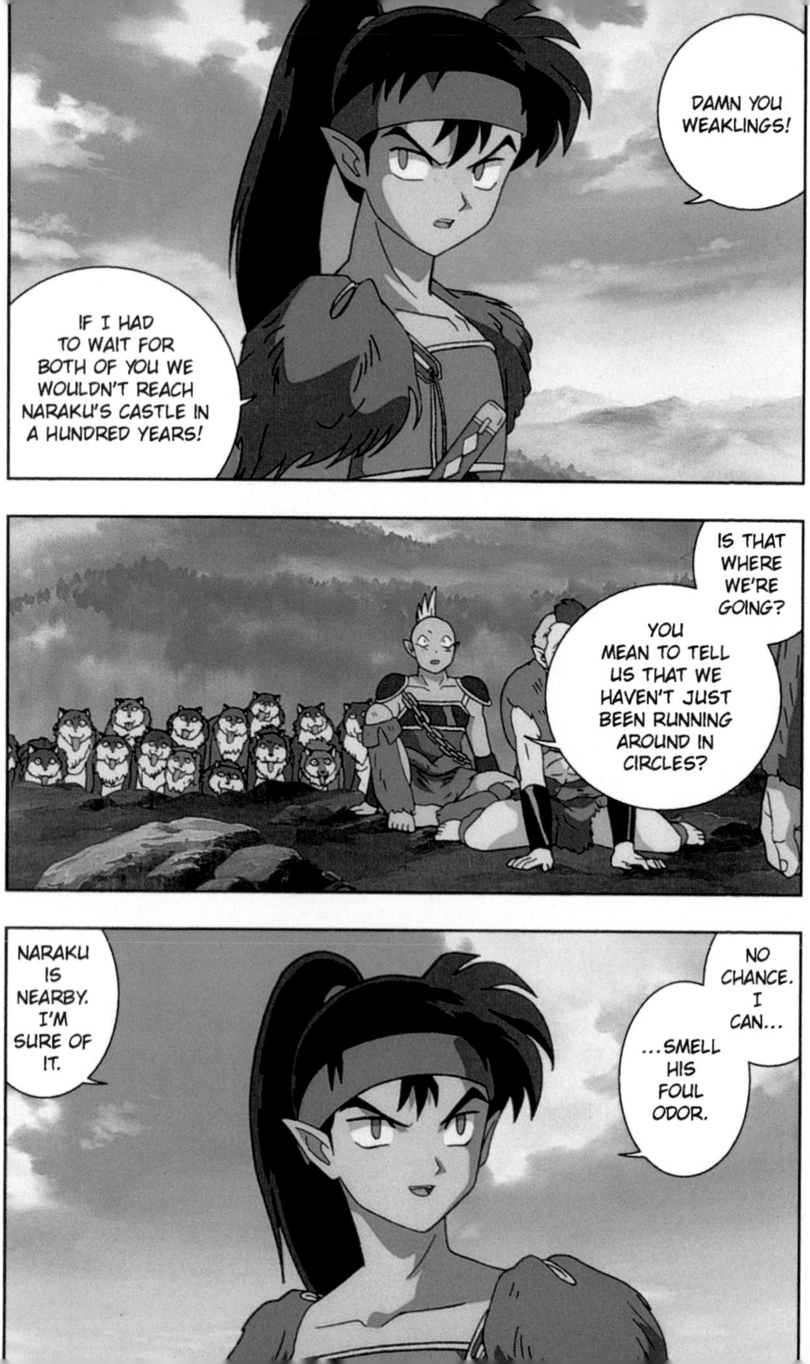
DAMN YOU WEAKLINGS!
IF I HAD TO WAIT FOR BOTH OF YOU WE WOULDN'T REACH NARAKU'S CASTLE IN A HUNDRED YEARS!
IS THAT WHERE WE'RE GOING?
YOU MEAN TO TELL US THAT WE HAVEN'T JUST BEEN RUNNING AROUND IN CIRCLES?
NO CHANCE. I CAN...
...SMELL HIS FOUL ODOR.
NARAKU IS NEARBY. I'M SURE OF IT.

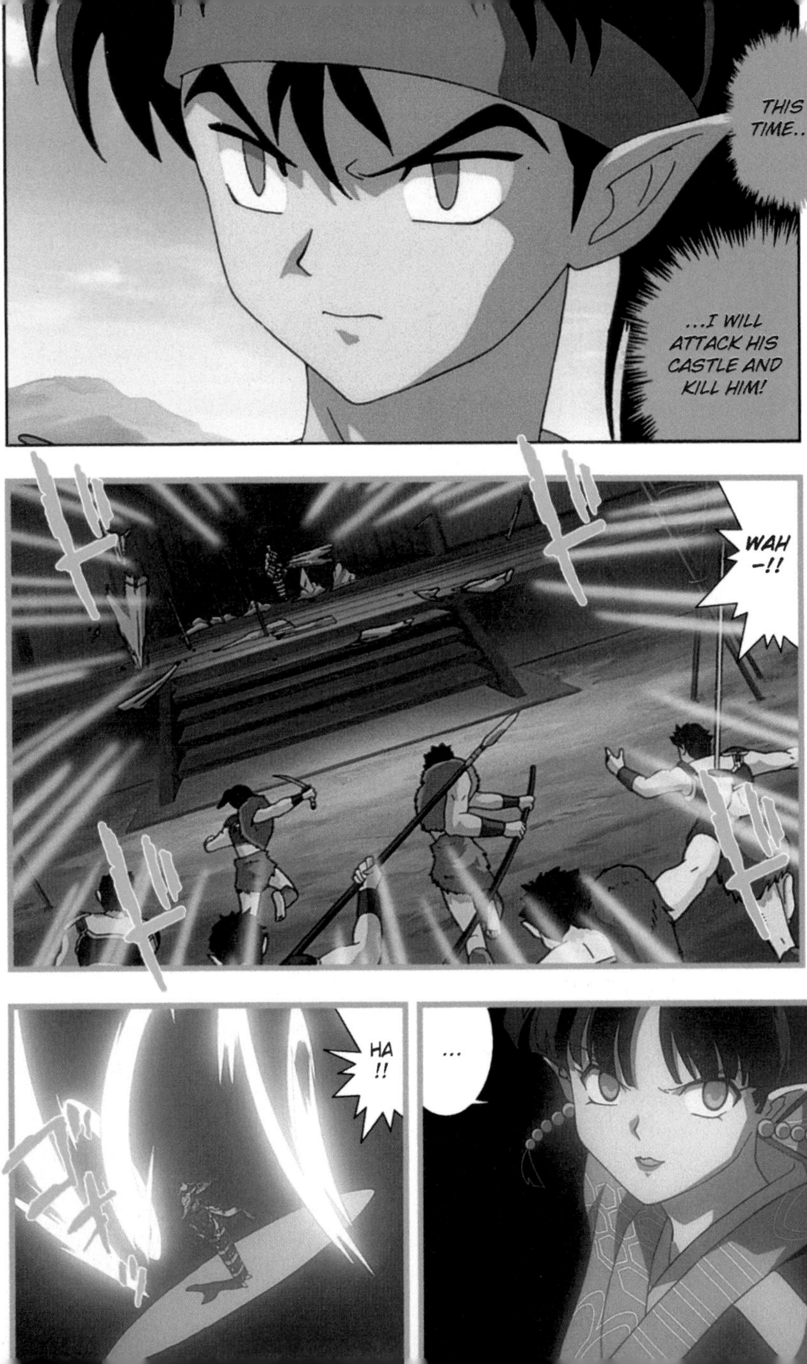
THIS TIME...
...I WILL ATTACK HIS CASTLE AND KILL HIM!
WAH-!!
...
HA!!

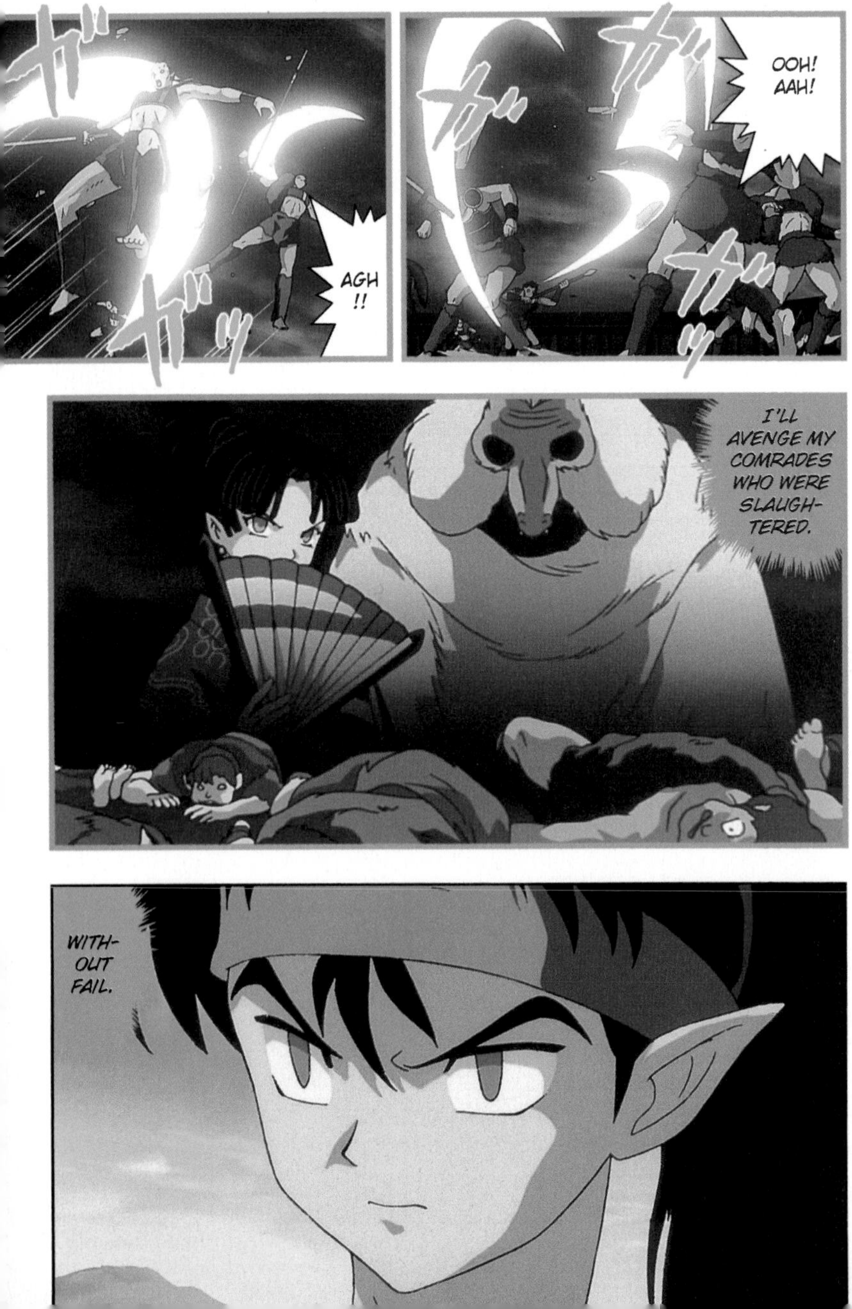
OOH! AAH!
AGH !!
I'LL AVENGE MY COMRADES WHO WERE SLAUGH-TERED.
WITH-OUT FAIL.

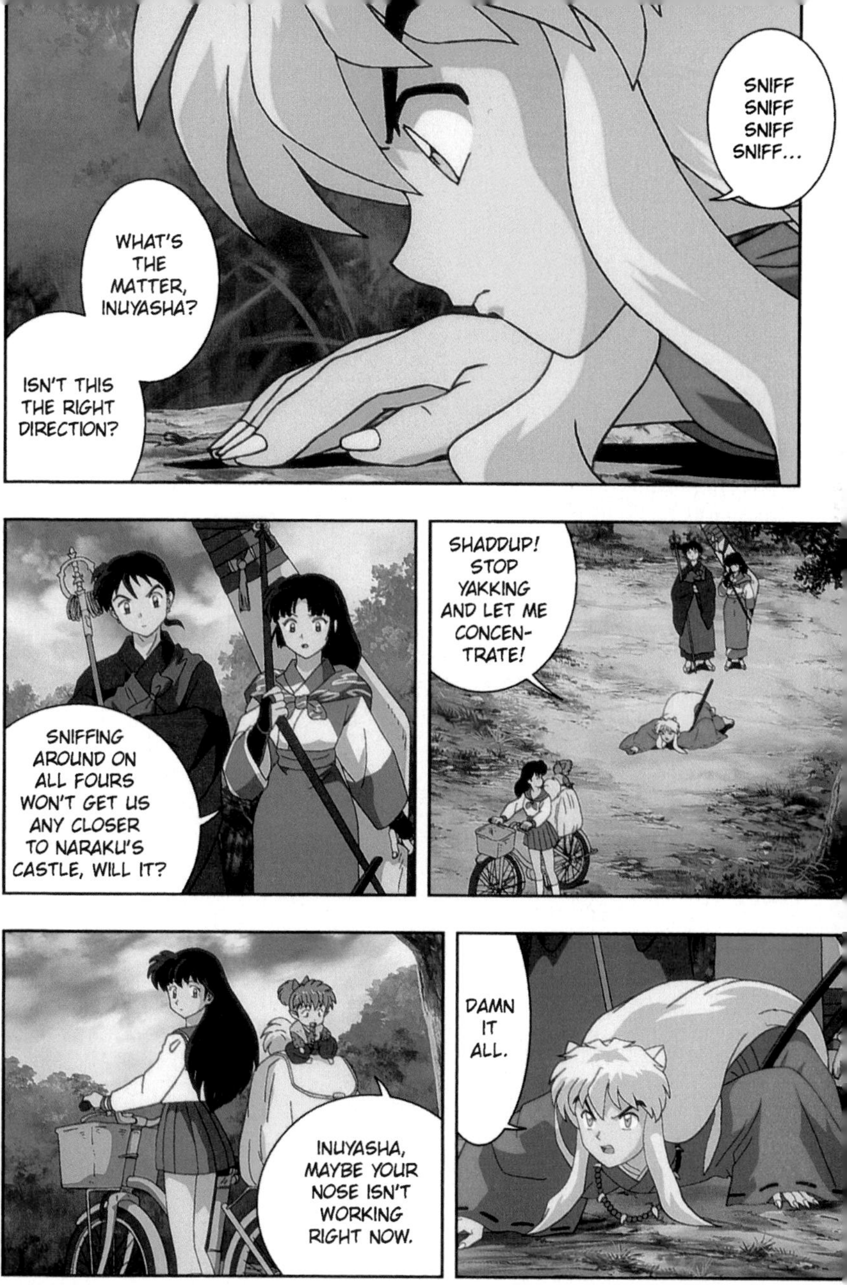
SNIFF SNIFF SNIFF SNIFF...
WHAT'S THE MATTER, INUYASHA?
ISN'T THIS THE RIGHT DIRECTION?
SHADDUP! STOP YAKKING AND LET ME CONCENTRATE!
SNIFFING AROUND ON ALL FOURS WON'T GET US ANY CLOSER TO NARAKU'S CASTLE, WILL IT?
DAMN IT ALL.
INUYASHA, MAYBE YOUR NOSE ISN'T WORKING RIGHT NOW.

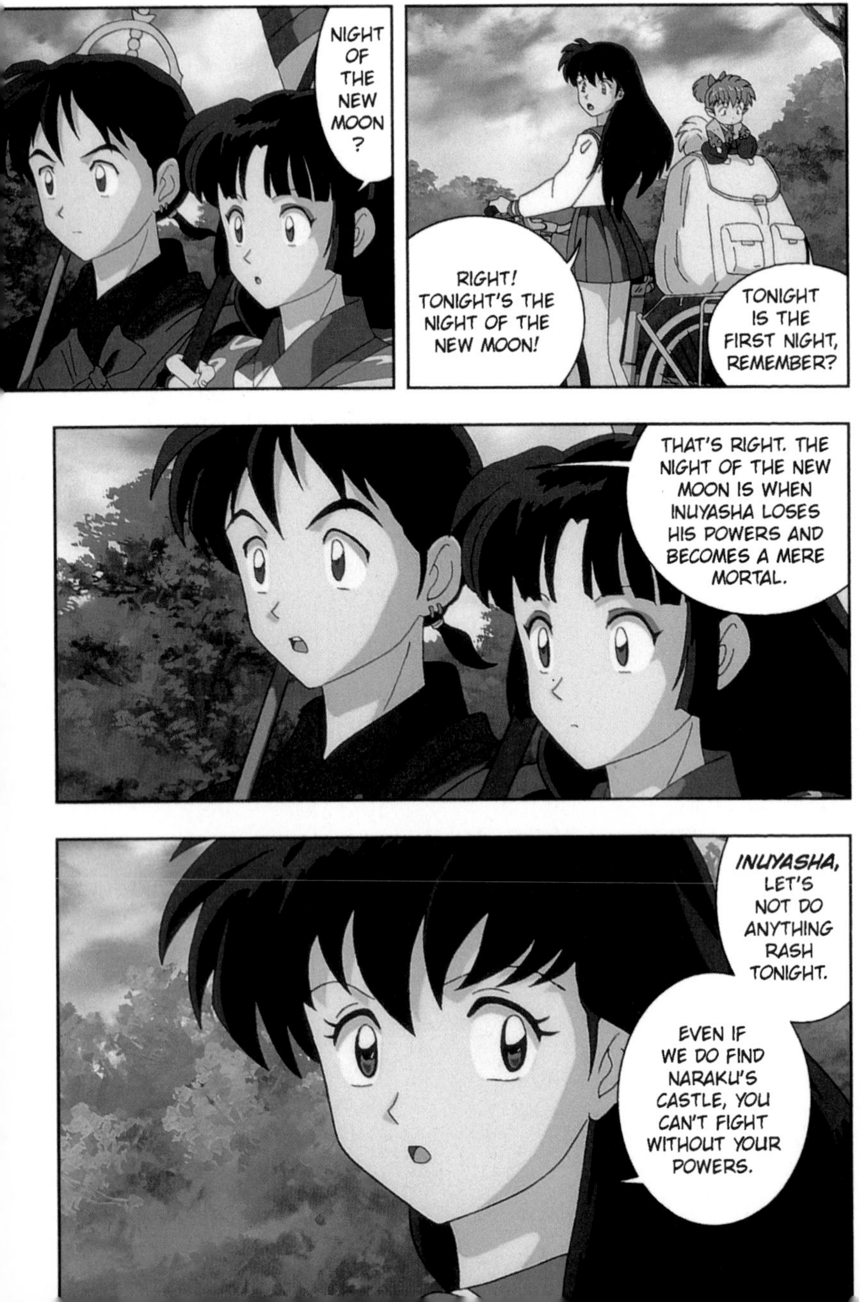
TONIGHT IS THE FIRST NIGHT, REMEMBER?
RIGHT! TONIGHT'S THE NIGHT OF THE NEW MOON!
NIGHT OF THE NEW MOON?
THAT'S RIGHT. THE NIGHT OF THE NEW MOON IS WHEN INUYASHA LOSES HIS POWERS AND BECOMES A MERE MORTAL.
INUYASHA, LET'S NOT DO ANYTHING RASH TONIGHT.
EVEN IF WE DO FIND NARAKU'S CASTLE, YOU CAN'T FIGHT WITHOUT YOUR POWERS.

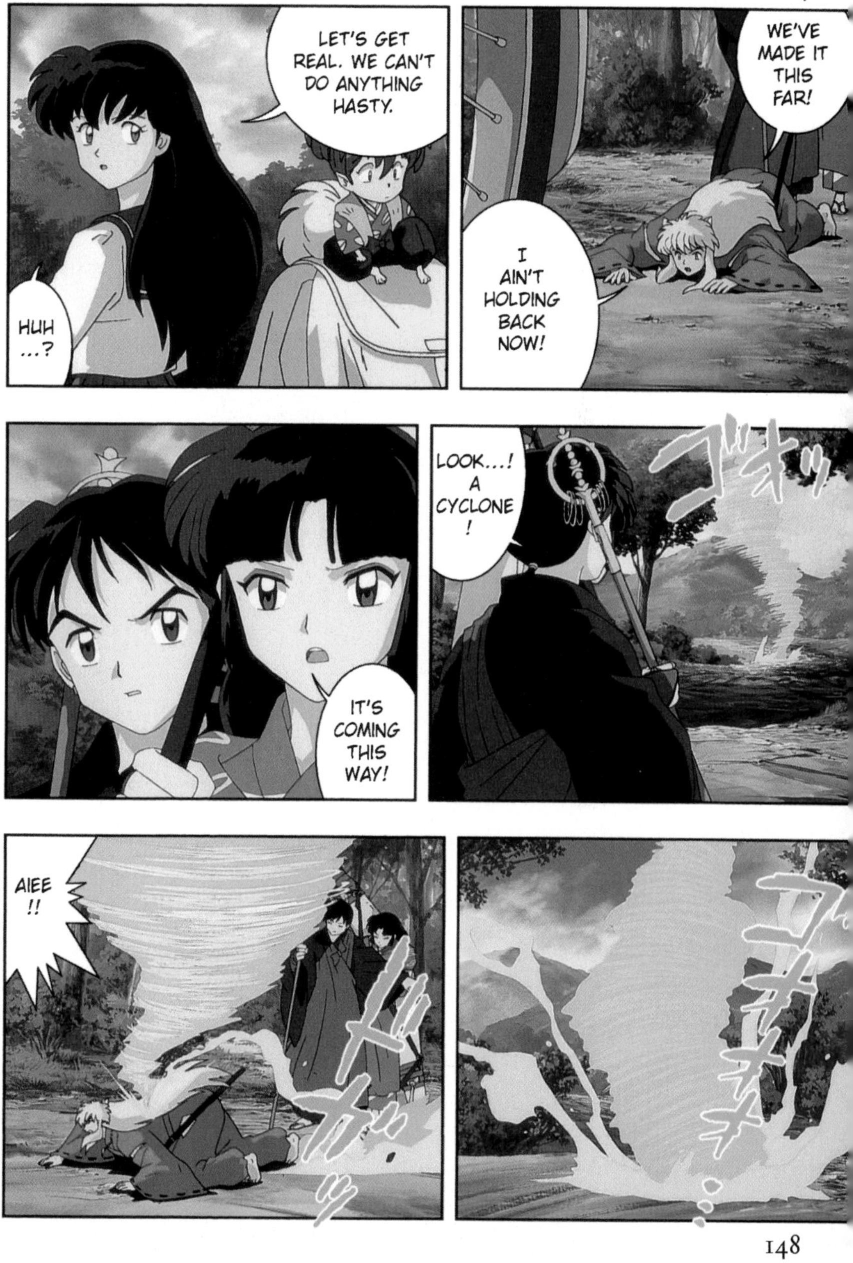
WE'VE MADE IT THIS FAR!
I AIN'T HOLDING BACK NOW!
LET'S GET REAL. WE CAN'T DO ANYTHING HASTY.
HUH ...?
LOOK...! A CYCLONE!
IT'S COMING THIS WAY!
AIEE !!

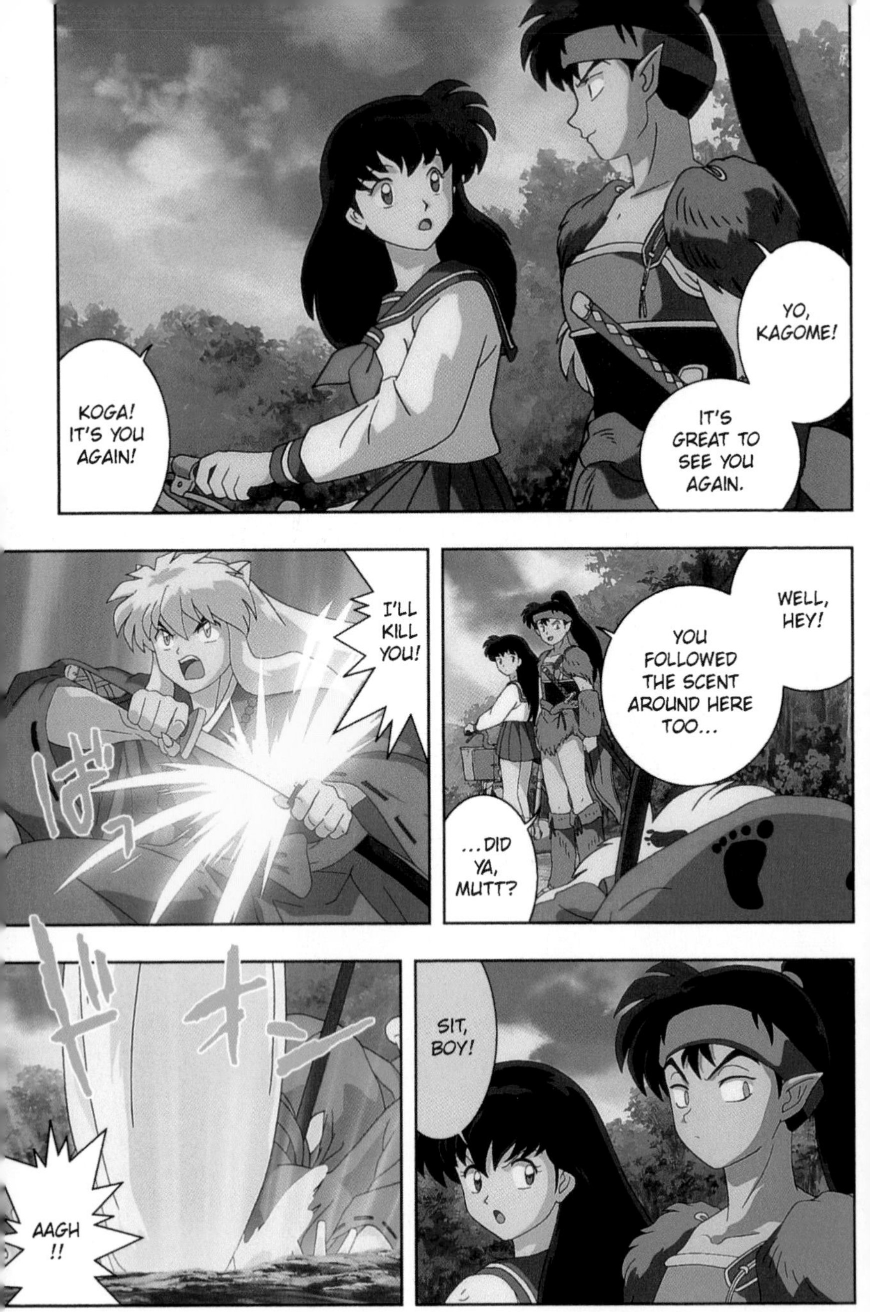
YO, KAGOME!
IT'S GREAT TO SEE YOU AGAIN.
KOGA! IT'S YOU AGAIN!
WELL, HEY!
YOU FOLLOWED THE SCENT AROUND HERE TOO...
...DID YA, MUTT?
I'LL KILL YOU!
ぱっ
SIT, BOY!
ドオーン
AAGH !!

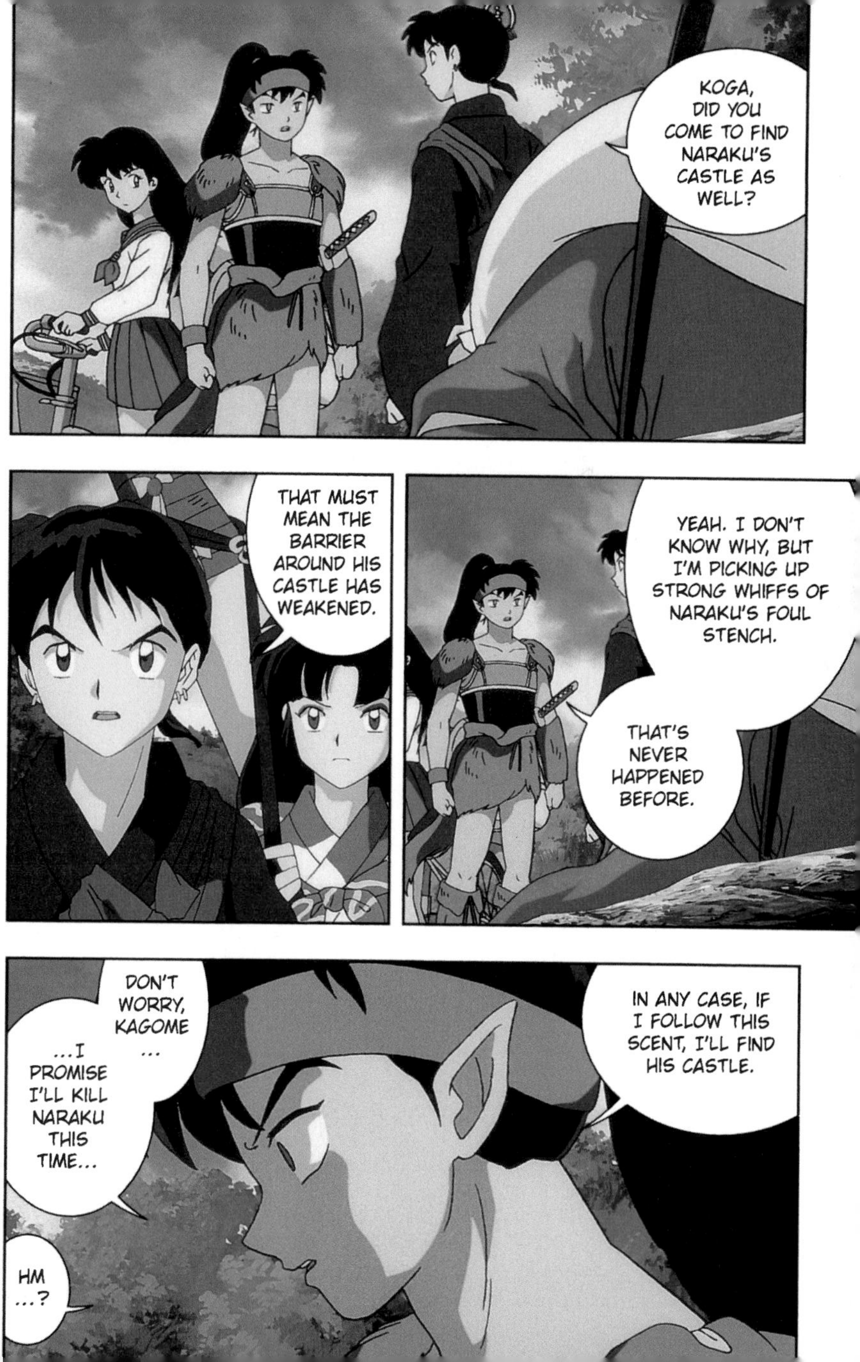
KOGA, DID YOU COME TO FIND NARAKU'S CASTLE AS WELL?
YEAH. I DON'T KNOW WHY, BUT I'M PICKING UP STRONG WHIFFS OF NARAKU'S FOUL STENCH.
THAT'S NEVER HAPPENED BEFORE.
THAT MUST MEAN THE BARRIER AROUND HIS CASTLE HAS WEAKENED.
IN ANY CASE, IF I FOLLOW THIS SCENT, I'LL FIND HIS CASTLE.
DON'T WORRY, KAGOME ...
...I PROMISE I'LL KILL NARAKU THIS TIME...
HM ...?

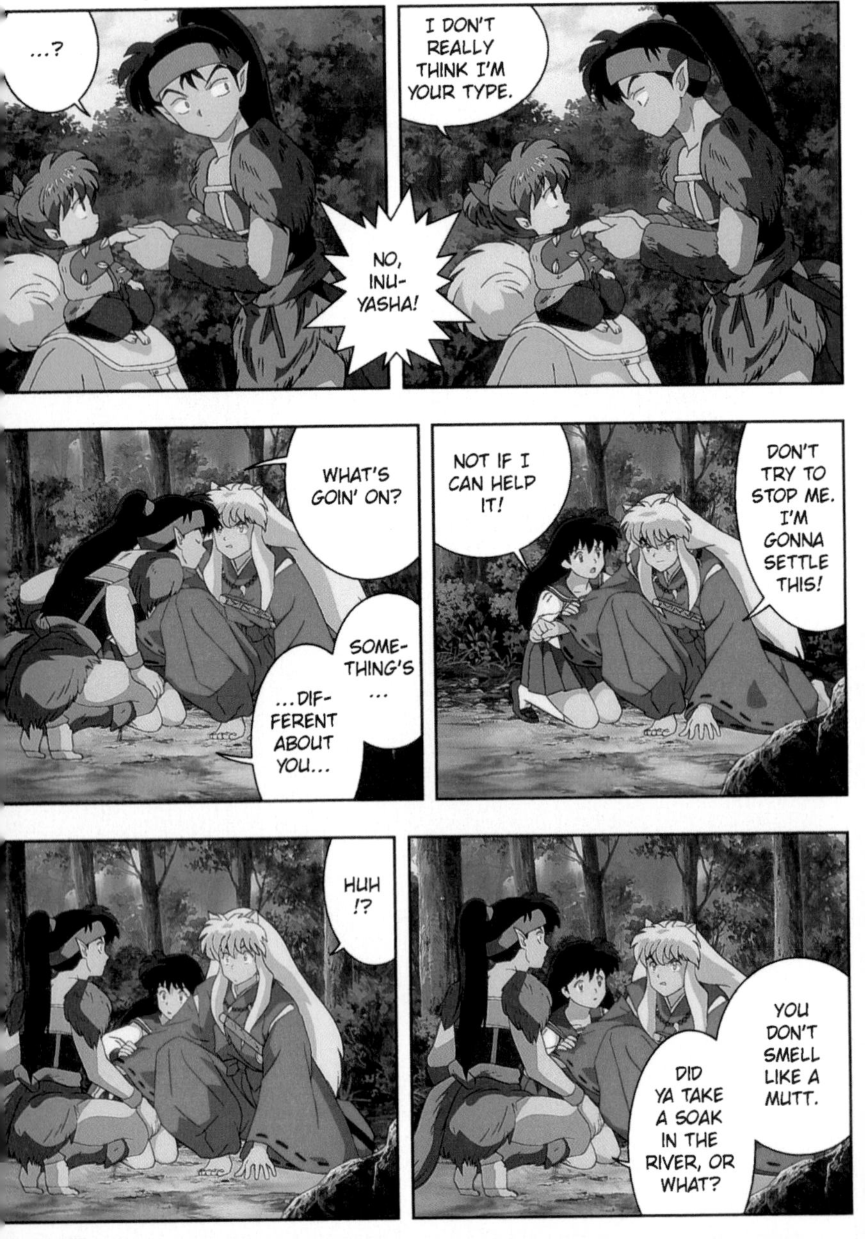
I DON'T REALLY THINK I'M YOUR TYPE.
NO, INU-YASHA!
...?
DON'T TRY TO STOP ME. I'M GONNA SETTLE THIS!
NOT IF I CAN HELP IT!
WHAT'S GOIN' ON?
SOME-THING'S ...
...DIF-FERENT ABOUT YOU...
YOU DON'T SMELL LIKE A MUTT.
DID YA TAKE A SOAK IN THE RIVER, OR WHAT?
HUH !?

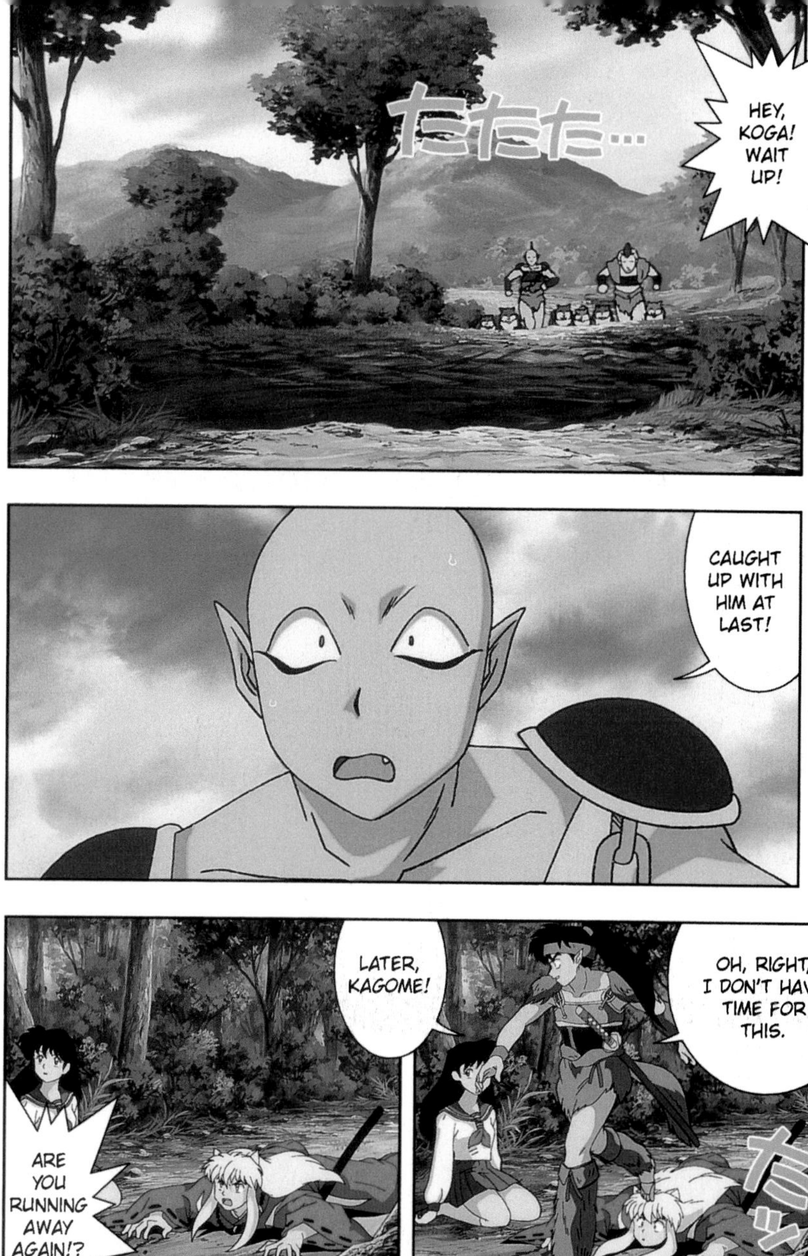

たたた…
HEY, KOGA! WAIT UP!
CAUGHT UP WITH HIM AT LAST!
OH, RIGHT, I DON'T HAVE TIME FOR THIS.
LATER, KAGOME!
ダッ
ARE YOU RUNNING AWAY AGAIN!?

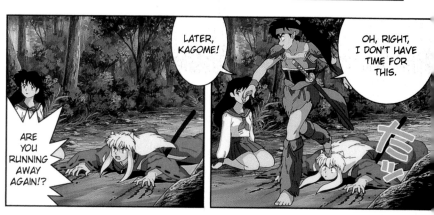

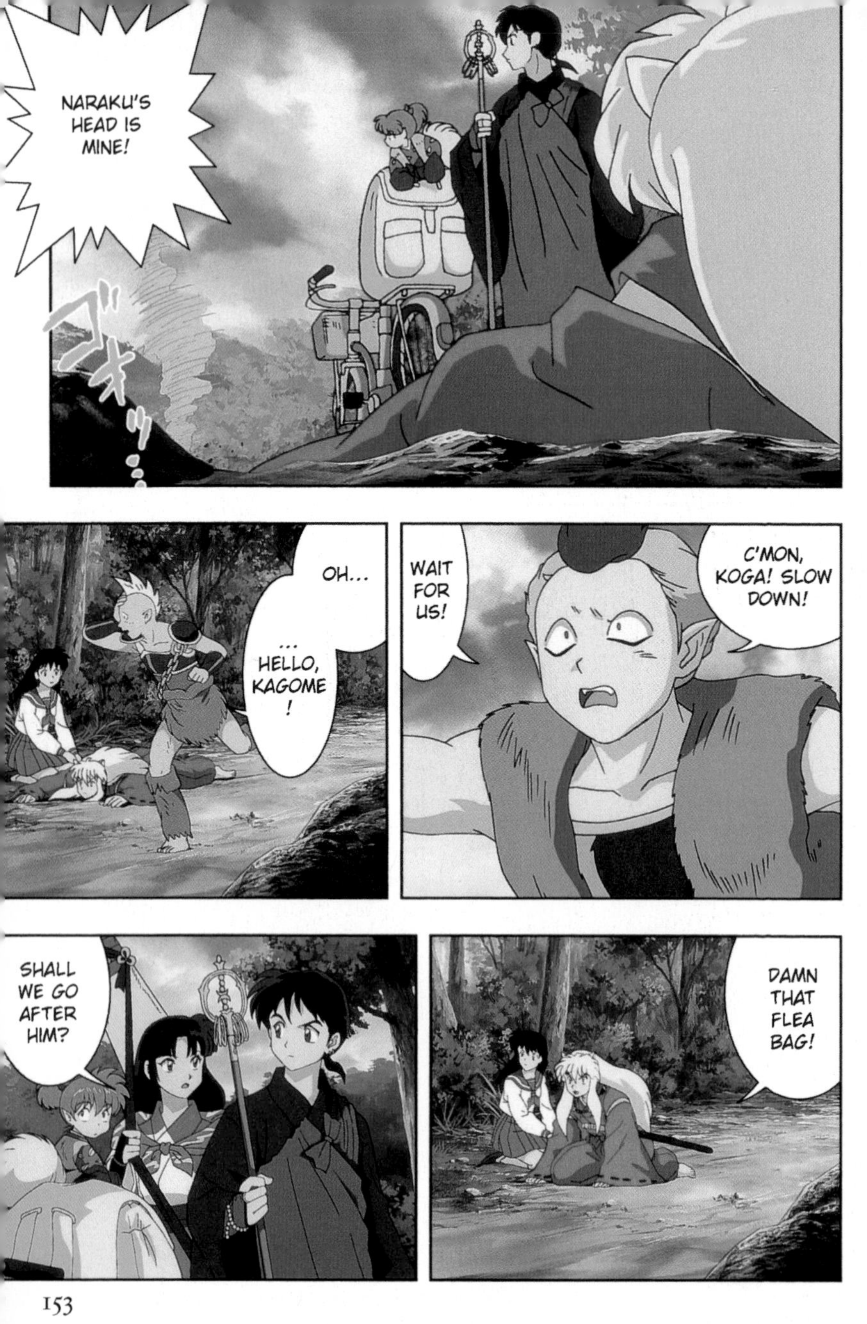
NARAKU'S HEAD IS MINE!
ゴォッ...
C'MON, KOGA! SLOW DOWN!
WAIT FOR US!
OH...
...HELLO, KAGOME!
DAMN THAT FLEA BAG!
SHALL WE GO AFTER HIM?

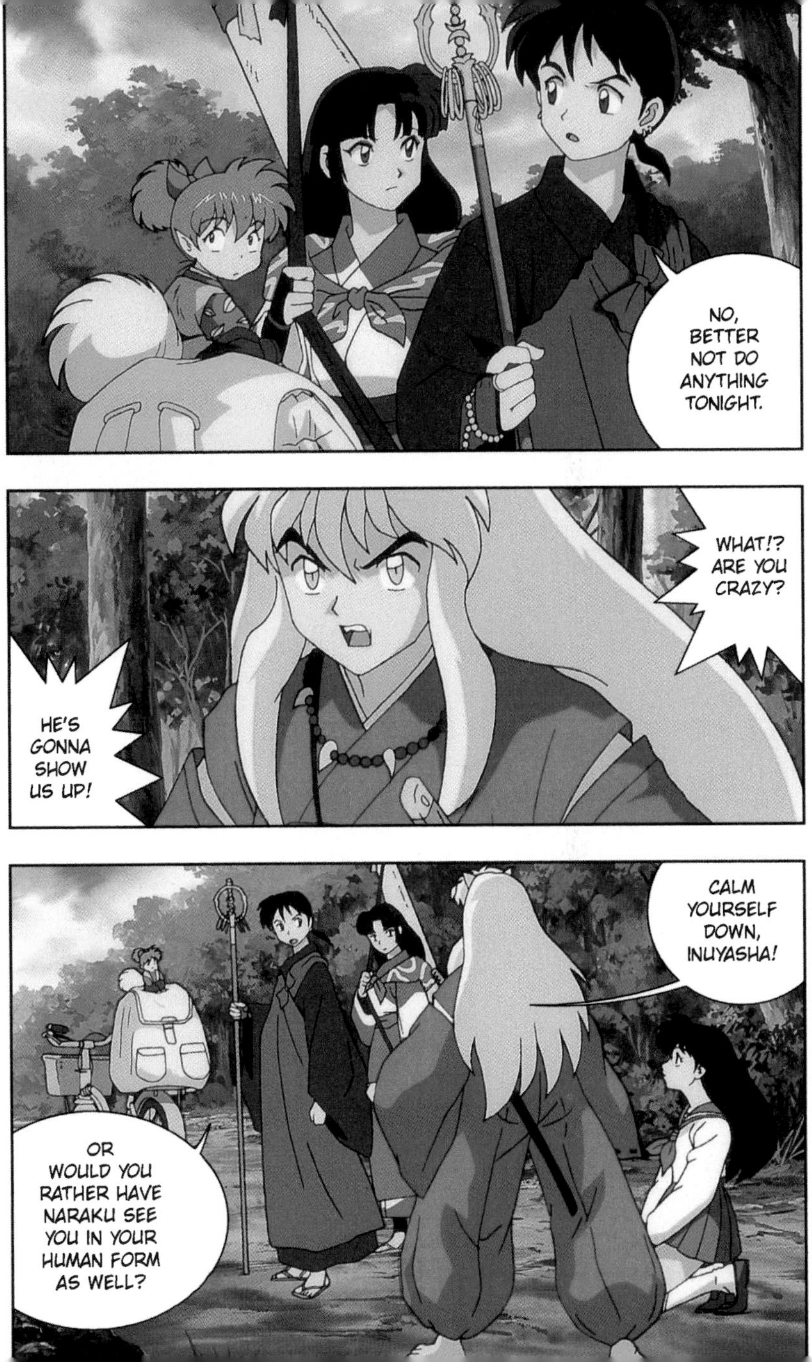
NO, BETTER NOT DO ANYTHING TONIGHT.
WHAT!? ARE YOU CRAZY?
HE'S GONNA SHOW US UP!
CALM YOURSELF DOWN, INUYASHA!
OR WOULD YOU RATHER HAVE NARAKU SEE YOU IN YOUR HUMAN FORM AS WELL?

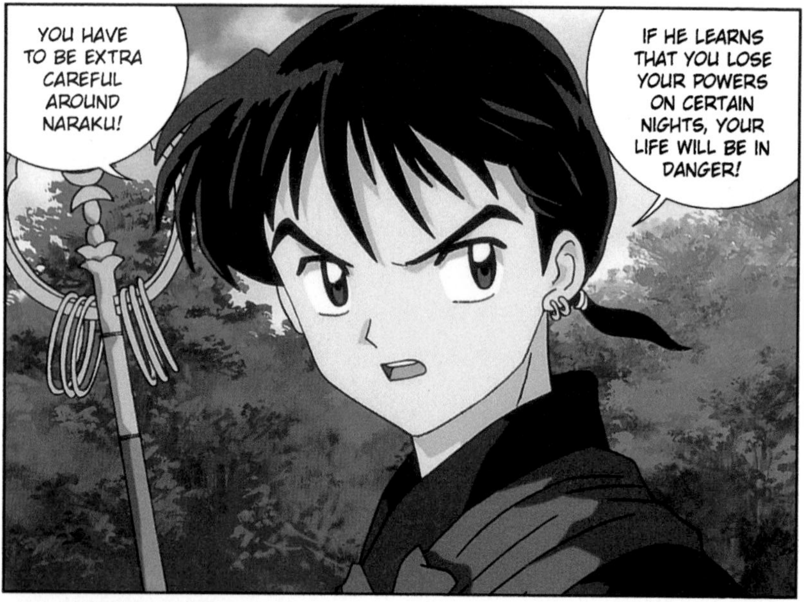
IF HE LEARNS THAT YOU LOSE YOUR POWERS ON CERTAIN NIGHTS, YOUR LIFE WILL BE IN DANGER!
YOU HAVE TO BE EXTRA CAREFUL AROUND NARAKU!

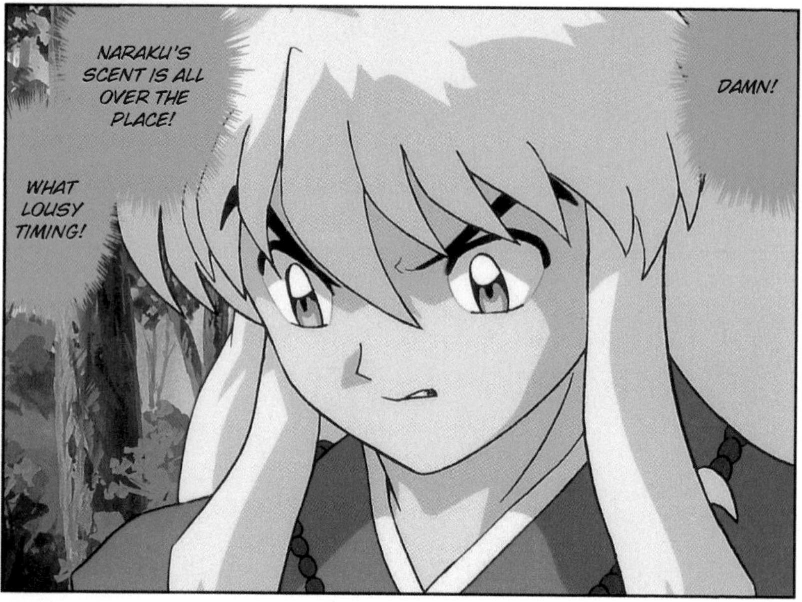
DAMN!
NARAKU'S SCENT IS ALL OVER THE PLACE!
WHAT LOUSY TIMING!

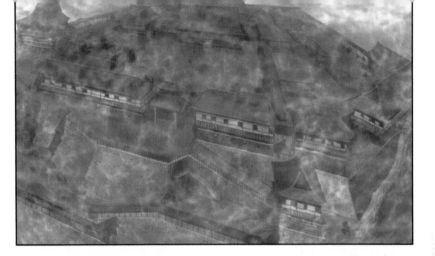

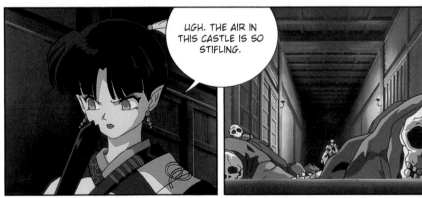

UGH. THE AIR IN THIS CASTLE IS SO STIFLING.

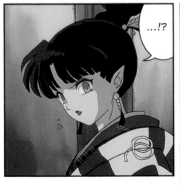

...!?

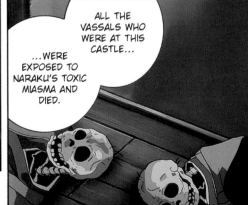

ALL THE VASSALS WHO WERE AT THIS CASTLE...

...WERE EXPOSED TO NARAKU'S TOXIC MIASMA AND DIED.

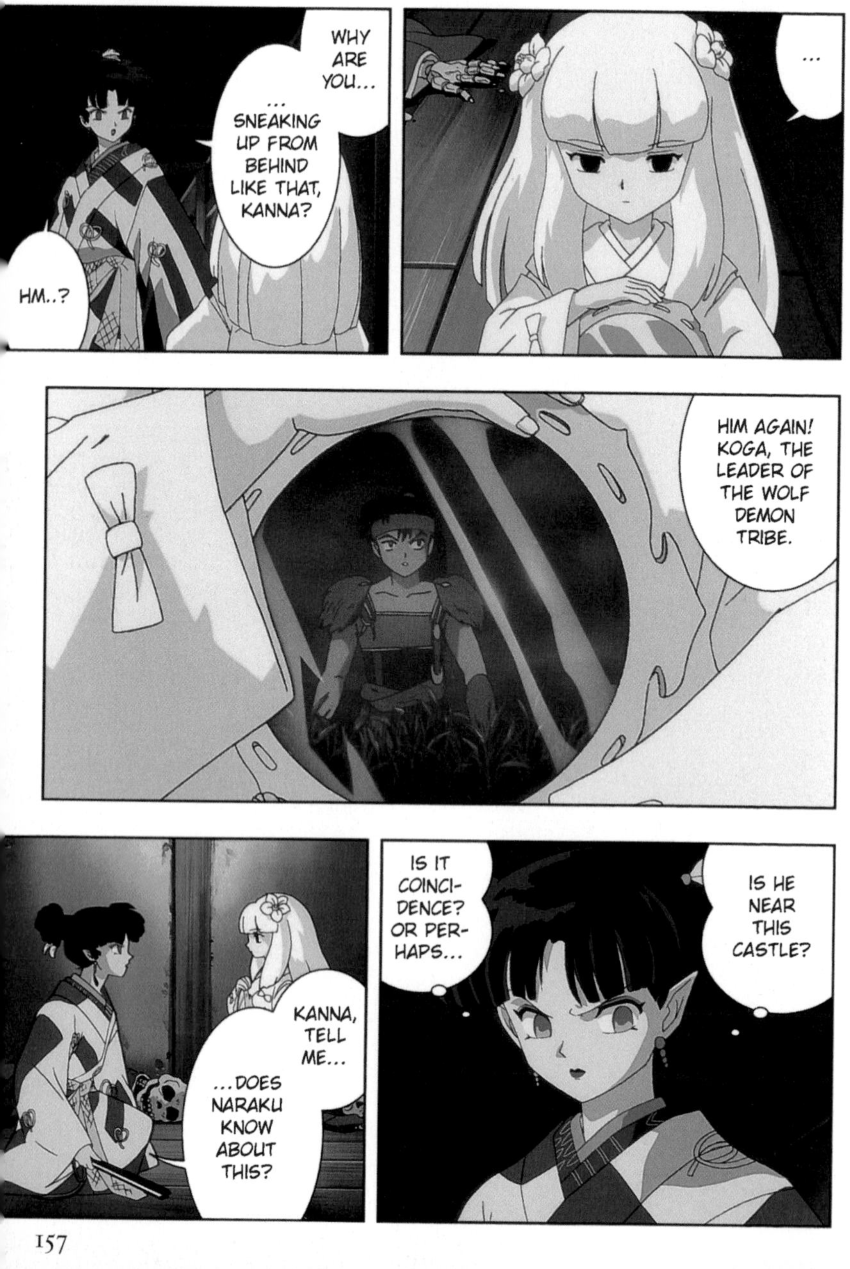
...
WHY ARE YOU...
...SNEAKING UP FROM BEHIND LIKE THAT, KANNA?
HM..?
HIM AGAIN! KOGA, THE LEADER OF THE WOLF DEMON TRIBE.
IS HE NEAR THIS CASTLE?
IS IT COINCIDENCE? OR PERHAPS...
KANNA, TELL ME...
...DOES NARAKU KNOW ABOUT THIS?

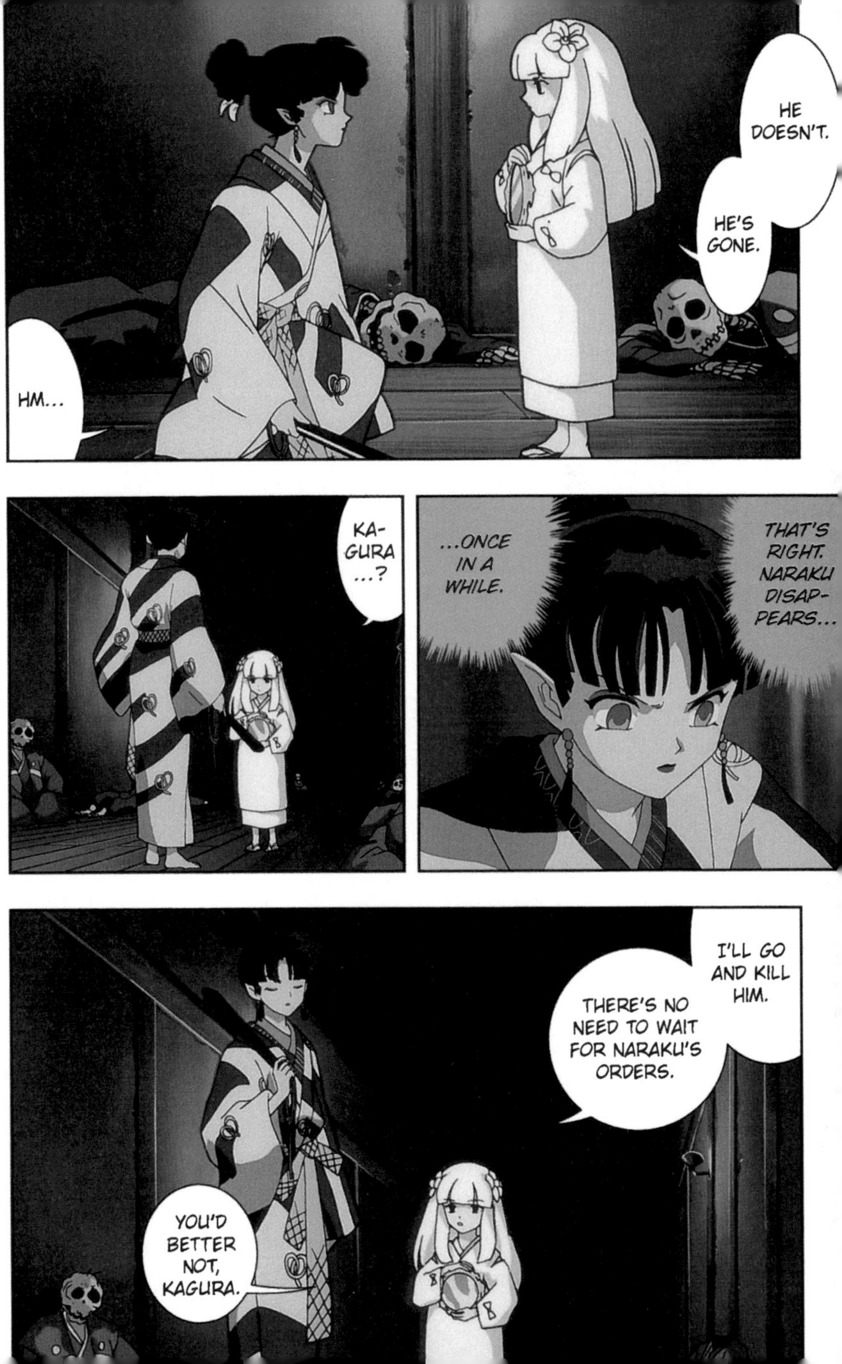
HE DOESN'T.
HE'S GONE.
HM...
THAT'S RIGHT. NARAKU DISAPPEARS...
...ONCE IN A WHILE.
KAGURA...?
I'LL GO AND KILL HIM.
THERE'S NO NEED TO WAIT FOR NARAKU'S ORDERS.
YOU'D BETTER NOT, KAGURA.

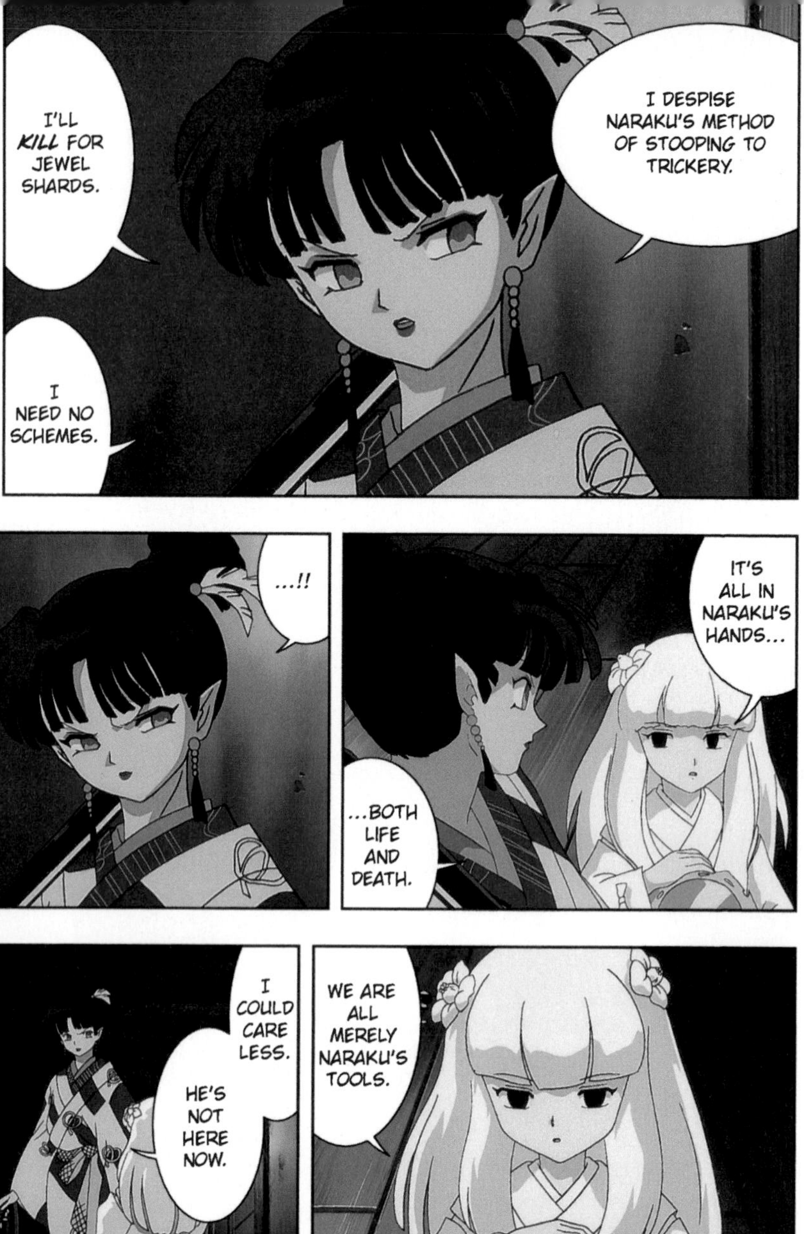
I DESPISE NARAKU'S METHOD OF STOOPING TO TRICKERY.
I'LL *KILL* FOR JEWEL SHARDS.
I NEED NO SCHEMES.
IT'S ALL IN NARAKU'S HANDS...
...BOTH LIFE AND DEATH.
...!!
WE ARE ALL MERELY NARAKU'S TOOLS.
I COULD CARE LESS.
HE'S NOT HERE NOW.

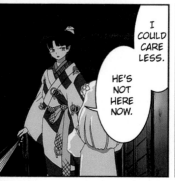

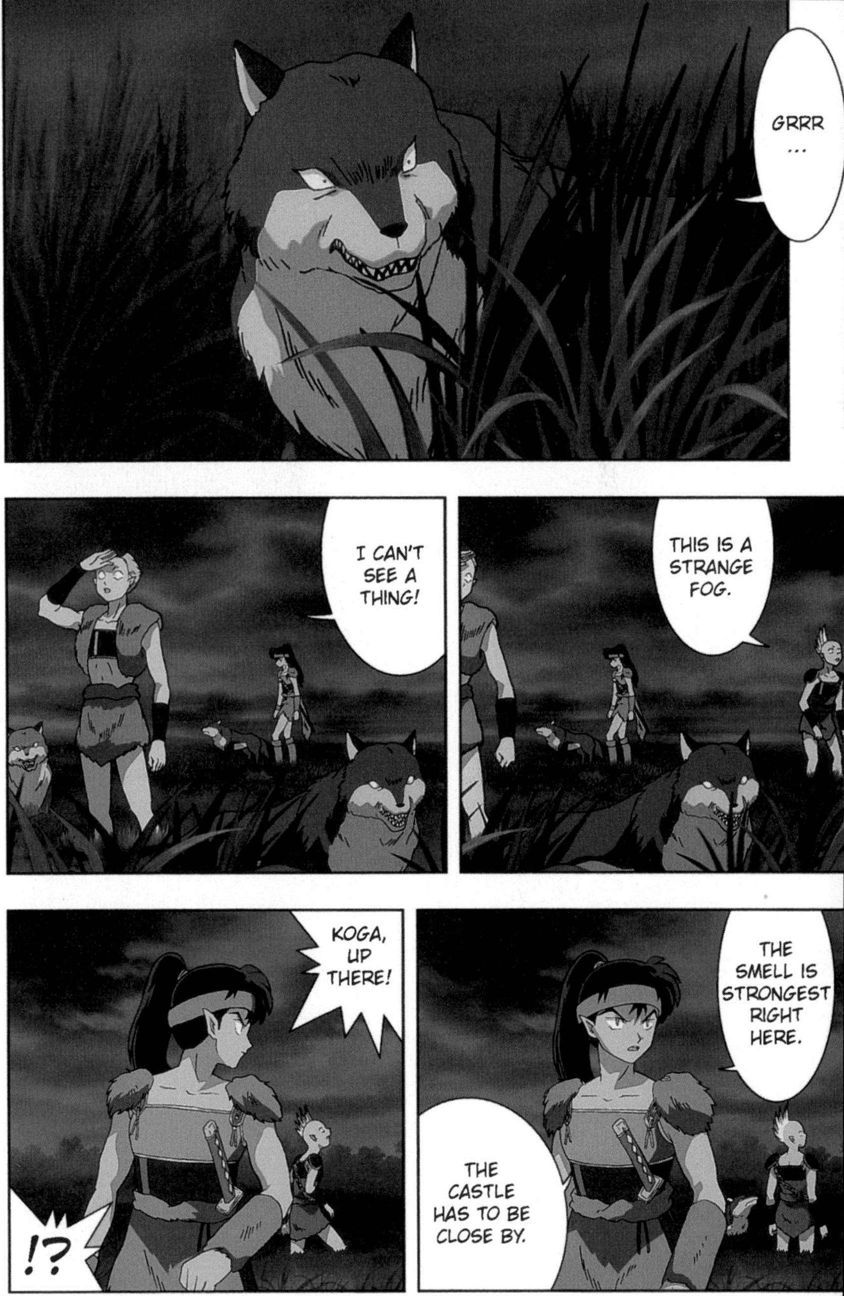
GRRR ...
THIS IS A STRANGE FOG.
I CAN'T SEE A THING!
THE SMELL IS STRONGEST RIGHT HERE.
THE CASTLE HAS TO BE CLOSE BY.
KOGA, UP THERE!
!?

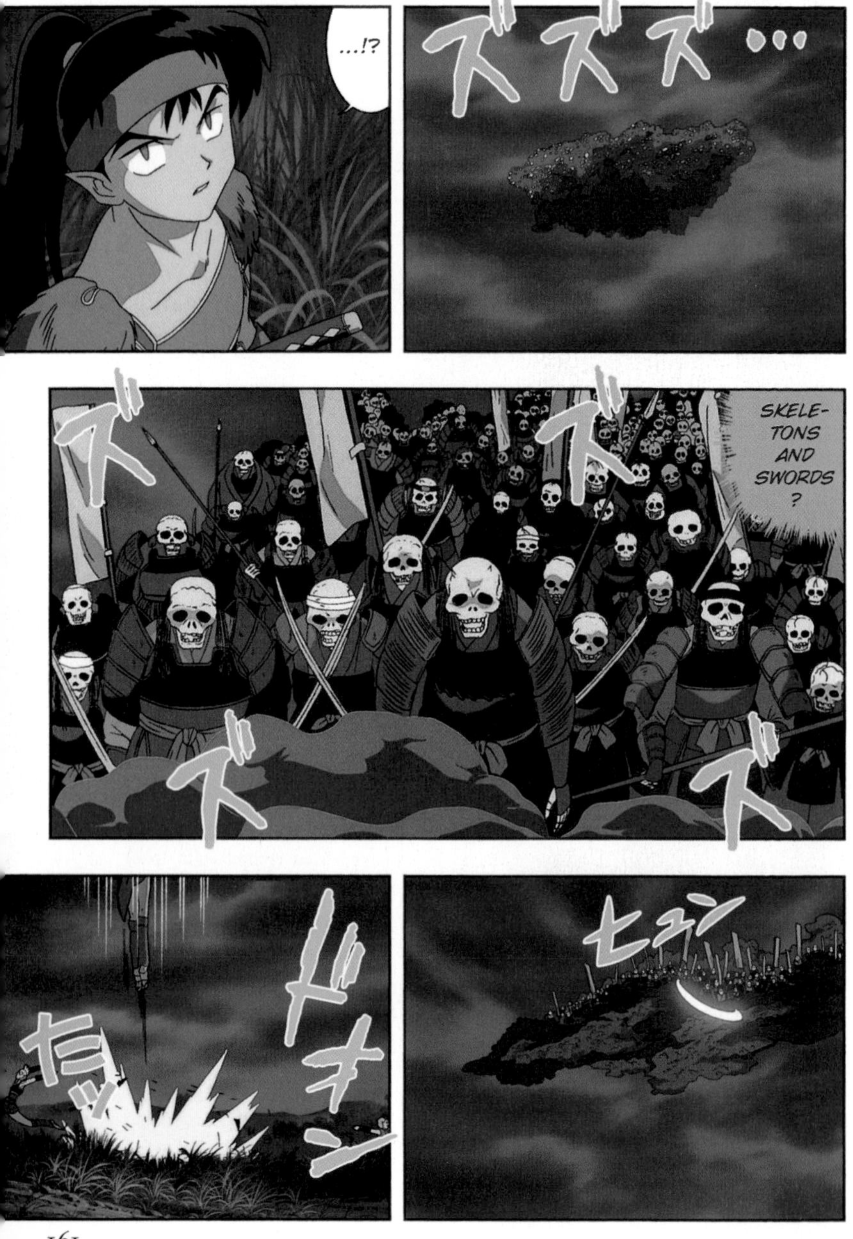
ズズズ…
...!?
ズ
ズ
SKELE-
TONS
AND
SWORDS
?
ズ
ズ
ヒュン
ドォン
たッ

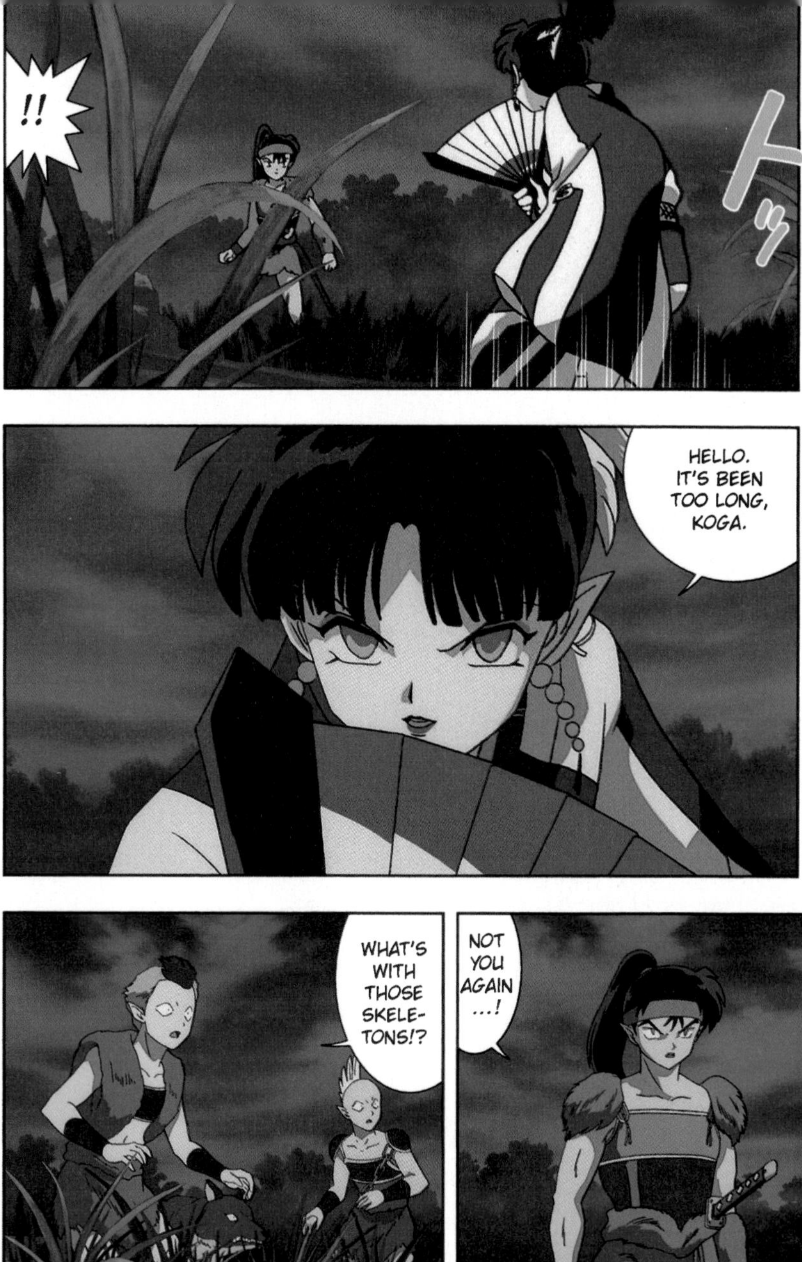
トッ
!!
HELLO. IT'S BEEN TOO LONG, KOGA.
NOT YOU AGAIN ...!
WHAT'S WITH THOSE SKELE-TONS!?

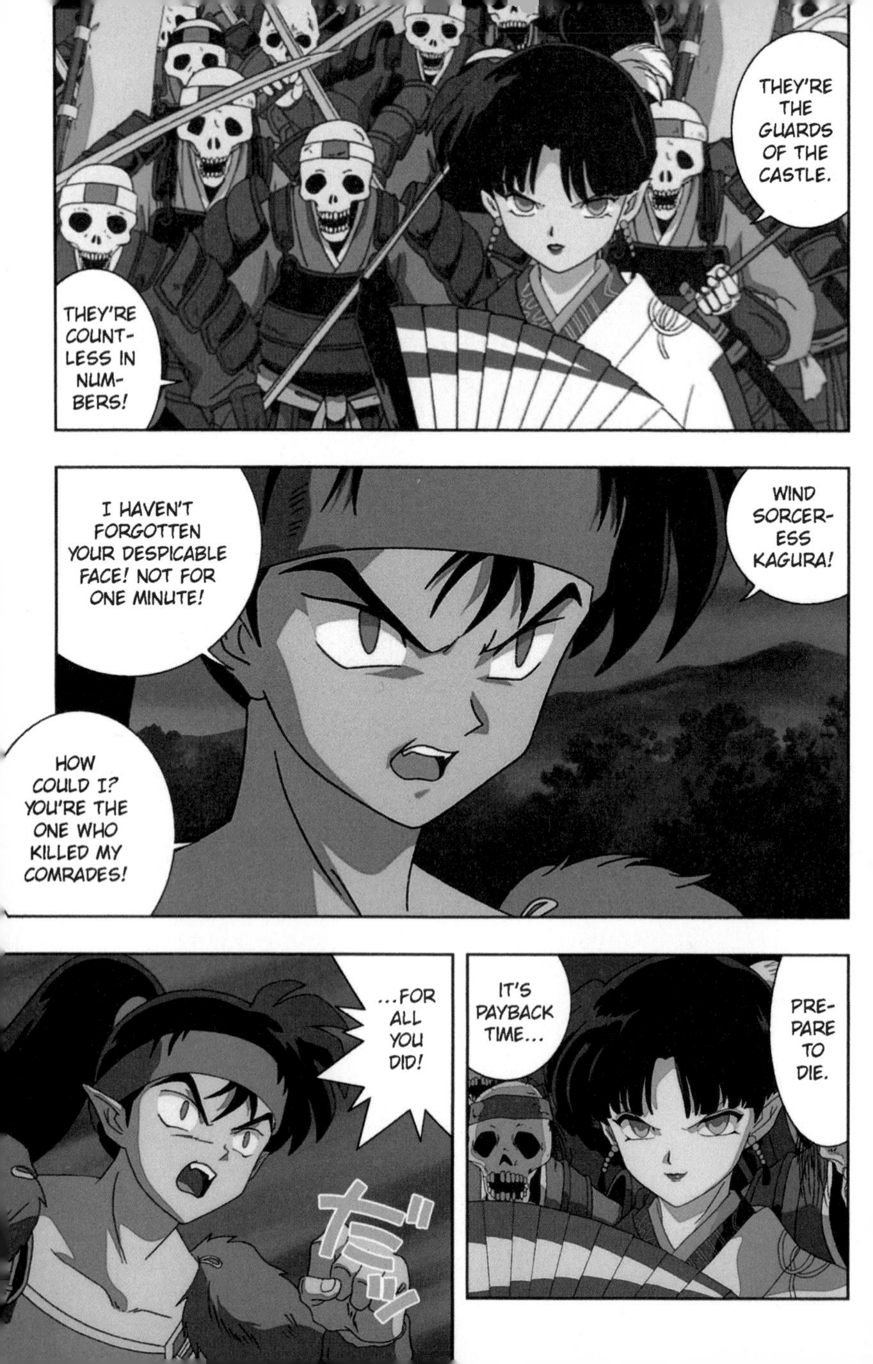
THEY'RE THE GUARDS OF THE CASTLE.
THEY'RE COUNTLESS IN NUMBERS!
WIND SORCERESS KAGURA!
I HAVEN'T FORGOTTEN YOUR DESPICABLE FACE! NOT FOR ONE MINUTE!
HOW COULD I? YOU'RE THE ONE WHO KILLED MY COMRADES!
PREPARE TO DIE.
IT'S PAYBACK TIME...
...FOR ALL YOU DID!

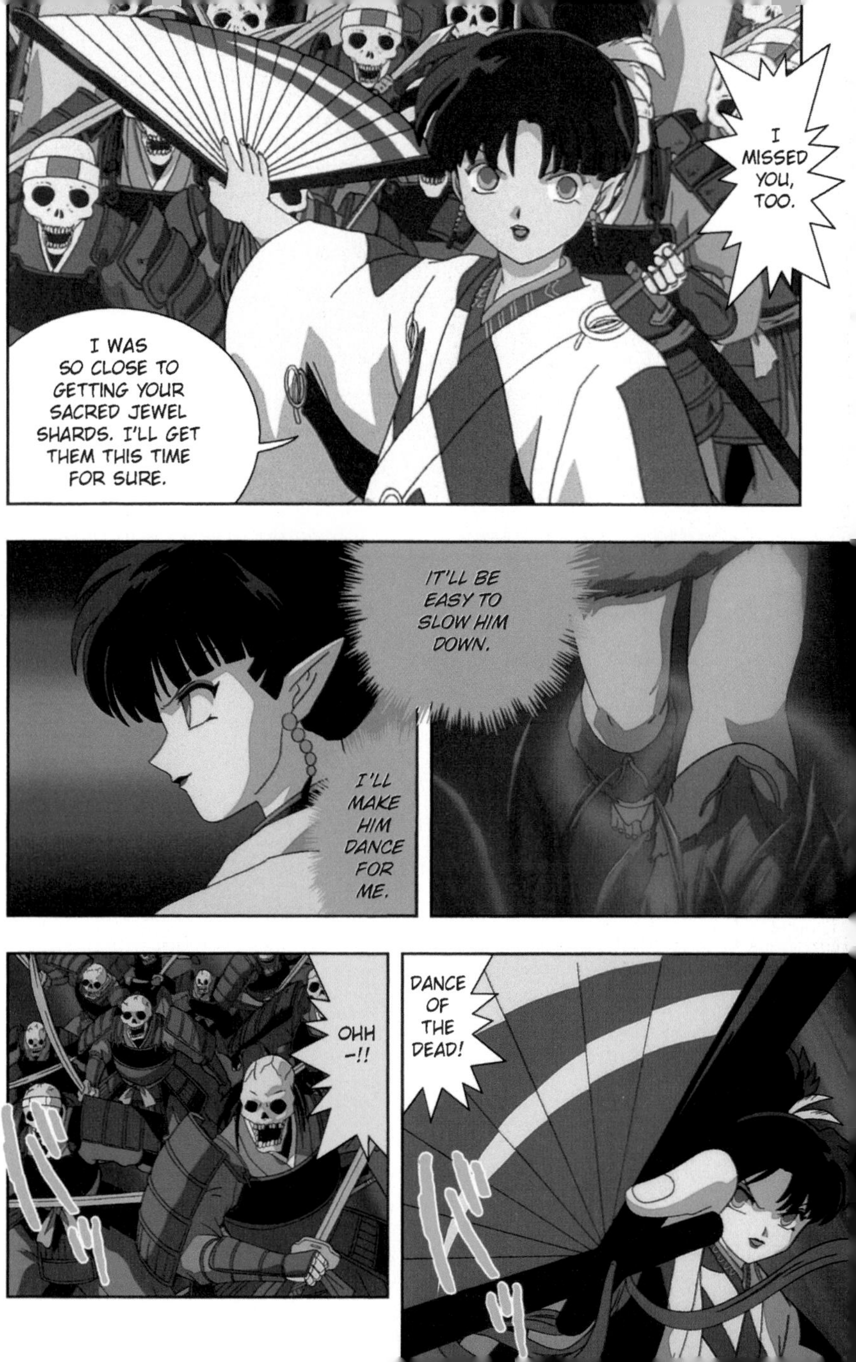
I MISSED YOU, TOO.
I WAS SO CLOSE TO GETTING YOUR SACRED JEWEL SHARDS. I'LL GET THEM THIS TIME FOR SURE.
IT'LL BE EASY TO SLOW HIM DOWN.
I'LL MAKE HIM DANCE FOR ME.
DANCE OF THE DEAD!
OHH-!!

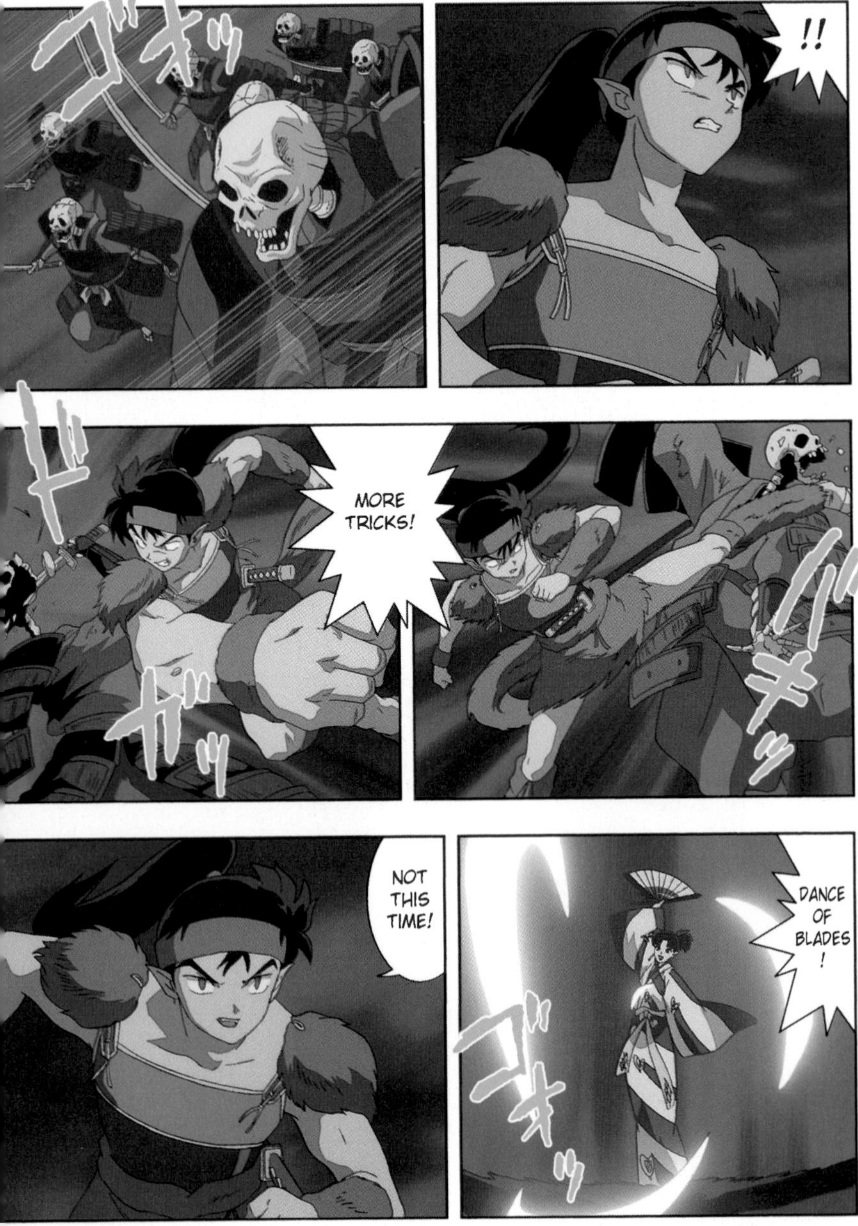
!!
MORE TRICKS!
DANCE OF BLADES!
NOT THIS TIME!

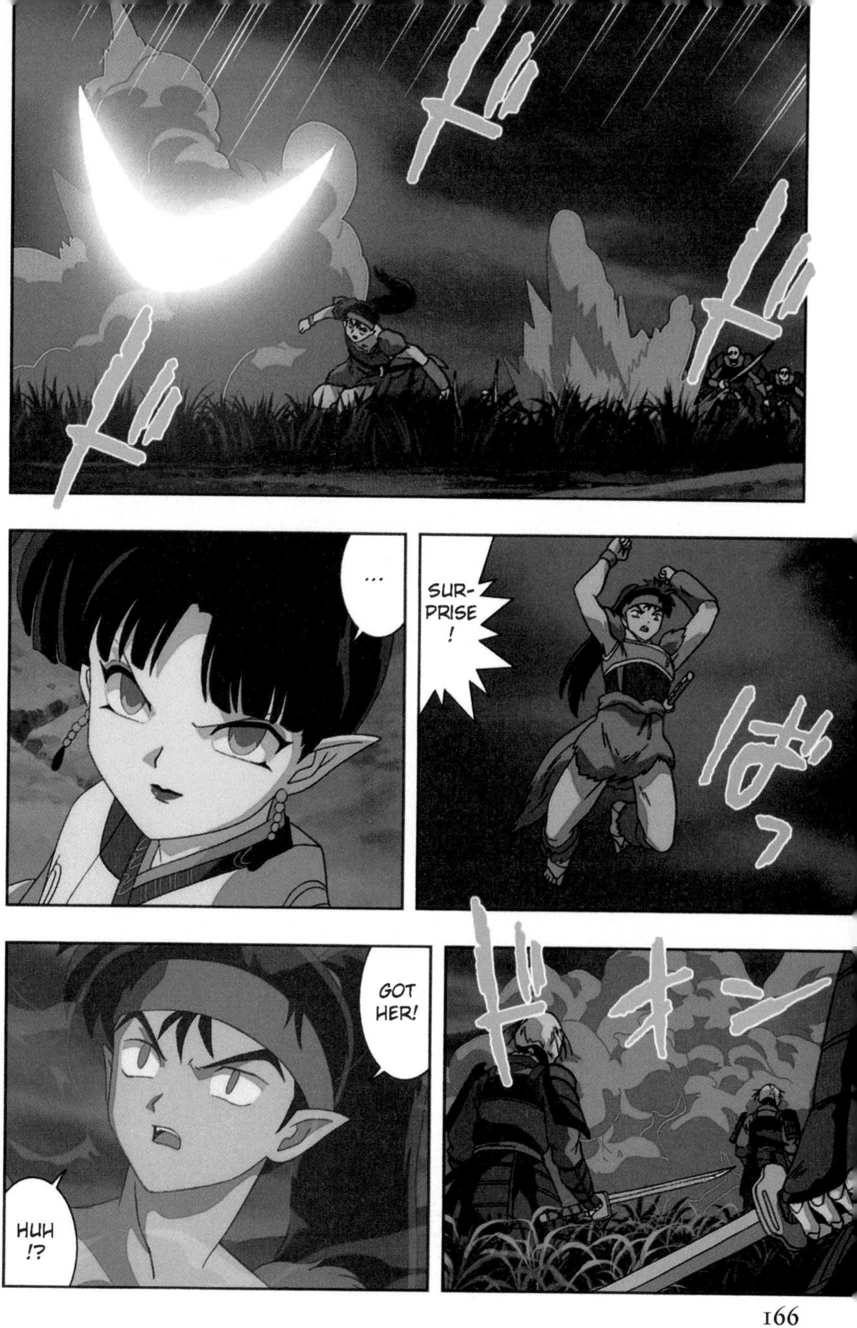
ドドドド
SUR-PRISE!
ばっ
...
ドオン
GOT HER!
HUH!?

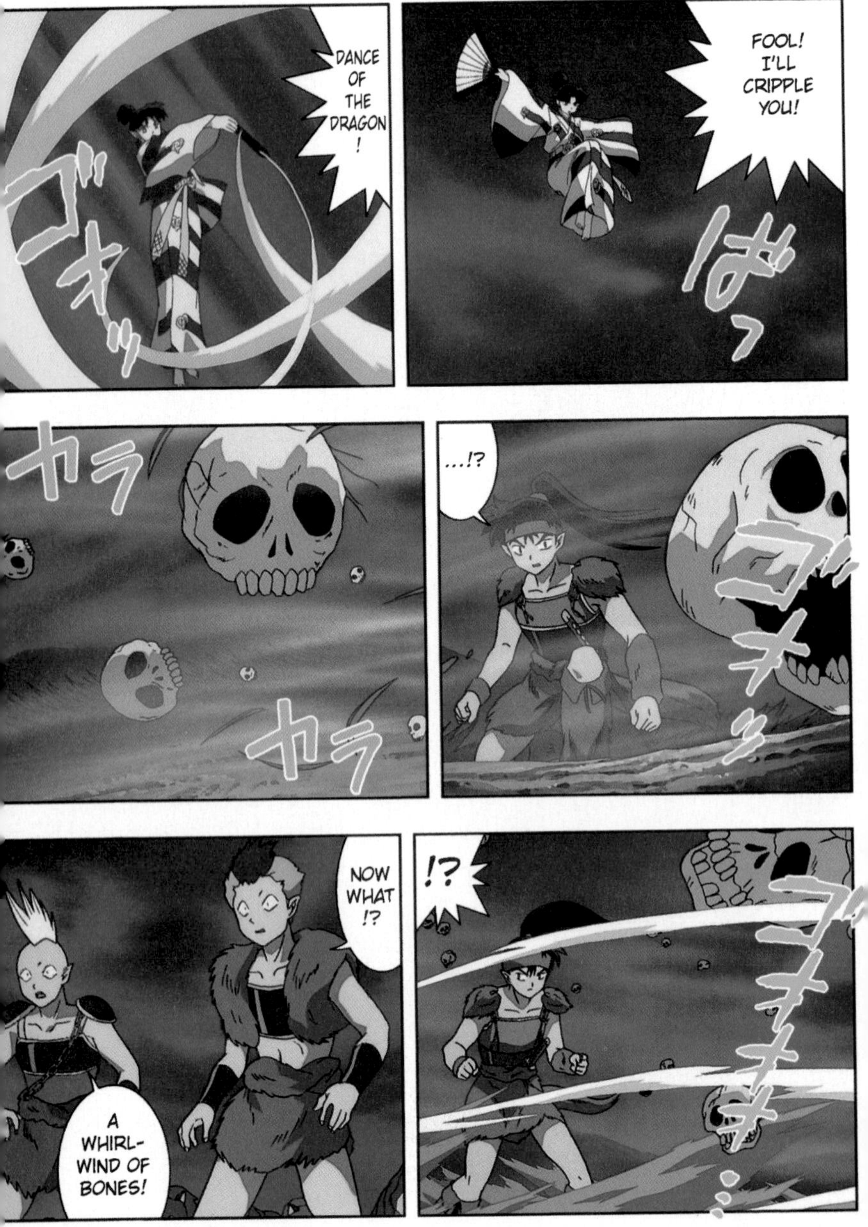
FOOL! I'LL CRIPPLE YOU!
DANCE OF THE DRAGON!
...!?
!?
NOW WHAT!?
A WHIRL-WIND OF BONES!

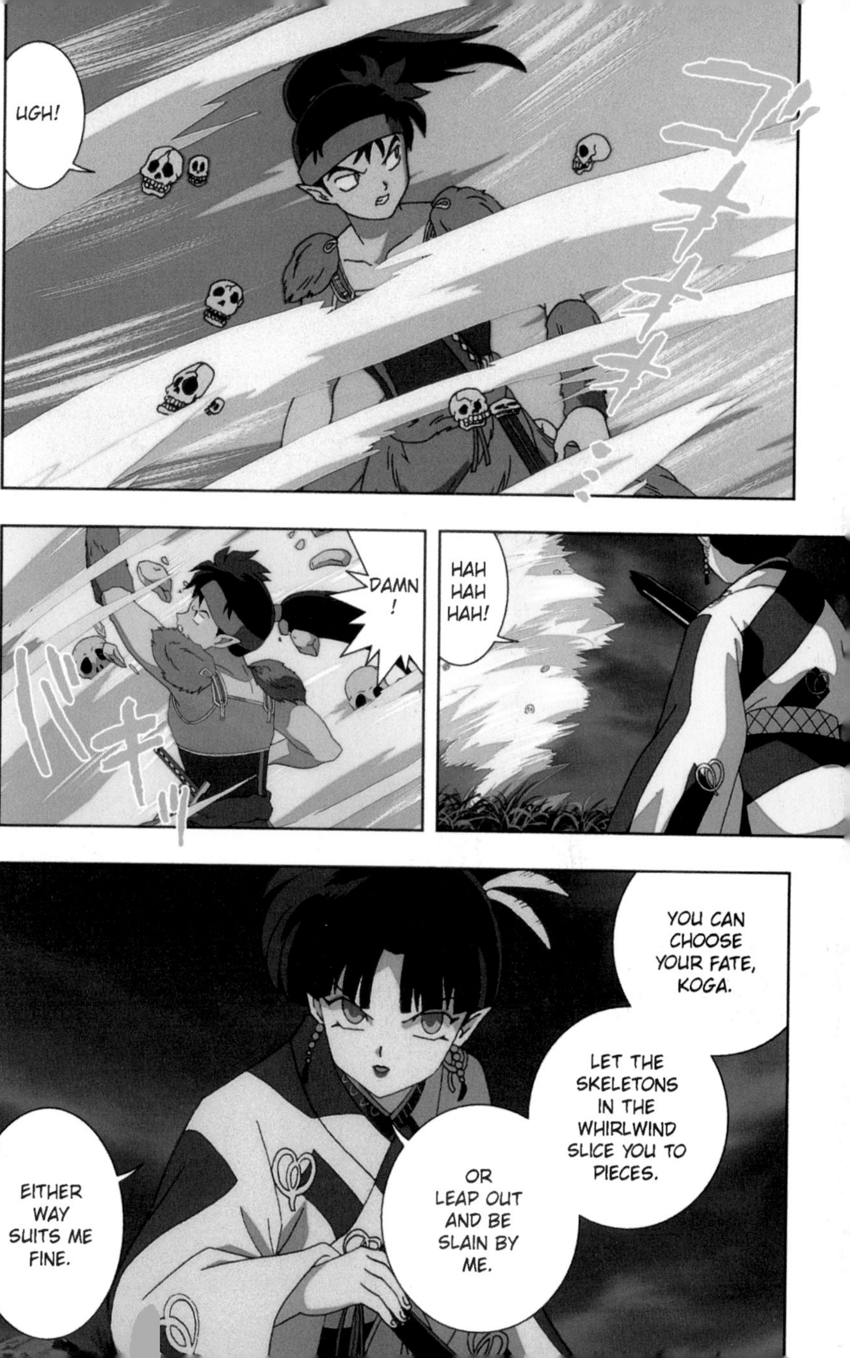
UGH!
HAH HAH HAH!
DAMN!
YOU CAN CHOOSE YOUR FATE, KOGA.
LET THE SKELETONS IN THE WHIRLWIND SLICE YOU TO PIECES.
OR LEAP OUT AND BE SLAIN BY ME.
EITHER WAY SUITS ME FINE.

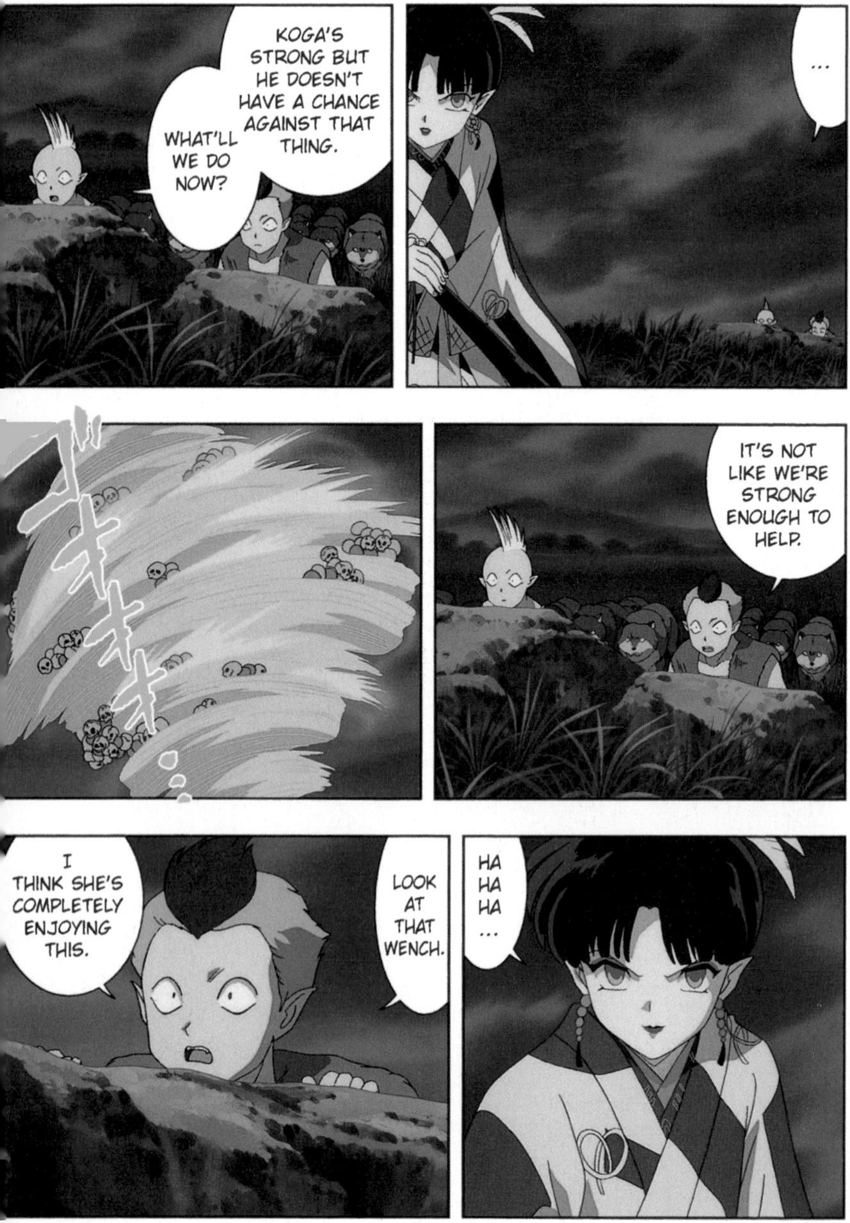
...
KOGA'S STRONG BUT HE DOESN'T HAVE A CHANCE AGAINST THAT THING.
WHAT'LL WE DO NOW?
IT'S NOT LIKE WE'RE STRONG ENOUGH TO HELP.
ゴォォォォ
HA HA HA ...
LOOK AT THAT WENCH.
I THINK SHE'S COMPLETELY ENJOYING THIS.

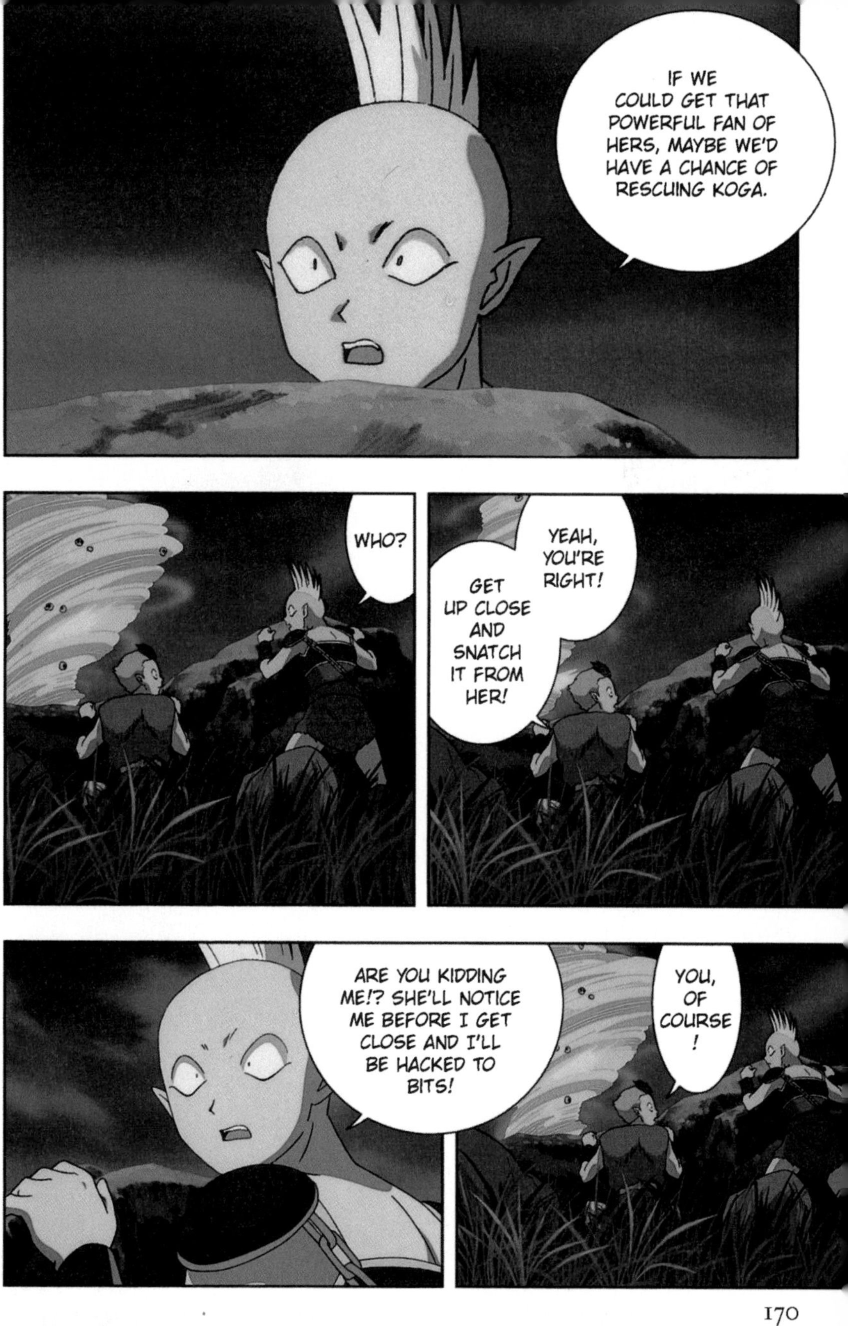
IF WE COULD GET THAT POWERFUL FAN OF HERS, MAYBE WE'D HAVE A CHANCE OF RESCUING KOGA.
YEAH, YOU'RE RIGHT!
GET UP CLOSE AND SNATCH IT FROM HER!
WHO?
YOU, OF COURSE!
ARE YOU KIDDING ME!? SHE'LL NOTICE ME BEFORE I GET CLOSE AND I'LL BE HACKED TO BITS!

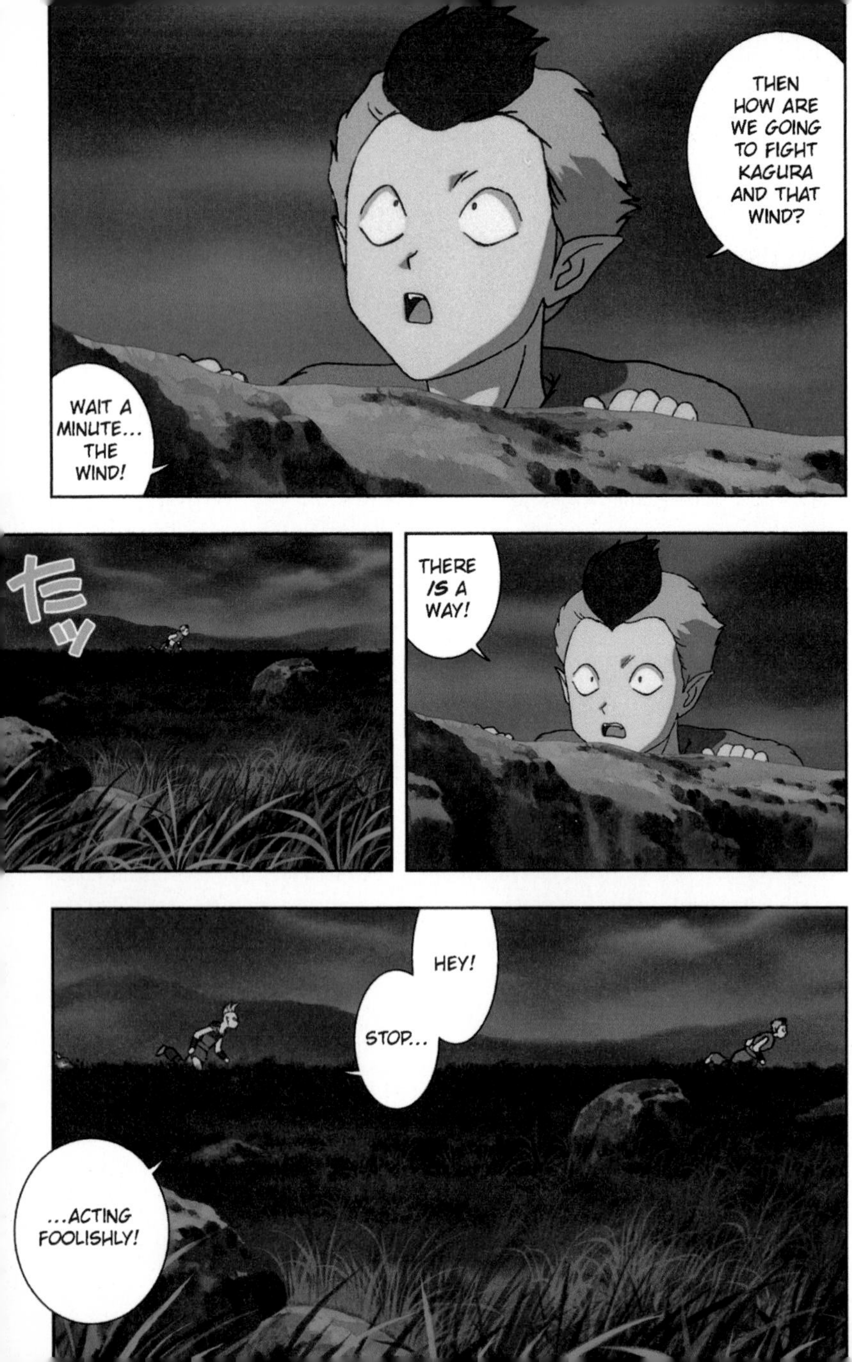
THEN HOW ARE WE GOING TO FIGHT KAGURA AND THAT WIND?
WAIT A MINUTE... THE WIND!
THERE *IS* A WAY!
タッ
HEY!
STOP...
...ACTING FOOLISHLY!

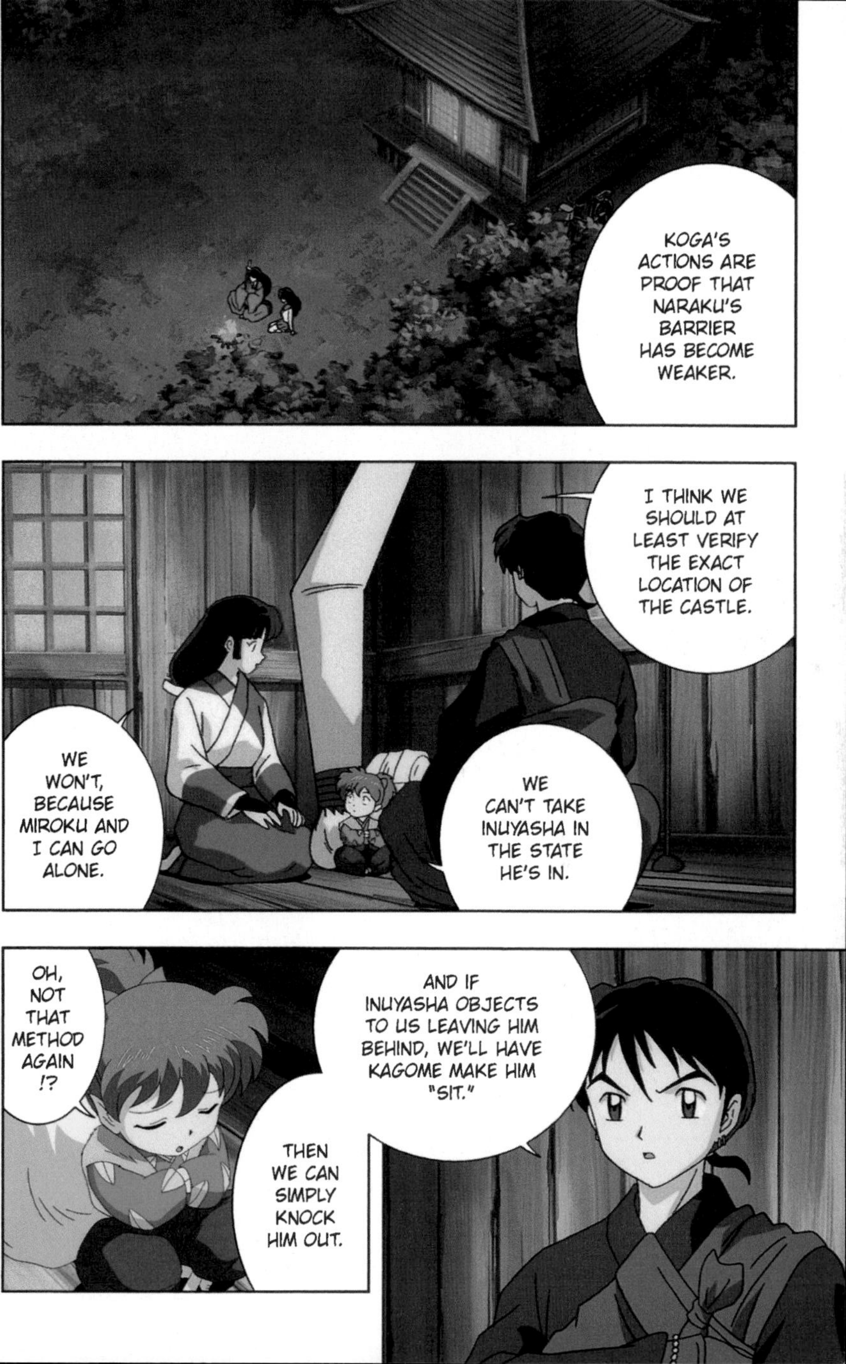
KOGA'S ACTIONS ARE PROOF THAT NARAKU'S BARRIER HAS BECOME WEAKER.
I THINK WE SHOULD AT LEAST VERIFY THE EXACT LOCATION OF THE CASTLE.
WE CAN'T TAKE INUYASHA IN THE STATE HE'S IN.
WE WON'T, BECAUSE MIROKU AND I CAN GO ALONE.
AND IF INUYASHA OBJECTS TO US LEAVING HIM BEHIND, WE'LL HAVE KAGOME MAKE HIM "SIT."
THEN WE CAN SIMPLY KNOCK HIM OUT.
OH, NOT THAT METHOD AGAIN !?

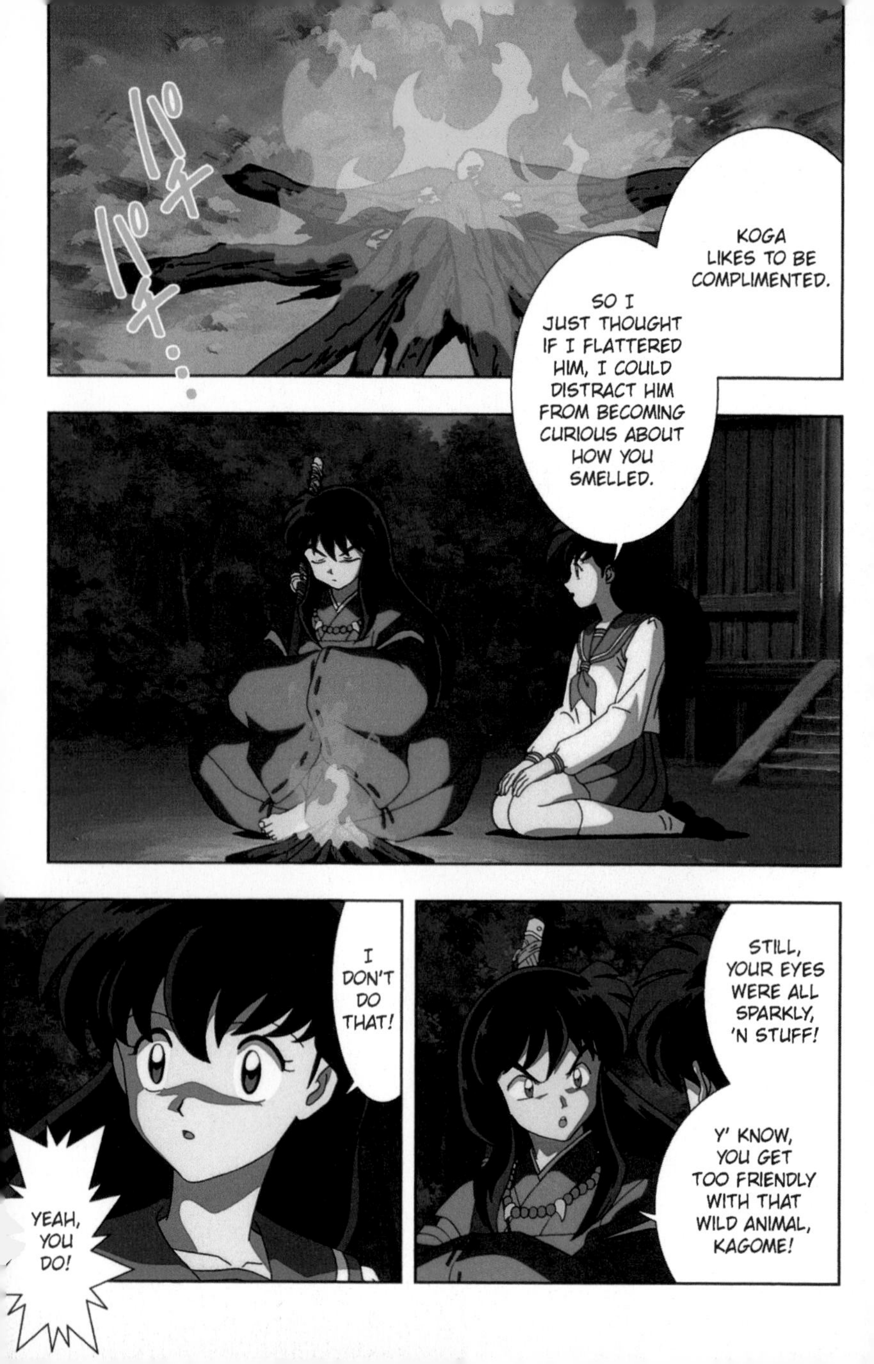
パチパチ…
KOGA LIKES TO BE COMPLIMENTED.
SO I JUST THOUGHT IF I FLATTERED HIM, I COULD DISTRACT HIM FROM BECOMING CURIOUS ABOUT HOW YOU SMELLED.
STILL, YOUR EYES WERE ALL SPARKLY, 'N STUFF!
Y' KNOW, YOU GET TOO FRIENDLY WITH THAT WILD ANIMAL, KAGOME!
I DON'T DO THAT!
YEAH, YOU DO!

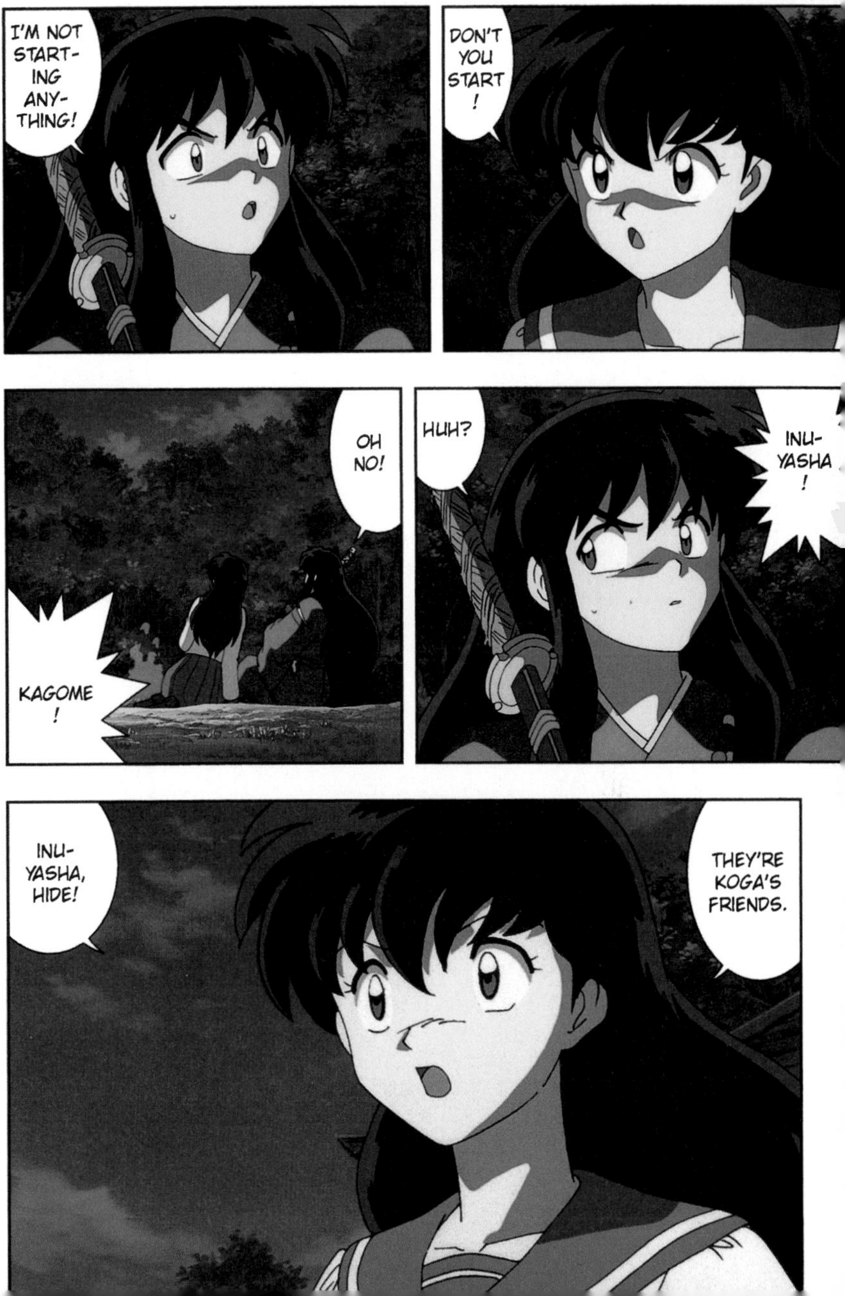
DON'T YOU START!
I'M NOT STARTING ANYTHING!
INU-YASHA!
HUH?
OH NO!
KAGOME!
THEY'RE KOGA'S FRIENDS.
INU-YASHA, HIDE!

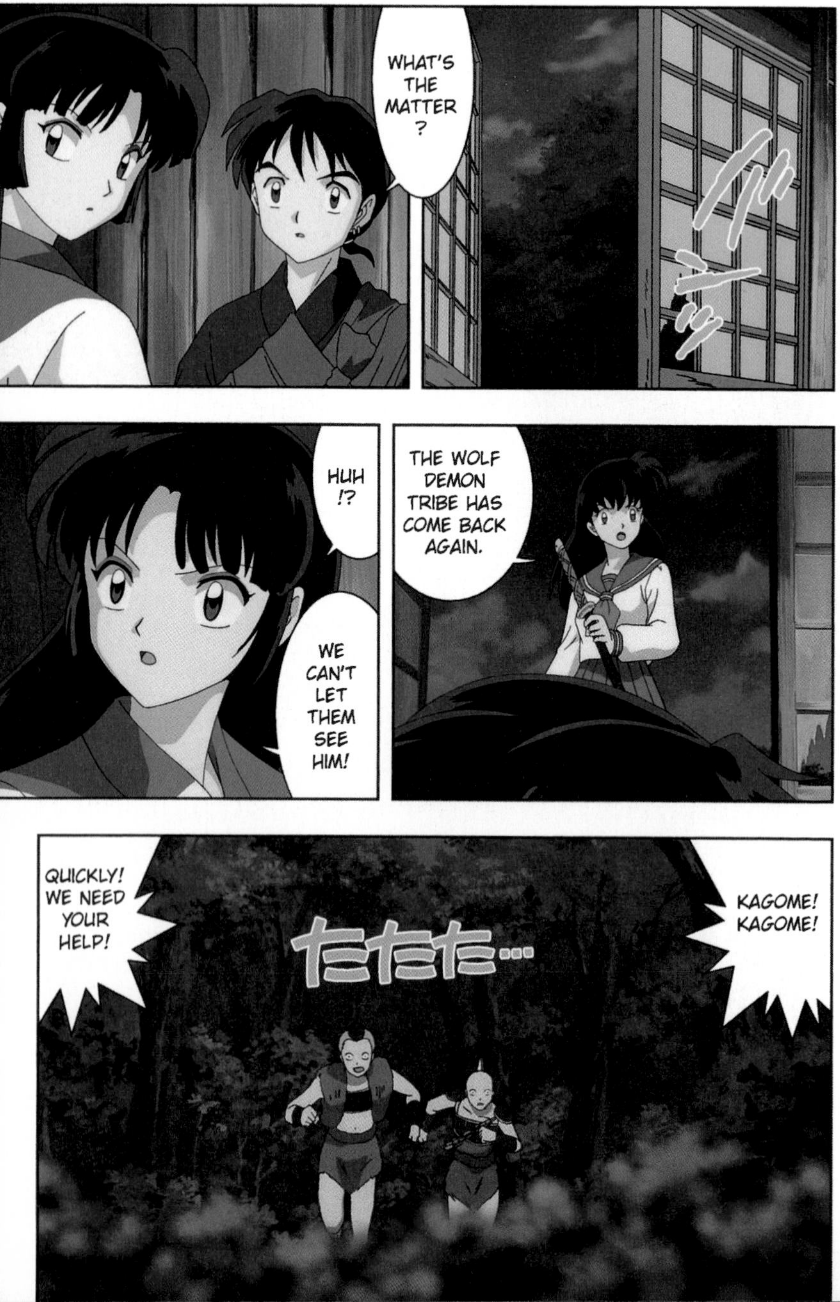
WHAT'S THE MATTER ?
THE WOLF DEMON TRIBE HAS COME BACK AGAIN.
HUH !?
WE CAN'T LET THEM SEE HIM!
KAGOME! KAGOME!
QUICKLY! WE NEED YOUR HELP!
たたた…

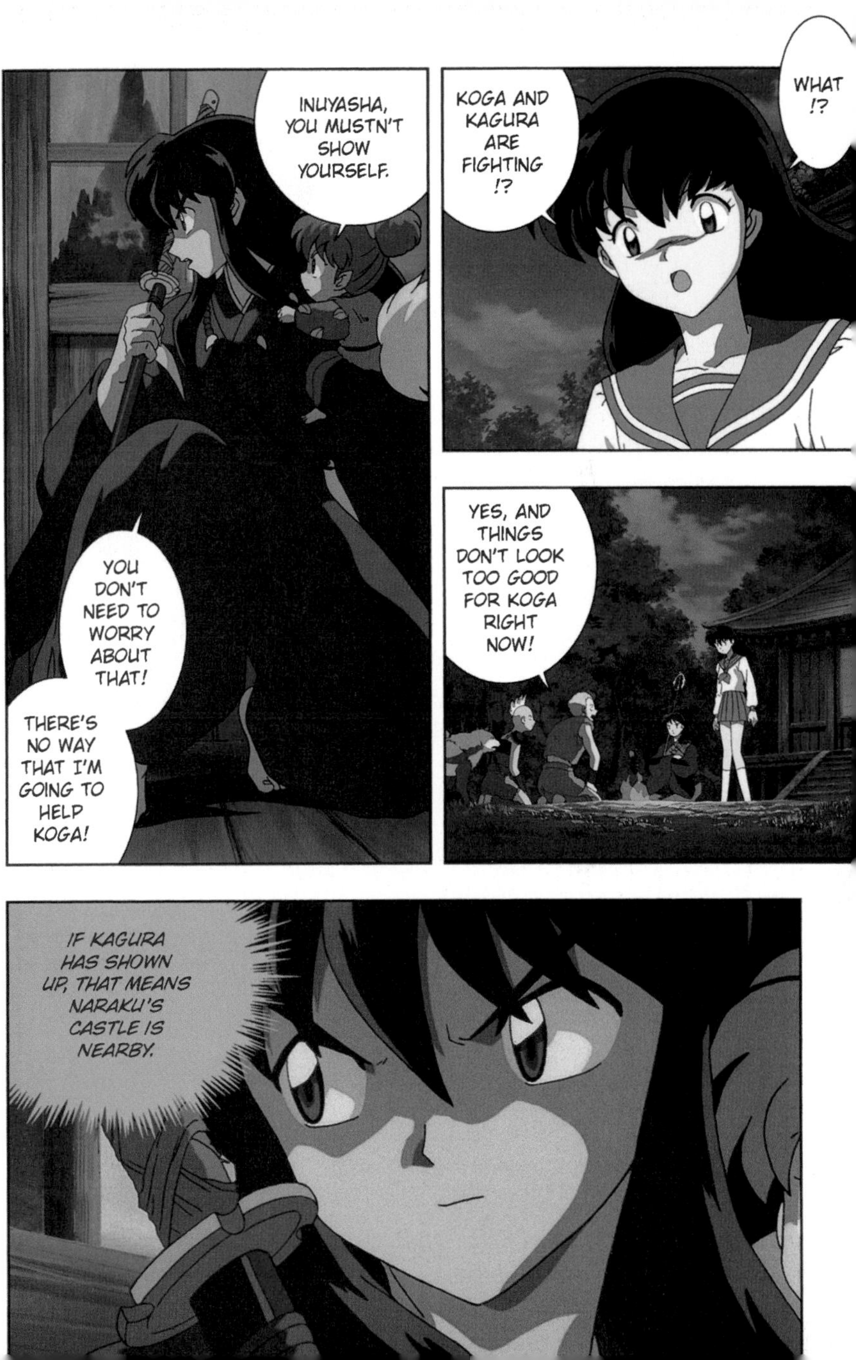
WHAT !?
KOGA AND KAGURA ARE FIGHTING !?
YES, AND THINGS DON'T LOOK TOO GOOD FOR KOGA RIGHT NOW!
INUYASHA, YOU MUSTN'T SHOW YOURSELF.
YOU DON'T NEED TO WORRY ABOUT THAT!
THERE'S NO WAY THAT I'M GOING TO HELP KOGA!
IF KAGURA HAS SHOWN UP, THAT MEANS NARAKU'S CASTLE IS NEARBY.

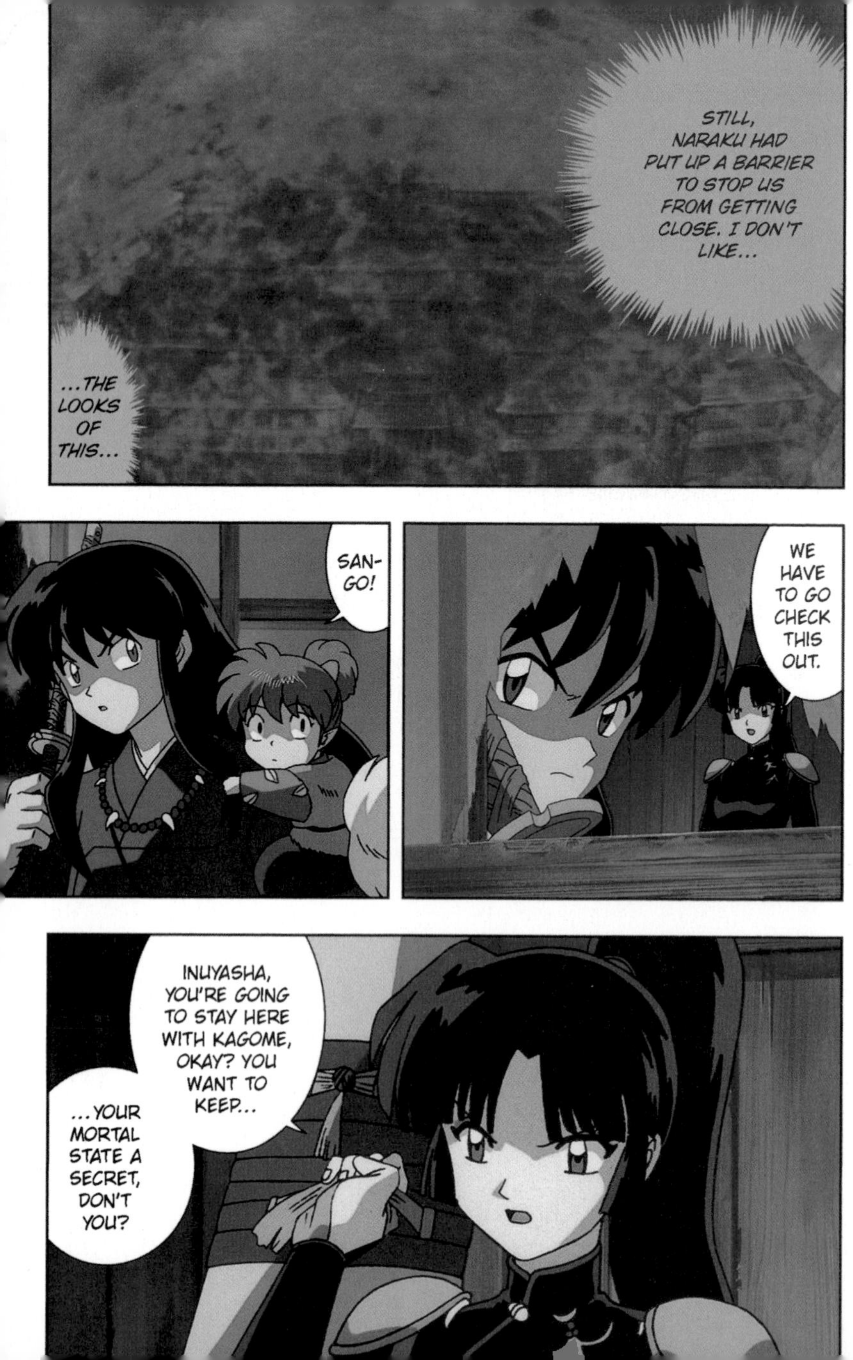
STILL, NARAKU HAD PUT UP A BARRIER TO STOP US FROM GETTING CLOSE. I DON'T LIKE...
...THE LOOKS OF THIS...
WE HAVE TO GO CHECK THIS OUT.
SAN-GO!
INUYASHA, YOU'RE GOING TO STAY HERE WITH KAGOME, OKAY? YOU WANT TO KEEP...
...YOUR MORTAL STATE A SECRET, DON'T YOU?

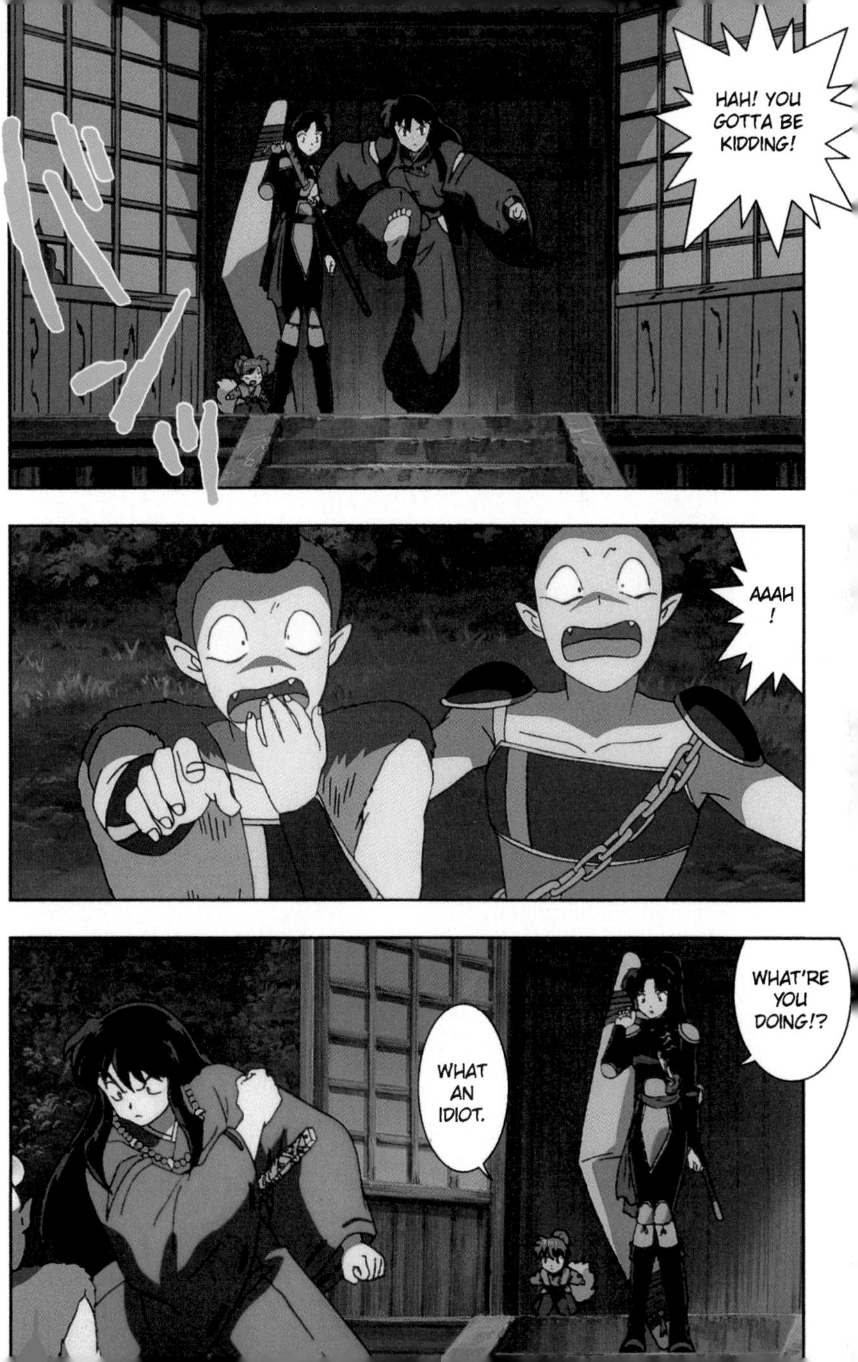
HAH! YOU GOTTA BE KIDDING!
AAAH!
WHAT'RE YOU DOING!?
WHAT AN IDIOT.

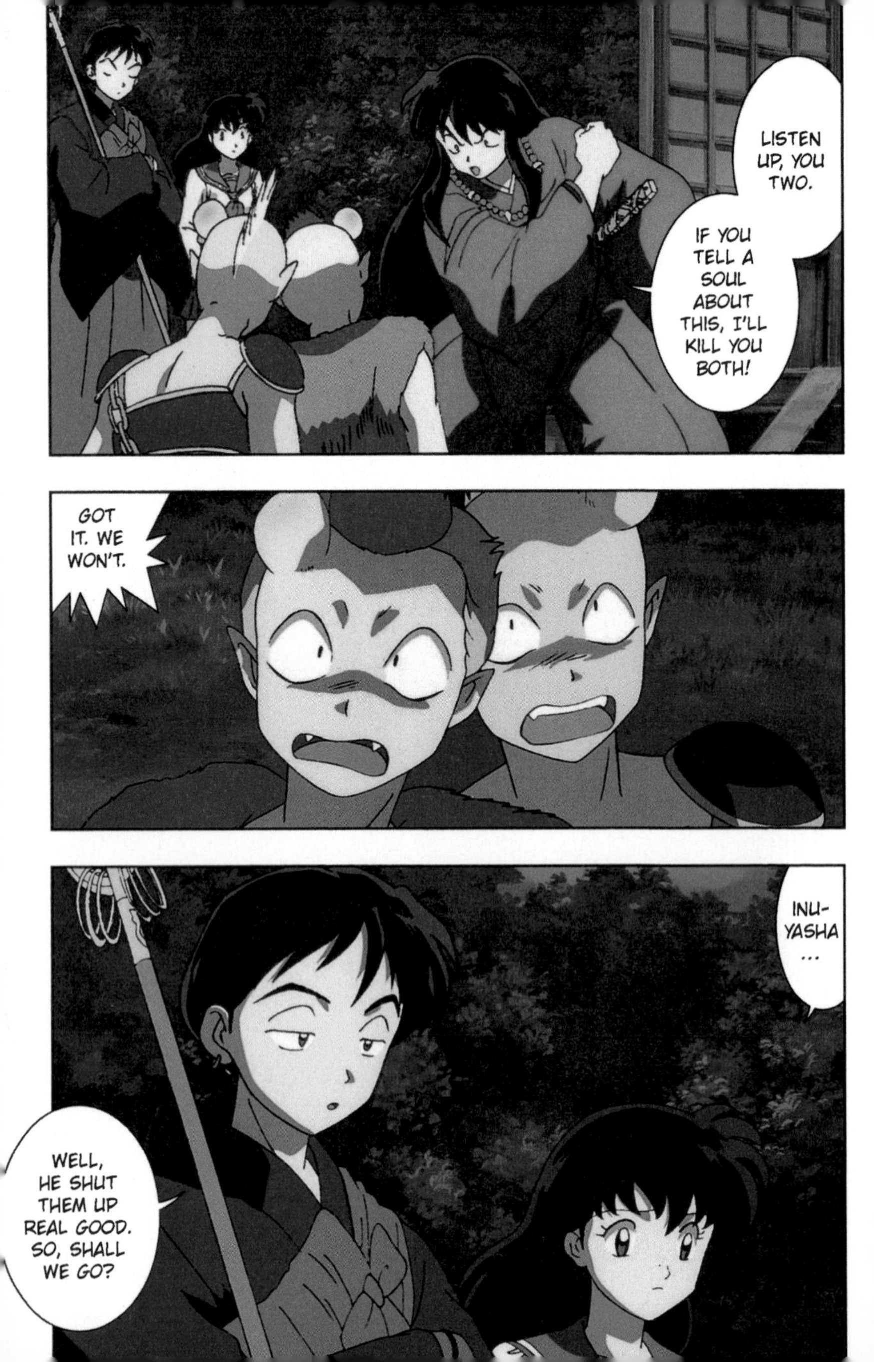
LISTEN UP, YOU TWO.
IF YOU TELL A SOUL ABOUT THIS, I'LL KILL YOU BOTH!
GOT IT. WE WON'T.
INU-YASHA...
WELL, HE SHUT THEM UP REAL GOOD. SO, SHALL WE GO?

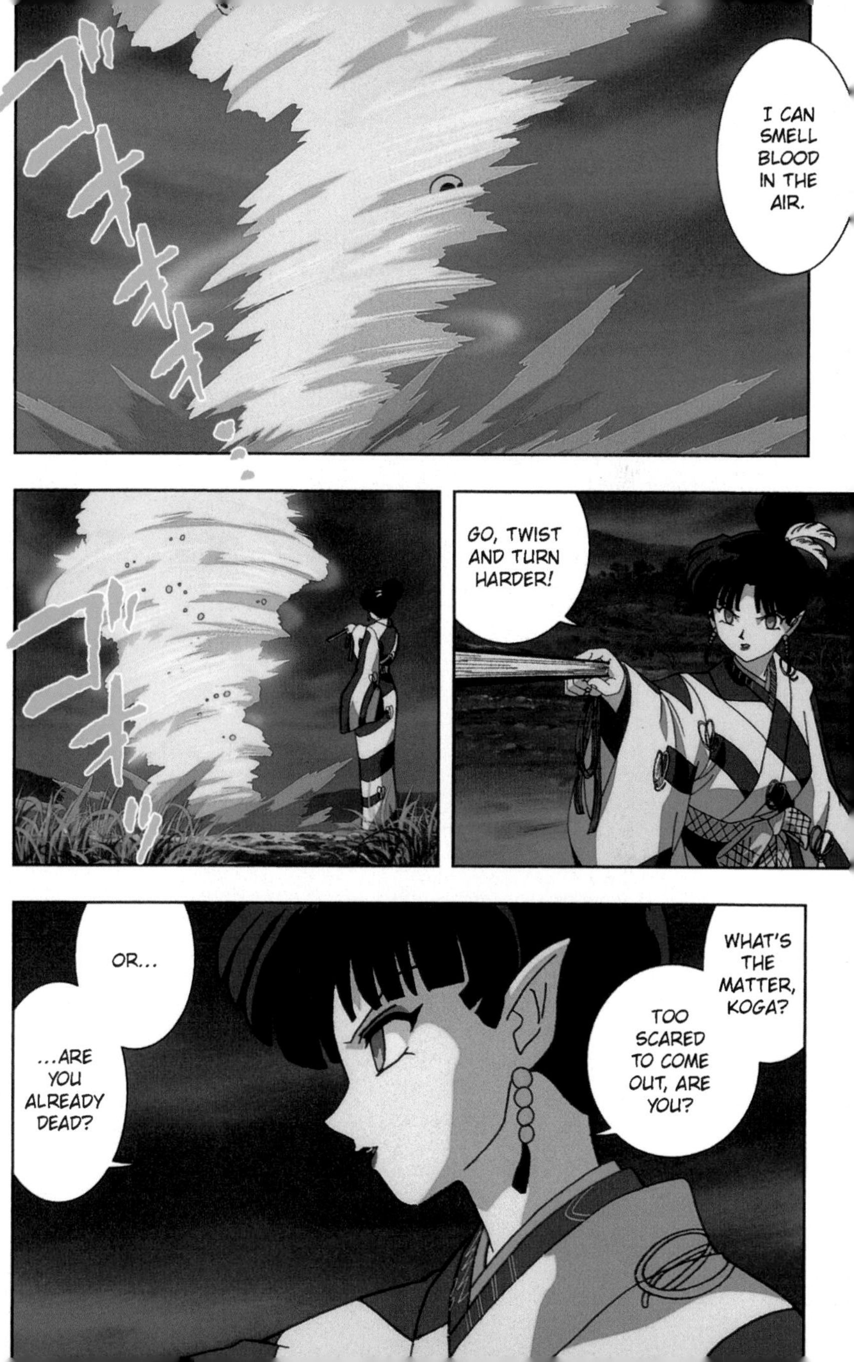

I CAN SMELL BLOOD IN THE AIR.
ゴオオオ…
GO, TWIST AND TURN HARDER!
ゴオッ
WHAT'S THE MATTER, KOGA?
TOO SCARED TO COME OUT, ARE YOU?
OR...
...ARE YOU ALREADY DEAD?

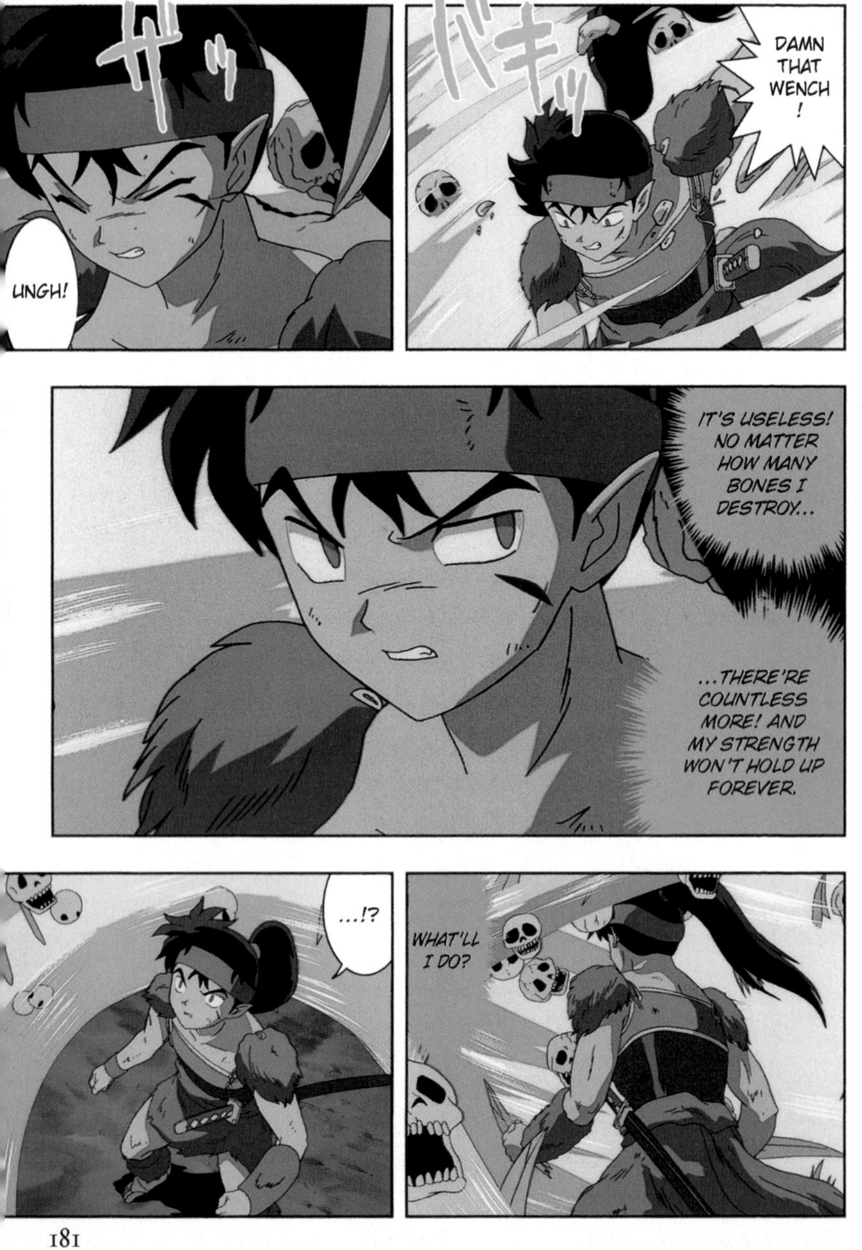
バキッ
DAMN THAT WENCH!
ザッ
UNGH!
IT'S USELESS! NO MATTER HOW MANY BONES I DESTROY...
...THERE'RE COUNTLESS MORE! AND MY STRENGTH WON'T HOLD UP FOREVER.
WHAT'LL I DO?
...!?

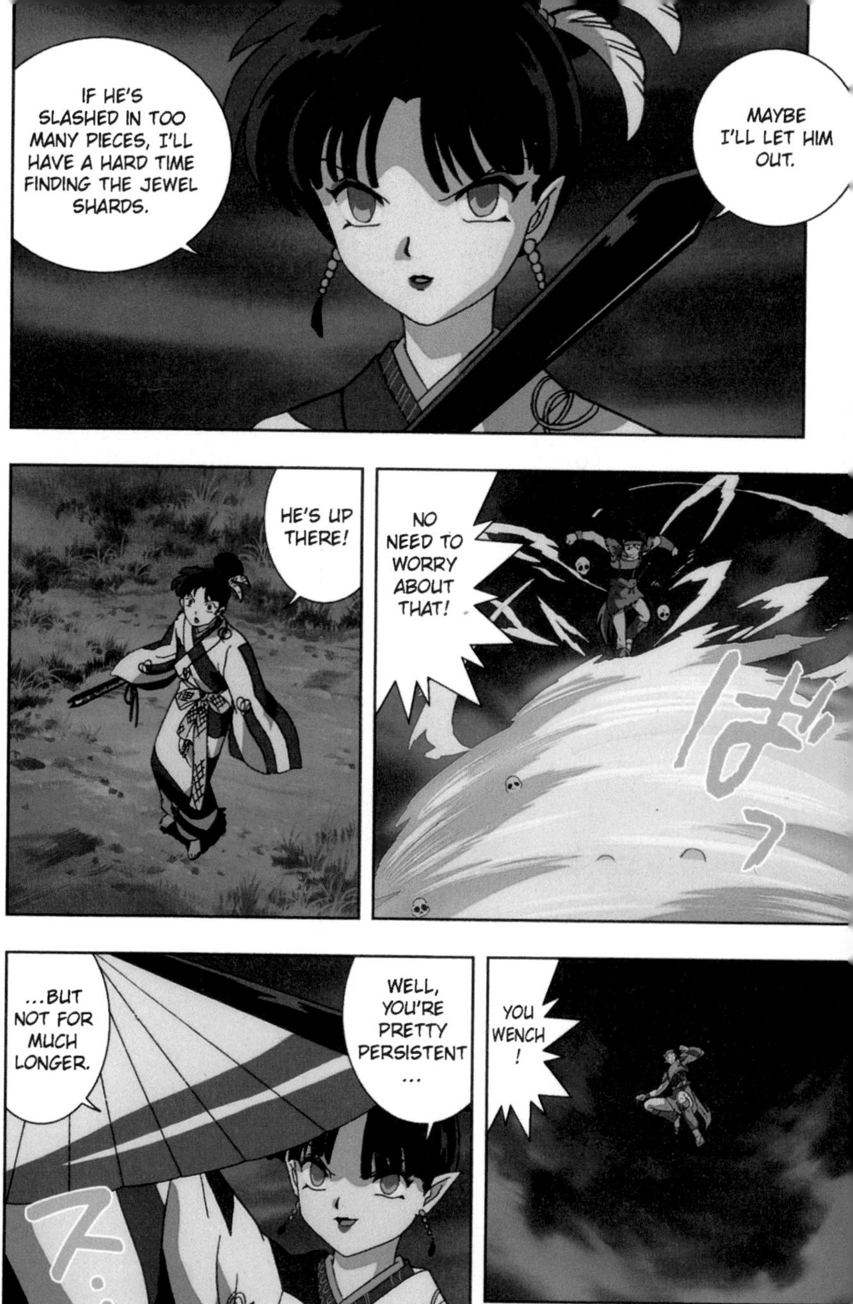
MAYBE I'LL LET HIM OUT.
IF HE'S SLASHED IN TOO MANY PIECES, I'LL HAVE A HARD TIME FINDING THE JEWEL SHARDS.
NO NEED TO WORRY ABOUT THAT!
ぼっ
HE'S UP THERE!
YOU WENCH!
WELL, YOU'RE PRETTY PERSISTENT...
...BUT NOT FOR MUCH LONGER.
ス...

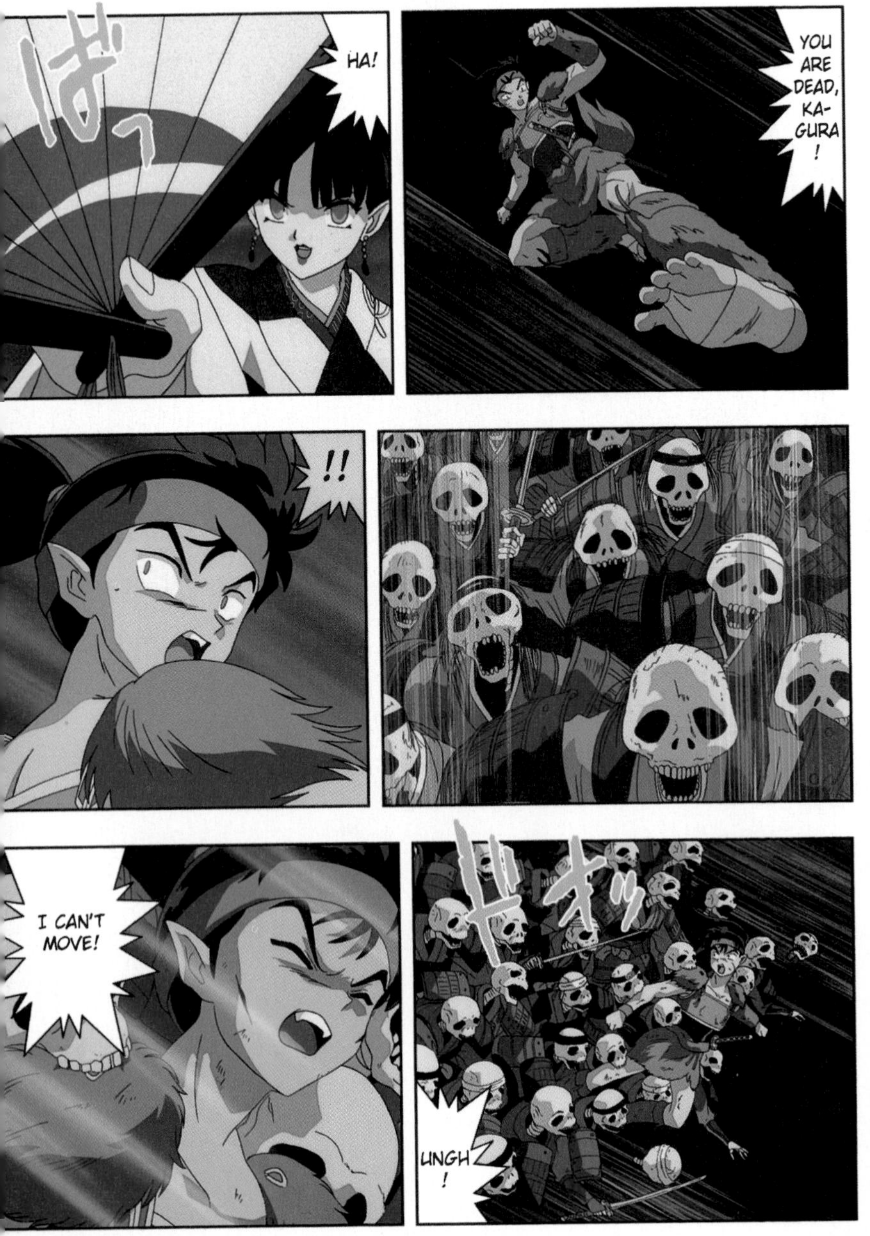
YOU ARE DEAD, KA-GURA!
HA!
!!
UNGH!
I CAN'T MOVE!

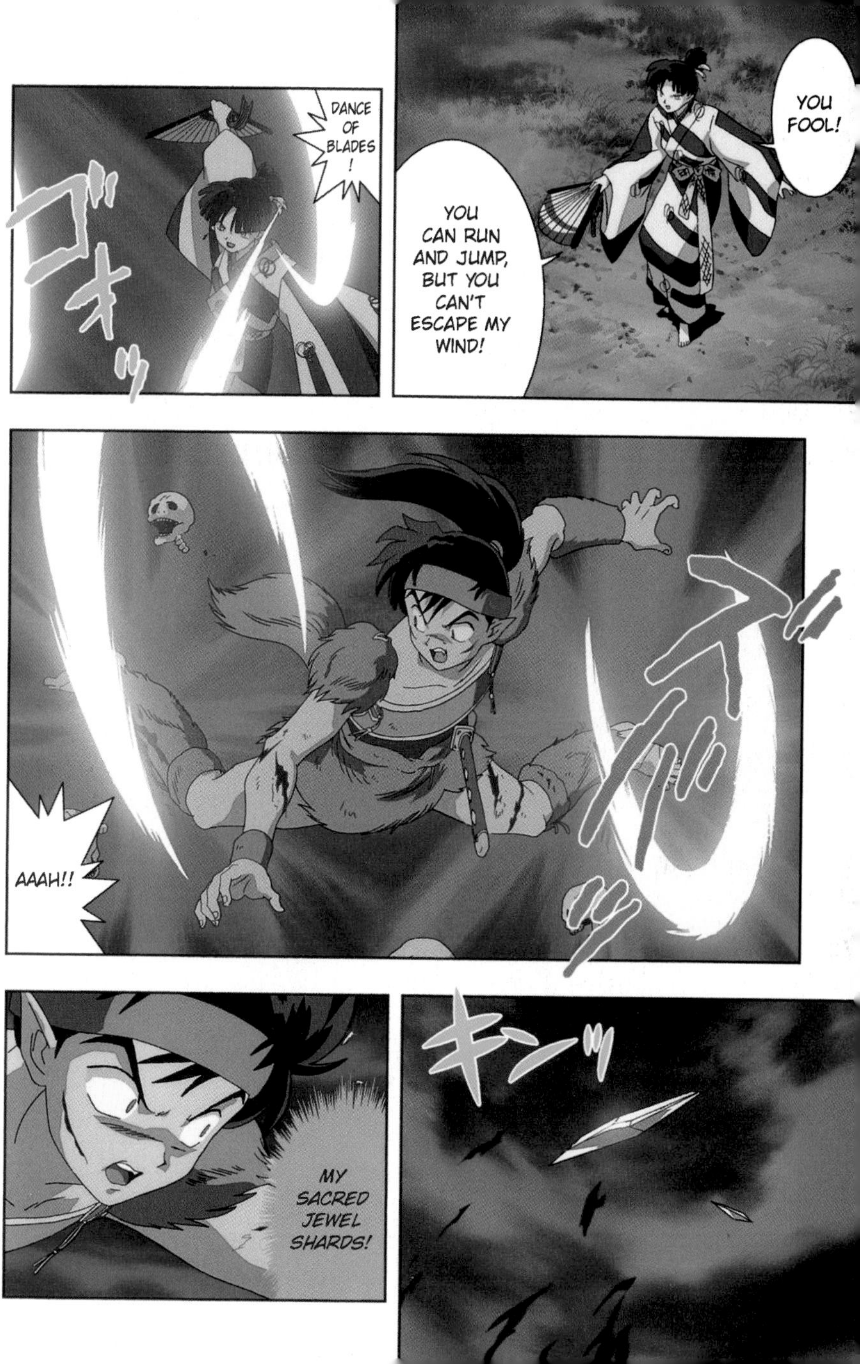
YOU FOOL!
YOU CAN RUN AND JUMP, BUT YOU CAN'T ESCAPE MY WIND!
DANCE OF BLADES!
ゴォッ
AAAH!!
キンッ
MY SACRED JEWEL SHARDS!

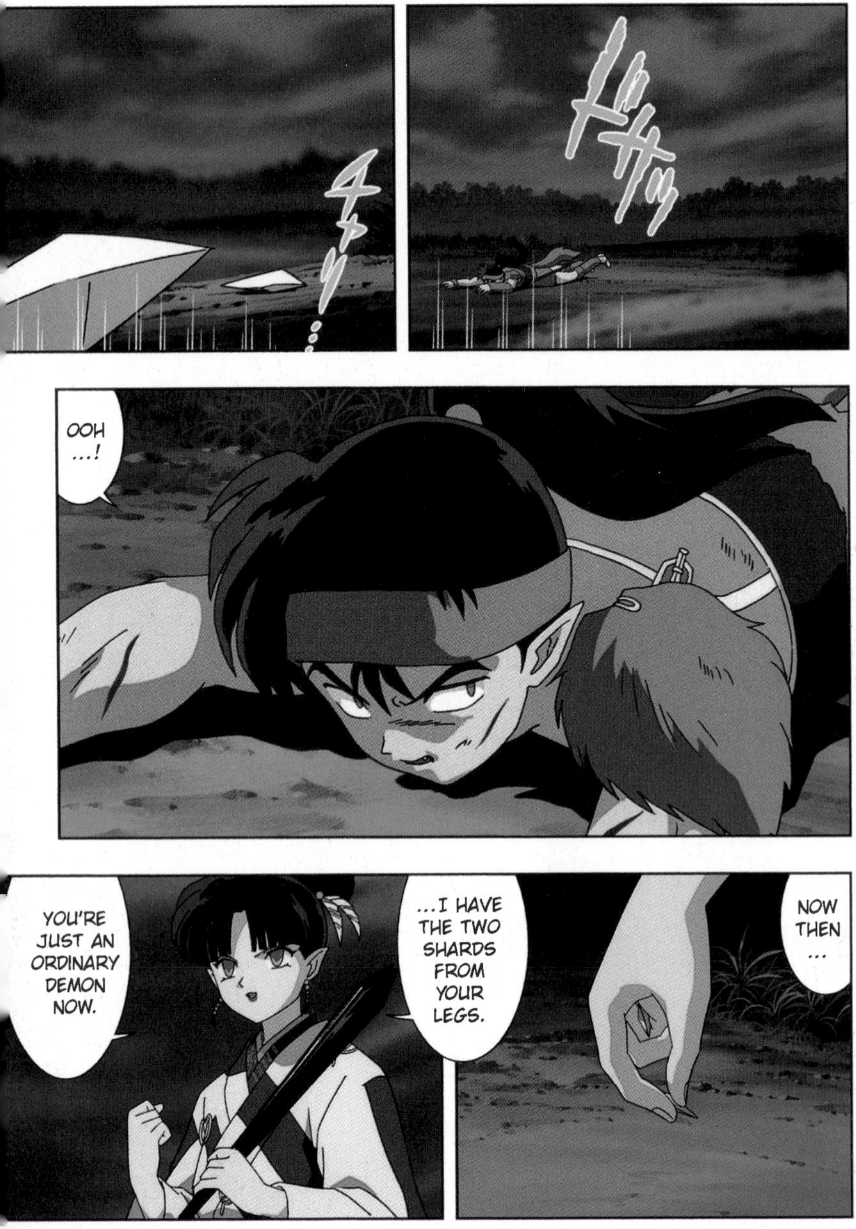
ドサッ
OOH ...!
NOW THEN ...
...I HAVE THE TWO SHARDS FROM YOUR LEGS.
YOU'RE JUST AN ORDINARY DEMON NOW.

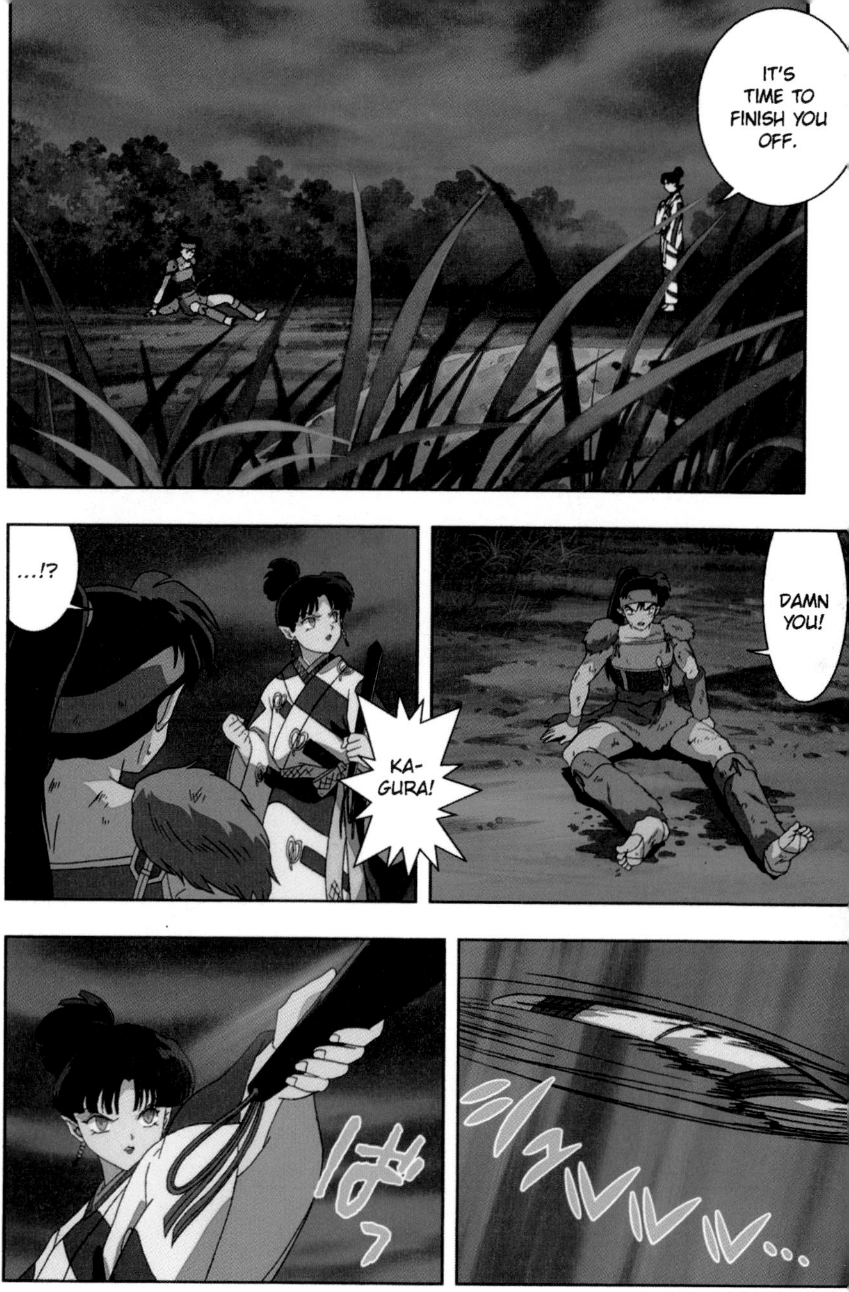
IT'S TIME TO FINISH YOU OFF.
DAMN YOU!
...!?
KA-GURA!
シュルルル...
ばっ

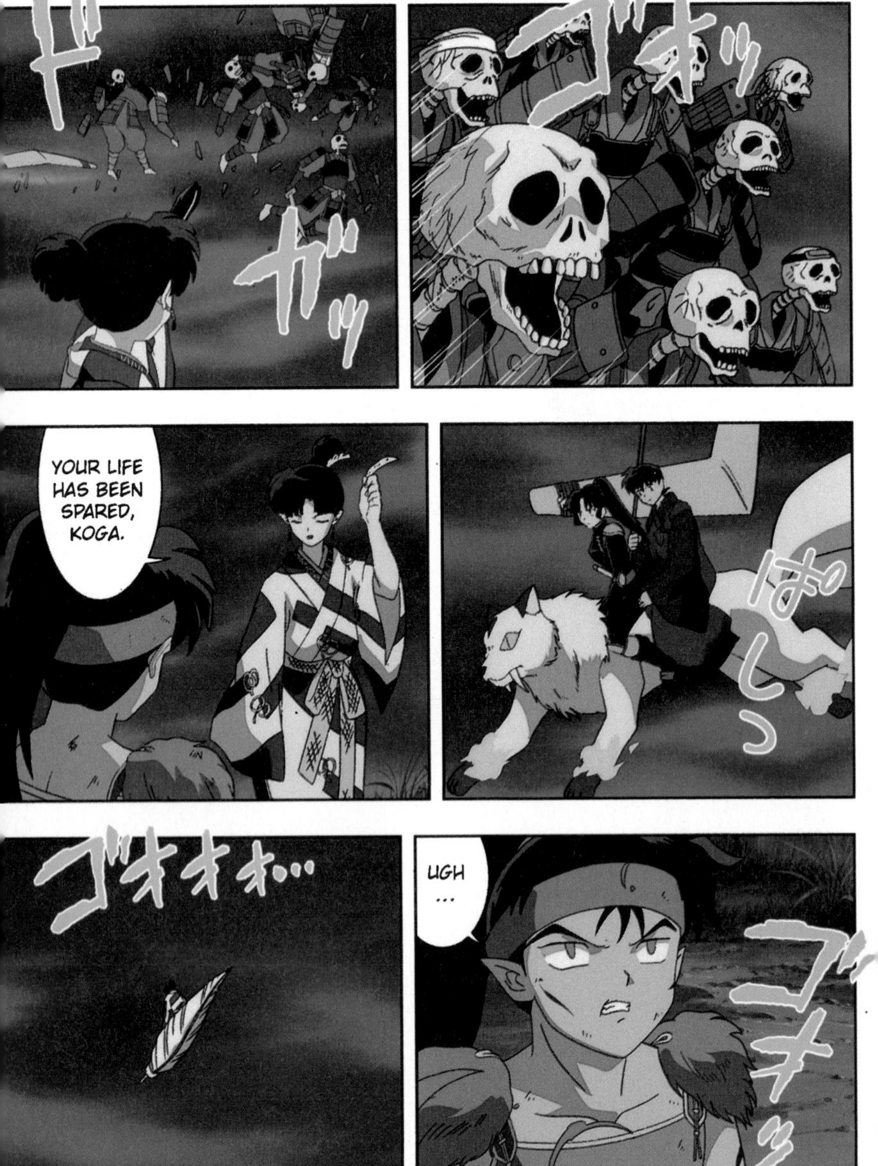
YOUR LIFE HAS BEEN SPARED, KOGA.
UGH ...

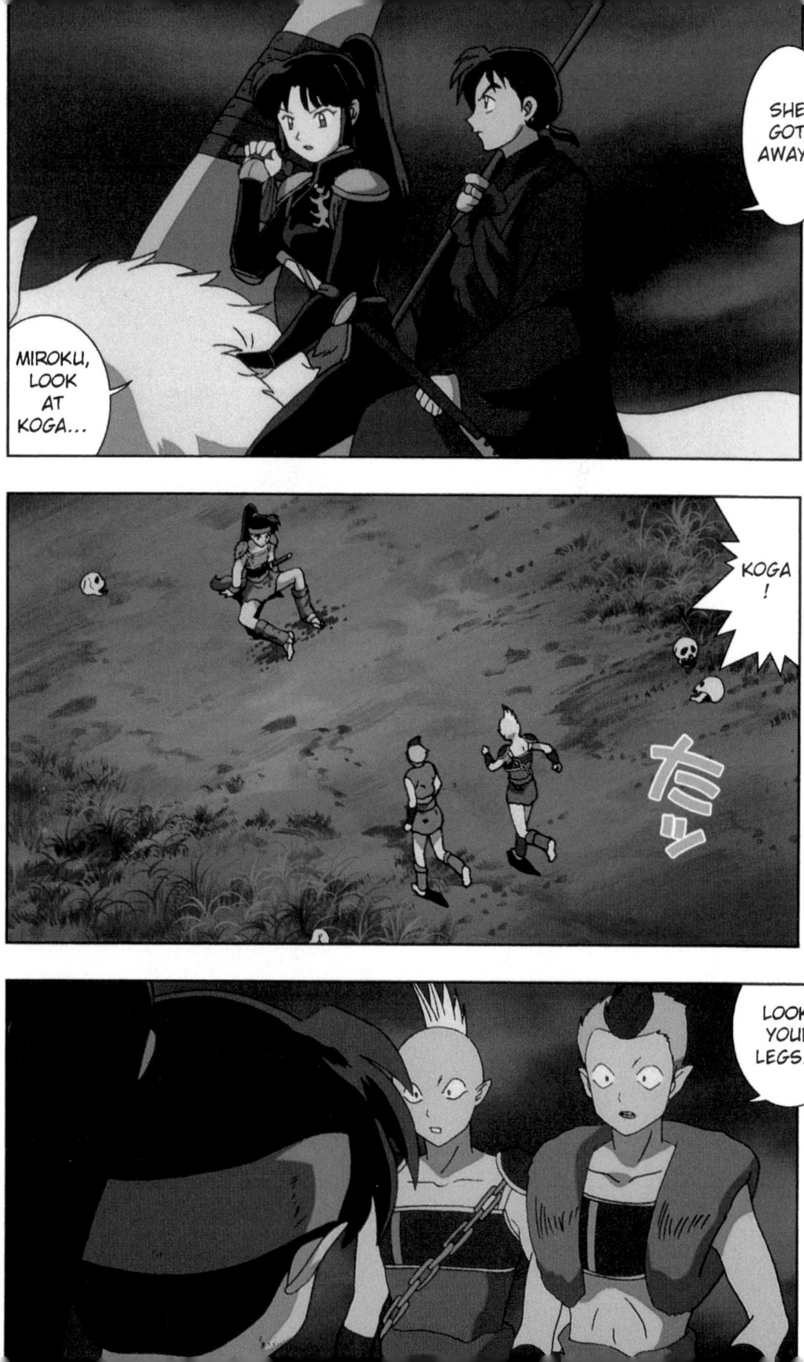
SHE GOT AWAY!
MIROKU, LOOK AT KOGA...
KOGA!
たッ
LOOK! YOUR LEGS...

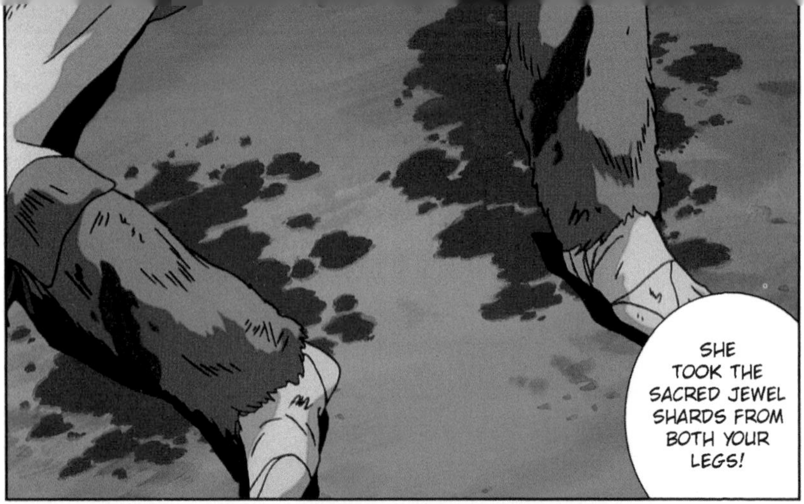
SHE TOOK THE SACRED JEWEL SHARDS FROM BOTH YOUR LEGS!

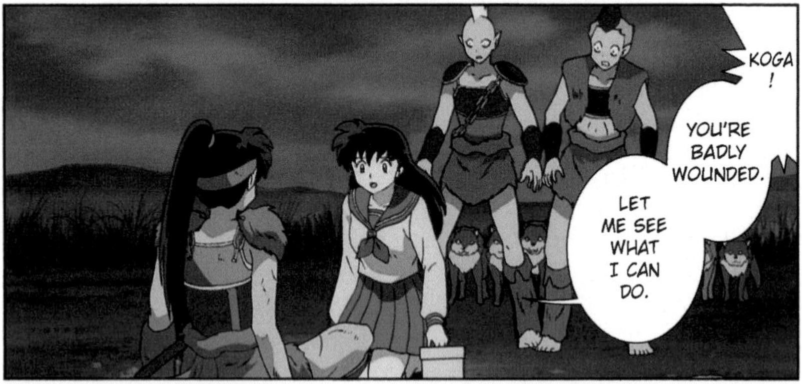
KOGA!
YOU'RE BADLY WOUNDED.
LET ME SEE WHAT I CAN DO.

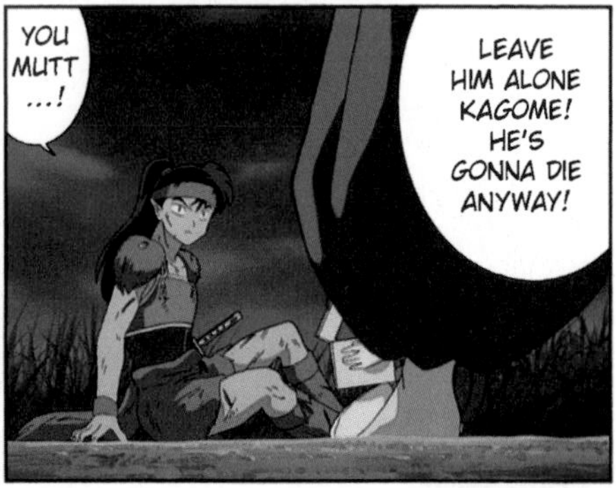
LEAVE HIM ALONE KAGOME! HE'S GONNA DIE ANYWAY!
YOU MUTT ...!

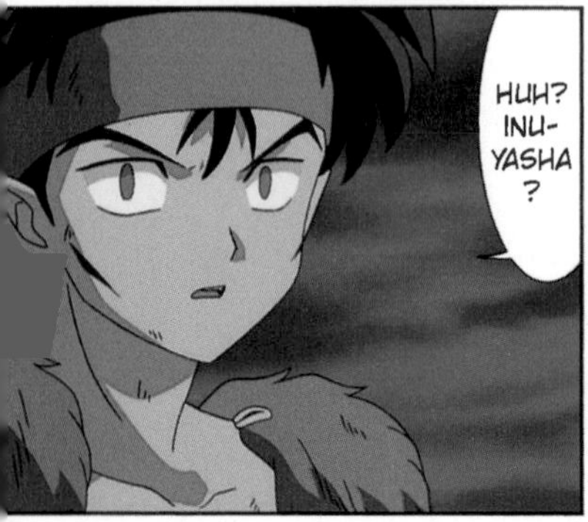
HUH? INU-YASHA?

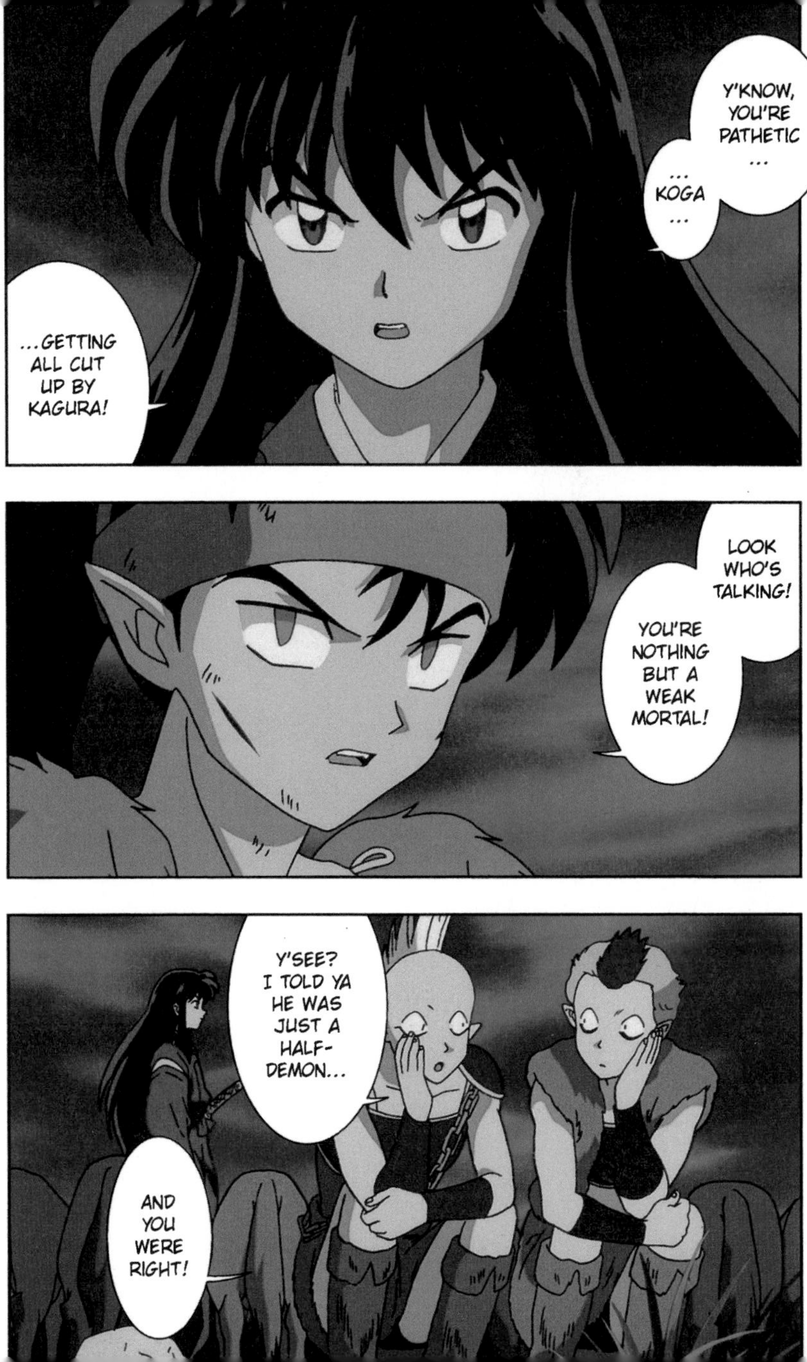
Y'KNOW, YOU'RE PATHETIC ...
... KOGA ...
...GETTING ALL CUT UP BY KAGURA!
LOOK WHO'S TALKING!
YOU'RE NOTHING BUT A WEAK MORTAL!
Y'SEE? I TOLD YA HE WAS JUST A HALF-DEMON...
AND YOU WERE RIGHT!

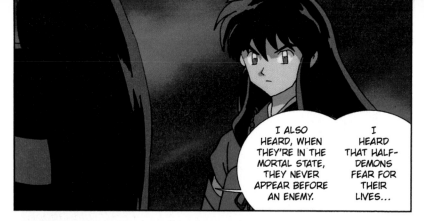

I HEARD THAT HALF-DEMONS FEAR FOR THEIR LIVES...

I ALSO HEARD, WHEN THEY'RE IN THE MORTAL STATE, THEY NEVER APPEAR BEFORE AN ENEMY.

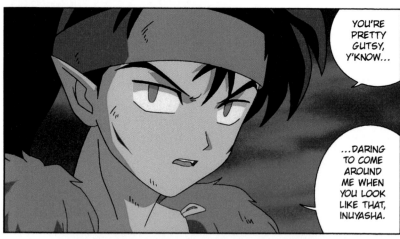

YOU'RE PRETTY GUTSY, Y'KNOW...

...DARING TO COME AROUND ME WHEN YOU LOOK LIKE THAT, INUYASHA.

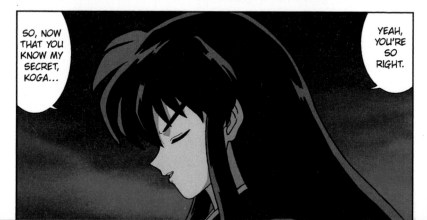

YEAH, YOU'RE SO RIGHT.

SO, NOW THAT YOU KNOW MY SECRET, KOGA...

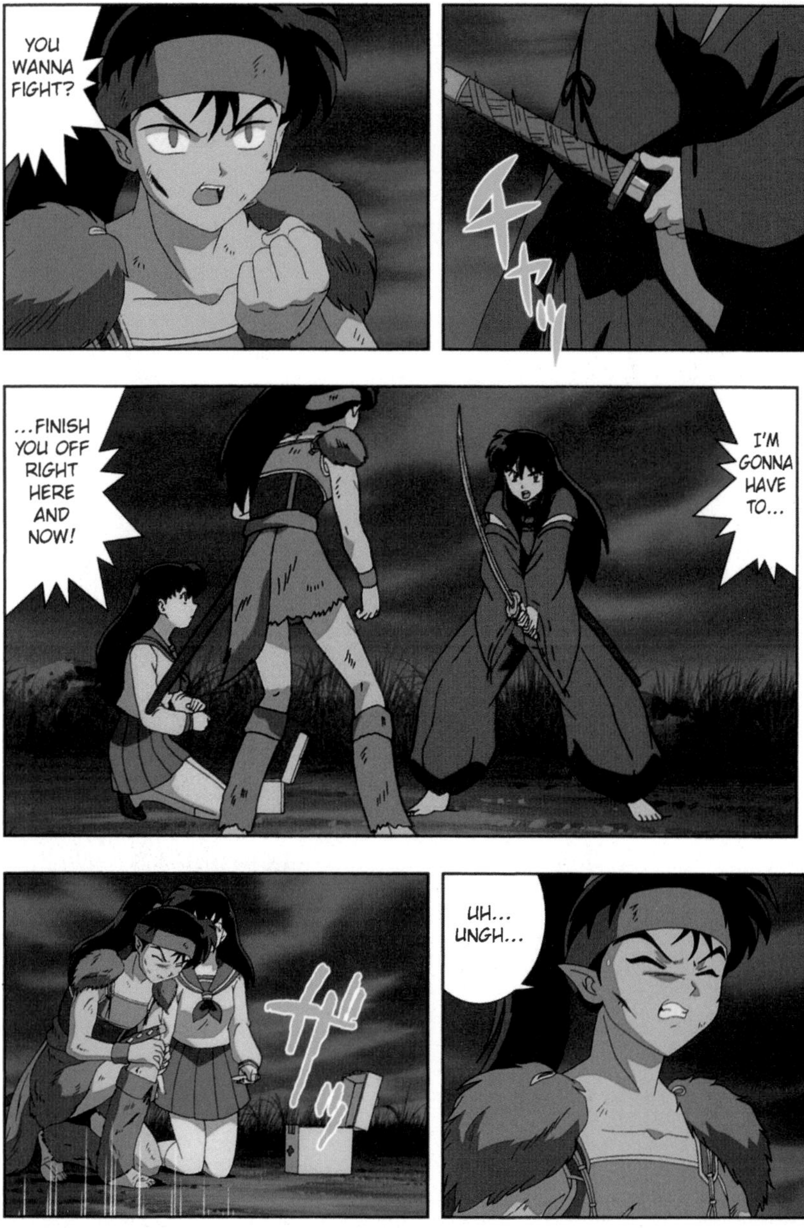
チャッ
YOU WANNA FIGHT?
I'M GONNA HAVE TO...
...FINISH YOU OFF RIGHT HERE AND NOW!
UH... UNGH...
ザッ

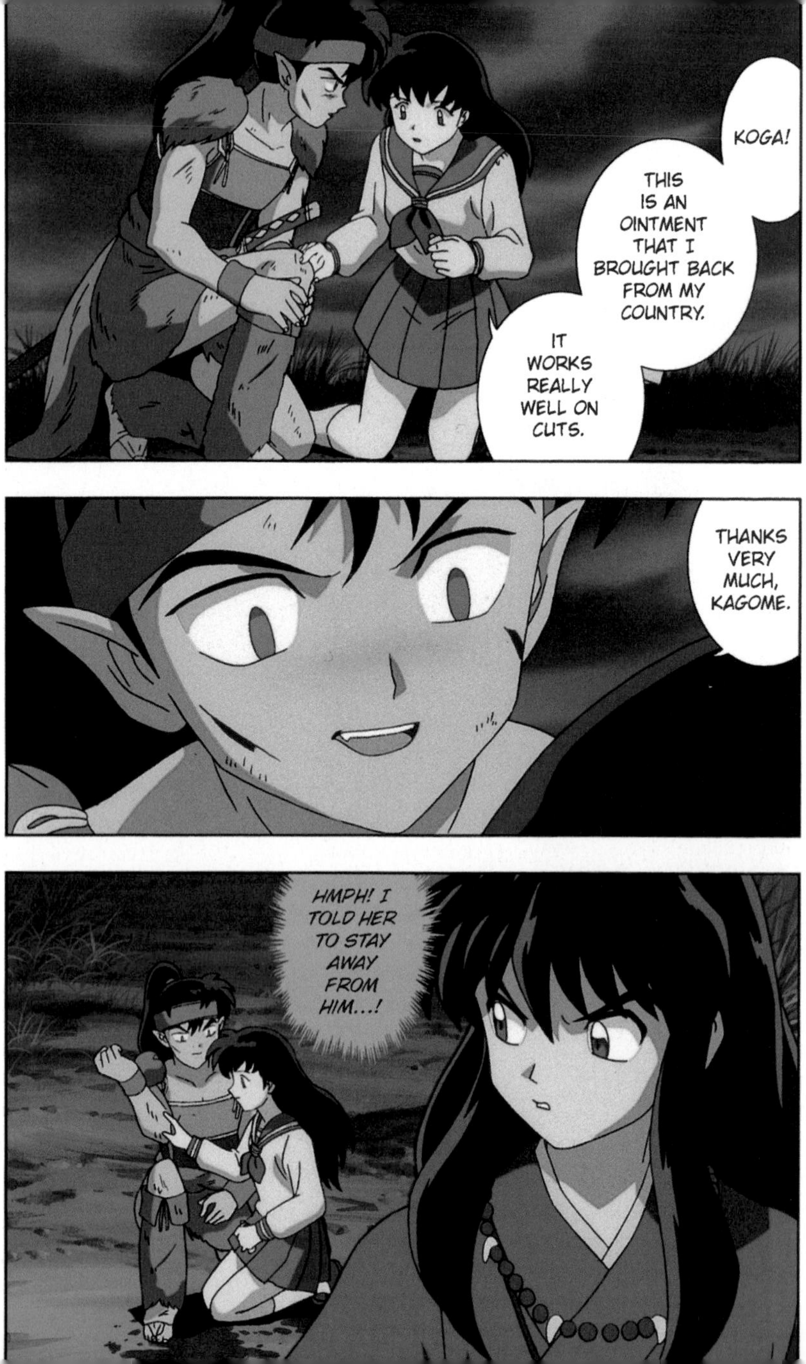
KOGA!
THIS IS AN OINTMENT THAT I BROUGHT BACK FROM MY COUNTRY.
IT WORKS REALLY WELL ON CUTS.
THANKS VERY MUCH, KAGOME.
HMPH! I TOLD HER TO STAY AWAY FROM HIM...!

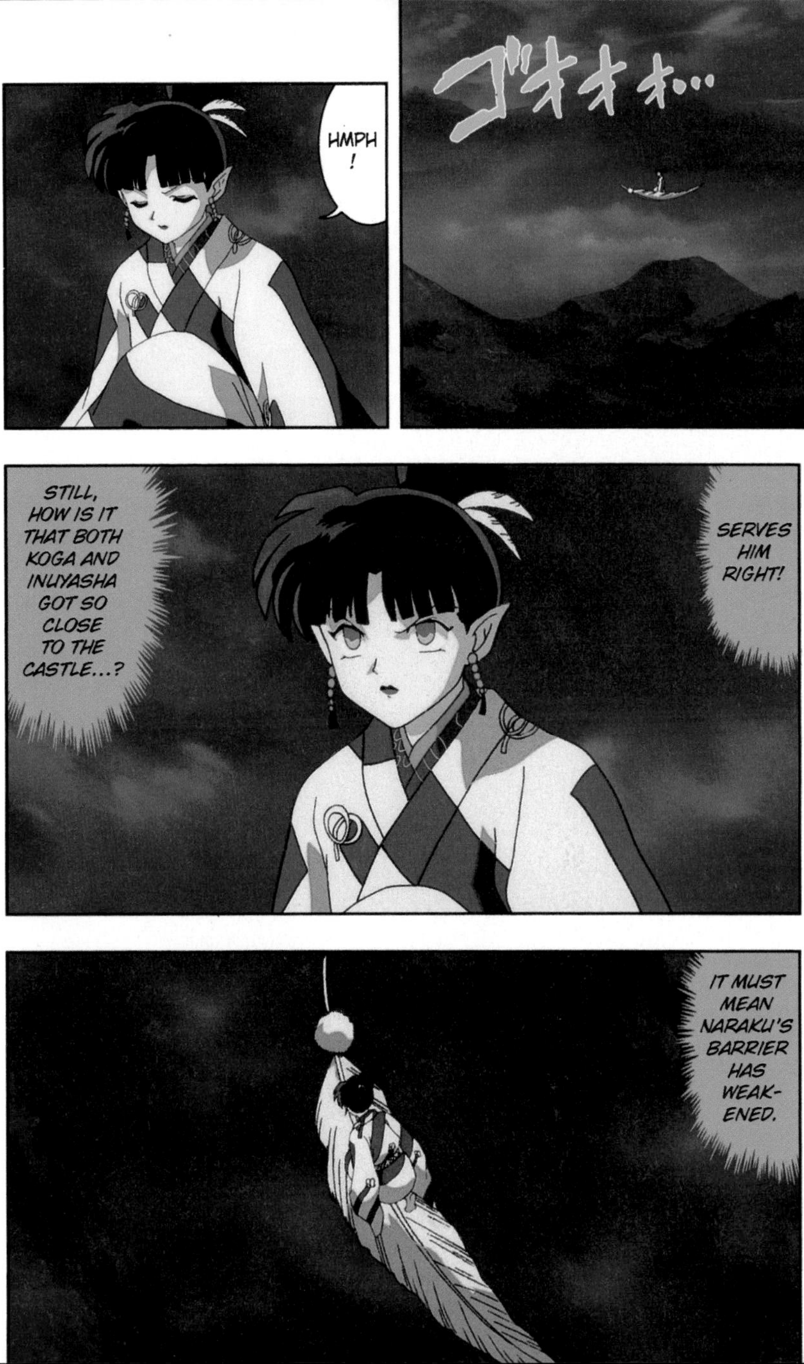
ゴオオオ…
HMPH!
SERVES HIM RIGHT!
STILL, HOW IS IT THAT BOTH KOGA AND INUYASHA GOT SO CLOSE TO THE CASTLE...?
IT MUST MEAN NARAKU'S BARRIER HAS WEAK-ENED.

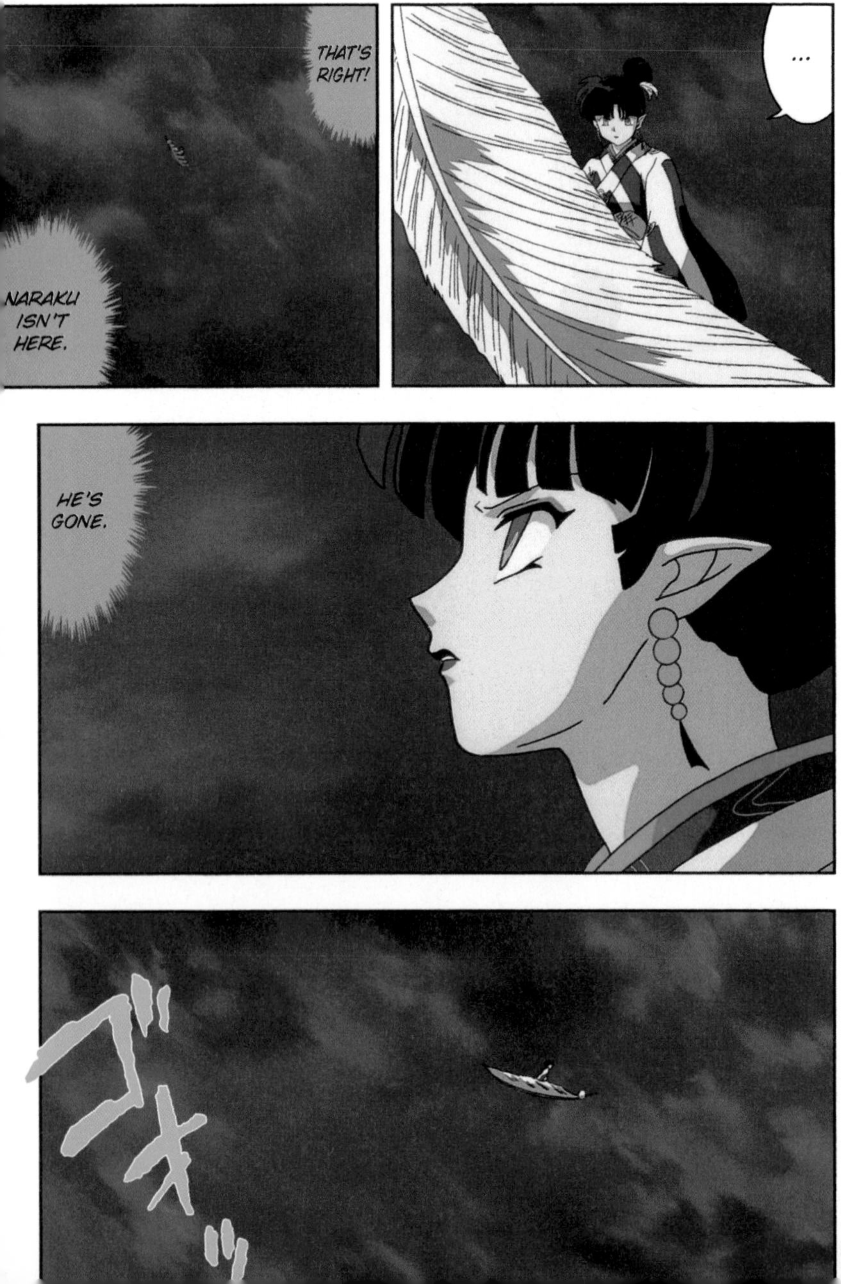
...
THAT'S RIGHT!
NARAKU ISN'T HERE.
HE'S GONE.
ゴオッ

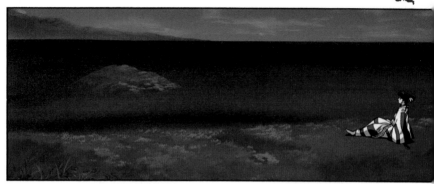

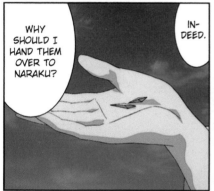

WHY SHOULD I HAND THEM OVER TO NARAKU?

IN-DEED.

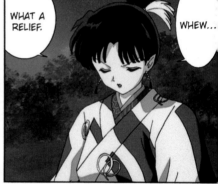

WHAT A RELIEF.

WHEW...

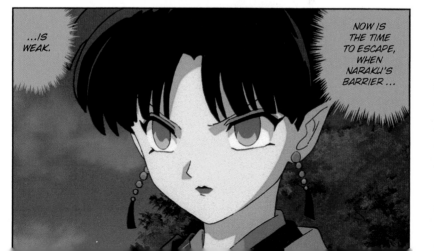

...IS WEAK.

NOW IS THE TIME TO ESCAPE, WHEN NARAKU'S BARRIER...

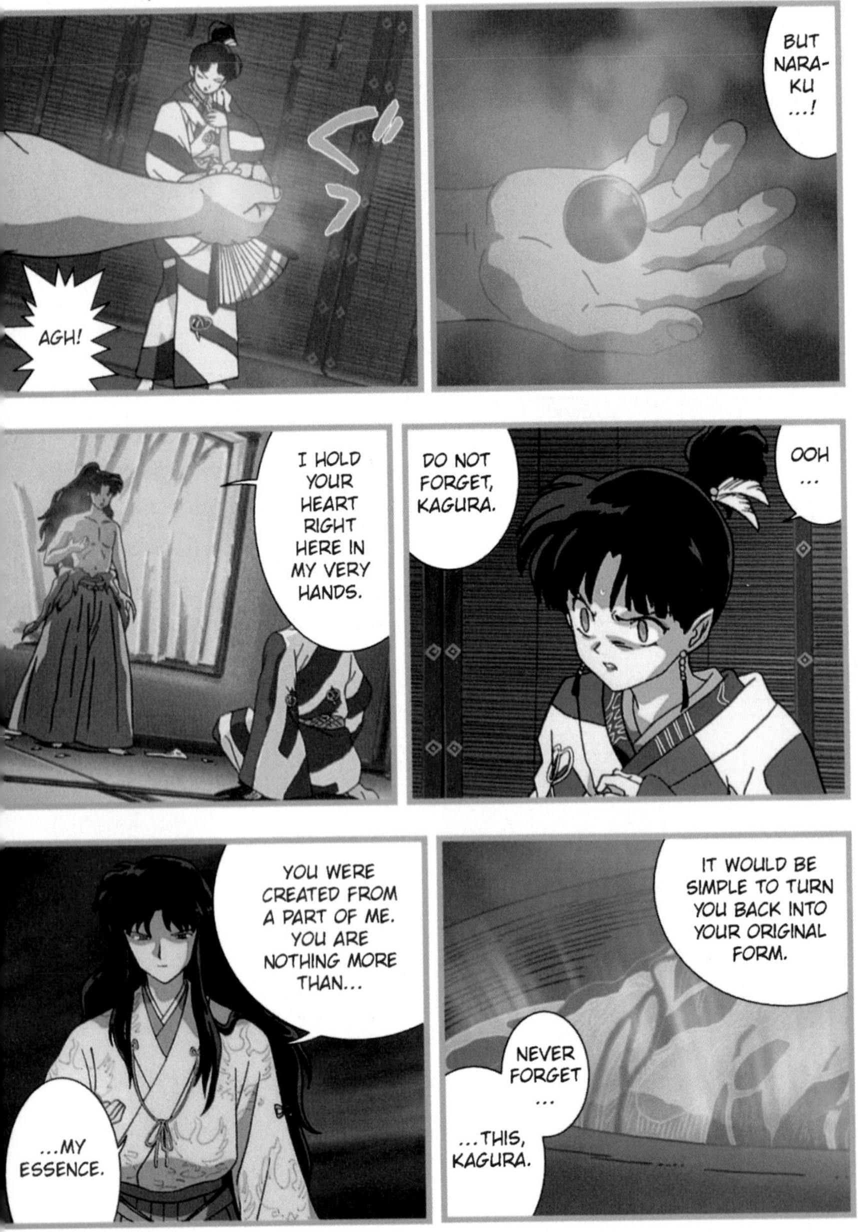
BUT NARA-KU ...!
AGH!
OOH ...
DO NOT FORGET, KAGURA.
I HOLD YOUR HEART RIGHT HERE IN MY VERY HANDS.
IT WOULD BE SIMPLE TO TURN YOU BACK INTO YOUR ORIGINAL FORM.
NEVER FORGET ...
...THIS, KAGURA.
YOU WERE CREATED FROM A PART OF ME. YOU ARE NOTHING MORE THAN...
...MY ESSENCE.

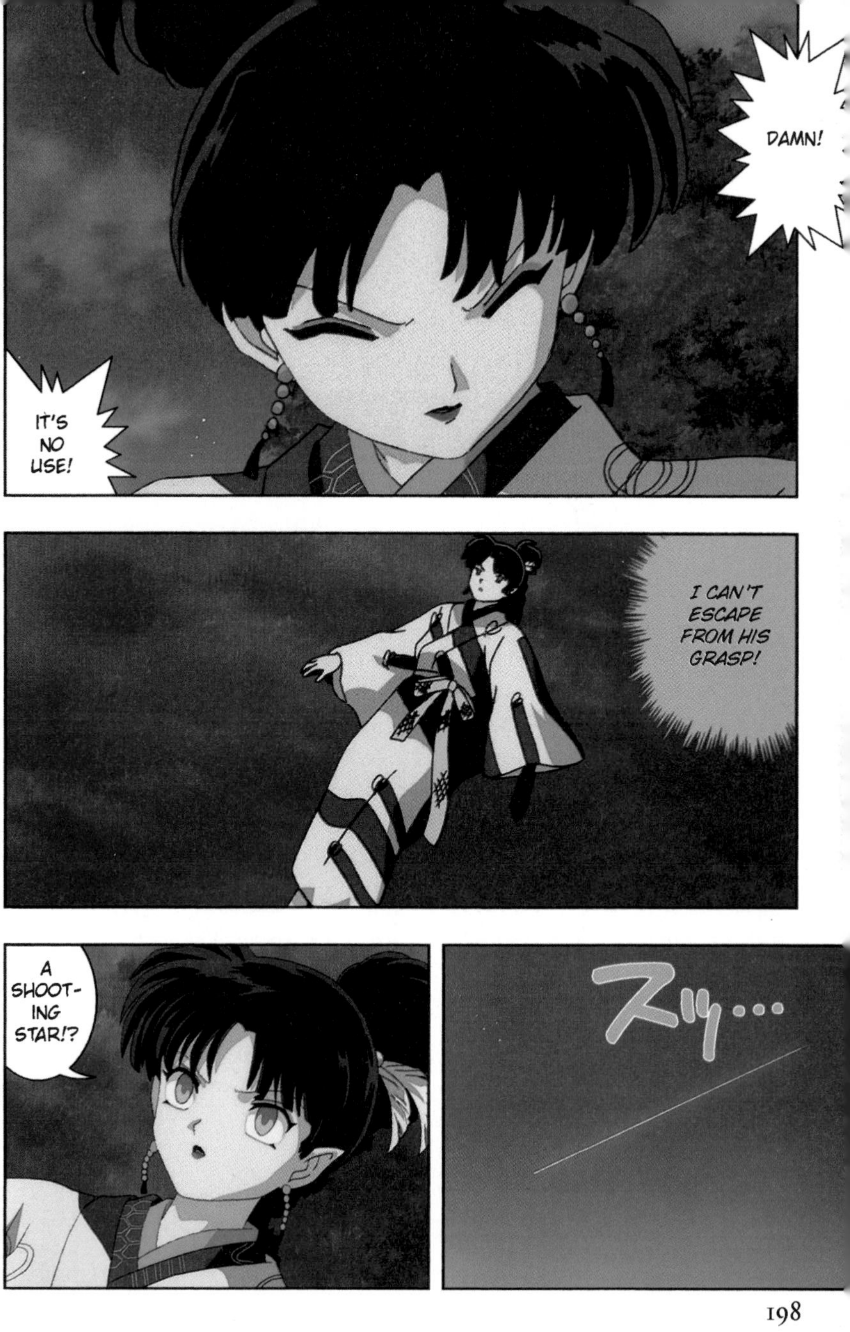
DAMN!
IT'S NO USE!
I CAN'T ESCAPE FROM HIS GRASP!
スッ...
A SHOOT-ING STAR!?

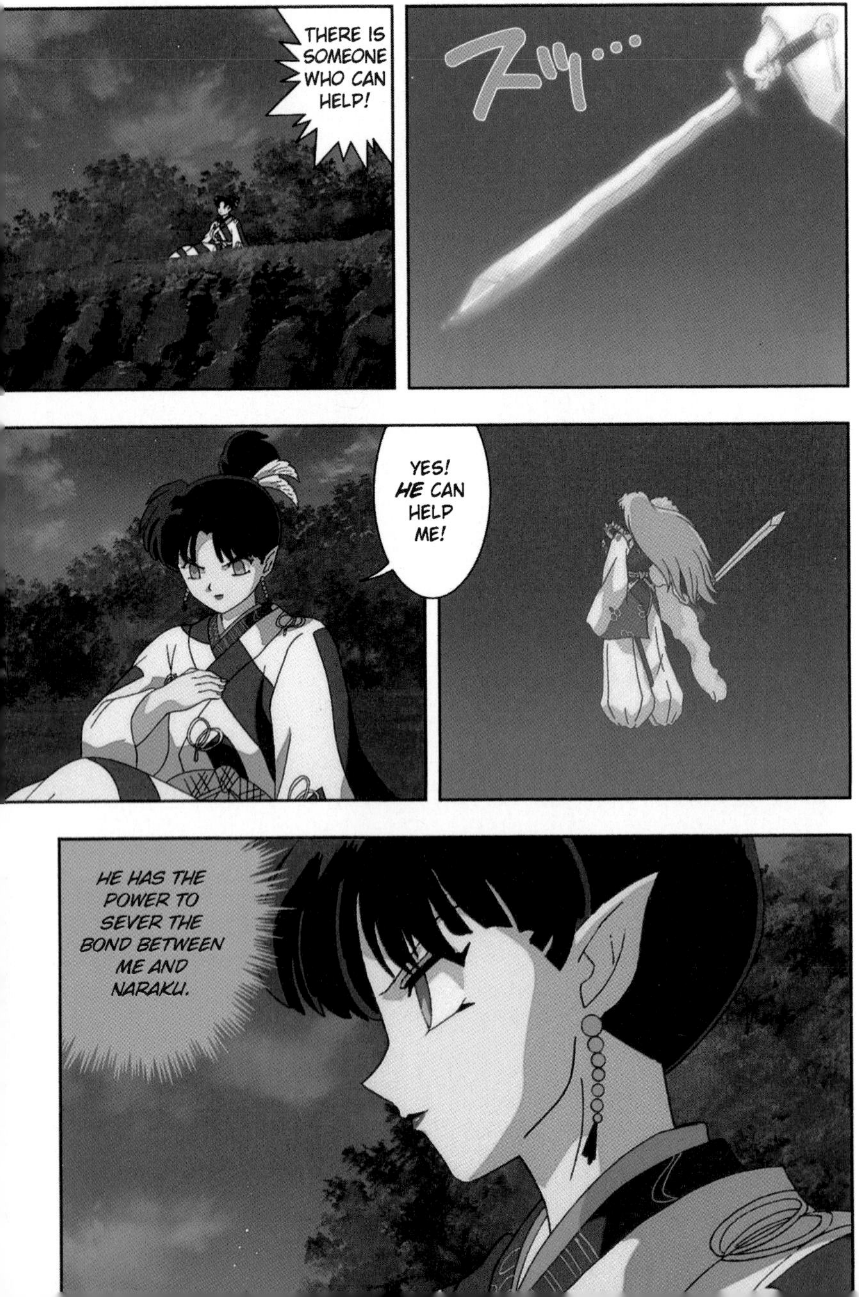
ズッ…
THERE IS SOMEONE WHO CAN HELP!
YES! **HE** CAN HELP ME!
HE HAS THE POWER TO SEVER THE BOND BETWEEN ME AND NARAKU.

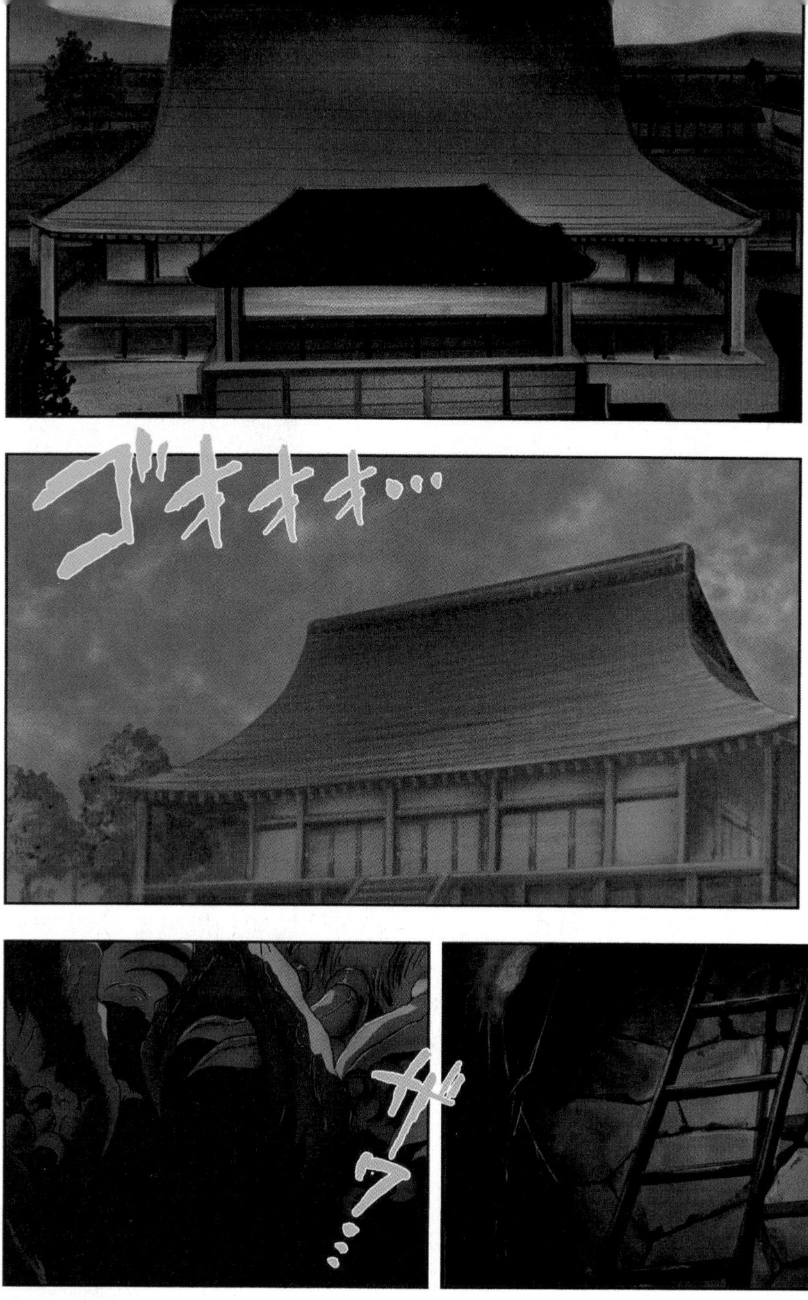
ゴオオオ…
ザワ…

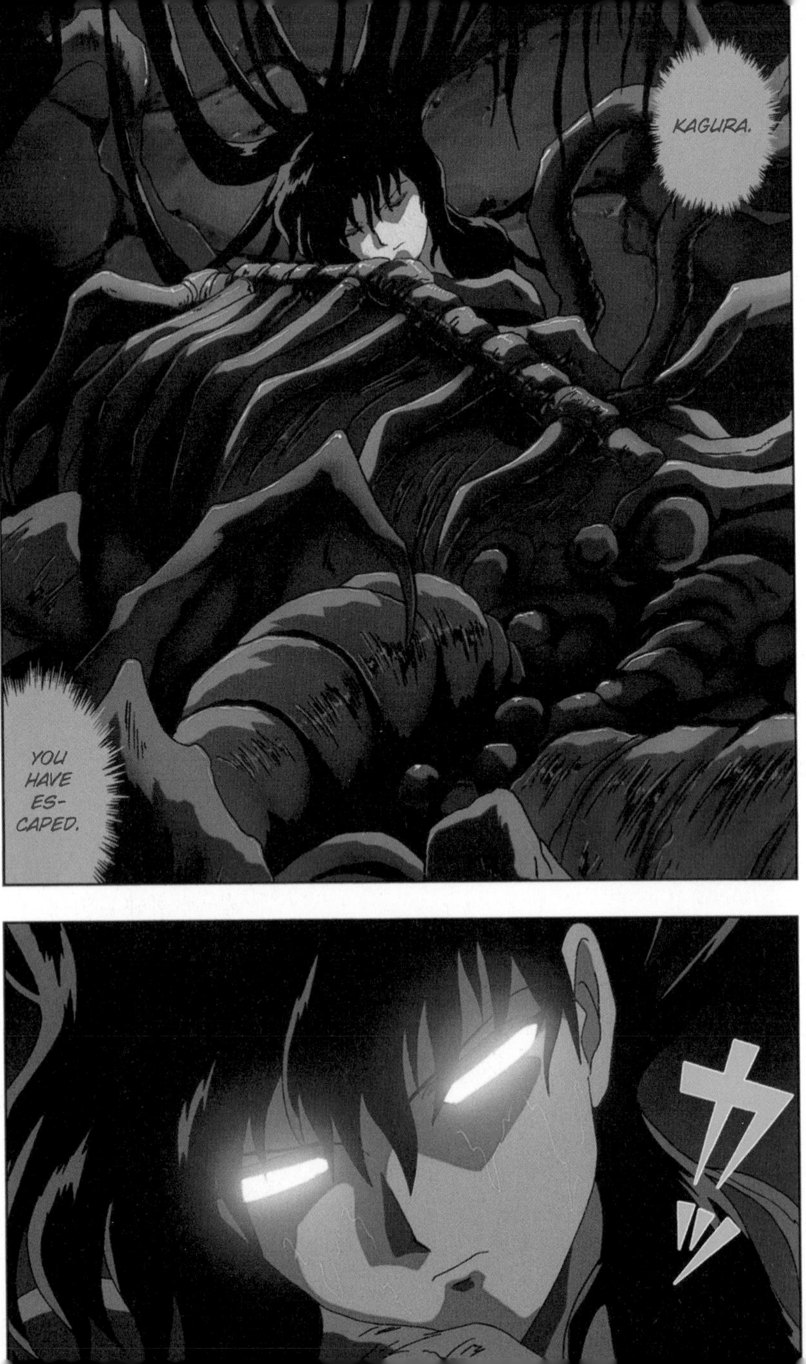
KAGURA.
YOU HAVE ES-CAPED.
カッ

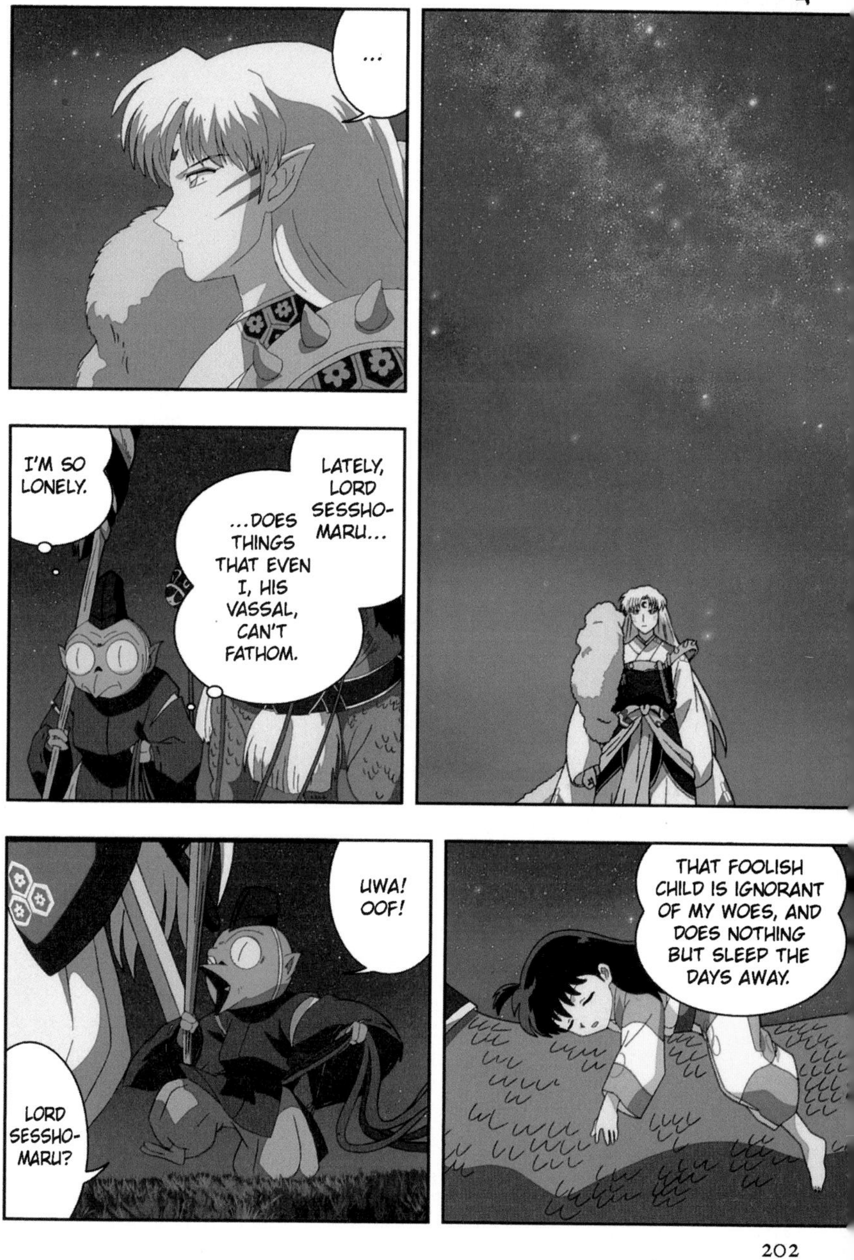
...
LATELY, LORD SESSHO-MARU...
...DOES THINGS THAT EVEN I, HIS VASSAL, CAN'T FATHOM.
I'M SO LONELY.
THAT FOOLISH CHILD IS IGNORANT OF MY WOES, AND DOES NOTHING BUT SLEEP THE DAYS AWAY.
UWA! OOF!
LORD SESSHO-MARU?

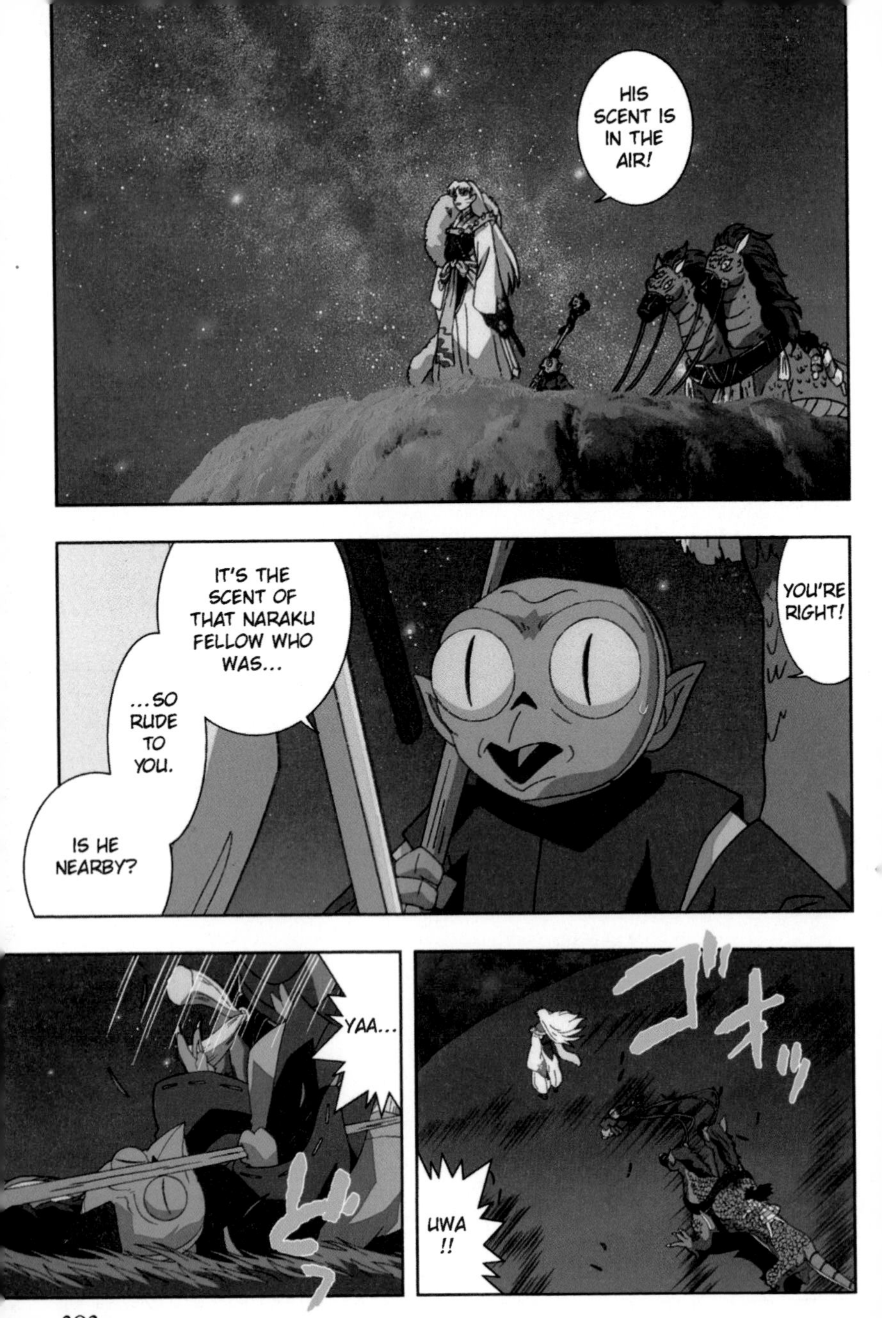
HIS SCENT IS IN THE AIR!
YOU'RE RIGHT!
IT'S THE SCENT OF THAT NARAKU FELLOW WHO WAS...
...SO RUDE TO YOU.
IS HE NEARBY?
ゴオッ
UWA !!
YAA...
どっ

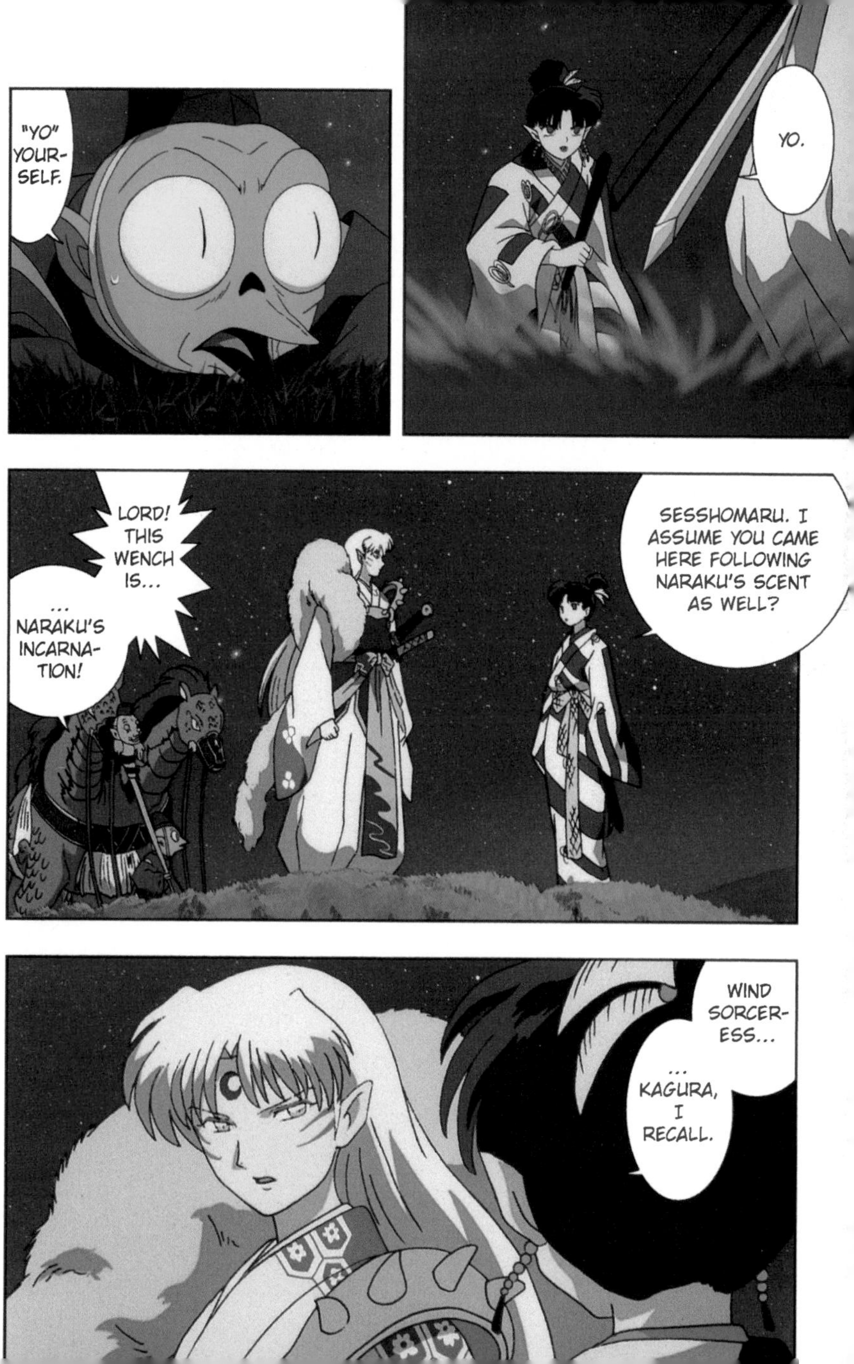
YO.
"YO" YOURSELF.
SESSHOMARU. I ASSUME YOU CAME HERE FOLLOWING NARAKU'S SCENT AS WELL?
LORD! THIS WENCH IS...
... NARAKU'S INCARNATION!
WIND SORCERESS...
... KAGURA, I RECALL.

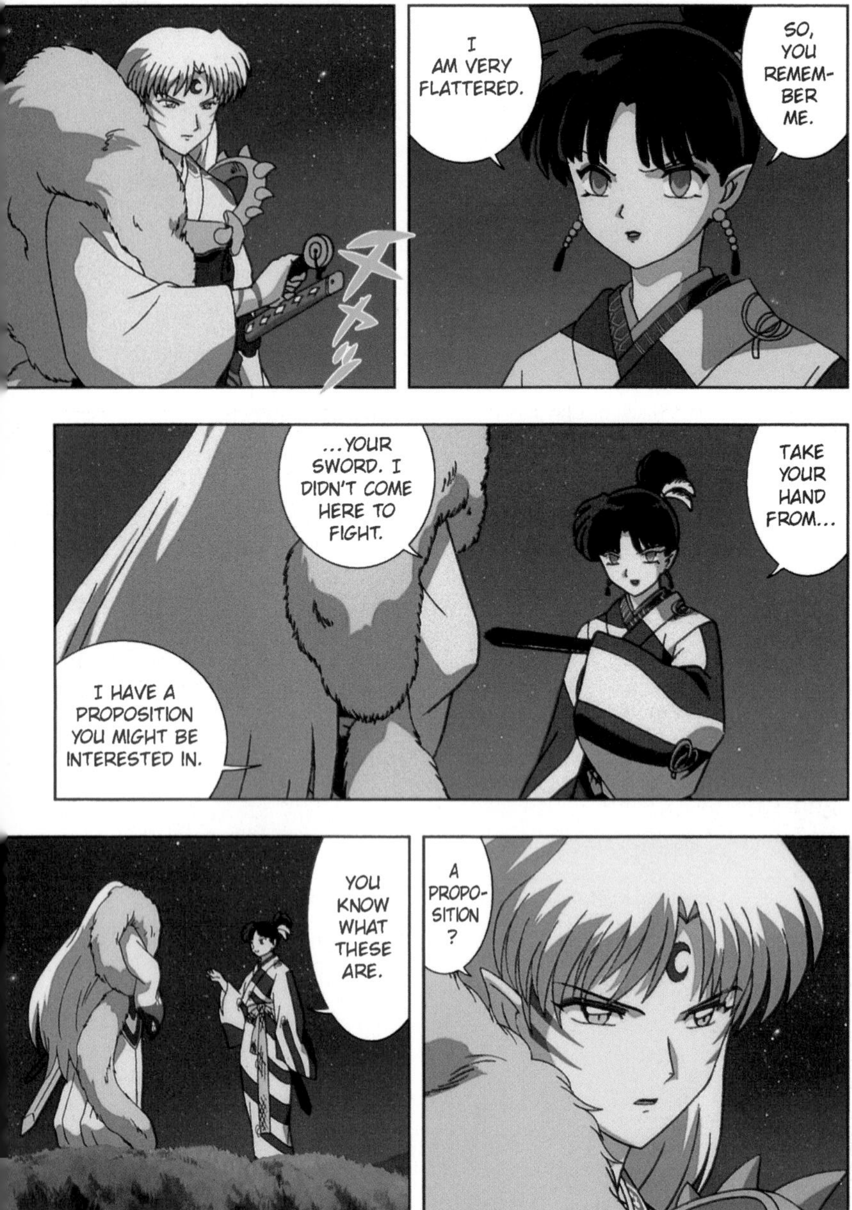

SO, YOU REMEMBER ME.
I AM VERY FLATTERED.
TAKE YOUR HAND FROM...
...YOUR SWORD. I DIDN'T COME HERE TO FIGHT.
I HAVE A PROPOSITION YOU MIGHT BE INTERESTED IN.
A PROPOSITION?
YOU KNOW WHAT THESE ARE.

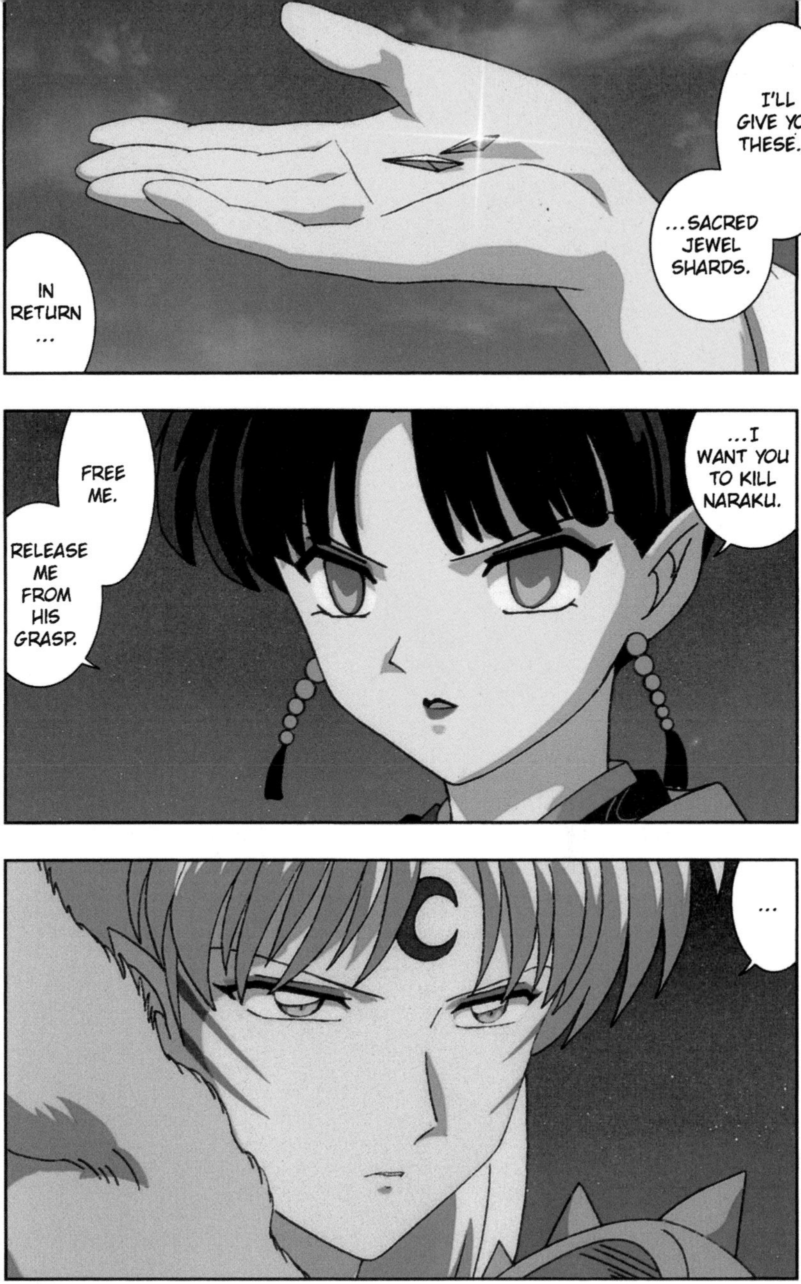
I'LL GIVE YOU THESE...
...SACRED JEWEL SHARDS.
IN RETURN ...
...I WANT YOU TO KILL NARAKU.
FREE ME.
RELEASE ME FROM HIS GRASP.
...

TO BE CONTINUED

Glossary of Sound Effects

Each entry includes: the location, indicated by page number and panel number (so 3.1 means page 3, panel number 1); the phonetic romanization of the original Japanese; and our English "translation"—we offer as close an English equivalent as we can.

20.3   FX: Gin (clang)
20.4   FX: Ga (samurai demon pushes back)

21.1   FX: Za (Inuyasha skids backwards)
21.3   FX: Doga (a mighty slash)
21.4   FX: Goh (blades whoosh)
21.5   FX: Doh doh doh doh (blades strike)
21.6   FX: Da (samurai demon rushes at Inuyasha)

22.1   FX: Doga (Inuyasha struck)
22.3   FX: Bun (Sango lobs her boomerang)
22.4   FX: Goh (whooshing)
22.5   FX: Buwa
         (blades and hairaikotsu hit each other)

23.2   FX: Dohn (blades strike)
23.5   FX: Zun (demon's blade strikes down to where
         Inuyasha just was)
23.6   FX: Ta (Inuyasha touches down)

24.1   FX: Kiri (Kagome knocks arrow)
24.2   FX: Gyun (arrow flies)
24.3   FX: Hu (arrow grazes Kagura)
24.4   FX: Shu… (Kaede shoots arrow)
24.5   FX: Shurururu… (arrow flies)
24.6   FX: Gin (Kagura deflects Kaede's arrow)

25.1   FX: Goh (whoosh)
25.2   FX: Doh (samurai demon's sword sticks itself
         in ground)
25.3   FX: Doga (Inuyasha strikes ground with blade)
25.4   FX: Doh (Wind Scar power sort circuits demon)

26.1   FX: Ba (demon explodes into shikikami)
26.4   FX: Gohh (Kagura whooshes up and away)
26.5   FX: Gohhh… (whooshing)

Chapter 64
Giant Ogre of the Forbidden Tower

6.1   FX: Ta ta ta… (running)

8.1   FX: Za (Inuyasha leaps through underbrush)
8.2   FX: Ta ta ta… (running)
8.4   FX: Za za (demons appear)

9.1   FX: Ba (demons attack)
9.2   FX: Da (Inuyasha leaps)
9.3   FX: Zuba (slash)
9.4   FX: Bun (Sango throws Hiraikotsu)
9.5   FX: Zan (Hiraikotsu slashes through demon)
9.6   FX: Hara… (shikikami flutter to ground)

10.1   FX: Pasha… (Shippo gathers water from river)

14.2   FX: Ba (Shippo struggles to free himself)
14.3   FX: Gashi (Momiji pulls Shippo's cheeks)
14.5   FX: Boso… (Miroku shuts his eyes and looks
         away in jealousy)

16.1   FX: Zan (slash)

17.3   FX: Ta (our heroes rush off)
17.4   FX: Su… (shikikami pick themselves up…)
17.4   FX: Goh
         (and whoosh themselves back to Tsubaki)

18.3   FX: Gii… (door creaking)
18.4   FX: Goh (whoosh as Kagura appears)

19.5   FX: Za (huge demon steps out of tower)

20.2   FX: Da (Inuyasha lunges)

46.3	FX: Ka (shining)
46.4	FX: Dohn (Tsubaki throws fireball)
47.3	FX: Goh (Wind Tunnel whooshes)
47.4	FX: Ka (shining of fireball)
47.5	FX: Ba (Miroku quickly closes Wind Tunnel)
47.6	FX: Doh (Fireball strikes)
48.1	FX: Kiri (Kagome nocks arrow)
48.2	FX: Shurururu... (arrow flies)
48.3	FX: Doh (arrow hits Tsubaki, but does nothing)
49.1	FX: Su... (the ogre's wound heals)
51.2	FX: Da (Inuyasha leaps)
51.3	FX: Bashi (Inuyasha repulsed)
51.4	FX: Bun (Sango throws boomerang)
51.5	FX: Bashi (Tsubaki throws another fireball)
54.1	FX: Kaaaa... (shining)
54.2	FX: Goh (whoosh)
54.4	FX: Gohhh...(whoosh)
54.5	FX: Kaaaa... (shine of ogre's eye)
56.1	FX: Ka (ogre's eye shines)
56.2	FX: Go go go (impacts)
58.2	FX: Ka (flash of light)
58.3	FX: Dohn (impact of fireball)
58.4	FX: Doh (lightning strikes)
59.1	FX: Dohn (lightning strikes)
59.3	FX: Ba (Inuyasha attacks)
59.5	FX: Goh (whoosh)
59.6	FX: Go go go (fireball flies)
60.3	FX: Goh (whoosh)
61.2	FX: Go go go (power washes over ogre)
61.3	FX: Doh doh doh doh (blows from the Backlash wave strike ogre)
62.1	FX: Gohhh... (Tsubaki as ogre whooshes away)
62.3	FX: Za (Tsubaki falls to earth)

29.1	FX: Ba (Inuyasha charges down the staircase)
33.1	FX: Pishi... (cracking)
33.2	FX: Ka (shining)
34.1	FX: Zu zu zu... (ogre tentacles break through)
34.2	FX: Ba (demon reaches out)
34.3	FX: Hara... (wind blows)
34.4	FX: Guohh... (demon roars)
35.1	FX: Shurururu... (demon enters Tsubaki's eye)
36.1	FX: Za (rustling)
37.3	FX: Ka (shining as Kikyo deflects Tsubaki's curse with her bow)
37.4	FX: Gohhh... (curse whooshes back toward Tsubaki)
38.2	FX: Ka (shining)
38.3	FX: Fuwa (Inuyasha flutters as he falls)
38.4	FX: Doh (Inuyasha lands hard on ground)
40.1	FX: Za (Kirara lands)
40.3	FX: Zuuu...n... (rumbling)
41.1	FX: Zu zu zu (rumbling)
41.2	FX: Zuzuzu... (rumbling)
41.4	FX: Ta ta ta... (running)
42.4	FX: Bari bari (lightning crackles)
43.2	FX: Kaaaa... (shining)
43.3	FX: Bun (ogre attack)
43.4	FX: Gohh... (whoosh)
43.5	FX: Ta (Inuyasha leaps)
43.6	FX: Dohn (power attack strikes)
44.2	FX: Ga (Inuyasha slams Tetsusaiga into the ground to make a Wind Scar)
44.6	FX: Dohn (Wind Scar strikes Tsubaki)
45.1	FX: Doh (Wind Scar noise)
45.5	FX: Ka (bright shining)

88.2	FX: Chu (slurping)
88.3	FX: Pashi (Inuyasha swats)
89.4	FX: Poi (Inuyasha tosses Myoga carelessly over his shoulder)
89.5	FX: Ju (Myoga lands)
90.4	FX: Kyoro kyoro (Myoga quickly looks both ways around the corner)
90.5	FX: Sa (sound awakens Miroku)
91.1	FX: Pyon pyon (Myoga sproings down the hall)
92.1	FX: Gishi…gishi… (footsteps in the hall)
92.3	FX: Su… (door to Miroku's room quietly slides open)
93.1	FX: Gishi… (child-spirit enters room)
93.3	FX: BA (Miroku leaps out of bed)
93.6	FX: Da (Miroku grabs little boy and runs for it)
95.1	FX: Gishi… (Miroku's door slides open again)
96.4	FX: Su… (Sango gets ready to attack)
97.1	FX: Doga (Hiraikotsu slams down)
97.3	FX: Ban (Miroku crashes through closed door)
97.4	FX: Ta (Miroku runs)
98.3	FX: Doga (Sango slams Hiraikotsu down)
100.1	FX: Ba (Inuyasha lunges for Sango]
100.2	FX: Dosa (Sango falls)
100.3	FX: Sawa sawa (grope, grope)
100.4	FX: Pashi (slap!)
101.6	FX: Hyoko (Myoga appears)
103.3	FX: Pyon (Myoga sproings over to Kirara)
103.4	FX: Koso koso… (sound of being stealthy)
104.3	FX: Zaku zaku (digging in the dirt)
106.2	FX: Ki (Miroku becomes possessed)
106.4	FX: Chari (Miroku's staff jingles)
107.1	FX: Bun (Miroku's staff slams down)

63.2	FX: Kaaa… (Tsubaki's right eye shines)
63.3	FX: Zuru… (Naraku's poison insects buzzing)
63.4	FX: Buuu…n… (insects carry Sacred Jewel away)
63.5	FX: Yoro… (Tsubaki is unsteady on her feet after jewel is removed)
64.2	FX: Bun (Sango throws her weapon)
64.3	FX: Doga (weapon kills insect)
64.5	FX: Pashi (fist closes around jewel)
69.1	FX: Zaa… (fizzing as Tsubaki dissolves)
69.2	FX: Za za za (Tsubaki dissolves)
69.3	FX: Basa (Tsubaki's clothes fly away)

Chapter 65
Farewell, Days of My Youth

74.1	FX: Goro goro… (strange rumbling in distance)
74.2	FX: Zawa… (rustling in grass)
74.5	FX: Za za za (rustling)
75.4	FX: Za za (rustling gets closer)
75.6	FX: Dogo (demon gets ready to pop out of ground)
76.2	FX: Goh (Centipede spits poison)
76.3	FX: Doh (Poison hits)
76.4	FX: Shuuu… (poison hisses)
77.2	FX: Za (Shippo pulled from danger)
77.5	FX: Cha (clang)
77.6	FX: Ba (Miroku strikes with staff)
78.1	FX: Goh (Whoosh)
78.4	FX: Shuuuu… (hissing)
79.4	FX: Zuhn… (Centipede collapses)
79.5	FX: Zu zu zu (Centipede collapses and dies)
81.1	FX: Wa—wa— (exuberantly happy crowd approaches)
83.1	FX: Ta (leads the way toward the village)
87.5	FX: Dosa (Inuyasha falls over backwards after having a full meal)

107.3 FX:Ta (Miroku runs)
107.4 FX:Bun (Miroku takes a swing with his staff)

108.1 FX:Ta ta ta… (running)

109.3 FX:Ta (running)
109.4 FX:Doga (Miroku slams his staff down)

110.1 FX:Pyon (sproing)
110.3 FX:Doga (strike with staff)

111.2 FX:Ta ta ta… (running)
111.3 FX:Ta ta ta… (more running)
111.4 FX:Dote (Miroku trips and falls)

112.3 FX:Pyon (flea hop sound)

113.2 FX:Sawa sawa… (grope grope)
113.6 FX:Doh (demon nears)

114.6 FX:Da (Inuyasha strikes at centipede)

115.1 FX:Goh (whoosh of Wind Scar)
115.2 FX:Dohn (centipede is struck)
115.3 FX:Zuuu…n… (centipede collapses)

116.4 FX:Ki (Inuyasha becomes possessed)
116.5 FX:Biku (Kirara looks up, shocked)

117.1 FX:Pyo—n (Inuyasha sproings off)
117.2 FX:Pyon pyon (sproing sproing)

118.4 FX:Da (Inuyasha leaps)

119.1 FX:Toh (Inuyasha lands)
119.2 FX:Za (Kirara screeches to a halt)
119.4 FX:Doh (Shippo goes flying)

120.5 FX:Su… (Inuyasha reaches out toward Shippo)

121.3 FX:Kyu (Inuyasha takes something off Shippo's nose)
121.6 FX:Doh (Inuyasha does face plant)

123.2 FX:Pyon (sproing)

125.3 FX:Sa sa (Myoga struggles)

127.2 FX:Gashi (Shoga grabs Myoga)

128.2 FX:Gashi (Shoga grabs Myoga)

130.2 FX:Bon (flea surprised, expressed by big blinks)

130.2 FX:Pachi pachi pachi (applause)

134.2 FX:Pyon (flea springs away)

135.2 FX:Pyo—n (sproi—ng)
135.3 FX:Pyo—n (sproi—ng)

136.2 FX:Pyon pyon (hopping)

Chapter 66
Naraku's Barrier—Kagura's Decision

138.4 FX:Su… (shooting star)

139.4 FX:Zawa… (rustling)

142.2 FX:Ta ta ta… (running)
142.3 FX:Za (Koga skids to a halt)

144.2 FX:Doh doh doh doh (sound of attack)
144.4 FX:Gohh (blades whoosh)

145.1 FX:Ga ga (blades hit)
145.2 FX:Ga ga (blades hit)

148.3 FX:Goh (far off whoosh)
148.5 FX:Goh (whirlwind sound)
148.6 FX:Doga (Inuyasha is knocked down as wind runs him over)

149.3 FX:Ba (Inuyasha starts to draw his sword)
149.5 FX:Dohn (Inuyasha does face plant)

152.1 FX:Ta ta ta… (running)
152.3 FX:Ta (Koga runs off)

153.1 FX:Goh… (Koga whooshes off)

161.1 FX:Zu zu zu… (skeleton army approaches via air)

182.2	FX: Ba (Koga leaps out of whirlwind)
182.6	FX: Su... (Kagura brandishes fan)
183.2	FX: Ba (Kagura strikes with fan)
183.5	FX: Doh (skeletons rush at Koga)
184.2	FX: Goh (whoosh of Kagura's fan)
184.3	FX: Zuba (slashing)
184.4	FX: Kin (shards pop out)
185.1	FX: Dosa (Koga collapses)
185.2	FX: Chari... (jewel shards pop out and plop to ground)
186.4	FX: Shurururu... (Hiraikotsu flies through air)
186.5	FX: Ba (Kagura brandishes fan)
187.1	FX: Goh (skulls are animated)
187.2	FX: Doga (skulls get broken)
187.3	FX: Pashi (Kirara lands)
187.5	FX: Goh (Kagura whooshes off)
187.6	FX: Gohhh... (Kagura whooshes into the distance)
192.1	FX: Chari (Inuyasha draws sword)
192.4	FX: Za (Koga falls to his knees)
194.1	FX: Gohhh... (Kagura flies along)
195.4	FX: Goh (Kagura whooshes off into the distance)
197.2	FX: Gu (Naraku abruptly squeezes his fist shut)
198.3	FX: Su... (a shooting star)
199.1	FX: Su... (Sesshomaru brandishes sword)
200.2	FX: Gohhh... (wind whooshing)
200.4	FX: Zawa... (barrier noise)
201.2	FX: Ka (Naraku's eyes abruptly start to shine)
203.3	FX: Goh (whoosh)
203.4	FX: Doh (Jakken topples over)
205.2	FX: Chari (Sesshomaru puts his hand on his sword)

161.3	FX: Zu zu zu zu (the skeleton army approacheth!)
161.4	FX: Hyun (blade hurtles through the air)
161.5	FX: Dohn (blade lands on spot where Koga just was)
161.5	FX: Ta (Koga dodges)
162.1	FX: Toh (Kagura lands)
163.5	FX: Da (Koga lunges for Kagura)
164.4	FX: Ba (Kagura brandishes fan)
164.5	FX: Ba (corpses rush in to attack)
165.2	FX: Goh (whoosh)
165.3	FX: Baki (Koga kicks corpse soldier)
165.4	FX: Doga (punch)
165.5	FX: Goh (whoosh)
166.1	FX: Doh doh doh (blades strike at Koga)
166.2	FX: Ba (Koga attacks)
166.4	FX: Dohn (impact)
167.1	FX: Ba (Kagura leaps)
167.2	FX: Goh (Kagura swishes fan)
167.3	FX: Goh (skull whooshes by)
167.4	FX: Kara kara (skull sounds)
167.5	FX: Gohhh... (whoo—sh)
168.1	FX: Gohhh... (whooshing)
168.3	FX: Baki (Koga punches at flying skulls and breaks some)
169.4	FX: Gohhh... (whirlwind whooshes]
171.3	FX: Ta (Ginta dashes off)
173.1	FX: Pachi pachi (fire burning merrily)
175.1	FX: Ban (Kagome opens door)
175.5	FX: Ta ta ta... (running)
178.1	FX: Ban (Inuyasha starts off down stairs)
180.1	FX: Goohhh... (whirlwind whooshing)
180.3	FX: Goh (whooshing)
181.1	FX: Baki (skeleton bones breaking)
181.2	FX: Za (Koga gets out)

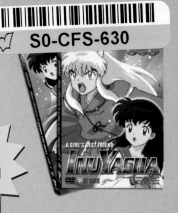
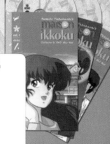
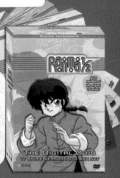